Living to One's-Self:
The Life and Poetry of William S. Trout
1909-1980

By

J. Terry Zeller

Ph.D., University of Minnesota
Professor Emeritus, School of Art
Northern Illinois University

Sincerely Yours,
W. S. T.

Published in the United States of America
Printed by Lightning Source

ISBN 978-0-9898434-1-6

Illustrations and book design by Diana Abreu

To the memory of my parents
John E. and Hazel H. Zeller

Table of Contents

Illustrations

Permission to reproduce these photographs was provided by the following individuals and institutions: Figure 1 (Courtesy of Glenna Kauffman Wilkey); Figures 2, 3, 6, 7, and 12 (Courtesy of Alice Trout Smith); Figures 4 and 5 (Courtesy of Coatesville High School); Figure 8 (Courtesy of Violet Baker); Figure 9 (Courtesy of Boston Symphony Orchestra Archives); Figure 10 (Courtesy of Donald Smith); Figure 11 (Courtesy of Emory Phillips); Figure 13 (Courtesy of Octorara High School); Figure 14 (Courtesy of Millersville University Archives).

Acknowledgments

This biography of William Trout would not have been possible without the generosity of his friends, colleagues, former students, and acquaintances, who shared their memories of him in personal interviews, telephone conversations, letters, and emails. The specific contributions of those who provided invaluable oral or written information are noted in the text. Special thanks are due to Donald Smith, Alice Trout Smith, Violet Baker, Robert and Jean Rentz, William Axe, William Snyder, Dianne Danz, C. John Bryer, and Betty Curtis. I appreciate the encouragement and varied contributions of Emory Phillips and David A. Johns, my friend of many years, in making the book a reality. I very much appreciate the comments, corrections, and suggestions for improvement made by those who read parts or all of the manuscript, specifically John Delli Carpini, Dennis Simmons, Scott Donaldson, and the late Byron Detwiler.

I am indebted to the institutions that assisted in my research: the Boston Symphony Orchestra Archives, Coatesville High School Library, Lancaster County Historical Society, Harvard University Library, New England Conservatory of Music, Boston Public Library, Chester County Historical Society, the Historical Society of Western Pennsylvania, the Graystone Society/National Iron & Steel Heritage Museums, and the National Archives. A special debt is owed to the staff of Millersville University Library and Archives. My debt to the important work of many scholars is apparent in the list of secondary works I consulted in an effort to place Trout's life and poetry within the context of twentieth-century social, cultural, and intellectual history in general and to situate him within Anglo-European and American literature. I am grateful to Audrey Skilton for proofreading of my prose. However, Trout's poems and extracts from his letters remain as he wrote them. Finally I want to thank Diana Abreu who worked her magic in turning a manuscript into a book. The product of her layout and design skills combined with her sensitive aesthetic judgment and artistry have given us not just a visually appealing book, but one that reflects its content through the use of color and the arrangement of suggestive imagery.

The poems "Blacksnake," "And still she sings, the Marschallin," "So safe it was," "There at the woods' edge," and "August Evening" were first published in *Rapportage*; "North of the old orchard" and "Summer Ending" in *descant*; "Commencement" and "The teacher of biology" in *Millersville Review*, and "Sur Le Noel" in *Cimarron Review*. I want to thank these publications for first bringing Trout's poetry to public attention.

Introduction

At nine o'clock on an early September morning in 1961 at Millersville State College in southeastern Pennsylvania, a tall, thin, stoop-shouldered man with a shuffling gait and wearing a dark blue suit and necktie and black shoes came through the door at the back of Classroom 1 in Wickersham Hall and took his place at the lectern in front of the blackboard. His tender but penetrating eyes, salt-and-pepper hair, and deeply furrowed, somewhat gaunt but gentle face bore a striking resemblance to Abraham Lincoln's. Speaking softly and flipping in circles a ring of keys on the long bony middle finger of his right hand, he made an immediate and deep impression on me, a freshman in English 11, Grammar & Composition I. This sensitive, reflective, unassuming man was in love with knowledge he was eager to share and steeped in subjects well beyond the one he was charged with teaching. His name was William Trout. This was the first of four courses I took with him, and, over time, a friendship developed. On a winter afternoon a decade later, he shared with me the poetry he had been writing for some thirty years or more but never sought to publish. While he did not have the luxury of pursuing his muse as a full-time poet, and never earned so much as a dime from his verse or saw any of it in print, he was no Sunday scribbler, no sing-song rhymester, as the quality of his poems testifies.

I see this biography of William Trout as part of a larger effort by literary scholars that has been going on since at least the 1980s to recover unknown, ignored, neglected, marginalized, or suppressed twentieth-century American poets in an effort to restore the rich diversity of America's cultural memory made necessary by the narrow and restrictive literary canon constructed by critics and academics from the 1930s through the 1950s. The formalism of experimental poetry that grew out of the poems and critical essays of Thomas Sterns Eliot and other High Modernists created the erroneous impression that modern poetry made a decisive break with past practice. Based on the evaluative criteria laid down by the New Criticism in the 1930s—predicated on the ideas and practices of High Modernism which viewed a poem as "ahistorical," "a purely aesthetic object" appealing to the intellect and not to readers' emotions, "purified of social influence and critique" and institutionalized in academe after 1945—the work of many twentieth-century American poets who made use of traditional forms and took as subject matter the personal; the individual; everyday life; or issues of race, gender, war, and social and economic justice was not recognized as belonging to the canon of Modern poetry. Such a restricted, "purist" interpretation of what constitutes Modern poetry has, according to Cary Nelson, not only led to the loss of contact with the rich diversity of twentieth-century American poetry but also to an unjustifiable dismissal of the quality of much of the poetry written between 1910 and 1945 (Nelson 1989).

As with many, if not most, writers of poetry and fiction, much of Trout's verse is autobiographical, not only the incidents and ideas related but also in the emotions conveyed. Although essentially a lyricist, who, for the most part, favored traditional fixed forms using meter and rhyme, Trout also wrote narrative verse and like many other twentieth-century American poets experimented with a variety of forms. The richness of his imagery makes him as much a poet of the eye as of the ear. He is a poet of solitude and reflection whose poems are not nostalgic but rather are affirmations that the past is part of the present. His poetry is contemplative; it is about the experience of living rather than just his experience of life; it values understanding over action, and while rooted in the intellect is leavened by emotion and intuition. The richness of his poems comes from the way in which they combine ideas, sensations, memories, reflections, and feelings. His imagination, informed as it was by his explorations of the unconscious, takes his verse beyond material reality and at times to the edge of the mystical or spiritual. His poems range from psychological suggestion to the exploration of psychological states. Bill's poems are about place and time; about family and friends; about people who doubt or suffer or are on the margins of conventional society; about illness, age, and death; and about exploring both the natural world and the landscapes of the mind. The poems document his keen observations of nature (its topography and flora, creatures, weather, moods), his intellectual interests (particularly classical music and opera, literature and visual art, philosophy and psychology, and the occult), reflect his political and social values, and testify to his spiritual quest and his struggle to come to terms with his personal doubts and demons. Because each of us has an inner life Trout's poetic exploration of his own can resonate with his readers. Still, he is not always an easily accessible poet. Like Emily Dickinson, Trout was unconventional and cryptic to the point of sometimes making it difficult to understand what his poems are "about." This quality makes it important to provide context for such poems, which is difficult given both his secretive nature and the paucity of documentary evidence about his personal and public life. Readers of Trout's letters and poems will find him by turns coming across as a realist, an idealist, a skeptic, an ironist, and, some would say, a cynic, but not a complete pessimist.

He valued poetic traditions going back to the Latin poets and the Elizabethans, and had a particular fondness for Catullus and John Donne; for Thomas Hardy, A. E. Housman, Walter de la Mare; for Emily Dickinson, Edwin Arlington Robinson, and Edna St. Vincent Millay. He is not a poet of the genteel tradition but a Modern poet, though not a Modernist, which I take to mean poets descending from the Eliot-Pound circle. He is a mid-twentieth-century poet who did not embrace wholeheartedly modernist aesthetics, subject matter, or practices, but at the same time could not keep from being influenced by them. While certain of his poems share characteristics of the American Confessional Poets, he can no more be grouped with them than he can with the practitioners of Projective Verse of the 1950s and 1960s. His poetry needs to be seen in relation to his own generation, meaning those American poets born between about 1900 and 1920, among them Randall Jarrell, Richard Eberhart, Theodore Roethke, and Winfield Townley Scott. His life and verse provides a new perspective on these and other Middle Generation American poets and their poetry. While he drew on major aspects of British and American poetry, Trout's voice is very much his own. He has things to say that his contemporaries did not often address and says things in ways different from other poets of his day. He merits recognition not only for the technical excellence of his verse, but also because he represents the many twentieth-century American poets who pursued their muse outside the mainstream literary circles, and whose voices must be heard if we are to have a more complete picture of American poetry in the middle years of the last century.

We may never know when Trout began writing poetry, though the first mention of it is in a letter sent to a friend during World War II. Unlike Emily Dickinson, he did not circulate his poems among relatives and friends. However, Virginia Eshelman, a fellow teacher at Christiana School, recalled that in the 1950s he sometimes called her on the telephone and read one of his poems to her; and in the 1960s his Millersville colleague Louis Jennings and at least one of his college students, William B. Snyder (who found one of his poems in a book Bill lent him), were aware he wrote poetry but were never invited to read it. Of the more than seven hundred fifty poems in Trout's oeuvre over half are typed final copies; the rest, also typed, are not marked "FINAL." Handwritten drafts or revisions may have been among the papers (including the journal Bill told me he kept) he asked his brother Frank to destroy after his death. However, crossed-out words and their substitutes in the margins of some poems indicate that he refined his work even after marking it "FINAL." Only a few of the poems are dated (and these in the 1960s); nonetheless, it is possible from internal evidence to assign approximate dates to a number of them. One might, for example, conjecture that much of his nature poetry, many poems related to childhood memories, and the "portrait poems" may have been written during the 1940s and 1950s while he was living in Gap. Those dealing with his aging mother and social-political commentary may date mainly from the early 1950s to late 1960s. His darkest and most "confessional" poems and those related to dreams probably date from the years after his mother's passing in November of 1967 at a time when he was reading and rereading the works of Carl Jung.

The intent of this cultural and intellectual biography is to introduce William Trout to the public and make his poetry more accessible to readers by placing representative poems within the history of ideas as well as in the context of his own life, work, and thought. My approach to Trout's poetry is more expository than critical, which seems to me the most appropriate way of introducing him to a wider public. The informality of the narrative, which is organized thematically, not chronologically, is as much a memoir or remembrance as it is a traditional biography, and might best be described as a life in context. I have made a concerted effort to keep the narrative free of academic and critical theory jargon. Chapter One focuses on Trout's family history, education, and life experiences as they relate to his poetry. Chapter Two examines the intellectual and socio-political influences in his life and work. Exploring his personality and private life in relation to his poetry is the primary focus of Chapter Three. Chapter Four is devoted to the role nature plays in his verse. Trout's interest in psychology and its influence in his life and poetry is the subject of Chapter Five. The role of visual art and music in his life and poetry is examined in Chapter Six. Chapter Seven looks into the literary influences of British and European writers on Trout's thought and poetry; while the influence of American writers on him is examined in Chapter Eight. Although an effort has been made throughout the book to place Trout's poetry within the wider context of Anglo-American poetry, Chapter

Nine is devoted to identifying the distinguishing characteristics of his verse, locating his work within the history of twentieth-century American poetry, specifically in relationship to his "Middle Generation" contemporaries, and to considering the possible reasons why he chose not to publish his poems.

Wanting the reader to experience Trout in all his complexity, I have included, in addition to the poems in the body of the book, an Appendix containing additional poems. In order to assess the literary legacy of any writer I believe it necessary to know all of the work the individual produced. But since it is not practical in a book of this nature and length to include all of the more than seven hundred fifty poems Trout wrote, I have included poems based on two criteria which are not necessarily mutually exclusive: literary quality and biographical significance. It is unrealistic to expect consistent high quality in the work of any poet, even those given canonical status. In addition to the excellent poems one finds in a poet's oeuvre one also comes across those that are notable for a particularly memorable line, or two, striking diction, or delicious rhymes or wonderful rhythm but which, overall, may be less than optimal. Original spelling and punctuation have been maintained in quotations from Trout's letters and college lectures as well as his spelling, spacing, line breaks, capitalization, and punctuation in the poems. Bill often used the British rather than the American spelling of words, and sometimes chose the second rather than the first spelling given in the dictionary. He also has a penchant for archaic words and those with French roots.

The trappings of scholarship are kept to a minimum so as not to render me guilty of "refrigerating the mind," as Bill said was so often the case with scholarly writing. I used *The University of Chicago Manual of Style* author-date documentation system as the most economical in space and the least disruptive method of citing print sources. Correspondents and individuals interviewed are cited by name and identified within the text, as are manuscript and archival materials. Along with frequent quotations from his letters, lectures, and marginalia in the books he owned, Trout's poems are intended to let him speak for himself about those events, experiences, and feelings that molded and colored his life.

Chapter One
Beginnings and Early Influences

For most of his adult life William Trout inhabited three worlds. There was the public world of convention, accommodation, and routine necessary to earning a living; the semi-private world of home, family, a few close friends, and student visitors; and the solitary world wrapped in the sights, sounds, smells, moods of nature, filled with books and classical music, and haunted by doubts, dreams, and memories. His childhood and adolescent experiences seem to have done much to shape and shade how he negotiated the three worlds in which he lived; however, documentation of his early years is sketchy at best. There are also few details of his adult life, with some periods for which there is no first-hand information whatsoever, save for what can be gleaned from his poems, which is just what this secretive man intended.

Born on 17 July 1909 in Salisbury Township, Lancaster County, Pennsylvania, William Stauffer Trout was the fourth child of Charles Edgar Trout (1875-1919) and Alice Gray Livingston (1875-1967), who were married on 5 June 1901. As the photograph of Bill's father as a young man shows (fig. 2), he was tall and thin, characteristics Bill apparently inherited judging from his 1940 Selective Service Card which lists him as 6 feet 3 inches tall and weighing 150 pounds at age 31. That Alice Trout was small in stature (something always remarked by those who knew her) is apparent in the photograph (fig. 3) taken of her, perhaps about the turn of the century, when she was in her twenties, posed between two tree trunks and a shattered stump.

Bill's ancestors on his father's side emigrated from Germany in the first half of the eighteenth century; one of them, Paul Trout, fought in the Revolutionary War. His grandfather, John Rutter Trout (1836-1901), and two uncles, Henry Markley Trout and A. Newton Trout, served as infantrymen in an emergency regiment recruited in Lancaster County and deployed along the Susquehanna River at the time of Robert E. Lee's invasion of Pennsylvania in the summer of 1863. In February of 1865, John Rutter Trout reenlisted, joining the 195th

Pennsylvania Infantry with the rank of sergeant, and served until mustered out on 31 January 1866. The regiment was posted to guard the B&O Railroad line in Berkeley County, West Virginia, then fords on the Shenandoah River, and ended its duty guarding public buildings in Washington, D.C. It never engaged Confederate troops in battle. The same was not to be the experience of Thomas Jefferson Bitzer (1843-1923), a farm boy from the Gap area whose sister Mary Elizabeth Bitzer (1838-1929) married Bill's paternal grandfather in March of 1873. Tom Bitzer enlisted in the Union army on 10 July 1861, when he was eighteen, and served as a private in Company B of the 30th Pennsylvania Volunteers (1st Reserve Infantry), part of the Army of the Potomac, until mustered out on 13 June 1864. He served in General George McClellan's Peninsula Campaign and saw action in many battles including Second Bull Run (in which he was wounded on 30 August 1862), Antietam, Fredericksburg, Chancellorsville, Gettysburg, and under U. S. Grant in the bloody battles of the Wilderness and Spotsylvania Court House, and was granted a pension of $6.00 per month under the Civil War [Veterans] Act of 1890 (Invalid), which benefit was increased under subsequent pension acts to $40.00 per month in 1918. It is reasonable to assume that Bill heard stories of Civil War experiences from his elderly relatives, though not his grandfather Trout, who died in 1901.

Bill's grandparents on his mother's side were William G. Livingston (abt 1827-1909) and Catherine D. Mong (1831-1919), his second wife, who bore him three sons and two daughters, Mary and Alice. Mr. Livingston, described as "an extensive dealer in livestock," owned property in the tiny village of Roseneath near Gap and was listed in the 1880 Federal Census and in county directories from 1884 to 1909 as a farmer and drover. Bill's ancestors on his mother's side, some of whom settled in Salisbury and Sadsbury Townships in the eighteenth century (including members of the Linvill and Hoar families, whose politics were Whig and Republican), were either members of the Society of Friends or disposed to their beliefs. William Livingston and his first wife, Rachael Ann Linvill, rest in the burial ground at Sadsbury Friends Meeting, part of the Hicksite branch of the denomination, which built its first place of worship in 1725 and replaced it about 1748 with a stone meeting house. Bill's spiritualism and values, among them, his attitude toward the military and war, may in part be traced to the influence of his grandmother Livingston, whose kindness he recalls in a letter written many years after her death. (Ellis and Evans 1883, 162, 179, 93-94, 193-194, 1047, 19-20, 1060-1061; Klein 1924, 840; Thomas J. Bitzer and John R. Trout Service Records and Pension Applications, National Archives).

Trout had both a strong historical sense and sensitivity to the nature of time. The novels of Sir Walter Scott he read, and which were read to him in childhood by his mother, and that he alludes to in his poems, among them "So safe it was to sit beside," fostered his interest in history. The books he read later in life and mentions in letters confirm his early interest in European and American history. In one of his scrapbooks, he filled ninety-two pages with quotations, in French, from Michelet's multi-volume *Historie de France*. For Jules Michelet (1798-1874) the common people were the heroes of history whose struggle against the oppressions of monarchs, the aristocracy, and the church he chronicled and whose rights he championed. He glorified the French Revolution of 1789 and deplored how its ideals, won with the blood of the lower classes, were subverted by self-serving politicians in later years. Trout took extensive notes on W. H. Herndon's controversial 1888 biography of his law partner, Abraham Lincoln. He also read David Donald's 1948 *Lincoln's Herndon*, and owned a set of Douglas Southall Freeman's three-volume *Lee's Lieutenants* (1942-44), as his student Dennis Simmons who borrowed it for a school report recalled. It may have been from his aging relatives and neighbors that Bill developed a life-long interest in history, a concern for the personal past, and a vividness of memory that inform his poems, many of which are memories, documents of events or individuals, or verbalizations of family photographs. He looked at the present through the lens of history and recognized the importance in our lives of the material culture of the past, as illustrated in poems like "Before the Sale" and "North of the old orchard, the house shambles." He kept a musician's sword, enlisted man's cavalry saber, and an 1853 model British Enfield rifled-musket (used by both Union and Confederate infantry) he told me (when he gave them to me in the 1970s) were picked up on the Gettysburg battlefield, presumably by Tom Bitzer, who had fought there.

Alice Trout took care of the childless Thomas Bitzer (1843-1923) and his wife Susan McIlvaine Bitzer (1842-1923) in their old age. The assets enumerated in the probate records of Thomas Bitzer's estate filed with the Lancaster County Orphans' Court in 1923 show him to have been a man of some means. The real estate consisted of about eight acres (appraised at $2500) with a two-story stone house with seven rooms and an attic and cellar, frame barn, tobacco shed, carriage house, "old stable," and "old stone [tenant] house" (appraised at a little more than $16,000). His bank balance and stock holdings amounted to a little over $12,900. He bequeathed $1000 to the Bellevue Presbyterian Church and gave legacies amounting to $9200 to relatives. The

$1000 he left to pay for a "suitable monument" to be erected on his cemetery lot turned out to be a large and impressive granite stone engraved with the names of six major Civil War battles in which he fought. Alice Trout received $1000 and title to the "home property" which included the Bitzer farmhouse and about eight acres of land, the orchard, fields, meadows, and woods of which provided fodder for many of Bill's poems. In time the importance for Trout of place and personal history would manifest themselves in his poetry, when the farm and surrounding countryside and his immediate and extended family, as well as neighbors and townsfolk were taken as subjects for such poems as "Signs," "Cold twilight still—but life begins to stir," "Country Sale," "Remember how the old woman used to chuckle," "Lark Descending," "Henry," "Grandmother" (a tribute to his paternal grandmother not included herein), and a childhood reminiscence of a November visit from a favorite "Great-Aunt" with apples to swap for flowers.

Small, glowing, bitter-scented,
November chrysanthemums
Against the pickets minted
Prim medallions.

Down through memory stalking
Carefully, with a cane,
Three apples in her apron,
On her cheek a brown stain,

She shuffled the frosted path,
To a creaking rocking chair
Beside the oven door,
Gray afternoons to share.

She clucked when we brought
Chrysanthemums to swap
For gingerbread and apples
Hoarded in her lap.

For most of his life Bill lived on the edge of Gap, a village of fewer than a thousand souls (the 2000 Census records a population of only 1,611 residents) in the rolling farmland and hedgerows of the Pequea Valley of eastern Lancaster County, situated about sixteen miles east of Lancaster, the county seat, and west some eleven miles from Coatesville in neighboring Chester

County. Both Lancaster and Coatesville were small cities, with Philadelphia, less than sixty miles from Gap, being the nearest metropolis. The land on which the village was built had been surveyed in 1701 by order of William Penn. The village is located at the eastern end of the Pequea Valley in the gap between Welsh Mountain on the north and the Mine Range (containing copper and nickel deposits) on the south. As early as 1726 there was an inn at "the Gap" on the main trail a day's journey from New Castle, Delaware, where immigrants landed on their way to new settlements in the West. Many of the early settlers to the area were Scots-Irish and German. The most important religious denominations among the "English" were Quakers, Presbyterians, and Methodists. The German settlers were members of Lutheran and Reformed congregations or belonged to "plain" sects, including the Church of the Brethren, Mennonites, and Amish.

A society for the abolition of slavery was founded in Pennsylvania as early as 1775, and in 1780 the state legislature passed a law for the "gradual abolition of slavery." Although the abolitionist William Wright of Columbia may have been the first person to organize Underground Railroad activity in Lancaster County, it is not surprising given its proximity to Maryland and to residents sympathetic to the plight of slaves, that "stations" on the route to freedom were established in the Gap-Christiana area. Although the Church of the Brethren held that slavery violated Christ's teachings, they did not actively engage in opposition to it. The Mennonites believed that slavery was sinful and forbade their members from owning slaves, but refrained from participation in Abolition or African Colonization movements. However, individual Mennonites were involved in helping runaway slaves, most notably Christian Franz (1805-1890), who belonged to a Mennonite church in Christiana and gave fugitive slaves shelter in his home and guided them north to freedom. At its monthly meeting in January of 1848, the Sadsbury Friends Meeting, located between Gap and Christiana, established a committee, including Sarah Pownall, and charged it to "confer and correspond" with other Friends Meetings to discharge their testimony "against the sin of slavery." Many of the farmers living in the townships of Bart, Salisbury, and Sadsbury were Quakers active in the anti-slavery movement who gave runaway slaves work or assisted them in escaping to Canada (Rettew 2006, 19-20).

The first blood of the Civil War was shed in Lancaster County in what became known as the Christiana Riot or Resistance. William Parker, a slave who escaped from a plantation in Ann Arundel County, Maryland in 1839 and settled in the Gap-Christiana area in the mid-1840s, where he rented a stone tenant house on the farm of Levi and Sarah Pownall, and earned his living by working as a hired man on the farms of other Quakers. Before dawn on the morning of 11 September 1851, a Maryland slave owner, accompanied by relatives and a deputy marshal with a warrant under the Fugitive Slave Act of 1850 arrived at the home of William Parker to seize three runaway slaves who were being sheltered there. Two Quakers, Elijah Lewis, a storekeeper and local postmaster, and Castner Hanway, a miller, tried to settle the matter peacefully, advising the marshall and his group to leave before the aroused armed blacks arrived at the Parker house. Those inside the house refused to surrender. Gunfire was exchanged, and, summoned by the sound of a fish horn Parker's wife blew from a second floor window (a prearranged signal to summon help from neighbors if slave catchers were in the area), Parker's black neighbors came from all directions carrying guns and corn cutters. In the melee the slave owner was killed and several people were wounded. Following the clash a number of Quakers helped the blacks to escape and flee to Canada, Parker among them. Thirty-eight men were charged with treason, among them Elijah Lewis and Castner Hanway; all were either acquitted of or had the charges against them dropped. The clash and subsequent treason trial received wide coverage in local and national newspapers (Ebersole 2006, 160-164; Ellis and Evans 1883, 1030, 1041, 71-73; Rettew 2006, 11-17, 32-37, 94, 111).

Although it is doubtful Trout ever met any of the men involved in the Christiana Resistance (the last survivor, Peter Wood, died in 1918), as a child he may have heard accounts of it from grandparents (His maternal grandmother, born in 1831, lived to age eighty-eight and his paternal grandmother, born in 1838, lived past her ninetieth year, dying in 1929.); his Rutter, McIlvaine, Hoar, Livingston, or Linvill relatives, some of whom were Quakers; his neighbors who would have been in their teens or early twenties at the time; or from Tom Bitzer, who was seven at the time and may have recalled family recollections of such a singular event in the life of the community. We also know from his poem "Forecast," which mentions a steel engraving of the abolitionist and Radical Republican Congressman Thaddeus Stevens of Lancaster hanging in the dining room of the Trout home, that Bill grew up in a family whose political affiliations had been for generations Whig and Republican and were supportive of African Americans (Ellis and Evans 1883, 1060). Stevens, who had been actively involved in the defense of Castner Hanway, advocated confiscating land from southern planters and distributing it in forty-acre plots to former slaves, was among those in Congress who championed the 13th Amendment to the Constitution, which ended slavery in the United States. When Stevens died in 1868 he was interred, as he had directed, in the only cemetery in the city of Lancaster that allowed people of all races to be buried there. In a letter of 6 September 1977 Bill told me he had been reading "lives of Thaddeus Stevens," and was then on his third.

An aerial photograph of Gap (fig. 1) and the surrounding countryside taken in 1951 shows the geographical universe Trout lived in for more than half a century. Most of the village is nestled between the curving tracks of the Pennsylvania Railroad, seen in the middle ground, and U. S. Route 30 (the Lincoln Highway) running at an angle from east to west through the landscape at the village's edge. Barely visible in the hazy distance toward the upper part of the photograph is Welsh Mountain. The two-story frame house in which Bill spent his early childhood is a few hundred yards east of the two-story stone Bitzer-Trout homestead, where Bill lived from the mid-1920s to 1961; both are along Route 30 to the east of the village and not visible in the photograph.

The Gap in which Trout lived from 1909 to 1961 was a typical agricultural community, the economy of which depended on the fertility of its rich limestone-based soil and the skills and work ethic of its prosperous and frugal farmers. It had a national bank, post office, and railroad station. J. C. Walker & Sons were important dealers in grain, lumber, and coal. Other commercial enterprises included hardware stores, a furniture store and funeral home (not an unusual combination for small towns of the time), a barber shop and a beauty parlor, a general store and drug stores, a clothing store; restaurants and bars, shoe repair and jewelry shops, creamery and dairy businesses, an ice plant, a greenhouse, saddle and harness shops, a coach and carriage shop, blacksmith shops, farm implement and machinery dealers, and by the early 1920s gas stations and automobile garages. There were a number of physicians practicing in Gap, including Dr. George W. Beacher, the Trouts' family doctor, but only one veterinarian, Dr. C. J. Bryer, and no attorneys or dentists. In the early twentieth century electrification came to Gap and with it, in 1906, trolley car service began, which continued until the last trolley left the village on August 20, 1932, when buses replaced the trolleys. The trolley ran from Center Square in Lancaster and basically followed Route 30 to Gap and then to Christiana, with a spur that continued to Parkesburg and Coatesville. Though the village in 1917 opened its new two-story, six-room school (fig. 8) to house grades one through eight (those who wanted to attend high school had to go to White Horse or Coatesville), it had no other educational or cultural institutions—no library and no movie theatre. However, sports were important to the community, particularly its baseball teams (Ellis and Evans 1883, 1044-1046; Lorenz 2002, 33-85).

In 1966 Carolyn Neuhauser Keneagy published a small book (*A Gap in My Memory*) about growing up in Gap which provides information and impressions that contribute to our understanding of the environment in which Trout, who was nine years older than Keneagy, spent his childhood and adolescence. She records that traveling medicine shows came to Gap every summer providing "corny" performances, the only public entertainment available to residents. In hot weather, kids went swimming in the reservoir behind the Gap Post Office, though that Bill Trout joined in the fun is unlikely. Because prices for farm products had dropped significantly after World War I, resulting in an agricultural recession that affected much of rural America before the more widespread depression of the 1930s, Carolyn Keneagy's father was forced to quit farming in 1921 and go to work in a steel mill in Parkesburg, an employer for a number of Gap bread winners. The farm economy in eastern Lancaster County during the '20s was not much different from the rest of the country. While truck farmers selling fruits and vegetables (which many Gap-area followers-of-the-plow did) fared somewhat better than those raising livestock and cash crops like grain and tobacco, by the early 1920s prices for agricultural commodities in general had collapsed as a result of overproduction. Many farmers had gone into debt purchasing machinery which along with falling income resulted in record numbers of foreclosures on family farms, but not among those belonging to "plain" sects, particularly the Amish whose frugality, use of horse-power over tractors, and limited involvement with the financial and other institutions of the mainstream society were insulated from the worst effects of the downturn in the agricultural economy. Yet there was truth in Harvey Green's observation that for American farmers "the sound of the Roaring Twenties was the howl of the wolf at the door." And things only got worse for farmers after 1929 (Keneagy 1966, 42-44, 9-10; Green 1992, 2, 42-43).

Keneagy's memoir also records the effects of the Great Depression on Gap residents, not only her father's layoff from the steel mill and unemployment, but also on specific Gap businesses that went under in the 1930s, among them a restaurant, a clothing store, and a shoe repair shop. "Most families in Gap," she wrote, "were struggling just as we were to get by." Her father was again unemployed during the winter of 1934-35. She recalled that during those lean years, "Our folks no longer had company on Sunday for meals" (Keneagy 1966, 51-52, 59). We know from his poems the economic hardships the Trout family experienced during the same period, but as schoolteachers they had secure jobs (albeit at small salaries), at least for eight months of the year. Even without economic hard times, during summer vacations it was difficult for the Trouts to make ends meet, thus necessitating some type of stopgap employment until September. But they could at least feed themselves from their garden and hen house and apparently sold the surplus eggs, fruits, and vegetables.

Bill came from a line of carpenters. His paternal grandfather, listed in an 1898 country directory as a carpenter, and two uncles helped build the Gap Town Clock Tower in 1892, still a prominent local landmark. His father is listed in the various county directories for 1909-1910 as either a carpenter or laborer but might best be called a general handyman. Alice Trout Smith—the daughter of Bill's older brother, Charles L.—recalled being told by her father that her grandfather, Charles E. Trout, while working as a carpenter during a barn raising, was seriously injured in a fall. This was just one of a series of accidents, serious illnesses, and deaths of family members and close friends that were to darken and trouble Bill's life. As his poems testify, he never forgot his rural working-class origins. The sights, sounds, smells of his childhood are painted in the poem "On the Back Porch" with its references to life on a small farm and to his father's trade. The flowers so loved by Mrs. Trout, the pump outside the kitchen door, the sounds of carpentry, and the Trouts' Jersey cow tended in its illnesses by old Doc Bryer (as his son remembered) all identify the scene as Bill's childhood home. This work embodies some of the salient characteristics of his poetry—realism and scrupulous attention to detail—and reveals him to be a master of diction and a consummate colorist. His knowledge and love of classical music come through in the musicality of his rhymes and rhythm:

> There in the sunny morning grew
> Nasturtiums, yellow, scarlet-streaked,
> Twistingly pungent, soaked with dew;
> And there the long pump-handle squeaked
> Laboriously, before the gush
> Rose from the cistern in a rush
> To cascade in the iron trough,
> Then whirl and gurgle and be off

To wet the crimson rambler's root.
The screen door slammed; the scolding wren
Stuttered at her tiny door;
Triumphant cackling of a hen
Punctuated the uproar
Of carpentry—hammer and plane
Gossipped; and up the stony lane
The Jersey cow, turned out to graze,
Mooed her delicate malaise.
No summer morning voice was mute.

When Bill was not yet two years old, his sister Susanna (1904-1911), who apparently was a delicate and sickly child, died of pneumonia on 14 April 1911, a few months shy of her seventh birthday. From the poems alluding to Susanna's death, one can surmise her loss was a profound and lasting sorrow for Alice Trout. She apparently shared her memories with Bill, and in old age her flashbacks brought on by senility contributed to the sorrowful tone of much of his verse. One of the poems suggests he had seen photographs of the little girl and recognized the similarities of her features to those of his mother and grandmother:

See, on the right, there just in the corner
Of the broad forehead, borne at least to three
Generations: lightly there is scored
The shadow of a curl that has freed
Its tangle from the cap.
                                        How early did
The small creature learn that darling laughter?—
But at the end, she must atone the forbidden
Daring, that calls down the whirring shaft—
Is it so? But no. The whole journey
Embraced six years, six months, and fourteen days—
Fourteen days of April.
                                        And April stirs—
Stirred just now—the curl. Yes, she must pay
That gaiety unfolding wings of silver,
Fledgling only, but daring the spring gust,
Daring the arrow from the cloud.

Until
Possibility defeat distrust,
Let's keep the curl's shadow, on the right,
Pencilling that forehead known, so known.—
Such talisman signs dim evangel, slight—
But not fastidious, he who goes alone.

Tragedy again struck the Trout household when Bill was not yet ten. His father, age 44, died of pneumonia on 14 February 1919—a victim of the 1918-19 influenza epidemic—leaving his wife to provide and care for their four sons, ranging in age from six to sixteen. Mrs. Trout was one of three Gap women widowed by the flu epidemic (Keneagy 1966, 9). Years later Bill recalled that dreadful afternoon in a poem he titled "Valentine Day":

At a time unnoticed, the chill house had become
Silent almost, inexorably, slyly.
Beyond the kitchen window, a grayness
Fluttered slowly near, circling assured.—
Then in the hallway door, the neighbor quietly
Beckoned, and we followed him, followed
Along the icy hall, and up the laddery stairs.—
I saw you kneeling by the bed, your face gray,
Stony with meaning I could not understand.
In both your hands you held the dark hand—
Limp, that hand, not pressing yours, even
To say good-bye. And your eyes were fixed
On the uncomprehending eyes, gone so dark.—
I knew that others stood about, two or three,
But who they were, I can not now remember.—
Later someone led us back, to that same room.
Order had come—a sort of order—and the sheet was drawn
Tautly over. That someone lifted the white cloth back,
To show us the face, a face gone vacant now,—
And the eyes remotely closed.
And from the other room, over low voices,
I heard your frail and brief, small, wailing cry.

Though the "laddery stairs" refer to those in the Trout house, and the kneeling figure by the bed is his mother, Trout moves beyond the personal, the private memory to universalize the experience of death in such a way that the "face gone vacant now" strikes a chord in anyone who has kept a deathbed vigil. In the "fluttering," "circling," "grayness" seen from the kitchen window, the subtle beauty of his words tells us that the angel of death has come. There are shades of Emily Dickinson (1830-1886) in this poem. Her poems "I felt a funeral in my brain" and "I heard a fly buzz when I died" come to mind in the stark economy and insightful detail with which both Dickinson and Trout sketch the death room. Something of the matter-of-factness of death one finds in Dickinson's "There's been a death in the opposite house" also informs Trout's "Valentine Day." As with Dickinson's poems, among them "Grief is a Mouse," many of Trout's were inspired by sorrow or pain and describe their psychological effects as in:

Grief is adroit in its suspended
Counter-attacks; it knows to bide
Until the unguarded mind, bending
Careful care, essays to guide
The chisel, or record the note.
Launched implacably then, the sleepless
Has the victim by the throat,
Outcry stifled by the leap.

Then the shameful blemish comes;
The face splinters to ugly planes,
The eyes are seared by meager salt,
The grudged tears of age. Wanes,
Waxes, wanes again the drumming
Confusion in the bony vault.

The number of poems Dickinson and Trout wrote on various aspects of death and dying (though she penned more than he) evinces their preoccupation with the subject, which for Dickinson, as Barton Levi St. Armand documents, was influenced not only by her personal religious beliefs and Calvinist theology but also by the popular culture and folk art of nineteenth-century America, and to the proximity of the Amherst town cemetery to the Dickinson home on Pleasant Street, where Emily lived during her late childhood and adolescence, and from which she could observe funeral processions and rituals. Both poets experienced the frequent loss of loved ones—family as well as friends. They witnessed and recorded the act of dying and the rituals that followed, Dickinson in poems like "I've seen a Dying Eye," "She bore it till the simple veins," "The Eyes glaze once—and that is Death," and "Twas warm—at first—like Us," and Trout in "Valentine Day," "Remembered," and "Autumn/Watching." They speculate on what lies beyond physical death, recall visits to the graves of the departed, commemorate those who have passed and record their own grief, and give form to the figure of Death as Dickinson does in "Death is the supple Suitor" and "Because I could not stop for Death" (Johnson 1955, chap. IX; St. Armand, 1984, 25-26, 41-42, 46-49, 53-58; Mudge 1975, 6, 45).

In addition to his sister and father, Trout lost close relatives including his maternal grandmother, Catherine Mong Livingston, who died in 1919; his paternal grandmother, who passed away in her ninety-first year in 1929; Thomas and Susan Bitzer, who died in their eighties in 1923; uncles and aunts and neighbors from the McIlvaine and Livingston families, among them his mother's sister, Mary Livingston at age 76 in 1949; and former students and young co-workers at Lukens Steel killed in World War II. Thomas H. Johnson's assertion that what links Emily Dickinson's poems about death is "the knowledge that death snaps the lines of communication with those we have known and loved, and creates the uncertainty in the minds of all mortals whether that communication can ever be reestablished," might also be applied to Trout's poems and helps explain his attempts to communicate with those who have departed this world (Johnson 1955, 204). However, communicating with the dead is not always a comforting experience for the living, and for Trout raises doubts about the Christian idea of Heaven and life everlasting, as one of his poems suggests.

> With supplicating eyes, the dead return
> Sometimes, diminished mendicants of alms
> From the bewildered destitute, who burns
> To acquit the adjuration of those palms
> Thrust from shadow. Here is all reversed
> The mythos of some bright Elysian day
> Eternal. And by bafflement dispersed,
> The haunted mourns, of penury the prey.
> Across the April clearing, underneath
> The shellbark buds unfolding, coloured fawn,—
> Among the bloodroot and rue anemone,
> The dead returned; and lonely life must see

Its guarded dream repudiated, drawn
Awry, and ripped from fraying hem to hem.

Edna St. Vincent Millay, another of Bill's favorite poets, also took death as the subject of many of the poems she included in her collection titled *Second April*, among them "Lament," "Elegy Before Death," "To a Poet That Died Young" (about Percy Bysshe Shelley), "Burial," and the five poems in "Memorial To D. C.," written about the death of her young Vassar friend Dorothy Coleman, a victim of the 1918 influenza epidemic. Considering the collection too morbid, Macmillan rejected *Second April*. It was, however, published by Harper Brothers in 1921. As Nancy Milford points out, the inspiration for these poems came from the Latin poets and the Elizabethans so beloved by Millay. After her mother's death in 1931, Millay worked out her grief in six poems on the subject, including "Valentine" (her mother was buried at Steepletop, Edna's home in the Berkshires, on Valentine's Day) which were published in 1934 (Milford 2001, 187-188, 340). One can reasonably speculate that the love Trout expressed for both the Latin poets and the Elizabethans in letters to friends indicates a source of inspiration for his poems about death that dates back farther than Dickinson and Millay. But unlike Dickinson or Millay, he, as will be discussed later, also explored ways of reestablishing contact with the dead, specifically his deceased mother, and sometimes used the hope for such contact as the subject for poems, as with "Come back, come back, across this wind" and in this one:

You seem to come between the page
And the eyes; you seem to lead away
A mind demoralized by age
Hourly, importunately.
All is gray, close around,
Becoming blackness, where I fear
To venture yet, whence no sound
Reaches the unwearying ear.
I halt, listen—lean to catch
The frail voice that calls, calls—
Seemingly; the book falls
Face downward, and the eyes search
The heavy dark.... But sound nor sight
Quickens the insensate night.

Church cemeteries and small country graveyards are a familiar part of the landscape of Lancaster and Chester counties. Bill once told me that a path he used to take home from school passed an old burying ground in which there was a towering ancient oak tree, the sight of which sent a shudder through him when he realized that its size and strength came from the human fertilizer sucked up by its roots. Both Emily Dickinson and Trout were familiar with neglected country burying grounds. Her poem "After a hundred years" questions whether a forgotten cemetery where "weeds triumphant raged" can preserve the memory of the dead. And in the poem "Time" Trout moves through the dry weeds of a rural graveyard and traces with his finger the weather-worn names on the headstones, thereby making tactile contact with the "unremembered dead."

Time is now this valley, a sombre rift
Sunk grimly in the ranges of the hills
That scrutinize, and then slyly shift
Point of espial, to align their wills
With those of their confederacy. Here
Day never comes; only dusk succeeds
To night, among these boulders—shades of fear
Reared menacing among the dry weeds.
Sometimes there is a stone ruggedly
Squared and smoothed, and bearing on its face
Letters that the dark forbids to read;
One can not know—however patiently
The finger-tips fumblingly re-trace—
The crumbling record of the unremembered dead.

Bill also made regular visits to his mother's churchyard grave. Often in these cemetery poems he uses the weather to set the mood and then paints a landscape in which nature flourishes among the dead, as in

Lulled by the drift of rain, the season pushed
Among the darkening stones above the sleepers;
Under the retreating thunder's rush
The sycamores fanned out their plumed sweep;
And all the spangled roadside brimmed over,
Starring the beggarly ditches with blue disks

Of wild chicory, with the sprawling clover
Escaped from hayfields, and with the Queen's mist.
And I remembered: such exuberance
You love always—whatever thrives and thrusts
Root and tendril, breeding flower and pod.
I thought: By contrast, only the interlude,
Of winter's slow reduction to the clod,
To the frosted husk—such only can I trust.

There is nothing remotely morbid or macabre about these cemetery poems. On the contrary, these are poems of soft sorrow, gentleness, reflection, and great beauty. In "Lulled by the drift of rain, the seasons pushed" life, regeneration, and beauty coexist with death. In "Visit," which contains some of Bill's loveliest imagery and turns of phrase, he recalls going to his mother's grave in the Bellevue Presbyterian Church cemetery (seen behind the church's pointed tower roof in fig. 1 in the left middle-distance just as the railroad tracks enter the curve) which can be identified by what he tells of its location: "Between the railroad [the Main Line between Harrisburg and Philadelphia that borders Gap] and the meadow / Between the highway [U.S. 30, the Lincoln Highway] and the west / Slopes this dull and spiky fallow":

Here the gray, shrouding chill,
A little gritted, a little grimed,
Wraps us, and beneath this hill,
At a time neatly timed,
Time breaks, obedient to the Will.

Between the railroad and the meadow,
Between the highway and the west,
Slopes this dull and spiky fallow,
Where only, and at last, is rest;
From here, these need not to go,—

No more need know dispersal, not
Dull integration in the weave,—
Unborn at last, unbegot,
Not to fear, not to grieve
Longer, by the world forgotten.

. . .

End? End, to all intent.
But yet the inference that I found,
Or seemed to find, as I bent
Long stare upon the secretive ground,—
This was the panther's blandishment?

The tone or mood of Trout's "Visit" differs from that which informs Robert Frost's "In a Disused Graveyard." Frost injects an element of cleverness or humor in his description of the people who come out of curiosity to read the headstones in a New England burying ground. The speaker notes the irony in the visitors' fascination with the cemetery and their unwillingness to acknowledge their own mortality. Though certain as they are of death, the absence of new burials leads the "marbles"—the dead—to ask: "What is it men are shrinking from?" Trout's speaker, on the other hand, visits a specific grave in a "spiky fallow"—not an anonymous cemetery but one located within identifiable landmarks—not out of curiosity but out of duty to a deceased loved one. There he says, "only, and at last, is rest," from which "these need not go / No more to know dispersal, not / Dull integration in the weave / Not to fear, not to grieve." It is clear that Trout's visit is neither casual nor brief, and that his "Long stare upon the secretive ground" has been a time both of personal remembrance and of unresolved philosophical contemplation ending in a question: "This was the panther's blandishment?"—evidence of Bill's skepticism about the flattering or cajoling promise symbolized by the panther. In the *Physiologus*, a beastiary written in the early Christian era containing descriptions of animals and fantastic creatures to which allegorical or symbolic meanings were attached, the panther is associated with awakening or rebirth, and by extention with the resurrection of Christ. This beastiary was an important source for medieval texts and religious art.

What little we know of Trout's childhood and adolescence comes mainly from his poems. Until his brothers Charles and John in the early 1930s installed a bathroom in the house his mother inherited from Thomas Bitzer, Bill never lived in a home with an indoor toilet. The pump opposite the kitchen door provided water for the household. His poems tell of a boyhood of hand-me-down clothes and making do with things others would discard; of simple meals and poorly heated rooms; of working in the vegetable garden and flowerbeds; of time spent with grandparents or aging aunts and uncles; of roaming fields, meadows, and woods where copperheads and blacksnakes lurked, sunfish might be caught, or partridge berries and wine berries found;

and of felling and decorating the family Christmas tree. And while presents were few, practical, and of the cheapest kind, there were always books to read or to be read by a mother who nurtured the minds and imaginations of her children. The names of friends and playmates have not survived, though poems like "Blacksnake" and "Sur Le Noël" suggest companions, perhaps Bill's brothers, and most likely the youngest, Frank, with whom he formed the closest attachment. One is left with the impression that as a boy Trout spent most of his time with family members or in solitary pursuits.

As his eighth-grade schoolmate Violet Baker remembered, Bill was polite and friendly and always able to answer questions in class the other students could not, but stayed in the classroom and read while the other children were on the playground at recess—evidence that from an early age he was a omnivorous reader and a loner. "We called him the thinker," Baker recalled and said that after repeated invitations to Bill to join them in play, to which he responded that "he had work to do," classmates just stopped asking. Was it shyness, a lack of interest or sense of inadequacy where sports and games were concerned, or some physical problem that kept him in the classroom at recess? Peter S. Walker, a life-long resident of Gap, who as a child knew him, recalled that Bill, who had a reputation for brilliance, was "really loved" and willingly helped others with their math problems.

Bill repeatedly made the honor roll during his years (1924-28) at Coatesville High School (known for the excellence of its language instructors), where he completed four years of Latin. Paired with a picture (fig. 4) of him as a baby (as were all the 1928 Coatesville graduates), his senior-year photograph (fig. 5) shows that he was a handsome young man with a thick head of dark shiny hair; large, gentle but penetrating eyes; a full, sensuous mouth; and a rather dreamy, distant look. Bill's reputation for brilliance led the 1928 yearbook staff to put this quotation from Oliver Goldsmith's poem "The Deserted Village" next to his picture: "And they gazed, and still their wonder grew / That one small head could carry all he knew." Summarizing his high school accomplishments, the yearbook went on:

> 'Bill' was valedictorian of our class. He hailed from Gap and had to get up at five o'clock every morning to catch the train. 'Bill' was very modest about his famous literary works. His best works were given in his contributions to the 'Spotlight' [the school newspaper]. He also might be remembered for his part in a sketch from 'Silas Marner' and for a debate in his Sophomore year. From his criticisms of books and

authors in English and Latin classes some of us thought that he would make a good literary critic.

That there was a vein of seriousness in Bill's personality early in life was recognized by Violet Baker and by other pupils at Gap and at Coatesville.

Three surviving pieces of Trout's high school criticism (all published during his senior year) appeared in "Literary Pick-Ups From English Classes," a regular feature in the bi-weekly school paper, *The Spotlight*, which show the promise later fulfilled in his poems, letters, and lectures. Compared with the other contributions to this column, the superiority of his essays in terms of style and content is apparent in his "No One Ever Understood Christmas As Dickens Did When He Wrote 'Carol' " and "Boswell's Life Of Johnson." In the humorous invention "Lady Macbeth Makes A Revelation," he wrote in a manner that brings to mind the atmosphere one finds in Symbolist paintings or literature while adding a touch of 1920s realism. He wrote that Lady Macbeth's revelation was made "in the Twilight Land that lies between Here and Beyond" while she "lolled in her chair in a graceful attitude, smoking a scented cigarette" on an afternoon "stifling with the subtle odor of scarlet poppies that flamed everywhere" as she and Shakespeare sipped tea "under wide-branched trees that cast long jet shadows over the grass and arched so thickly into green dusk overhead that no patch of blue was visible." She chided Shakespeare for never telling "the truth about me," of leaving her "an unfinished portrait," explaining as she flicked "an ashen cone from her cigarette": " 'Anyone with any sense would know I killed the whining ninny' "—Duncan—after discovering Macbeth's cowardly inability to do the deed. The characteristics of Trout's "voice"—wit, rich vocabulary, an appreciation for imaginative realism and attention to telling detail, an ability to conjure-up marvelous images that spark the reader's imagination and intellectual interest, sympathy and admiration for those who overcome adversity, the importance of historical context to an understanding and appreciation of literature, a belief that literary works should teach lessons and reflect core human values—are already apparent when at eighteen he wrote of Boswell's famous work:

> If anyone will take the trouble to pry about among the family book shelves, he will probably find, marshalled in the dusty battle line beside the ancestral Shakespeare, Milton and Bunyan, two stout, sturdy volumes. He will pull them out, glance at the title—"Boswell's Life of Johnson," and exclaim "Could anything be more interesting?"

> But should he have the courage to open them—what a difference!
>
> The whole eighteenth century—that glorious period of powdered wigs and embroidered waist-coats, of gorgeous dresses and towering coiffures, of hot blooded love affairs and rapiers gleaming in the moonlight—opens in a rainbow vista before him. A nasty motley crowd of scholars, beaux, macaronies, blue-stockings, actors, revolutionists and artists troop out from between those dusty pages.
>
> He meets Davy Garrick, the greatest Shakespearean actor the world has ever known, Sir Joshua Reynolds, the artist, John Wilkes, the famous radical leader. Hannah More, that formidable woman, who wrote the driest stories one could ever hope to read, in her long cloak and wide beaver hat, breakfasts with fat old Johnson for the reader's especial pleasure. He sees dapper little Goldsmith, locked in his room by an irate and unpaid landlady, and witnesses the rescue by Johnson, which brought the "Vicar of Wakefield" to light.
>
> But, towering above all the glamour of the age, he sees a man, borne down by almost every handicap that ever tormented mankind, rise from poverty to the highest literary position in England. He sees an inhabitant of Grub Street sought after by the proudest nobles of the land, loaded with honors, yet keeping his head through it all.
>
> It is a book to read and re-read, because it is human, because the lessons it teaches will be true for all time, because it teems with the red blooded life of the century, and last and possibly least, because it has been, since it was written, the standard for all biographies.

If Bill as a teen also tried his hand at poetry, no evidence has survived; however, his acknowledgment later in life that during his school days he had read Edna Millay and Walter de la Mare would make it likely that an adolescent as sensitive and precocious as he would have experimented with verse.

In a 1976 letter to the widow of the British poet Ralph Hodgson (who became a U. S. citizen and owned a farm near Minerva, Ohio), whose work Bill had known for many years and which, he says "dims almost to extinction the work of other moderns," he relates that his mother started teaching school in 1893 at the age of seventeen, "in order to prop a quavering household." But where she taught is not stated, and Salisbury Township School District records for that year do not list her among its teachers. He also mentions that his maternal grandmother, whose maiden name was Catherine Dorcas Mong, was a schoolteacher who grew up in Waynesburg, Ohio. When he was a child, he says, she showed him "such kindness as I do not forget." According to Salisbury Township School Board minutes, Alice Livingston was appointed in June of 1898 to teach at Gap Hill [Primary] School for the 1898-1899 school year and at Roseneath School for the years 1899-1900 and 1900-1901. The district's salary range for teachers at this time was $30-$40 per month for the seven-month school year, with the specific salary determined by the Board on an individual basis. When in June of 1901 the School Board approved the list of teachers for the 1901-1902-school term, Alice Livingston's name was not among them. She had married Charles Edgar Trout on June 5, 1901, and left the classroom. Occupied by her responsibilities as a wife and mother to a growing family, she did not teach again for eighteen years.

In February of 1919 Charles E. Trout died intestate, and according to a court decree his widow received only the family house, which had previously belonged to her father-in-law, John Rutter Trout and which he had sold to his son and only child in April 1901. Thrown on her own devices, she decided to return to teaching, and on June 7, 1919, was elected by the Salisbury Township School Board as one of two primary teachers at Gap Centralized School for the 1919-1920 school term. Teachers' salaries though conforming to the State mandated schedule for minimum compensation were set on an individual basis at the discretion of the Board. However, according to Board minutes, during the late teens and early twenties, Salisbury Township School District was plagued by recurrent financial problems and had to reduce teachers' salaries. In 1918 the School Board had approved a new salary schedule for teachers which provided a formula for base pay according to the type of teaching certificate one held, as well as an additional three dollars per month to those receiving a "mark of One" on the County Superintendent's assessment of "Practice of Teaching." Those teachers holding the lowest level of certification—a Provisional Certificate—were paid $30 per month. Mrs. Trout, as her Millersville transcript shows, had not graduated from high school and therefore likely held only a provisional certificate. It may well be that the new salary schedule encouraged or required her to seek more formal education, which she did by being admitted to Millersville State Normal School, where in 1921 she received the one-year professional certificate for teaching primary grades.

For more than twenty years Alice Trout taught first grade. Her sister Mary Livingston (also a Millersville graduate) taught grades 7 and 8 and was the school's Principal (fig. 6) until her retirement, hastened, perhaps, by reports of strange behavior. Mrs. Trout, according to Violet Baker, was adored by her pupils and loved and admired by her neighbors. A measure of the positive impression she left on her pupils is that about thirty years after she had her as a teacher, Carolyn Keneagy wrote, "Don [her brother] and I both remember with affection our first grade teacher, Mrs. Alice Trout." Among her memories was that "Mrs. Trout could peel the skin from an apple in one continuous length. We kids would crowd around her each lunchtime and ask her to peel our apples like that" (Keneagy 1966, 36). Former students would surround her and hold onto both her arms when she passed through the halls or visited her sister's classroom, Violet Baker recalled.

A photograph (fig. 6) of Alice Trout wearing a black armband, her son Frank (who was born in 1913 and looks to be about six years old), and Mary Livingston, shows them standing next to a frame building (either Bellevue Presbyterian Church parsonage in Gap or another church) with gravestones in the background. Judging from the grim expressions, black arm bands, and Frank's age it was likely taken in 1919 at Charles E. Trout's funeral, on Easter Sunday (since the trees in the background seem to be in early leaf and the figures wear no outer-garments), or at the funeral of Bill's maternal grandmother, Catherine Mong Livingston who passed away that year. In this photograph the petite and pretty young Alice Trout seen in fig. 3 has become a work-and-worry-worn widow and mother of four boys, her drawn and deeply lined face—evidence of the hardships and sorrows she has suffered—making her look older than her forty-three years.

Though dogged by poverty, Alice Trout not only cared for the aging Bitzers, but also provided a home for her mother-in-law until her death in 1929. She apparently supplemented her teaching salary by selling produce from her garden, which the ninety-four-year-old Peter S. Walker (whose first grade teacher was Mrs. Trout), referred to as a "truck patch." In spite of economic difficulties, she was committed to seeing that all of her children received an education. The expenses involved in sending Bill to the larger and better-staffed high school in Coatesville in neighboring Chester County rather than to the smaller one in nearby White Horse, had no doubt taxed his mother's financial resources.

Beginning in the fall of 1928, Bill commuted via trolley to the state normal school at Millersville (renamed Millersville State Teachers College in 1929) near Lancaster. The realities of his economic situation (made worse after the stock market crash of 1929 sent the nation into the Great Depression), and the need to find secure employment in the shortest period of time dictated his choice of the two-year curriculum for rural teachers. As is apparent from the college catalog, most of the classes were pedagogical not academic or subject matter courses, and were all at an introductory level. In addition to courses in teaching arithmetic, geography, social studies, and reading, the curriculum required courses in: English (grammar and composition), Art (materials and methods), Music (for children and basic instruction in piano), Psychology and Child Study, Handwriting, Nature Study and Agriculture, Educational Biology, Rural Sociology, Juvenile Literature and Silent Reading, Health and Hygiene in Rural Schools, Educational Measurements, several classes in general teaching methods, and, no doubt to his great displeasure, four semesters of Physical Education. Building on his four years of high school Latin, he elected to take Latin in his final year at Millersville. He received his two-year teaching certificate in 1931.

Returning to Millersville in the summer of 1932, he began working on his B. S. in Secondary Education with a major in English and a second required field in social studies. Having to teach during the regular school year to support himself and his mother, it took him fifteen years as a part-time student (teaching duties and war work at Lukens Steel kept him from taking any classes from 1940-1946) to complete his bachelor's degree, which he received in 1947. His transcripts list the courses he completed for the baccalaureate, including twenty-one credits in English consisting of one-semester courses in American Literature, English Literature, Romantic Literature, Short Story, Novel, Contemporary Poetry, and Teaching of English. His grades were excellent. Though he received four "Cs" (two each in Music and P.E.) out of fourteen courses in his first year, he earned "As" in all of his other certificate and baccalaureate classes. He took six additional classes in 1948-49. Judging from the course titles (three of which were in education), they were probably required to make his Pennsylvania teaching certificate permanent. Given his shyness and low self-image, as well as the long commute to and from Gap, it is not surprising that, save for his transcripts there is no record of Bill's student years at Millersville. There are no photographs of him as a college student, no mention of college friendships, no indication that he joined clubs or participated in any aspect of campus life except attending classes. In spite of the intelligence all who knew him testified to and his excellent high school and college record, Bill genuinely believed that he was poorly educated, intellectually inadequate, and a failure in life. "I was born thinking, 'I'm no good', and I never got over it," he told William Snyder, one of his Millersville students in the 1960s.

Early in 1931 Bill began his teaching career in the one-room Mt. Airy School on Welsh Mountain, when he was elected by the Salisbury Township School Board to complete the term of a teacher who had resigned at the end of February. His salary was $110 per month, of which he took home $106.33. At the next Board meeting he was given a regular eight-month contract. From 1931 through the 1935-36 school year, his monthly salary was $115 for eight months. The 1936-37 school year saw him move to Gap Centralized School to replace his aunt, Mary Livingston who had retired. He received several small raises over the years and in April 1939 the School Board appointed him the principal of Gap Centralized School. In addition to his administrative duties, he continued teaching grades seven and eight. By 1941-42 he was earning $140 a month. At the School Board meeting 18 August 1942, Alice Trout, having reached the mandatory retirement age, was one of several teachers who resigned. At the same meeting Bill met with the Board to ask for a salary increase, which they declined to approve after considering his request "from all angles," whereupon, he resigned effective immediately. His resignation was accepted. That Trout requested a salary increase after having received one only a year earlier was no doubt an attempt to help compensate for the loss of his mother's salary, which would strain the family's finances since her pension was quite small.

After working in the mill at Lukens Steel in Coatesville during most of World War II (see Chapters 2 and 3), Trout took a position teaching junior and senior high school in Christiana, a town a few miles from Gap. When Pennsylvania's school districts were consolidated during the 1950s, Christiana School became part of the Octorara School District, and Bill went there to teach high school English and served as adviser to the school's student newspaper.

Trout's career as a public school teacher came to an end in 1958. With the clear understanding that he would not be required to obtain a master's degree, he was, at age 48, recruited in 1958 to the English faculty at Millersville State Teachers College by the department's chair, Dr. L. S. Lingenfelter, who had been one of his professors. After he joined Millersville's English Department, his sense of inadequacy may have deepened by being surrounded by Ph.D.s whose presence may have made him uneasy about teaching at the college level with only eighteen credits in survey English literature courses. But, as he wrote a friend, he had not sought the job. No doubt he accepted the position knowing his college teaching schedule would be more flexible, with fewer classes and no extracurricular activities to supervise. Then, too,

Millersville was only a short drive from their Lancaster apartment, to which he and his mother moved in 1961. Apartment living involved no yard work or household maintenance. And perhaps most important, hospital care was a few blocks away, as was the office of his mother's cardiologist.

Bill's brother Frank also received his teaching certificate and bachelor's degree from Millersville State Teachers College, and like Bill began his teaching career at Mt. Airy School before taking positions in other Lancaster County districts and then moving to Maryland, where he ended his teaching career in the 1970s. Charles, the eldest brother, went to Stevens Trade School in Lancaster, and after his marriage graduated from Drexel Institute of Technology in Philadelphia. John spent a year at Pennsylvania State University and later became a successful building contractor. The four brothers were very different but, according to Alice Trout Smith, all had a tendency to depression. Charles and John worked in the world of business and were outdoorsmen who enjoyed hunting and fishing. Bill and Frank were teachers and bookish in their interests.

According to Bill's niece, Alice Trout Smith, there was a serious falling-out between the brothers at some point, probably in the early 1940s, the cause of which is unclear but may have been related to the care and financial support of their mother, who had recently retired from teaching and soon after developed health problems. Charles and John, who were married and had families, sided together. Frank, whose brief marriage after World War II to a lady dentist from Christiana ended in divorce, and Bill, who was a life-long bachelor, remained close and eventually shared an apartment in Lancaster after their mother's death and Frank's retirement. That the split between the brothers was a bitter one was apparent to Alice Trout Smith who recalled that when she and her parents went to Gap to visit her grandmother, Bill and Frank retreated to their rooms when they saw their older brother's car pull up to the house. Apparently Bill harbored resentment against his two older brothers for the rest of his life. When Emory Phillips, one of Trout's Christiana students in the 1950s, inquired about Bill's brother, John, he was told "that is a name never spoken in this house."

Bill lived with his mother all her life and cared for her at home until she passed away in her ninety-second year on 26 November 1967. Her kindness, sacrifices, and selfless dedication to her family and love of learning account for his deep devotion to her, and explain why she figures so prominently in his poetry. One understands why his sense of duty to a parent was offended when, as he told me, one of his Millersville colleagues justified putting her parents in an old-folks home because having to take care of them "interfered with her life-style."

Trout's life-long love of literature and words came from his mother. In the course of one of the afternoons we spent together, he told me that in his childhood his mother read to him from an old volume of Shakespeare (it in fact belonged to his maternal grandmother and was inscribed with her name, and was among the books he gave me in the 1970s) as she worked at the kitchen table and he sat on the floor next to her. And in a letter to me of 19 April 1977 he says: "Once when we were sick from measles, my mother (poor, burdened, over-worked child) read Gulliver to us. Yet, yet I see so clearly the sickroom, the kerosene lamp, and her intent face, as she sat on the edge of the bed." He gives voice to such memories of his mother and the difficult economic circumstances of his childhood, writing:

So safe it was to sit beside
Your chair, to lean against your knee,
To listen, eyes and ears wide
To con the enchanted company
Your voice evoked from black lines
In order to and fro marching
The rustling pages: bright designs
Of danger, of unfortunate kings,
Of houses built in trees, of gold
Coins that spilled from broken chests
In ruined abbeys, of captives sold
Into slavery. Bequests
Such as these the years yield—
Honey-hexagons safely sealed—
Good harvest from a little field.
What mattered at all the scanty meal,
Holes in shoe soles, coat too small,
The north wind with its blade of steel
Probing our too timorous hall?
We curled under the quilt, and shook
Till warmth began to cumulate;
But we could think about the book,
And cogitate and speculate.
Wise in this, as wise in all,

You knew, you understood, you dared—
And life left you no interval
For questioning; you were spared
No subtle ambush, no attack;
But never did your courage quail,
Although the wall at your back
Was fate's ironical entail.
Heiress of centuries, your largess
Endures like silver, year to year,
And in the darkening wilderness,
Is the last gleam to disappear.

Bill's description of ill-fitting clothes, shoes with worn soles, scanty meals, an ill-heated and drafty house, and the selfless sacrifices his mother made for her children while all along nourishing their minds and imaginations, reminds one of Edna St. Vincent Millay's poem "The Ballad of the Harp-Weaver," where she tells of the poverty and maternal self-sacrifice that she experienced in her childhood, a poem which Millay's friend and literary critic Edmund Wilson at first believed "verged on the sentimental" but later found "profoundly moving" (Milford 2001, 212, 216).

The quiet dignity, grace, and courage of the elderly Bill commemorates in his verse can be seen as the equivalent of qualities found in poems celebrating young love and youthful beauty. The years as companion and caregiver to his mother resulted in some of the most beautiful and moving of his poems and make him a poet of old age. Even at the moment of his mother's passing he recalls her wisdom and the love of literature that bound them together over so many years:

"You always think that, when I close my eyes,
I'm asleep"; so it was you said,
Half-smiling, half-protesting, when I read
Aloud to you—not from the pseudo-wise—
Rather from Pickwick, Copperfield, or poems
Remembered from far childhood, so that you
Could say a chance phrase. (Even now
The brightness gleams a moment, flashing through.)

At the last kiss, at the final touch
Of disbelieving fingers on your hair,

The lashes did not stir, the dim eyes
Did not open, to protest across
A smile.—Now time on unresisting flesh
Shoals, and the mind goes groping—where
Blindness remembers that you were always wise.

In "Now Anonymous," a poem written after Bill and his mother had moved to an apartment in Lancaster City in 1961, he recalls both his mother's frugal habits born of poverty and the grief faced by the elderly who must leave their homes. He also records his own anger and bitterness at an unfeeling, uncaring God who allows such things to happen. Again, he takes a deeply personal experience and turns it into one of the sad realities of living too long that many of us are destined to experience:

For long a widow, taciturn, observant,
Her family reared at cost that only she
Could itemize, though very far from her
Would be the reason, she lived frugally.
Penuriously, she saved everything:
Compact cardboard boxes, spans of string;
Damaged curtain rods, off-size nails,
Radios discarded, wooden pails. . . .
But those who mocked were glad enough to hear,
When some minute imperative shouldered near,
Her "Wait a minute," to see her go assured,
To vanish for a little while, immured
In miscellany only she could thread,
To issue, calmly bearing what was needed,
The imperatively relevant detail—
Devil's-horror hair-pin, horseshoe nail.
  When suddenly the Lord's perplexing whim
Sent her wandering, lost, adjacent streets,
And turned her to a bundle, staring dimly,
Her kin transferred her, swiftly and discreetly,
To the nursing "home." Then how the magpie nest—
"My house," she always said, with impassive
Pride—was scattered, at the auctioneer's suggestion;
The patient years flew off, in far less

Than no time.—God, not yet satisfied,
Keeps her living, but in the night she cries.

Women, particularly old women—his two grandmothers, aunts, and neighbors—played a central role in Trout's childhood and appear frequently in his poems. Beginning in childhood Bill had an unusually close relationship with his mother, who, according to her granddaughter Alice Trout Smith, relied upon him much more than on her other sons after her husband's death, and goes so far as to suggest that her grandmother's sorrow in losing Susanna, her only daughter, may have resulted in her trying to make Bill a replacement for the little girl. Thus early in life Bill was tethered to his mother by her hand *and* his. Hints of just how close mother and son were are found in these exerpts from the poem "Forecast," which tells about "our abortive picnic on a dull Sunday of late August" (which probably took place about 1913-1914 given the reference to the "moody, sturdy baby," who would have been Bill's younger brother Frank, born in 1913):

Excursion long planned, broodingly meditated, repeatedly
 discussed
With you, but healthily deprecated
By the feared, long-legged father, and by the brother,
Callously bumptious, impatiently jeering such concerns for the
 precious details—
Would the basket hold everything? Would the icing be spoiled
 on the chocolate cake?
What would you wear?
. . . .
You, I remember dimly, but so surely: you wore a light dress,
 carried
The moody, sturdy baby on one arm,
And managed all with efficient simplicity and with your simple
 grace.

But when they arrived at their picnic site in a woods beside a stream, the overcast sky gave way to rain and to the "querying glance" of the young neighbor who had driven them there in his car, "father jerked his head / Abruptly, toward home ..." They ate their "sandwiches of devilled eggs" in the dark dining room, "shaded by the apple trees," "beneath the sternly contemptuous gaze of Thaddeus Stevens, in the steel engraving," while "In front of father, the chocolate cake—always your master-piece— / Lolled in regal and unsmutched princeliness." The implication here is that the father will cut the cake and distribute the pieces. That there were problems between Bill and his father is hinted at in the poem's final lines: "But I knew very well that my slice / Would be parsimoniously sparing." The poem suggests the father's lack of sympathy for his third son's sensitivity. Might Charles Edgar Trout have seen Bill as a mommy's boy, not "masculine" like his older brothers who liked hunting small game, as a "sissy" perhaps who showed too much interest in books, music, and womanly things? One might speculate that the source of Bill's life-long sense of failure and self-loathing was, at least in part, the result of a boyhood perception of inadequacy, of his inability to please and win the respect of his father, whose early death robbed him of the opportunity to "prove himself" and thus gain his approval. But there is another poem with an unidentified male—"tall, thin, sinewy"—as the subject, who is said to earn his living by "saw and hammer." The references to the man's physical appearance and occupation lead one to assume it is Bill's father. However, recalling what is said about the father in "Forecast," one wonders whether the man who deferred to the boy "even in a village crowd" and whom the boy was "always proud" to have as a friend (note not a father), is in fact Charles Edgar Trout. If it is, the two poems taken together hint that Bill may have had conflicted and unresolved feelings about his father. If it was another man, his identity remains unknown.

Tall, thin, sinewy, twisted dry;
Easy in speech and motion; accurate
With his tobacco juice; with small brown eye,
Shrewd and cynical in estimate,
Under the black hat, pulled sinister
And low: him I was always proud
To have for friend; oddly he would defer
To me, even in a village crowd.
By saw and hammer, he fed what he had sired,
A brood suspect in almost every way,
Whose lapses he blandly blinked, if he knew.
Sundays in autumn he roamed the countryside,
Slow and sharp. And I might wheedle and pray—
He never told me where the dittany grew.

Referring to his mother in letters to Don Smith sometimes as "Allie," "Die alte Marschallin," or "Die alte Frau" (allusions to Strauss' opera *Der Rosenkavalier*), and affectionately to other friends as "my old lady," Trout gives hints in letters of how closely they were bonded in occasional glimpse into their life together: her hospitalizations and doctor appointments, her moods, and "reading [to her] murder thrillers (Ellery Queen!) we both relish," and the way they "roared" over a funny passage in one of Arnold Bennett's novels. Jeannette Dillman, the private duty nurse who cared for Mrs. Trout in the last year of her life when Bill was off teaching, remembered that the desk he worked at in their Lancaster apartment was in her bedroom, and that when he came into the room after school it was filled with a palpable atmosphere of mutual love. His mother's death in November 1967 was for Bill what Emily Dickinson in her poem "After great pain, a formal feeling comes" calls "the Hour of Lead," a profound emotional numbness born of a traumatic experience. She also recognizes in the poem "Pain—has an Element of Blank" that the loss of a loved one could open a life-long and possibly debilitating void in one's life, something Bill experienced after the passing of his mother and expresses in "Afterward."

These rooms are severely orderly
And very quiet, since no need is rife:
Now has been altered the denominator
Of the intransigent fraction that is life;
Tardily and desultorily withers
The hope uprooted, and the mind learns
Fumblingly, as surrender gathers
Its groping impetus—learns, and turns
At last impassive. Possibility,
By a past tense, signals its yesterday.

From the many poems he wrote about his mother after her passing it is clear that Trout was a "constant mourner," who suffered from what Emily Dickinson in her poem "It did not surprise me" likens to carrying a "coffin" in the heart. His brother Frank in a May 25, 1980, letter to Don Smith confirms that Bill never outlived his "Hour of Lead": "I have a feeling that since my mother's death he merely tolerated life," Frank wrote. In a letter to me of 20 January 1971, Bill confirmed what Frank suspected. "My mother said to me," he recalled, "rousing from a profound drowse, 'They are all gone into the other world. How can I live without them?' And the protracted witnessing of sufferings that I could do so little to palliate filled me with a bitter hatred for life that does not seem to abate."

But there may be another explanation for the frequency with which he alludes to his mother in so many of his poems. In "Through Shadows of the Shadowless," "Come back, come back, across this wind," "The groping mind turns back to May, where bides," "Here I cling, threading maze," and other poems Trout casts himself as a traveler or wanderer and his mother (even after her death) as a guide to lead him to the other side. Thus his dependence on his mother continued even after her passing.

Bill may have recognized that he suffered from an unhealthy attachment to his mother, what psychologists refer to as a "mother complex," something he would probably never have admitted. According to the Swiss psychiatrist Carl Gustav Jung (1875-1961), "Mother complexes are extremely common in America and often very pronounced, probably because of the strong maternal influence in the home and the social position of women generally." An individual who has "freed himself insufficiently, or not at all from his childish environment" and his parents is, Jung maintains, "incapable of living his own life and finding the character that belongs to him." For a son who is unable to separate himself from his mother, Jung points out, the result is "all kinds of neurotic fears—that is to say, a general fear of life. The more a person shrinks from adapting himself to reality, the greater becomes the fear which increasingly besets his path at every point" (Jung 1956, 186, 284, 297). All of the passages from Jung quoted here were both underlined by Trout and marked with multiple vertical lines in the margins of his copy of Jung's *Symbols of Transformation*. What is more, Bill also marked passages dealing with the "mother complex" in the other books by Jung he owned.

Alice Trout struggled to support and educate her children in a home filled with love; she took care of her in-laws in their old age, was generous to William Henry Brown (a poor African American hired man) and others, loved children (who adored her in return), took joy in nature and gardening, showed kindness to animals, was known by all who met her for her goodness and sincerity, and was admired by them for bearing the burdens of widowhood without complaint or recrimination. In a world Bill saw as lacking in sincerity, loyalty, compassion, generosity, and selflessness his mother was the gold standard by which he judged people, not only those he met in person but literary figures—like the humble, caring, principled reddleman Diggory Venn, a character in Thomas Hardy's novel *The Return of the Native*—and other public persons from artists and musicians to politicians. It may well be that it is his mother's example that in part accounts for his admiration for such writers as George Sand, Emily Dickinson, May Sinclair, Charlotte Mew, Edna Millay, and Edwin Arlington Robinson.

With the exception of "Valentine Day," which focuses more on his mother than his father, and an occasional mention or allusion to Charles Edgar Trout (in "Forecast" and "Tall, thin, sinewy, twisted dry"), Bill's father is conspicuously absent from his poems. This may well be due to the fact that his father died when Bill was only ten years old; but one suspects, given the reference in "Forecast" to "the feared, long-legged father," that there were other reasons, including fundamental differences in temperament and values. Trout's self-sacrificing dedication to his mother, together with more than one hundred and fifty poems in which she, though never directly identified, is the principal subject (and others in which he refers or alludes to her), document his mother-fixation. In these poems he addresses not only her virtues and her struggles with poverty, widowhood, illness, and death, but also—drawing either from things she told him or family photographs—her childhood and youth. In part these poems are an attempt to hold onto the past, as he suggests in the last two lines of the poem, "To Have and To Hold" (not included herein): "To net you in a phrase, a line, / To hold, one moment, the fleet divine." And he makes a similar admission in the poem "Grandmother" (not included herein): "So much I hoard the memories, fragile, evanescent." While some of the poems about his mother get dangerously close to the syrupy sentimentality, but not the cheery optimism, of Ella Wheeler Wilcox, whose poetry Trout disparaged in letters, others bring to mind Alfred Lord Tennyson's *In Memoriam* (a poem he urged me to read at a time of grief in my life) in which the British Poet Laureate memorializes his dead friend Arthur Henry Hallam, and in the process worked through his own grief. Like Tennyson, Bill uses verse to try to come to terms with his mother's death, but he also, again like Tennyson, weighs the possibility that life may be just a cruel hoax perpetrated by an indifferent or unfeeling God. Trout's poems about his mother thus move beyond the merely private, the personal to explore wider philosophical and psychological issues. From the life experiences of childhood, adolescence, and early manhood that played such a significant role in shaping his character we turn to the intellectual influences that find expression in Trout's personality, professional life, and poetry.

Chapter 2
Ideas, Beliefs and Values

The political, economic, social, philosophical, and literary underpinnings of Trout's poems are crucial to understanding them. As noted near the end of the previous chapter, "Now Anonymous," for example, suggests a jaundiced view of organized Christianity. According to Alice Trout Smith (Bill's niece who as a child slept in her grandmother's room during visits to Gap), Mrs. Trout read a chapter from the Bible every night before going to bed, something Bill refers to in this short poem which makes more explicit his religious skepticism:

> Are you assured no luminous behest
> Came by night, across the snow, or through
> The beating of the rain?—No querulous question
> Unjustified—believe, believe—of you
> Prompts the query: it is honest, sad,
> Twilit speculation only. Here,
> In this thick book, whose savage chanting had,
> For you, such power to calm dismay and fear,
> To bring you peace, patiently I read—
> Only to see the mocking hope recede.

He did not find that the "twilit speculation" or the "savage chanting" of the Bible calmed his fear and dismay nor gave him the peace his mother found in Scripture. Patient reading of the Bible only showed him "the mocking hope recede." Kenneth Gibble, one of Trout's Millersville students, recalled a class discussion that turned to religion, perhaps in relation to George Eliot's agnosticism, in which Bill told the students that "his mother was a devout Christian believer, and then he said something like: 'I really wish I could also be a believer, but I find it impossible to have that assurance of faith.' "

Question marks, skeptical comments, but few affirmations, fill the margins of Bill's copy of Sir Thomas Browne's *Religio Medici* (1642) in which he expresses amazement at Browne's "pose of exaggerated humility," his credulity, hypocrisy, and unquestioning faith in a just and merciful God who allows cruelty and suffering to be inflicted on human beings made, as Browne insists, for no "other purpose than his glory" and "from whom he might receive his homage," which Bill calls "a degrading idea." Yet in an intolerant age, Browne expressed hope that through self-examination people may come to see others as not so different from themselves and treat them with understanding, charity, tolerance, and goodwill; something Trout acknowledges in his marginalia.

There is no record that William Trout was baptized or joined a church. Baptismal records exist at Bellevue Presbyterian Church in Gap for his brother Charles and sister Susanna but not for Alice Trout's three other children. Mrs. Trout apparently attended Bellevue Presbyterian, but how frequently is not certain. His poem "Lark Descending" suggests that Bill was in church at least once as a teenager, but there is no evidence that he ever darkened the door of a church again until his mother's funeral. His letters and the recollections of friends document that Bill, though he knew the Bible well (as his Gap student James Cauller remembered) and owned a copy of the *Manual of Prayers for the Use of the Catholic Laity* in which he noted specific passages, had serious doubts, and was perhaps an agnostic who put no faith in organized Christianity. Such doubts may have been fed by his reading of Nathaniel Hawthorne (1804-1864) and Herman Melville (1819-1891) whose novels and short stories drew on pre-Civil War (1830-1860) reform tracts, penny newspapers (which first appeared in American cities in 1833), and popular literature to explore the paradoxes of American society by exposing the irony and moral ambiguity revealed in the disconnect between what Christian zealots professed and how they lived. The admonitory and didactic intent of antebellum reform imagery is transformed by Hawthorne, and particularly Melville, who went beyond mere descriptive reportage to engage in philosophical reflection by using symbolism and the figurative language of metaphor to plumb the dark side of human psychology and to "lift the veil" hiding the moral ambiguities and contradictions of human behavior—the tippling temperance reformer, the lechery of moralizing clergymen, the northern abolitionist who turns a blind eye to wage-slavery in American industry—and the evils and corruption inherent in society. Hawthorne's novels and short stories, among them *The Scarlet Letter*, "The Rill from the Pump," and "The Minister's Black Veil," and those of Melville, including *Tepee*, *White-Jacket*, and *Moby-Dick*, subverted the respectability and authority of mainstream elites by exposing their "villainous or tabooed" activities, and as David Reynolds observes, make a case that "the strict insistence on moral rectitude ironically leads to immorality and violence" (Reynolds 1988, 114-134, 48-52, 135-165, 173-174). But Trout knew of more recent examples of how surface morality could mask the hypocrisy of Christian preachers and congregants.

Billy Sunday (1862-1935), a professional baseball star turned evangelist, who drew huge crowds at his revival meetings during the first two decades of the twentieth century until radio evangelists began to siphon off his audience in the 1920s, was widely reported in the press. A champion of the 18th Amendment and supporter of women's suffrage, he also opposed child labor and never forgot the poor, though his dramatic platform performances and colloquial sermons earned him loads of money, won invitations to dinner at the White House from Theodore Roosevelt and Woodrow Wilson, and the friendship of John D. Rockefeller, Jr. and Herbert Hoover. He was a sharp dresser and hobnobbed with the rich and famous, including movie stars (see McLaughlin 1955). Billy Sunday was the quintessential example of what H. L. Mencken called "cow-state Messiahs."

Even more renowned during Bill's youth and early manhood was Aimee Semple McPherson (1890-1944), an evangelist who began her preaching career by touring Canada and the United States holding tent-revivals: but later, though staging rallies all over the country, based her ministry in her 5,300-seat Angelus Temple in Los Angeles and took to the airwaves in weekly radio sermons. Her brand of corporate Christianity included publishing a weekly paper, a monthly magazine, and, beginning in 1924, owning her own radio station, KFSG. Her rallies and practice of faith-healing and speaking-in-tongues, were widely reported in the press. While her platform performances were theatrical and employed props, sets, an orchestra, and show business techniques, she denounced the secularization of society, opposed teaching evolution in the schools, and criticized card playing and dancing. She supported prohibition and women's suffrage, integrated her services at Angelus Temple by welcoming blacks, and during the Great Depression gave food and clothing to the poor and opened soup kitchens in Los Angeles. But she also made piles of money and lived the life of a Hollywood celebrity, in 1929 commissioning an architect to build her an Art Deco mansion—"Aimee's Castle"—in fashionable Lake Elsinore, California (see Sutton 2007). The character of the evangelist Sharon Falconer in Sinclair Lewis' novel *Elmer Gantry* (1926), a book Trout most certainly knew, was based on McPherson.

Such examples of hypocrisy and religious huckstering, as well as those he witnessed in his everyday life, in part account for Trout's reaction to organized Christianity, something Dennis Rittenhouse recalled fifty-five years after he and other Christiana students visited Trout at home one Saturday morning. As they observed through the living room window the arrival of long black limousines as part of the entourage setting up a tent revival meeting in the field across the highway, Bill quoted Scripture: "Take all thou hast and give it to the poor." And yet as so many of the poems about his departed mother suggest, Bill could not entirely abandon hope in a life after death, and some poems, such as "We gathered cress" contain subtle religious imagery. There are other poems that suggest he retained, however tenuously, some religious beliefs. In the poem "Through the ebbing fumes of midnight wine" he sees in a pink geranium, a "Miniature Damascus" (a reference to Paul's conversion experience on the road to Damascus), a "Bold assertion printed vehemently / Upon the tangible fastness of doubt." And in "Onset" he finds in a rose a symbol of love, "A pentecostal power"—an experience of grace akin to the descent of the Holy Spirit upon the Apostles and other followers of Jesus as described in the second chapter of the Book of Acts.

Trout tells his young GI friend Donald Smith (a Gap native) in a letter of 8 May 1943: "Of course my sympathies are all with Tuck [Don's girlfriend and future wife] in her quiet revolt from the outworn and corrupt practices of conventional religion. But I would never by any word or deed, willfully shake another's beliefs. My own view is pretty limited (what could be expected from a country Ichabod Crane whom the army turns from in horror). But I think [Edwin Arlington] Robinson formulated my idea best when he said [in a letter to Harry Peck of *The Bookman*] the world was not a prison house but a 'kind of spiritual kindergarten, where millions of bewildered infants are trying to spell 'God' with the wrong blocks.' " Jean Rentz, who for a time after the war shared a classroom with him at Christiana School, remembered that Bill hated doing the mandatory daily devotions before classes began and asked her to read the Bible and lead the Lord's Prayer. Writing to Don Smith in April 1944, about a Sunday afternoon New York Philharmonic radio broadcast of Beethoven's *Missa solemnis*, Bill says:

> This was the second hearing for me; the first took me quite unawares, and I recall being at first startled, then a little scared, and then unasham-

> edly weeping; and then becoming merely a kind of shallow vessel into which those exalted sounds poured and overflowed. As irreligious, I suppose, as it is possible for anyone to be, twice in my life I have been, seemingly, near understanding the divine frenzy of the devout, and both times music was the vehicle: once in March 1934 when Toscanini and the Philharmonic broadcast the Beethoven Missa [solemnis], and at my first [J. S. Bach] Saint Matthew [Passion].

Though obviously a deeply spiritual man, Bill seems to have spent much of his life searching for faith but always finding joy, solace, and spiritual nourishment in classical music. While he could not believe, he was not comfortable in his unbelief.

Having read Emily Dickinson's poems and letters, Trout was well aware of her struggles with faith—in part caused by the illnesses and deaths of those she loved—and may have found in them support for his own doubts and spiritual quest. Though fed on Puritanism and Transcendentalism, Dickinson's theology was her own, not the Calvinist orthodoxies preached from pulpits. Throughout her life she questioned New England Calvinist theology and rejected its moral sermonizing. Of the five members of the Dickinson family Emily alone refused to join the church even in the face of the religious revivalism that swept New England and in spite of pressure she experienced as one-by-one her classmates at Mount Holyoke Female Seminary became professing Christians, leaving her among those labeled "without hope." While at first she continued attending services, by her mid-twenties she gave up going to church, as confirmed in her poem "Some keep the Sabbath by going to Church." She kept it by staying home and visiting the family orchard and listening to birds sing. Like Melville and Hawthorne, Dickinson was influenced not only by the popular pulpit preaching of her day, particularly the new sermon style of such preachers as Henry Ward Beecher, Martin Leland, and especially Charles Wadsworth, but also by parodies of the new preaching style published in the penny press and humor periodicals of the day, which as David Reynolds claims, account for her "mixing the sacred and the secular, the Christian and the pagan" in her poetry and manifested in her use of colloquialisms, imaginative and emotional language, and help explain her "weird images, jolting rhythms, and half rhymes," that may have confirmed Trout's views on institutional Christianity and left its mark on his poetry. She held views of God and Jesus that were clearly heterodox. In her letters and in poems like "I know that He exists" she expresses doubts about heaven and immortality and the efficacy of prayer. Poems such as "What is—'Paradise'" poke fun at the conventional religious ideas of her day, and in "I never felt at Home—Below" she confesses "I don't like Paradise— / Because it's Sunday—all the time— / And Recess—never comes." She dismisses prayer in the poem "Of course—I prayed." In "That after Horror—that 'twas us" and "It always felt to me—a wrong," Dickinson questions why mere mortals should trust a God who snatches life away so capriciously or who denied his faithful servant Moses entry into the Promised Land and sacrificed his Son on the cross. She rebelled against the Calvinist God who played cat and mouse with peoples' lives and souls and accused Him of "Duplicity" in "'Heavenly Father'—take to thee." "Is immortality true?" Dickinson asked several of her correspondents, including Thomas Wentworth Higginson, and as late in life as 1882 in a letter to Washington Gladden. But it is in her poem "This World is not Conclusion" that Cynthia Griffin Wolff maintains one finds a systematic examination of the "leakage" and final loss of faith by Dickinson. As Barton Levi Saint Armand asserts, "Much of Dickinson's poetry was a continuing dialectic that used the imagery, premises, and metrics of Puritan hymnology as a basis for a personal psalmody of questioning and protest" (Johnson 1955, chaps. I and X; Mudge 1975, 118, 153-155, 159-160; Reynolds 1988, 31-37, 471; Wolff 1986, 98, 143, 148-149, 262, 269-270; St. Armand, 1984, 47, 127, 158). Her poems and letters provide a much more extensive documentation of her religious views than anything Trout has left us about his. Still, what we have shows that both were skeptics when it came to organized Christianity. They raised some of the same questions, though they may not always have arrived at the same answers.

In an undated letter from the early 1950s to Jean Rentz, Trout says of Dickinson: "She outgrew her theology but never relegated it to the attic; she rather used it to swing her tenuous but tough bridges across the infinite." Her religious skepticism, which left her "standing alone in rebellion," as she told her friend Jane Humphrey in a letter of 3 April 1850, was born of the disconnect she saw between the promise of a loving and caring God and the realities of earthly suffering. Trout records the same discrepancy in his poems "Now Anonymous," "Are you assured no luminous behest," and "Trust in neither god nor man." In his lecture notes for a course he taught at Millersville State College, he says of the poet of Amherst: "She turns the same irony, the same skepticism upon religion: D[ickinson] was not an ordinary woman, nor was she an obedient believer. Like Voltaire, she harries God with acid criticism, taunts, gibes; she puts thumbtacks on the Eternal Throne. She could not accept her father's religion. She said [of her family]: 'They pray to an eclipse.' All her life she was caught between conflicting tides of faith and open disbelief and some of the most memorable of the poems chronicle her predicament." Much the same can be said of William Trout as a person and a poet. His views on religion may also have been influenced or confirmed by reading the works of the Swiss psychologist Carl Jung, particularly his *Aion* (1951) and *Answer to Job* (1958), which Trout underlined and filled with a blizzard of marginal commentary.

As Jung affirms in his autobiographical *Memories, Dreams, Reflections*, the issue of God's ambivalence, His duality, His "tragic contradictoriness," raises the question of who is responsible for the sufferings of God's faithful servant Job and for the sins for which Christ is crucified, and by extension for the sufferings of humanity. Although he addresses this question in *Aion*, Jung makes it the main theme of his *Answer to Job*. At the very beginning of the book, he points out that Scripture gives many examples that Yahweh is a God who "lacks moderation" and who admits he is "eaten up with rage and jealousy." His nature combines "insight" with "obtuseness, loving-kindness along with cruelty, creative power" and "destructiveness." "Such a condition is only conceivable," Jung maintains, "either when no reflecting consciousness is present at all, or when the capacity for reflection is very feeble and a more or less adventitious phenomenon. A condition of this sort can only be described as *amoral*." Job recognizes that "God is at odds with himself," that He is a unity combining both evil and good. In abandoning Job, "Yahweh displays no compunction, remorse, or compassion, but only ruthlessness and brutality. The plea of unconsciousness is invalid, seeing that he flagrantly violates at least three of the commandments he himself gave out on Mount Sinai." Job looks upon God as a "moral being" and trusts in divine justice; yet, as Jung says, God "merely flaunts might over right." Beyond the "agonizing death" God allows his son to endure, Jung observes, "we are appalled by the incongruous attitude of the world creator towards his creatures, who to his chagrin never behave according to his expectations," next to which in the page margin Bill wrote: "the wounded soldier propped lurchingly against a shell-riddled wall" and "the 5 or 6 who die each night in the cancer ward" (Jung 1973, 216-217; Jung 1958, 3, 7, 10, 14-16, 53).

Trout rejected the clerical argument that even in the face of evil and suffering people should hold fast to their faith—in the words of an old gospel hymn, "trust and obey"—since God's ways are beyond human understanding. This view may in part account, as his Millersville student Dianne Danz recalled, for why he so liked Stephen Crane's poem "A man said to the universe" in which a man asserts his own existence, which the universe acknowledges but replies: "The fact has not created in me / A sense of obligation." In both his poems and letters Trout affirms an "existentialist" view that we are all on our own in a purposeless universe. Though people can find no help from an indifferent God or the impersonal universe, Bill would have agreed with Pascal that man is a weak but "thinking reed," and that even if the universe crushed him he still knows he dies. However, Trout seems less assured than Pascal of the nobility of human beings. His skepticism and stoicism are not concealed in a poem that also makes a subtle reference to his mother:

> Trust in neither god nor man
> Remains to landmark leagues, where now,
> Coldly counter to law's ban,
> Eyes strive to find the faded brow
> Lovely underneath its crown
> Of soft hair. Only hate
> Roams, where undefined Renown
> Lolled regent in Its veiled state.
> Into query, alone I go,
> And, outcast where you take no heed
> Of long courage overthrown,
> I dare the desolate—no recourse,
> Since faith had failed at the source,
> Leaving only a withered creed.

That Trout's "faith had failed" can in part be explained by the physical suffering and death of those most dear to him. About a year before her retirement in 1942, Alice Trout began suffering from heart problems and other ailments and was hospitalized in January of 1941. Later, according to her granddaughter, she broke her left hip three times and hobbled around with a cane. Bill tells Betty Curtis, a former Millersville student, in a postcard in January 1964 that his mother, just home from eight weeks in the hospital, "can no longer walk. Needs much care." "During the last 8 years, 4 mo. of my mother's life," Bill relates to Mrs. Ralph Hodges in a letter cited earlier, "I worked as nurse, housekeeper, doctor (often), as well as teacher. Since I was not discharged, [from teaching] my work apparently did not fall below 'subsistence' level. But the psychic malformation consequent upon that fate is patent in such screed as this. However, near the end, one seems to care little about anything." To me he confides in an October 1971, letter: "For almost thirty years, I did not dare to become ill, and I did not miss a day of school. What insanity. And for the last decade—1958-1967—I was ridden by horror lest I become protractedly ill (a stroke) or die before...." In a January 1979 letter he mentions to me that his mother had been hospitalized eighteen or nineteen times over the years. And in a letter to Jean Rentz in the mid-1950s he recommends Emily Dickinson's poem "Elysium is as far as to," saying, "if you have ever waited for news from the operating room, that poem will make you wince ... and reach shyly for Emily's hand." The despair that any caring child must feel in witnessing a parent's descent into dementia is reflected in one of Bill's few dated poems, written on 30 January 1966, about fifteen months before his mother's death. His patience, gentleness, and weariness come through in anguished words of helplessness in the face of the inevitable in the sonnet:

> Her endless, silent monologues of age,
> Accompanied by tears, shed or unshed,
> Tangle metaphysics, and cloud with rage
> My mutely somber, treasonable head.
> Eyes faded to the neutral gray of rain
> Stare past me into the Past, peopled now
> With vanished ones, coaxed by the tired brain—
> A torment that the mocking Powers allow.
> The soft mouth falters, and the fingers shake,
> Pressed to stay the faltering; her gaze
> Questions my presence, intrusion that unmakes—
> However sadly—the glimmer of those days.
> Through meager tears, the tacit syllables
> Beg the bright lies that Time the Pedlar sells.

The long years of day-to-day experience Bill had in caring for his mother helps explain why his poems about old people seem so much more personal, more intimate, more sensitive, and more insightful than Robert Frost's few poems about old age, which while sympathetic to the plight of the elderly and emotionally moving, lack the directness of concerned firsthand knowledge. In "An Old Man's Winter Night" Frost tells us of a man alone in his house on a winter's night. Everything about the poem suggests the aging process and end of life: darkness; a broken moon; frost; snow; icicles; empty, creaking rooms; logs reduced to ashes in a stove; sleep. He conveys the isolation and loneliness of the elderly man who was "a light ... to no one but himself" and whose confusion and failing memory suggest the beginnings of senility. Yet Frost's observations turned into metaphors seem somehow detached and rather clinical, almost generic when compared to Trout's observations of the elderly in poems like "Now Anonymous," "You always think that, when I close my eyes," "Great Aunt," "Her endless, silent monologues of age," and this one (written in 1971) recalling his mother's last years:

> The small face shrivels, and the eyes grow strange;
> The wrists are twigs, clothed with delicate,
> Pathetic sheathing, subdued by a brown stain;
> The hands are the claws of a bird tense with fright.
> Endlessly, the thread of voice goes on,
> Confusing people, times, generations.
> Shocked, the listener quakes: in a weird dawn,
> All those dead feet, hurrying on their way.
> —I make this doggerel in another dawn—
> Implacable materiality—
> Only to grope to There, where you have gone,
> So long ago—four remorseless years.
> The mind veers back: confronts the shrivelling,
> Feels the bird-claw tighten on the wrist;
> Remembers saying inly, "To go on living
> After. . . ." Dull confusion must desist.

Writing of his aunt, Mary Livingston, who suffered a stroke in 1945, Bill describes her in hospital as "lying a shriveled, shattered old woman; her mind wanders, her body is almost completely out of control." And yet thinking of all the young victims of World War II who "never had a chance to live," he goes on to tell Don Smith, "you don't pity [her]; you merely hope for the speedy end, which will not come." The many agonizing hours he must have spent in hospitals with his mother, aunt, and others are reduced to a poetic snapshot, "Semi-Private Room," of the patient who shared the room, which is redolent with irony, bitter humor, and social commentary:

> In a shabby dressing gown—her gray-streaked hair
> In straight meagre pig-tails, her mouth pinched tight—
> She sat grimly by the window; her spare

Hands gave an inkling of how right
Her bankbook looked, and spoke of the three farms,
Lavish in their profitable charms.

Proudly beside her, in a little vial,
Reposed two gall-stones, at which the bishop stared
In three-jowled fascination, and made trial,
About his paunch, of how his dinner fared. . . .
Neither noted the six gladiolus sprays,
Lavender, spinning the light into laughing maze.

Trout aims a bolt of not so subtle social criticism at the "business" of death in the United States by questioning the ways in which people are required at their moment of greatest sorrow to surrender grief to deal with "calculation's sly gaze."

Quietly insistent, importunate,
Present themselves intently at the sill,
The doctor, the mortician, and the State,
The Law, professional about the will;
This one is deferential, alludes to fate;
Another brings an official form to fill;
A third prescribes a capsule to abate
Pain; the fourth calmly presents his bill.
How have we passed, then, the primordial,
Distanced the dumb nomad and his ways
Of jackal, that we surrender, and concord
Grief and calculation's sly gaze?—
In, in, huddled beside the dead,
The central thing stoops the bewildered head.

But it is not only the deaths of family and the sufferings of his beloved mother that account for Trout's troubled view of life. Running through most of his correspondence is evidence of persistent low self-esteem, a topic that will be explored more fully in Chapter 5. Exactly when in life this negative self-perception developed—and why—is uncertain, but it may help to explain why he became increasingly reclusive over the years.

The poetry of Emily Dickinson and William Trout is profoundly home-centered. Jean McClure Mudge explores the many manifestations of domesticity related to Dickinson's imaginative inner-world and the tangible world of her everyday life expressed by the themes, imagery, and diction of her poems. As with Dickinson, some of Bill's poems make references to or are set in specific domestic spaces: the back porch, kitchen, dining room, parlor, hallway, or bedroom. Domestic activities like tending the garden, gathering watercress and making sandwiches, a simmering soup pot and jars of currant jelly set out to cool, and eating a picnic lunch in the family dining room when rain aborted an outing are memories of daily life in the Trout household that provide insights and carry significance important for understanding Bill's personality and poetry. Both poets were introverts who found in home and family a refuge and a prison. While they were devoted to family members, each feeling obliged to care for an invalid or aged parent, there is evidence in their letters and poems that reveals the stresses and resentments such responsibilities created, as well as a sense of having sacrificed their own lives for others. Expressions of loneliness and unfulfilled desires are also found in their letters and poems. With his knowledge of Jungian psychology Trout could recognize in Dickinson's correspondence and verse the symptoms of neurosis, particularly because he was also neurotic, as will become apparent in Chapter 5. (Mudge 1975, xvii-xviii, 67-69, 173-174, 190-192).

While Dickinson does not seem to have regretted turning her back on the outside world (a conscious choice given poetic voice in her poem "Renunciation—is a piercing Virtue" in which she says "Renunciation—is the Choosing / Against itself") there were times when Bill seems to have had second thoughts about his decision to renounce the world beyond his home and family. There is for instance a deep sense of melancholy in what he says to Don Smith in a July 1942 letter: "The tyrannical obduracy of time haunts one insistently as he grows older—so much that might have been done, so many unborn memories murmuring accusations; 'on this short day of frost and sun' it is a sad thing to have 'slept before evening.' " Here he is quoting from the Conclusion of Walter Pater's *The Renaissance: Studies in Art and Poetry* (1873), a work in which the critic and Oxford don asserts: "Not the fruit of experience, but experience itself, is the end." He goes on to urge upon readers the idea that "To burn always with this hard, gemlike flame, to maintain this ecstasy, is success in life." And finally admonishes them that: "Not to discriminate every moment some passionate attitude in those about us, and in the brilliancy of their gifts some tragic dividing of forces on their way, is, on this short day of frost and sun, to sleep before evening" (Pater 1907, 249-250).

Thus already at age thirty-three Bill had begun to believe life had passed him by, that he had not seized the day and made it his own. "I don't know how it is," he writes to Don Smith in 1943, "but daily I grow more of a recluse, more timid of subjecting myself to alien and probably hostile scrutiny and criticism" [and] "my own failure to stand life's varied acid tests is most humiliating, and daily I long to stick a change of underwear and a pair of clean socks in my pocket, and be off [quoting Tennyson's "Ulysses"] 'beyond the sunset, and the baths of all the western stars.' But I guess it is too late 'to seek a never world.' With three or four people in the world I can be comfortable, but with most I suffer tortures—no kidding." Sadness and frustration about missed opportunities in life come out again in his letter of 22 July 1945 to Smith: "I sometimes dream about a rocky coast with green water and white foam and gulls and silence, and me hugging my knees in a windy nook and staring out to sea, and not even thinking about the past or the future ... especially not about the past. But all the sea I'll get will be in Sibelius," whose symphonies and tone poems evoke the stark beauty of the ocean and the Finnish coastline and landscape of lakes and marshes, meadows and forests. Already in his mid-thirties, Bill had begun to have regrets and to see himself as one of Edwin Arlington Robinson's "clerks of Time."

That he loved visual art, classical music and opera, and spent much of his time alone reading and listening to music, may have contributed to an unspoken perception among some of the residents of Gap that Bill was a little strange or eccentric. No doubt compounding the sense of isolation and alienation he may have experienced was the knowledge that his radical social and political views, his religious skepticism, and, perhaps, a secret that dared not speak its name were seriously at odds with the mores of the conservative and convention-bound community in which he had to earn his bread. Only in his poems, letters, and conversations with the few people he trusted did Bill hint at or confide his thoughts and beliefs.

His double Xs marking Thomas Hardy's "Drummer Hodge" (so different from the saccharin idealism of Rupert Brooke's 1914 God-and-Country poem, "The Soldier") reveal both Trout's sympathy for those who fight their country's wars and his admiration for this poem about a Wessex farm boy killed in the Boer War (1899-1902) and thrown, "uncoffined," into a South African grave. Yet his question, "Why did he write it? Why" written next to Hardy's 1917 patriotic poem, "A Call To National Service" reflects the distaste Bill felt not only for the sentiments expressed in the poem and the use of art to support a war, but by extension his objection to the flag-waving-remember-Pearl-Harbor-patriotism that swept the United States after 7 December 1941.

While most Americans apparently never questioned the ways in which the government and the censored news media reported and the mass culture—popular songs, magazines, commercial advertising, and particularly Hollywood films—depicted the conduct and realities of the war in an effort both to justify what was being done and to keep up the morale of service personnel and civilians, Trout's critical spirit saw through the misrepresentations, euphemisms, evasions of wartime actualities, and shallow high-minded (and at time disingenuous) rhetoric about democracy and preserving civilization. He recognized that individuality and the freedom to question and dissent were casualties of the war, eroded by the conformity, uniformity, anonymity, blandness, and shallowness that pervaded the culture of wartime America. Irony, satire, subtlety were hard to come by in the writing of the period, whether literary or journalistic, where so much was formulaic, stated in terms of stereotypes, clichés, or unexamined binary absolutes—good versus evil, bravery versus cowardice, friend versus foe, freedom versus fascism—and written mainly in monosyllables. It was a time of slogans—"Wage War on Waste," "The Great Crusade," "Rap the Jap," "Grow More in '44," and "Freedom Is a Habit," the title of a poem by Carl Sandburg (1878-1967), one of the nation's most popular poets and a promoter in the tradition of Walt Whitman of all things American.

But Trout's skepticism concerning the motives and actions of the government did not keep him from fretting about, sympathizing with, and supporting the troops (among them his brother Frank), characterizing them in a letter to Don Smith as "all Galahads and Lancelots and Cavalier Baynards, sans peur et sans reproche..." (fearless and irreproachable knights). He carried on an extensive correspondence with his brother and a number of young GIs, among them Don Smith, whose thirty-seven letters from Bill between 1941 and 1946 are crucial to understanding this complex man.

Bill's experience with his local draft board left him angry and bitter, something he expressed in letter to Don Smith on 19 January 1942. Ashamed of having failed several army physicals and being classified 4-F, but relieved that he would not have to turn the care of his mother over to strangers, Bill no doubt felt his rejection for military service was yet another of his failures in life. Yet during World War II he sometimes worked eleven-hour shifts, from 5:30 in the evening to 5 in the morning, operating an electric drill in the machine shop in the mill at Lukens Steel in Coatesville, as he told Smith in a Fourth of July letter in 1942. If Paul Fussell's claim is correct that the most vigorous soldierly contempt was directed not at conscientious objectors but at those found physically unfit for military service, Trout's 4-F classification no doubt deepened his already low self-esteem and explains his telling Don Smith that he is someone "whom the army turns from in horror" (Fussell 1989, 116). He laments in another letter to Smith how absurd it is that someone as "garden variety" as he is rejected for military service while Smith, a talented young music student at Oberlin, is "sacrificed, and for what? For the benefit of a minority class, for the ruthlessly greedy, the diabolically ambitious—and with what bravado the young go out to death; not having lived, they pour out life, their only possession, in defense of a living lie, going so valiantly away [quoting from Aeschylus' *Agamemnon*, part VII] 'to sleep at Troy the sleep of swords.' "

As one by one his former pupils and the young friends he made in the steel mill were drafted, Trout's melancholy and disillusionment deepened. Writing to Smith on 10 June 1944, he tells him of "Chick, the slight, gray-eyed Nijinsky who was lost to the ballet by one of those criminal wastes of life; [and of] little Bob, the eighteen-year-old Ephrata Dutchman with the sturdy body and engaging accent ... so they go." A working-class Irishman in his twenties named Jim is mentioned often and at length in Bill's letters to Smith. But it was the death on 22 November 1943 in a military airplane crash in Morocco of his handsome, popular, and fun-loving (he rode a motorcycle) former Gap pupil Sgt. Parke J. Bair, Jr., nicknamed "Hookie," that devastated Bill. Hookie's "unfailing and regular" letters over three years, "were sunny spots in life's pretty uniform grayness, and his visits were in the nature of holidays," he tells Don Smith early in December 1943, saying: "I never knew anyone who lived quite so buoyantly and freely; the eagerness to clutch at life gave him the hint of being winged ... With him goes, now, much of the light, and almost all of life's rare gaiety ... such people shouldn't be hurt; and the senselessness and evil of existence are verified past question." Nearly two years later the pain of Bair's death persisted as Trout, in a letter to Smith, reflects: "for years I have never lived thru an October such as this. It cuts across your nerves like a sudden electric shock. Coming home at evening thru the crisp dry air and the smell of smoldering leaves, I kept remembering Hookie. This weather always seemed to suit him." Bill's anxiety about his brother Frank and his young friends in the military led him to admit in a January 1944 letter to Smith: "I don't pretend to be emotionally stable these days. Life for me isn't worth the attempt at preserving any equilibrium."

Bill was very fond of Frank (fig. 12). He felt "loss and desolation" with Frank away in the army, he writes Smith in June 1943, confessing that on "sleepless nights I used to go into his room and sit there trying to shame myself into having more courage." He tells Smith in a letter postmarked 20 September 1943, that "Frank is sensitive to natural beauty and likes autumn," and that his (Bill's) "whole life" is "balanced on the successful return of two or three people from this their journey into Inferno." But his grief and sense of loss went beyond family and close friends. He "cried like a fuckin' baby" at the news of the D-Day landings, and when FDR died "wept as I would for a friend," he admits to Smith.

But Trout was not yet a total pessimist. He had faith, as he assures Smith in September 1943, confident that after the war the intelligence and resourcefulness of young people would take the nation in a different direction. He could not think that they "will resign the wealth of this country, and its place in international life, to the financial interests which have heretofore steered this nation from calamity to catastrophe." However, by June of 1945 he held a jaundiced view of the credibility of the news media, characterizing as "muck" that which is "hurled at us hourly by the press and radio." And by early September 1945, his guarded optimism about postwar America has been shaken not only by the Republican Party's "defamation of FDR's character," but by the growing "evidence of re-action" in the United States and the betrayal of the sacrifices made by those who had fought. "It looks as tho Americans died to give every American woman two pairs of nylon stockings before Christmas and every American family two Ford cars," he fumes to Smith. Anyone who has paged through the ads for consumer products in such popular magazines as *Collier's*, *The Saturday Evening Post*, and *Life* during the last eighteen months of the war will understand where Bill got his cynicism. GIs in foxholes from Italy to the South Pacific are shown in ads dreaming of new houses, plates heaped with ice cream, Brooks Brothers suits, new cars, kitchen appliances, and any number of other consumer goods. At the end of September 1945 he declares to Smith: "There is a dangerous social levening (should be 'leavening') process going on here; and no unity, no cohesion, no goal; class against class; urban against rural; property against labor. The disbanding of the armed forces is engendering a terrific bitterness; and the supposed aims of the last four years are hopelessly obscured."

The possibility of nuclear annihilation ushered in when the United States dropped atomic bombs on two Japanese cities in August 1945 fueled Trout's pessimism. He mentions "the Bomb" in several letters to Don Smith, advising him in January 1946: "Don't—ever—live in the future, in the sense of denying present happiness for the sake of the vague rosy glow beyond the hill. Is the Bomb any more of a menace than the skidding car, pneumonia bacillus, et al?"

William Axe, a student of Trout's at Christiana School from 1946-48, who enlisted in the Marines and served in a combat unit in Korea, remembered that Bill was very critical of both the U. S. policy that led to the Korean War and to its conduct. As with World War II, Trout sympathized with and supported the troops but blamed politicians and bureaucrats for sacrificing so many lives in what he believed was an unjustifiable war. Axe recalled that as early as 1953-54 Trout expressed concern about the dangers posed by the American "military-industrial complex" years before President Eisenhower's farewell address to the nation on 17 January 1961, in which he warned of the negative consequences—"economic, political, even spiritual"—inherent in the "conjunction of an immense military establishment and a large arms industry." The "military-industrial complex," the President pointed out, has "grave implications" in its "potential for the disastrous rise of misplaced power." Trout also pressed Axe, a self-confessed "gung ho" Marine, to explain how or why it was possible for so many young men to be so uncritically accepting of the military mind set that they would not question the reasons or motives of those sending so many of them to their deaths.

Even earlier, Bill's antipathy to the military surfaces in an undated one-page homily titled "To A Young Friend in Celebration of a Singular Event: First Anniversary of Army Service" sent to Don Smith, probably in June of 1944. While acknowledging that military service may have given Smith discipline, made him more understanding or accepting of others by bringing him into contact with people different from himself, taught him "not only to appreciate friendship but also to offer friendship" and make some "wonderful friends," and refined his sense of appreciation of the "little things that can mean so much when you don't have them"—Bill clearly saw the negative experiences as outweighing the positive ones. He congratulates Smith for being able to put up with things he himself could not. "I am trying to put myself in your shoes, trying to imagine myself, at 21 again, suddenly torn out by the roots, from surroundings I loved and appreciated, thrown into the company of 'masses' whom I hate … forced into a mould, forced to do stupid things over and over again, things I hate because of their brutal dullness and dull brutality!" He may have learned from his brother Frank and young soldier friends about what Paul Fussell describes as the varieties of "chickenshit" service men have to endure (Fussell 1989, 79-95). Then, too, only the most naïve or credulous of American civilians could swallow as truth what newspapers and magazines fed them about combat. Paul Fussell, who led a rifle platoon in France and was badly wounded in 1945, documents the not infrequent "f-ups" of military planners that resulted in significant casualties as well as the sanitizing of the war by the news media, most notably the photographs in *Life*, which never showed landing beaches and battlefields strewed with body parts, but only occasionally the clothed and intact bodies of dead GIs. In battles fought with tanks, machine guns, and high explosives, dismembered bodies were common. And yet severed arms, headless, legless, or disemboweled cadavers, were never showed to the public (Fussell 1989, 268-273). Thus there are legitimate grounds for Bill's cynicism. Whether or not he was a pacifist is moot since he never used the word in his extant correspondence, or to my memory in our conversations. Yet he saw nothing in war as noble or worth celebrating, but believed there was good reason to take anything the government or the media said with a pillar of salt.

In a 2005 interview, the ninety-three-year old George Hoar, a retired insurance agent and former Republican Party committee man in Salisbury Township related to the Trouts through marriage, told me that Bill was a registered Republican, which is no doubt true given the fact that most of the elective offices in Lancaster County, including local school boards, were a virtual monopoly of the GOP. No doubt Bill's voter registration decision was influenced by necessity. His party membership did not reflect his politics. For most of his life Bill's anti-capitalist views were fed by his experiences, what he observed around him, and what he absorbed from socially conscious writers like Dickens, Hardy, E. A. Robinson, H. M. Tomlinson, and what he read in the *Manchester Guardian*, *The New York Times*, and magazines. Some of his most revealing statements about his own values and beliefs are the comments he penned in the margins of the books he owned, written in reply to some point made by the author. One such comment written in his copy of J. W. N. Sullivan's book on Beethoven, in response to the discussion of the composer's financial problems with his publishers and creditors, reflects both Trout's rejection of communism and his anti-capitalist sentiments: "The Communist 'morality of deceit' is merely 'business morality.' " "Let no one ever tell you," he warns me in a letter of 2 May 1971, "that poverty … fortifies the character and expands the spirit. That admonition is an ecclesiastical beneath-the-board connivance with rapacious capitalism."

Dates written in his copy of the Modern Library's *Nine Plays* by Eugene O'Neill document that Trout read them during April of 1948, drawn to them presumably by the playwright's explorations of the psychological struggles of modern men and women with failed aspirations, frustrations, passions, and the inability of materialism, science, or religion to give meaning to their lives. Although his annotations are sparing, those lines he did mark or underscore tell us something of his ideas and attitudes toward Western Civilization and religion. Responding to the advice of General Bayan, in "*Marco Millions*," that he invade and conquer the West, Kublai, the Great Kaan, replies that the West "... must be a pitiful land, poor in spirit and material wealth. We have everything to lose by contact with its greedy hypocrisy. The conqueror acquires first the vices of the conquered. Let the West devour itself." Later in the same play Bill underlined Kublai's observation: "My hideous suspicion is that God is only an infinite, insane energy which creates and destroys without other purpose than to pass eternity in avoiding thought." He again reveals his attitude toward organized religion by marking a passage in *Mourning Becomes Electra* in which Christine (the wife of General Mannon) says to Hazel Niles in a tone of "bitter longing": "If I could only have stayed as I was then! Why can't all of us remain innocent and loving and trusting? But God won't leave us alone. He twists and wrings and tortures our lives with other's lives until—we poison each other to death!"

Bill's scrapbooks are filled with quotations and notes he took from books he read, and with clippings on cultural subjects, current events, and advertising, often annotated in ways that reveal his attitudes and values. H. M. Tomlinson was a British journalist and novelist, who, in addition to fiction, wrote on current events, nature, and his travels in a reflective, meditative manner, about events and the people he observed. As Frank Swinnerton, who knew him, wrote: "He had always been a philosophic observer in the vein of Thoreau" (Swinnerton 1956, 207-208). While rereading Tomlinson's *The Turn of the Tide* (written during World War II and published in 1945) in 1976, Bill copied into one of his scrapbooks five pages of quotations from it, suggesting his sympathy with the author's point of view, among them the following: "Men of business terrify me more than Hitler ever did. As politicians, they are never right. Service of Mammon and the people at the same time cannot be done" (p. 81). "The State and its edicts have been substituted for God and a moral order. The State is an impersonal monster with a heart of gun-metal and bowels of steel piping. Its only rule is expediency" (p. 82). "It is taking us too long to learn that politics and finance are two aspects of the same thing" (p. 121). "If the war [World War II] does not bring us to unity in the cause of mankind, then we fail, and are wasting life and treasure"

(p. 126). And near the end of the book, Tomlinson makes another point with which Trout could concur, one that was made more than twenty years before the environmental movement got under way: "What is this conquest of nature we boast about? It begins to look very much like the suicide of mankind" (p. 170).

Not only had Bill experienced poverty firsthand during childhood, he had seen it up close in his first teaching job in the one-room school at Mt. Airy on the southern slope of Welsh Mountain some miles north of Gap. After receiving his two-year rural-school certificate in 1931, he taught all six grades at Mt. Airy School from 1931-1936, when he joined his mother at Gap Centralized School. His students at Mt. Airy were predominantly children of the rural poor—white, black, and multiracial. As early as the mid-eighteenth century, Welsh Mountain, extending for some twenty miles through Lancaster, Berks, Lebanon, and Chester counties in eastern Pennsylvania, offered refuge to escaped slaves who intermarried with the local Native Americans and descendants of Welsh and Irish immigrants. More blacks settled there in the nineteenth century, as did poor whites, building small log cabins, ramshackle board shacks, and dugouts, and eking out a subsistence living farming the mountain's thin, stony marginal land or working as charcoal burners making fuel for area iron furnaces. Some owned their land, but others were squatters with no clear title to the land they occupied. Multiracial families were not uncommon in the area. As Joan Lorenz points out: this "interracial community" fostered "a deep chasm of fear, prejudice, and suspicion … between the apparent chaos of mountain living and the apparent order of [Pequea] valley life" (Lorenz 2002, 212). In the decades just before and after the Civil War Welsh Mountain became home to outlaw gangs—the Buzzard family being the most notorious—who engaged in everything from chicken stealing and cattle theft to armed robbery and bounty hunting for fugitive slaves.

"A Mission for Outlaws," a report in *The New York Times* (21 November 1898), claims that for years portions of Welsh Mountain in Lancaster and Lebanon counties "have been the home of people ignorant of God and Christianity, with thievery and outlawry generally their principal vocations, and an utter disregard of law marking their daily lives." For a time, beginning in 1898, the local school board stopped providing education to African American children on Welsh Mountain. But the founding of a Mennonite mission aimed to reform residents of the area. In 1899 the Mennonite Church began mission work among the impoverished black and mixed race residents on the mountain, intending to improve their economic circumstances, redeem their souls, and end their reputed lawlessness. The Mennonites bought land and paid locals to clear it. A mission building was constructed to house training and employment opportunities for black and biracial residents in shirt making, carpet weaving, broom-making, and farming methods. In 1906 they began monthly preaching services. In 1914 a Sunday School was opened. Their efforts, however, produced disappointing results, and by 1924 only the broom making and farming operations survived.

In January 1924, a Lancaster newspaper carried a story titled "Murder Will Not Dim Light Of Mennonite Mission That For 25 Years Has Sought to Guide Lawless Welsh Mountain Negroes," which reported the death of Arthur Moyer, the Mennonite Mission's superintendent for the previous eleven years. Moyer was shot down by a group of black youths as they were stealing corn from the Mission's barn. No doubt playing on the recent crimes of Bonnie and Clyde, John Dillinger, and Al Capone, the *Lancaster Sunday News* in January of 1935 ran a story titled "Children Of The Wilderness Survive: Welsh Mountain Retains Its Traditions In A Complex Age of Gangs and Guns." As the story explains, "moonshining was one of the mountain's first callings, so when prohibition came along it sprang into real popularity." Buying or stealing apples from local orchard men to make their reputedly "splendid" applejack, the moonshiners made their hooch at night and peddled it in jugs concealed in bags of charcoal. It was in this environment in 1931 that the twenty-two-year-old William S. Trout, fresh out of college, took up his duties as the lone teacher in the integrated one-room public school in Mt. Airy on Welsh Mountain. Unfortunately, there are neither eyewitness accounts nor written documentation of Trout's five years at Mt. Airy School.

At home Bill came into personal contact with William Henry Brown (fig. 7), who may have been a former slave. According to the Census of 1910 and that of 1920, Brown was born either about 1842 or 1852 in either Pennsylvania or Maryland. Both censuses list him as single, able to read and write, and, according to the county directories beginning in 1884, as a laborer who did odd jobs. Beginning in 1884, the Salisbury Township tax books list Brown as a laborer who resided on various farms in the Gap area, including that of Thomas Bitzer, who according to the 1923 probate records bequeathed to Brown $50 and the small stone tenant house where he lived from 1906 until his death in October 1936. Bill took this house as the subject of his poem "North of the old orchard, the house shambles." Brown's annual taxes varied from twenty-five to fifty cents. There were apparently times when Brown ate at the Trouts' table. Alice Trout Smith remembered occasionally going with her uncle Bill to take Brown food that her grandmother had cooked. Brown had no known relatives: thus Alice Trout was named administrator of his estate, valued at $203.97. Local tradition has it that Mrs. Trout paid Brown's funeral expenses and had a head stone erected to mark his grave.

Like Edwin Arlington Robinson, Bill was interested in people neither as types nor (as with T. S. Eliot and other modernists) as "everyman" or "mass-man," but as individuals. Both poets created memorable verse portraits: Robinson's "Aaron Stark," "Charles Carville's Eye," and *Captain Craig*, are in part imaginative fictions whereas Trout's come from real-life people, such as Lizzie in "Lark Descending," his "Great-Aunt," and Harold Weirich in "The teacher of biology." William Henry Brown was the subject of "Henry," one of Trout's longest poems.

1. Indication

"No, ma'am, I thank you," Henry always said,
When you insisted on another cup
Of coffee, and he shook his bald head,
Black and round. Then, getting up
With slowness deferential—courtesy
Demanding thus—he peered, to make sure
That knife and fork were crossed circumspectly
Upon his plate. That habitude allured
Child-scrutiny, but Henry never would
Have answered question, even had one dared
To query—inconceivable hardihood—
And such might probably have well been spared.
Whence came that gesture, simple and unerring
As the autumn west wind, detaching from an arch
Of maple bough, one leaf,—faithful as spring
Greening the wheat fields on the hills of March.
Peasant gratitude for bread unhoped,
The monk's punctilio—or further back—
The half-brute nomad's untaught sign, to cope
With gliding shadow?
The stubby-fingered, black
Hand was planet-punctual to place
Fork over knife, in silent prayer for grace.

2. Late Afternoon

Worm-fence, rain-runnelled, weathered gray,
Lurching; a glossy chestnut tree,
Demurely Japanese; a ray
Of sun, slanting sleepily
On the well-curb, spent and sagging;
An apple tree, gypsy-ragged,
Bohemian complacently,
Where water-sprouts lanced untrimmed;
Wine-berry thicket, whereto skimmed—
Arrowed, elegantly slim—
The wood-thrush: all this before
Crumbling stone, battered door,
Near whose threshold sat and drowsed
One whom time had ravaged, bowed,—
And freed from all but the last care:
Old—as the Bartlett pear
That braved the years, courageous still
To keep its watch beside the well—
Henry slept, and smiled in dream,
Waked, stared, and dreamed again;
Waked smiling, when the gray squirrel leaped
Fearlessly, to pose and nip
A crust held in the knobbly hand;
Murmured when the field mouse crept
To take the crumb with delicate lip,
Crumb that the robin, shining-eyed,
Grudged as theft, contraband.
But when the child, in grass-stained dress—
Eluding watch preoccupied
With baking—stole beneath the fence,
And touched his knee, he creakingly
Rose, to forestall distress,
And led the vagrant down the tide
Of evening, home; and bowed to take
A proffer of hot coffee-cake—
Supper, then.—Sacraments
Are made of such—sometimes of less.

3. Requiescat

Infrequently on that great tree, untrimmed,
Had been discerned a blossom, never an apple;
And so it was one never knew the kind.
Its province, then, was just to shade the well,
On the steep southern slope; to canopy
The lurchingly resigned, decrepit shed
That was the porch (obliging sage entry,
Past the findings stowed there, in scattered
Magpie-garner); and then to serve as vantage
For the squirrel tribe, for crow, wren, and robin,
Housing near—pensioners, mendicants,
Seemingly, but only friends convene
For colloquy, as these took possession
Of Henry's stooped shoulders, his knobbly knees,
His black, knotted hands. The band would come—
Across the pear-bloom-scented wash of breeze
In May, or through a blue noon of October—
For chestnuts, sunflower seed, handfuls of crumbs
(Of course, no wrens in autumn).
But a sombre
Knot of mourners, peering shyly dumb—
Tree and squirrel, robin and crow—one day,
Watched the still strangeness hurried away.

In this portrait poem Bill captures the noble simplicity, courteousness, gentleness, and love for animals of this field hand with the same simplicity, economy, and attention to precise details of physical appearance and personality he used to limn his "Great-Aunt," his own mother, or any of the other old folks he took as subjects for his verse.

Trout's "Henry" brings to mind Robert Frost's "The Death of the Hired Man," a poem about Silas, also a farm hand. As in their other poems with similar themes, there are important differences in the approach they take to the subject, which can in part be attributed to differences in their life experiences and values. Trout's poem, using an actual person as subject takes place over time, beginning on a day in the kitchen where a family meal has just been shared with the old field hand, then moving out of doors in front of the small stone house where Henry lives and where he sits, snoozing then waking to feed breadcrumbs and seeds to assorted birds, a squirrel, and a field mouse. A speaker who remembers Henry from childhood narrates the story. "The Death of the Hired Man" is invention (albeit drawing on Frost's experience), a dramatic narrative that takes place on a single night on the porch of a farmhouse, where the hired man, Silas (asleep in the kitchen), is the subject of a dialogue between a farmer and his wife.

While Trout gives us details of Henry's physical appearance—his "bald head / Black and round," "stubby-fingered" and "knotted hands," "knobbly knees," and body "ravaged, bowed" by time and years of manual labor—Frost tells us only that Silas is "worn out," "a miserable sight," and jumbles "everything," mixing one thought with others. The poets show us men with very different personalities and characters. Henry is described as courteous and deferential, kind to children and animals, contented, and by implication hardworking and deserving of a restful old age. By contrast, Silas is depicted as unreliable, easily lured away by promises of pocket money, a little boastful and argumentative, making promises he doesn't keep, and with "nothing to look backward to with pride, / And nothing to look forward to with hope," has but "one accomplishment," his skill in building a load of hay. Warren, Silas' employer, voices Frost's conservative socio-economic values, those of the self-reliant Yankee man of property when he asks "what good" Silas is now that he's old and can't do much work. Since he can't afford to pay fixed wages, he also expects Silas to be content with room and board, but does acknowledge a man's right to better himself. Mary's compassion for Silas (though even she says he is "Worthless" and "the kind kinsfolk can't abide") allays her husband's cynicism enough that he seems ready to give the hired man a home in which to die. In the end, albeit grudgingly, Frost like Trout acknowledges the importance of respecting the worth and dignity of even the least among us. Yet the way Henry is viewed and treated by those more fortunate than he stands in stark contrast to the attitude of those to whom Silas (no more to them than the "worn out" stray hound who came to them out of the woods) goes for help.

Nature figures less prominently in Frost's poem than in Trout's. Only in the interlude, when Warren goes into the house to see Silas, is nature mentioned as Mary spreads her apron to catch the moonlight and touches the damp morning-glory strings. While Silas' connection to nature is primarily economic—harvesting and clearing land—Henry is shown to be an integral part of nature, at one with its trees and wildlife, its moods and rhythms. While it is only Silas who is shown to be old in Frost's poem, Trout's is filled with suggestions of aging and decay: a weathered, worm-eaten fence, "the well-curb spent and sagging," a "crumbling" stone house, a "battered door," and a "lurchingly resigned decrepit shed," each in its way a metaphor for Henry and a reminder of the decay of material things and our own mortality. The written image of the old black man approaching the end of his eighty-plus years is in stark contrast to his photograph (fig. 7), probably taken when Henry was in his forties. In the snapshot he poses confidently for the camera, his eyes fixed directly on the viewer, feet planted firmly on the ground, hat cocked on the back of his head, hands on hips, and a pistol tucked in his belt.

In terms of style, "Henry" and "The Death of the Hired Man" are very different. Trout's poem written in irregular rhyme is divided into three parts. His diction is a combination of literary and everyday language. Frost wrote in blank verse using the colloquialisms of homey speech and a tone and manner of speaking typical of New Englanders.

Early in Trout's career at Millersville State Teachers College, Betty Curtis, a twenty-seven-year-old army veteran and one of the few African American students at the college in the 1950s, remembered him as someone with whom she felt comfortable. Her roommate, another African American student, had recommended Trout to her. Curtis said she found him "accepting" and interested in the "inner person," not in anyone's race or economic status. His encouragement led her to a life-long love of Anton Chekhov's plays. She and Trout exchanged occasional letters and postcards for nearly two decades after she graduated. She sometimes sent him books and articles on literary topics she had copied for him. In a postcard he sent her in January 1964 he recommends to her several of Gustave Flaubert's works as well as the writings of Lafcadio Hearn (a newspaper correspondent and writer of Irish-Greek ancestry who lived in the United States for nearly twenty years before settling in Japan as a teacher in 1890), since she was about to be sent on assignment to the Far East. And in his last letter to her, dated 19 October 1977, he tells her: "And of you, I think often. Your poise, grace, intelligence, adventurous spirit remain so clearly in my memory. Perhaps most of all, your sensitivity to human values—you are a true daughter of Tchekhov."

We know from Trout's letters to Don Smith that he worked in a "mill" during the summers when there were no school paychecks. The years Bill spent during World War II laboring full-time in the machine shop and welding department of Lukens Steel brought him into protracted daily contact with urban-dwelling members of the industrial working class. He experienced first-hand the long hours of regimented physical labor doing repetitive tasks in the dirt, heat, and noise typical of work in American heavy industry. During these years he worked side by side with men from varied ethnic backgrounds and traditions, including men from all over the United States who came to Coatesville to do war work, among them many African Americans. For a time he worked the night shift, sleeping during the day and doing "pure labor … where you can't sit down and are too weary to think, only calling for a strong back and a weak mind—so you see I fill the bill admirably," he explains in a letter to Don Smith. Not only did lack of sleep and the dust and smoke of the mill at times give him violent headaches and sinus problems, but he tells Smith, millwork also makes his hands swell, accounting for his illegible handwriting. In a letter to Smith postmarked 13 December 1943, he recounts life at the mill in a trenchant, yet poetic manner: "Work, grease, noise, the roar of the torches with their turquoise flames oddly lovely in all that sordidness, the clangour of the cranes, the crash of falling steel; profanity, obscenity, the human animal at his emptiest in one sense, at his greatest usefulness in another, since it is the steel that must bring at least a few of the lads back again." From what he relates to Smith about his fellow steel workers, with some of whom he formed close personal relationships, at least at work, it is clear that he respected and liked them. Some confided in him, among them fathers worried about their servicemen sons, and others—like the sixteen-year-old boy from the hill country of North Carolina whose dialect he describes in correspondence to Don Smith—he gives a few bucks to tide them over until payday. That Bill identified with these working-class males is patent. An affectionate quip reveals both his sense of humor and his own self-image: "All the gutter-snipes cling to me, recognizing a fellow." Working in a steel mill helped mold Trout's social-political values and beliefs and contributed to his concern for the fate of the individual in a society where technology, mass-production in a depersonalized and regimented workplace, standardization, and corporate capitalism were its defining characteristics and influenced its values and all aspects of its citizens' lives. Trout's experience growing up in a single-parent family with a working mother, his years teaching the rural poor of Welsh Mountain, and his work as a steel mill hand assured he would neither look upon the lower classes with condescension nor sentimentalize them.

The roots of the crisis in human values and the alienation of twentieth-century man from himself and his fellow beings are addressed in Erich Kahler's *The Tower and the Abyss: An Inquiry into the Transformation of the Individual* (1957), a book Bill recommended to me in the 1970s. (Kahler was a refugee from Hitler's Germany and a close friend of Thomas Mann). One of Trout's longest and most powerful poems, and arguably his most pessimistic about human beings and the society in which he lived, is "Then perhaps it has always been so: we have embroidered," which reflects the influence of both Jung and Kahler, as well as hints of T. S. Eliot.

I.

Then perhaps it has always been so: we have embroidered
Lust and death with sentiment—bridal veils and consolatory
    anthems;
Impulses to be feared, naked and monstrous, we have tried to
    propitiate,
Called the Furies "Good Ladies," more to hush
Our own despair than to confirm comprehension of
Such race-conjured entities.
                And having broken
Infancy's confident faith, how are we to believe again
In anything? All, perhaps,
Is greed, then—toad's gray belly, rattler's head
Couched sleepless on loathsome folds. And Cinderella's
        godmother
Will not arrive in time; the magic tinder-box
Is permanently lost; and all the slick garrulity
Jangles false, drowned in this black and icy rain.

II.

We have fished up from the paleolithic slime of dreams
These vestiges of a racial past that we struggle to repudiate;
But—in spite of the morning shower, of the scrubbing, of the
    shaving,
In spite of deodorants, of newsbroadcasts, of editorials—
The hooting troglodyte stares from the mirror, and swings with
    us on the bus.
Where is the secret of that vision, fragile as frost crystals,
    tougher than steel delicately alloyed
(Francis' dream, and Mozart's—cosmos spun about attenuate fingers)
To twist the kaleidoscope, to impose order on
Chaotic vileness, the wreckage of this century?

III.

No time remains now to evolve a system:
Already at work in the blood the impersonal
Anti-human virus dissolves the delicate tissue
And the fragile receptors; the complex mechanism
Of tendrils interlaced softly disintegrates.

Soon we shall look up from the absently
Attended book, to see the stranger in
The familiar room, and how he entered here
We shall not know.
                              Immediately will begin
The nervous, grave debate, rising to rage
Of accusation and recrimination,
To end in acquiescence, as we go,
Hatless and coatless, with him into the storm.

IV.

Not by framing with the horizontal
Girder, nor perching chaos serenely on
Severe supports chastely vertical,
To snare the sunset and to arrest the dawn,

Shall we domesticate disintegration:
That trick has been tried before, and long ago.
Nor yet to launch a spired aspiration,
Of stone and spirit, will dispense the throe.

Only acquiescence—no assault—
Suffices here: to lie defeated, prone,
In the immense shadow. Shaft or vault,
The stone assuages, and the shadow on the stone.

V.

In the widening expanse of the darkening sky at evening,
Borne on the lift of air from the primeval, impersonal hills,
An illumination—sought so long through silent desperation—
Breaks on the crippled mind: this crucifixion
Is perhaps birth and growth; perhaps only so the mind

Finds the bizarre gate, the unique exit
By which the edict permits it to go out
Into the impersonal darkness, into the expanse of evening sky,
Into the primitive night.

Trout's resentment at what American society had become and was doing to the young, with whose Vietnam War protests he sympathized, emerged in his letter to me of 30 May 1971: "It is the thrice accursed materialistic education (irony) of the era that has paralyzed. I can well understand the revolt of this new generation, understand—of course better than they understand—the savage resentment of the condemnation to starvation; that—instead of the nourishment for the spirit (it exists—that creature)—they are proffered what the frightful advertising of the age offers them—the poison bait on the trap." That "poison bait" was the lure of materialism and the chance to live in a little suburban box and fit into the gray flannel suit of American corporate-consumer culture and accept the conventions, platitudes, and self-deceptions peddled by the mainstream media. By the 1960s, American education was being marketed as the way to land a better paying job and to own more things rather than as preparation for a life enriched by the care and feeding of the mind through the liberal arts. General education was being eroded and watered down to make more room in the curriculum for specialized vocational courses. In a letter to me in 1976 Bill refers to present-day America as "this soul-less era." Among the newspaper clippings he kept was an ad for *Fortune* magazine in the 3 January 1978 *New York Times* titled "Jerry tackles Jimmy [Carter]. Only in the new *Fortune*," featuring a large photograph of President Gerald Ford. Trout annotated it with three biting comments: "All together, boys ... "Gobble-gobble-gobble"; "The Fat Boy in Pickwick Papers says 'I wants t'make yer flesh creep' "; and "Can you not see the wires by which Finance causes the puppet to jump?" In a letter to me in the spring of 1979 Bill broods: "One stares incredulous at the lying league (finance-politics) and the idiot (and ultimately damned) public."

From the vantage point of memory, Trout assessed American society in the late twentieth century and found that its institutions, values, and material and technological advances are incapable of fulfilling deeper human needs. What has been lost by such "progress" he suggests through a neat bit of irony and not so subtle satire are the well-springs of our true "Social Security," the title he gave to his poetic reflections. He finds in herbicides, tourism, and hourly news broadcasts not contributions to our well being, not "advances" to celebrate but symptoms of what ails modern American culture, which has lost those qualities that contribute to a healthy natural and social environment.

There, at least, the birds have not yet been annulled,
Not yet the honey-bees, by the weed-killing sprays;
The wren still finds the green cabbage worms in the dew-soaked garden,
And in the hayfield, where the well
Watches mysteriously, the rose-red clover
Bobs to receive the traders black and amber,
With them exchanges commodity, but no secrets—hence is never prone to tell
The squint diplomacies of the infinite.
In that republic, dim no longer, memory
Can move with more assurance now, since bitter winds have swept away
The smell of cucumbers (so one scented where the copperheads,
Our only Eden vipers, slipped beneath the laurel).
There, there at least,
Come no tourists in sun-glasses; there the glib priests
Of news-on-the-hour do not bark
Their horrours, in the garrulous staccato.
Harried by grief, and by eclipsing dark, age hurries back
For only there does loneliness belong.

While he supported the anti-Vietnam war protesters, Trout was apparently troubled by the more extreme elements of the feminist movement of the 1970s. Next to the color plate of Bruegel's painting "Mad Meg (Dulle Griet)," in his copy of Wolfgang Stechow's 1968 book on the artist, he wrote: "It is the 'liberated woman' of 1978." It would, however, be simplistic and inaccurate to conclude from this comment that Trout was a misogynist. The love and dedicated care he gave his mother, the admiration and affection his female friends and students had for him and he for them (Jean Rentz, Betty Curtis, and Dianne Danz, only three of many), and the high regard in which he held such women writers as George Sand, Charlotte Mew, May Sinclair, Edna Millay, and Willa Cather—all of whom were "liberated" in their thought and lifestyle—testify to his respect for strong, independent women. And yet there is some evidence, like his comment about Bruegel's *Mad Meg*, to suggest that while Bill certainly didn't hate women, he may have feared, or at least been wary of those Dylan Thomas once referred to as "brassy-bossy men-women." Such evidence comes in the form of comments found in his books, for example: "More than half the capital in America (U.S.) is in women's hands"—a quotation from Jung that can be interpreted in a number of ways, among them an affirmation of the economic acumen of women or a fear of their financial power—that he wrote on the fly leaf of his copy of Jung's *Symbols of Transformation.* In his copy of C. S. Lewis' *Surprised by Joy* he underlined part of the author's observation: "You may add that in the hive and the anthill we see fully realized the two things that some of us most dread for our own species—the dominance of the female and the dominance of the collective" (Lewis 1955, 8-9). For an admirer of Thoreau and Hazlitt the dominance of the collective was certain to send shivers down Bill's spine.

An avid student of history, particularly the French Revolution of 1789, Bill identified with Danton, who was instrumental in ending the monarchy but opposed the bloody excesses of Robespierre and paid for his opposition with his life. He questioned traditional schools of historical interpretation, including Jeffersonian myths, calling Aaron Burr "my old hero" and in the same April 1944 letter to Don Smith denounces Burr's betrayal by General James Wilkinson "into the slimy paws of Thomas Jefferson." On the jacket of his recording of Beethoven's Third Symphony, which contains biographical information on the composer and clichéd generalizations about the work's philosophical content and meaning, Bill mockingly wrote: "twaddle," "asinine claptrap," and "threadbare, dreary, windy vapidity." The author of the cover copy linked Beethoven's political philosophy to that of America's Founding Fathers, whom Trout quips might more aptly be called "The Finagling Fathers"; thus taking yet another irreverent swipe at what he regarded as the popular American myth that the signers of the Declaration of Independence and framers of the Constitution actually believed in "liberty, equality, fraternity" and were more committed to championing freedom than they were in protecting the vested interests of landed and commercial elites.

Trout was suspicious of social and economic privilege because of its tendency to result in the misuse of political power by financial elites or by a "hero" turned tyrant who manipulated the ignorance, gullibility, and narrow self-interest of people. He mistrusted both the mob and the aristocracy, whether of wealth or birth. While Edwin Arlington Robinson railed against Prohibition in poems like "Demos," "Dionysius in Doubt," and "Demos and Dionysius," in large measure because he saw its wider implications for government intrusion into people's lives and movement toward more standardization and greater public complacency in America, Trout worried that consumerism, corporate controlled mass-media, and popular culture were taking the nation down the road to mediocrity and conformity (Donaldson 2007, 357-358). Unlike both Robinson and Edna St. Vincent Millay, who wrote poems on specific political and social issues of the day, Trout's socially critical verse is not targeted at specific events or policies. Rather, as in "All are headed for the river that drives on down there, in dank" and "Asylum" such poems address what he saw as endemic evils: war, prejudice and intolerance, indifference to the poor and the elderly, and the corrupting power of society's addiction to materialism and the influence of wealth in politics. He did not write poems either championing or attacking specific political actions or policies.

Nonetheless, he was deeply suspicious of government, indeed any institution that might curtail individuality and personal freedom. The scent of the British essayist William Hazlitt (1778-1830) can be found in Bill's views on religion, politics, and social issues. He would have agreed with Hazlitt when he wrote that truth "is not one, but many." And like Hazlitt he was not given to accepting either intellectual or moral absolutes but rather based his judgments and approach to life on common sense, feeling, and experience, and used imagination rather than strict adherence to logic or reason as his guide. Believing that human behavior could not be explained by "reason," as his letters and conversations testify, he would have concurred with Hazlitt's assertion: "To refuse to avail ourselves of mixed motives and imperfect obligations, in a creature like man, whose 'very name is frailty,' and who is a compound of contradictions, is to lose the substance in catching at the shadow." Hazlitt was no slave to convention, no adherent of prevailing style or opinion. Trout admired his intellectual independence and integrity in refusing to surrender his convictions for financial gain or to curry popular favor in the pursuit of fame. Hazlitt was no trimmer. "His aggressive individualism," as Herschel Baker observes, "stamps itself on everything he wrote," including inspiring "his contempt for 'corporate bodies'—academic, political, and ecclesiastical." Bill also shared with Hazlitt an aversion to authority, utopian reformers, and meddling do-gooders (Baker 1962, 324-326, 392-393, 396-397, 462, 466-467, 470, 472-473).

And there are certainly echoes of Henry David Thoreau (1817-1862), another unregenerate individualist, in Trout's thought. Thoreau wrote scathing attacks on contemporary American culture, both criticizing the conventions of his day and warning of the dangers posed by the misguided zeal of reforming do-gooders. Thoreau's "ideal of living deliberately" resonated with Bill (Reynolds 1988, 97-103). His copy of *Walden* has certain passages, which he delighted in quoting from memory, underlined and emphatically marked with multiple heavy lines, among them: "I would rather sit upon a pumpkin and have it all to myself, than be crowded on a velvet cushion." And: "If I knew for a certainty that a man was coming to my house with the conscious design of doing me good, I should run for my life" (Thoreau 1910, 47, 96).

Not surprisingly for one who admired the independence of Hazlitt and Thoreau, Bill seems not to have found the social views and politics of Thomas Carlyle (in spite of Carlyle's contempt for *laissez faire* economics and the "Gospel of Mammonism") particularly congenial, and certainly didn't like his tone, as he explains in a letter to me of 31 October 1971: "Under duress," he says, "I read Carlyle's P & P [*Past and Present*], read for a course in Vic. Lit. [Victorian Literature] that was cast at me once at MV [Millersville]. But the only C[arlyle] that now I recall without distaste is the Reminiscences. I discovered early that he offended me at a sensitive point; always I have detested being roared at, and C[arlyle] roars like an Auld Licht [Old Light] minister" (a member of the conservative, strict Calvinist faction of the Church of Scotland in the late eighteenth century).

Both Trout's library and letters shed light on the intellectual currents that influenced his socio-political views. He owned a copy of Alexis Carrel's (1873-1944) best-selling *Man, the Unknown* (1935), which he may have read the year it was published since he wrote that date on the book's copyright page. However, the fact that he wrote his mother's initials (A.G.L.T.) and the date 1973 in the margin on page 130 documents that he also read the book after her death. Carrel was a French surgeon and biologist who won the Nobel Prize in Physiology/Medicine in 1912, was for a time on the faculty of the University of Chicago and the staff of the Rockefeller Institute of Medical Research, and received honorary doctorates from seven universities, including Princeton, Brown, and Columbia. But he was also sympathetic to fascism and advocated the implementation of eugenics policies by France's Vichy government.

Trout's heavy underlining of Carrel's *Man, the Unknown* shows that it contained ideas that interested him whether or not he agreed with them. Carrel's hostility to the "brutal materialism of our civilization" that "crushes the affective, the gentle, the weak, the lonely, those who love beauty, who look for other things than money," and the negative effects of modern technology and corporate capitalism on the individual likely struck a responsive chord in Bill. He would have agreed with Carrel's observation that "Modern business methods take no account of the personality of the workers. They ignore the fact that all men are different." And he might also have been sympathetic to Carrel's belief that the commercialism and popular culture of modern society had undermined ethical and moral standards (Carrel 1935, 317, 245, 131-133).

Given his interest in Jungian psychology (to be discussed in Chapter 5), Trout would have shared Carrel's objection to the arbitrary separation of the "physiological and the mental"—though not with eugenic considerations in mind—and his insistence that "Neither the soul nor the body can be investigated separately." Carrel's claims that "Clairvoyance and telepathy are a primary datum of scientific observation" and that biologists and physicists have not "taken into account the existence of metaphysical phenomena," might also have won Trout's agreement. However, the number of question marks Bill put in the margins of Carrel's book indicates his unwillingness to accept many of his assertions. It appears that Trout questioned some of Carrel's generalizations and was uncomfortable with certain of the claims he made on behalf of men of science. The question marks Bill put in the margin whenever Carrel made positive statements about Mussolini may be taken to indicate his disagreement, and the big one he awarded Carrel's silly statement that "Men of genius are not tall. Mussolini is of medium size, and Napoleon was short," indicates not only the contempt Bill had for such absurdities but his unwillingness to admit the genius of the likes of such men (Carrel 1935, 118-119, 124, 62). While Trout could share Carrel's belief that modern industrial civilization had lost its spiritual and moral moorings, it does not follow that he shared his politics.

He tells Don Smith in a letter of 8 May 1943 that he has, like jumping into a swimming hole, "plunged, ass first, into Spengler's Decline of the West." In November 1943 he was reading John Donne's poems "for the 300th time and creeping about in Spengler like a maggot in a cheese." Later in the year he tells Smith that in Spengler, "one crawls about among the ruins of great cultures and listens to the winds of our doom wailing among the monoliths." And in March 1944 he admits to Smith that Hitler's rise to power and the "decadence of Britain and France ... and a certain spiritual affinity with Spengler completed my disillusionment" with Europe.

Replying to something Don Smith wrote about Henry Adams (1838-1918), Trout, in a letter of 6 June 1945 mentions that he first read *The Education of Henry Adams* (published in 1907) in 1931 and immediately identified with Adams' views on technology and his discomfort with life in a mass society, saying he noted a certain "sympathy" between Adams and Spengler. "All in all," he observes, "I think that he was the first to see that the machine is to be our doom. He was a skeptic and a stoic [so, too, was Trout], impressed by nostalgia as he looked back to the 13th century [in his book *Mont-Saint-Michel and Chartres*], impressed and frightened as he surveyed the dynamos of the twentieth. I'll have to confess that his book left me only with a confirmation of mystery and despair ...." A sentence in *The Education* Bill says always stuck in his mind: "Nature has educated herself to a singular sympathy for death." Trout shared Adams' tragic sense of life, and no doubt agreed when he observed that, as a result of its optimistic national creed, "America has always taken tragedy lightly. Too busy to stop the activity of their twenty-million-horse-power society, Americans ignore tragic motives" (Adams 1918, 416). Bill was "grateful" that knowing Adams led him to the Saint-Gaudens memorial for Adams' wife (who had committed suicide in 1885, plunging Adams into protracted mourning and reinforcing his neurasthenia) in Rock Creek Cemetery in Washington D. C. "I think that hooded figure expresses all some of us will ever know; but no one can think of it without drawing courage from it," Bill told Don Smith. In time he wrote a poem about the Adams Memorial.

It is significant that Trout read *The Education of Henry Adams* for the first time when he did, in 1931. That he was fresh out of college and teaching the children of the rural poor at Mt. Airy School during one of the bleakest years of the Great Depression must have made Adams' pessimistic view of modern American society ring true to the twenty-two-year-old country schoolteacher. A direct descendant of two American presidents and the son of Charles Francis Adams (a diplomat President Lincoln sent to London during the Civil War to assure British neutrality), Henry Adams was a historian and writer who, as a discerning witness to the transformation of the United States during the second half of the nineteenth century, recorded in his autobiography the despair he felt as he saw mechanization and materialism become the new gods worshipped by turn-of-the-century Americans. And nowhere were the idols of these new gods more apparent than at the world's fairs of the period, which contrasted "civilization"—exhibits of dynamos, farm machinery, flush toilets, and mass-produced household furniture—with "savagery"—Social-Darwinist anthropological exhibitions and midway villages featuring "primitive" peoples, among them scantily-clad representatives of South Pacific Islands and African tribes (Commanger 1950, 132-138; Rydell 1993, 19-31). Adams visited the Columbian Exposition in Chicago in 1893, and said after seeing the machinery hall in which giant dynamos provided electricity to power the machines that "the dynamo became a symbol of infinity," an "occult mechanism," and "he began to feel the forty-foot dynamos as a moral force, much as the early Christians felt the Cross" (Adams 1918, 380). For Adams, according to Alan Trachtenberg, the Chicago World's Fair represented "subliminally at least, the defeat of the 'simple industrial,' the final victory of the centralizing, mechanical, and incorporated society of capitalism" (Trachtenberg 1982, 219-220). Adams was even more dismayed by the shallowness, extravagance, and waste of the colossal amounts of money spent on the 1904 St. Louis Louisiana Purchase Exposition, "lighted by thousands on thousands of electric candles," and in the end concluded: "Had there been no exhibits at all, and no visitors, one would have enjoyed it only more" (Adams 1918, 466-467).

In a technological and corporate society controlled by robber barons of industry and finance like Andrew Carnegie, John D. Rockefeller, Jay Gould, Jim Fiske, and J. P. Morgan, only acceleration, change, efficiency, profits, and success mattered; "education counted for nothing" and the "administrator, organizer, manager" reign supreme, Adams concluded. For him the twentieth century was an age of "multiplicity," of "hysteria," of "chaos." In it everything had been shattered, from the methods of production to social values, to the new psychology's splitting of the personality "into complex groups, like telephonic centers and systems that might be isolated and called up at will." The new American, Adams said, was "the child of incalculable coal-power, chemical power, electric power, and radiating energy, as well as new forces yet undetermined." The initiative and individuality of Americans had fallen victim to the power of corporate capitalism, Adams maintained: trusts and corporations "were obnoxious because of their vigorous and unscrupulous energy ... They tore society to pieces and trampled it under foot." And, what is more, science, technology, materialism, and the relentless competition created by corporate capitalism, Adams believed, did much to diminish spiritual, intellectual, and aesthetic values in American society (Adams 1918, 239-240, 380-381, 433, 466-467, 496-500). This must have been heady stuff for a young country schoolmaster like Trout. As he read Adams' *Education* in 1931, the stock market crash, bank failures, closed factories and failed businesses, unemployed workers, the shanty towns of the homeless, and soup kitchens all brought on by greed and the excesses of corporate capitalism made possible by the failure of government to regulate banks, the stock market, and big business, could not have been far from Bill's thoughts. They no doubt influenced his social and political outlook for life.

It may be that Bill's passion for books and reading from childhood on fostered in him a critical liberalism that in part accounts for his disappointment with and alienation from the realities of everyday life. He gives poetic voice to his social philosophy and political views in a number of poems some people might call deeply pessimistic, among them "The Road," "All are headed to the river that drives on down there, in dank," and this one, which reveals his horror of political violence, religious intolerance, war, man's arrogant efforts to conquer outer space, and humanity's apparent inability ever to learn lessons from its follies:

> They must reverse the arrogant pilgrimage,
> Come back (the Voice from the Hill speaks serenely)
> Back from the moon, even (low laughter from the Hill),
> Return mendicant, begging meanly,
> Across an ailing Lent, the strato-coach
> A pumpkin rotting under falling snow.
>
> Time, turning prayer-wheel with a drowsy finger,
> May set a ploughman following ox in furrow;
> A shawled woman toting eggs, and bringing
> Tea from town; a soup-pot swung to simmer
> Over the oak-coals glowing on the stone—
> Though aeons first must spiral up the cone.
>
> They faulted, then?—Yes. They never learn.
> The bludgeon splits the bone; the fox-priest raises
> A crucifix before the heretic burning;
> The guillotine shaves close; the Bomb braises
> The tender suckling. But they never learn.
> And the Wheel turns—even now is turning.

Trout's outlook, like Thomas Hardy's, was rooted in a "tragic conception of the universe," a view that sees it controlled by an "unconscious will ... entirely oblivious to moral values," which is beyond the ability of human beings to understand or control (Pinto 1951, 43-44). He questions a "Cosmic Plan" that makes life a struggle while allowing its creatures to dream of a better future in the poem:

> The three-legged ant totes painfully
> Its yearly grain of mouldy wheat,

Happily adds it to the heap,
And pegs away, to scrounge again,
Ant-psyche dreaming of a stair
Far as the Ethiop's starry Chair—

Whence ingenuous emmet can,
In company with ennui's Queen,
Decode at last the Cosmic Plan,
Glimpse (two nebulae between)
Absconditus—and question why
The ant must amputated ply.

Bill's compassion for and personal identification with society's "failures"—victims of America's corporate capitalism, which stresses competition and measures success by status and the accumulation of money and material things—is another characteristic that he shared with Edwin Arlington Robinson. Consider for example his poem "Asylum," a work perhaps sparked by passing Lancaster County's "home" for destitute elderly on his trips to and from Gap, which reflects his view of life as a crapshoot.

A dirty fragment of the ace
Of diamonds lay upon the grass
Near the pavement, in a sunny space
Next the corner at which one must pass
The county's home for the indigent and the old.
Who played the ace, and lost? Around,
Above, the opulent season dreamed—
Riches, seemingly without bound.
And beyond the pickets crept those we deemed
Worth our charity: faded, hunched, cold,—
The silent, the defeated, those who had played
And lost, of humanity's few graces flayed.

Perhaps part of Bill's dislike of Robert Frost, to be discussed in Chapter 8, owes something to the New England poet's conservative social and political views, which manifest themselves in such poems as "A Lone Striker," "Two Tramps in Mud Time," "Provide, Provide," and even in "The Death of the Hired Man," all of which run counter to the sentiments Trout expresses in letters and in poems like "Asylum" and "The three-legged ant totes painfully."

What is more, Trout's portrait poems, which are based on the lived reality of relatives, friends, and neighbors, are much more forgiving and compassionate than the way Frost treats people in his poems, and are more insightful than his when it comes to human psychology. Trout's mastery in capturing the psychological underpinnings of a subject's behavior—the roots of his or her personality—is revealed in "Old Maid," which reflects his sympathy for and understanding of the difficulties, sacrifices, and flaws, as well as the toll taken on individuals who assume responsibility for others, something both his mother (who is alluded to in the last line of the poem) and Bill himself experienced firsthand.

> She ordered the four farms with unrelenting
> Rigor, which reclaimed the ultimate tithe
> From labourer and tenant; slightly bent,
> She moved as menacing portent against the sky
> For those rarely placid. The brood of seven
> Orphans of her blood she ruled as well,
> Replacing the mad mother, called to heaven—
> That gentle one whose earth had been a hell.
> Darkly impelled, and therefore darkly sure
> And mute, she loved that sister the mother called
> The 'judgment baby,"— whose death begot a wild,
> Suppressed storm, that drove her to your door,
> Dragging her grief across the crimson fall,
> Because she knew you mourned a dead child.

In another of his portrait poems, "Lark Descending," which, like "Henry," reminds one of E. A. Robinson, Trout's sense of humor comes through both in the text and in his witty adaptation of the title of Vaughn Williams' short piece for violin and orchestra (*The Lark Ascending*). Even as he pokes good-natured fun, Bill sympathizes with Lizzie, whom townsfolk viewed as something of an oddity—an attitude not unlike their indulgence of his own eccentricities. But at the poem's end, there is no humor when a greedy brother and his pliant lawyer ship off to the county poor house this kind and self-sacrificing woman whose only joy was song. Violet Baker, for more than eighty-five years a member of Bellevue Presbyterian Church, identified Lizzie as Elizabeth Townsend, a Gap spinster, who in the mid-1920s loosed her full-throated soprano voice in Sunday services wreaking havoc with choral and congregational singing and putting the minister, The Rev. David A. Reed (pastor from 1923-1926), in a difficult position between rebellious choir members and the indignant Lizzie, who was asked to leave the choir. As much as "Lark Descending," another of Trout's long poems, may make us chuckle, it is a poignant reminder of the shabby treatment people all too often dole out to one another, particularly to those who are "different."

> Undoctored human justice would require
> (Celestial justice is another thing)
> That Lizzie, central in a golden choir,
> Be bathed in light—and be allowed to sing.
> Once, when competition was not strong,
> Lizzie was permitted to ascend
> The choir loft; but not for very long
> Did rigour absent-mindedly relent,
> For Lizzie's voice (one struggled not to cringe)
> Pierced, oblivious of all nuance,
> And loitered, past the modulated fringe
> Of cadence, and her Amen rang alone.
> Even the village base at last rebelled,
> Endorsing the contralto's blunt, forthright
> Ultimatum; and Lizzie's joy was quelled,
> Past appeal; the preacher fled from light
> To some dusk corner of the pastoral soul,
> When caritas pleaded diplomacy.
> In Lizzie, anger dimly took control;
> But, rejecting all humility,
> She braved chagrin at last, and from her pew,
> Lifted, as of old, with disregard
> Of time and tone, a soprano voice imbued
> With Christian fervor only the very hardened
> Declined to grant—and those, one fears, were most.
> Charity, just a scrap, would have allowed
> Understanding: her hour was at cost
> Of slavery's furrow with fidelity ploughed—
> The paralytic mother, the imbecile
> Father, and the brother narrowly
> Avaricious,—a task not to beguile

Poor wit for long from destined overthrow.
(But lapse came later, when Lizzie's task was done—
At least, her earthly task.). Easily
One knows the satisfaction with which she donned
Her hat—creation incredible—and slyly
Avoided her brother's eye, to cross the sombre
Fields to church.—Not long resentment smouldered,
Quelled by the joy of song. Coldly, however,
To preacher, at the door of his neat fold,
Bidding his flock God-speed, Lizzie deigned,
Eyes steadily ahead, to brush the extended
Hand with a dry finger that maintained
Uneasy memory of wrong unmended.
    When jesting time had taken to the grave
Lizzie's charges, her brother thought it wise,
With the connivance of a lawyer friend,
To act decisively: so Lizzie ended
Her gray life where the county compromised
To house the indigent with the mad, thus saving
Too burdensome taxation by a wise,
Deft economy. And pastor hence
Need not longer darkly compromise
With needling doubt, commanding recompense.
(No matter—they said—how Sunday church bells rang
Across the town, Lizzie never sang.)

Chapter 3
On Living to One's-Self

Anyone who has escaped from small-town America or has read the novels of Sinclair Lewis recognizes (in spite of the good things small towns can offer) the subtle tyranny inherent in such places, particularly those in conservative areas like Lancaster County, Pennsylvania. Given Bill's innate shyness, solitary pastimes, religious skepticism, and social-political views, it is no wonder he became increasingly withdrawn over the years. And yet there may have been another possible reason why he protected his privacy, something also characteristic of the British poet A. E. Housman (1859-1936).

Trout owned copies of Housman's *A Shropshire Lad* (1896), *Last Poems* (1922), and *A. E. Housman: More Poems* (1936). But of all the poetry books in Bill's library, none was more obviously studied than his 1956 copy of *The Collected Poems of A. E. Housman.* The majority of its poems, including all but one from *A Shropshire Lad*, he analyzed in detail. He scanned many of the poems, noting the rhyme scheme, the diction, and Housman's skillful use of alliteration. In the *Name and Nature of Poetry*, the Leslie Stephen Lectures Housman gave at Cambridge University in 1933 (a copy of which Trout owned), Housman says: "And I think that the transfusion of emotion—not to transmit thought but to set up in the reader's sense a vibration corresponding to what was felt by the writer—is the peculiar function of poetry." Later he observes: "Poetry is not the thing said but a way of saying it … Meaning is of the intellect, poetry is not." He insists that, "Poetry indeed seems to me more physical than intellectual," which goes far toward explaining why he believed that simile, and metaphor are "things inessential to poetry," and why "satire, controversy, and burlesque" should be used "with great parsimony and tact" (Housman 1938, 8, 35, 37, 45, 10, 16-17). Housman's poetic style included a renunciation of "romantic embellishment" in favor of concision and simple, precise diction inspired from his study of Latin and reading of Classical literature. Likewise, there is much of Trout's poetry that reflects the influence of his study of Latin. What is more, George Watson characterizes Housman's poetry as "repetitive in theme," "disciplined," and with "an intensity of single experience long secreted"—all of which are characteristic of much of Trout's poetry as well (Hawkins 1958, 83; Watson 1957, 9).

According to Maud Hawkins Housman's lyrics are autobiographical, "a series of passionate outbursts against the frustrations and disorders of his own experience, which he generalizes as the common fate of all." This is a view shared by George Watson, who claims, "the characteristic feature of Housman's poetry was its power of defining emotions peculiar to him in terms that were just as valid for others." But, he warns, one should not "regard his overt subject as necessarily the real one," nor "infer his whole meaning from the apparent drift of his words" (Hawking 1958, 141-142; Watson 1957, 175). The same observations might well be made of Trout's verse.

Just as Trout's religious faith was shaky at best and his skepticism of human institutions all too apparent, so Housman cannot be counted a believer as his "Easter Hymn" and "The Laws of God, the laws of man" make clear. Both were lonely men, shy and intensely private, whose domestic lives were spartan. While the hardships and sorrows Bill had experienced taught him fortitude, he may have found in Housman the spiritual and aesthetic value of stoicism that characterizes so much of his poetry. Each had a strong attachment to his mother, was an introvert with a natural propensity to melancholy and despair, and was devoted to the writings of Thomas Hardy and read and reread Marcel Proust. "Embarrassed by admiration and repelled by curiosity," Housman, Watson points out, "lived remote from the literary world and a recluse from his fame" (Watson 1957, 9, 81-82; Hawkins, 1958, 32, 174, 197, 214, 84, 16, 201). As Hawkins asserts, "Death was to be the polyphonic background of Housman's poetry, with many variations in the foreground of his compositions ... the deaths of soldiers, or lovers, or suicides, or criminals." And she also maintains that his melancholy came from his "predilection for memory and recall, which in him amounted to tragic brooding." References to the West or "going west," which in the British vernacular allude to death, and in general connotes ending, are found frequently in Housman's verse, as in "The West," as well as in Trout's poems (Hawkins 1958, 84, 86). That Bill at least knew of the Hawkins and Watson biographies of Housman (and may even have read or owned them) is suggested by the full bibliographical information for them he wrote in his copy of Housman's collected poetry.

As Paul Fussell points out, Housman was part of the pre-World War I poetic tradition of erotic interest in attractive young men descending from

Walt Whitman (whom Edward Carpenter made known to British audiences) through Gerard Manley Hopkins to Housman. In the years just before the outbreak of the 1914-18 war, as Fussell notes, the book that was "in every pocket" was Housman's *A Shropshire Lad.* "In the Great War diction," Fussell observes, "there are three degrees of erotic heat attaching to three words: men is largely neutral; boys is a little warmer; lads is very warm." The theme of "beautiful suffering lads" that runs through much of Housman's verse seems to have "licensed" expressions of male bonding with hints of homoeroticism by war poets like Siegfried Sassoon, Robert Graves, and most famously, Rupert Brooke and Wilfred Owen, both of whom were young, pretty, and perished during the war (Fussell 1975, 160, 280-283, 286-309).

Like Housman Bill seems to have been attracted to handsome young men. The "lovely lads" Housman wrote about—young soldiers and athletes—were working-class males who came from "the barn and the forge and the mill." On his first trip to London, when he was sixteen, Housman made an unintended but revealing admission in a letter to his mother in which he lists the sights he has taken in (among them Westminster Abbey, the British Museum, St. Paul's Cathedral, Trafalgar Square), and ends by saying "but I think of all I have seen, what has impressed me most is—the Guards. This may seem barbarian, but it is true." Like many gay middle- and upper-class Englishman of the period, he was sexually attracted to soldiers (Watson 1957, 59-60, 118-120; Hawkins 1958, 85, 91-94, 105, 108, 122-124; Cook 2003, 19, 26, 38). Though a Classical/Latin scholar, it was not research that later in life drew Housman to the Greek galleries of the British Museum (a popular cruising area for homosexuals) but the nude male sculptures, with one of which, a beautiful "Grecian lad" "many loved in vain," he avoided making eye contact lest he "perish" like the boy who fell in love with himself and drowned when he slipped into a forest well while looking at his reflection in the water (Cook 2003, 33-35; Housman 1956, 52, 38, 28). Although Bill did not make young men the subject of any of his extant verse, one of his poems, "Milkweed," does contain veiled eroticism suggestive of masturbation or male genital desire:

> Through the smells of fish and mint,
> Of cow's dung dried, and redolent husk
> Of shorn hayfield, dreams the tint
> Of timid rose, breathes the musk—
> Odor: then in midnight hush,

Evocation miraculous—
The conjuration of a weed.

Corollary, appears the child
Who stared, levelly, at the cluster
Of small cameos, touched the mild
White sticky sap that oozed with lush
Indulgence (theophanic bush)
From a leaf broken. Milkweed then,
But now, in night's impersonal hush,
A kind of figurative Amen.

The poem's diction ("evocation miraculous," "conjuration," "indulgence," "theophanic," and "Amen") creates a magical, mystical atmosphere while its sensuous, even sensual language hints at a dream or childhood memory of a nocturnal bucolic experience either participated in or witnessed. Trout may also have used loaded metaphors in "Blacksnake" to mask a homoerotic encounter or desire. At the risk of reading too much into these poems, one is tempted to posit that both relate to homoerotic experiences or perhaps just fantasies or dreams in which the object of desire may have been an African American male, given the reference to the scent of "musk" in "Milkweed" and the way in which the blacksnake "oiled his skin and combed his hair."

From mid-life on Bill's letters are filled with what John Cowper Powys calls "masochistic humility." He demeaned his intelligence and abilities, scoffing at any suggestion that he had anything to offer anyone, as he did in the Fourth of July letter in 1942 responding to an apparent complement by Don Smith: "You musn't say foolish things about me—sometime soon you will be meeting real people of intelligence and understanding and sincerity, and will understand what a shabby and confusing (and confused) brain I have." Praise of any sort made him very uncomfortable and elicited a sharp reproof. In later years he objected to being called "Professor," always referring to himself as "a country schoolmaster," which, of course, he had at one time been. Believing himself to be unattractive and clumsy may in part account for the pleasure Bill took in the company of good-looking young men, many of whom were also athletic, out-going, and self-confident. Apparently self-conscious about his physical appearance, he once referred to his "ugly face" in a letter to Don Smith, and, as noted earlier, thought of himself as Ichabod Crane. Washington Irving describes the schoolmaster protagonist of *The Legend of Sleepy Hollow* thus: "He was tall, but exceedingly lank, with narrow shoulders, long arms and legs, hands that dangled a mile out of his sleeves, feet that might have served as shovels, and his whole frame most loosely hung together" [and might have been mistaken] "for the genius of famine descending upon earth, or some scarecrow eloped from a cornfield." Though clearly an exaggeration, this was the unflattering image Bill had of himself.

Although Trout avoided cameras whenever possible, the few photographs we have of him confirm the physical characteristics most people who knew him remember: his tall, lanky build, stoop-shoulder posture, and large narrow feet and bony fingers. He had a long rather narrow face with a mole on his left cheek and a full lower lip. Several people, among them his niece Alice Trout Smith, recalled that he wore high-button shoes long after they had gone out of fashion, suggesting that he may have had some difficulty with his feet. However, Rhoda Hostetter Clemens and other of his pupils at Gap Centralized School remember him striding around the playground at recess or lunch and going up the school stairs three at a time. Bill's interest in Abraham Lincoln, noted earlier, might in part be explained by similarities in their rural origins and early poverty, commitment to self-education, and the sorrows of personal loss, as well as by physical characteristics they shared, which in Lincoln's case gave rise to vicious comments and cartoons by contemporaries about his appearance and lack of refinement. Trout's physical characteristics may in part account for his self-consciousness and low self-esteem, as well as providing possible clues as to why he repeatedly failed military physicals during the 1940s.

Given his physical characteristics it is worth speculating (as some scholars have also done with Lytton Strachey and Abraham Lincoln) that Bill may have suffered from Marfan syndrome (or a related disorder with similar skeletal traits—Multiple endocrine neoplasia type 2B), a disease of the connective tissue first described in 1896 by the French physician Antoine Marfan (1858-1942), the genetic cause of which was not discovered until 1991. Although the most serious symptoms are related to malfunctions of the heart valves due to the abnormality of the chemical makeup of the connective tissue, Marfan syndrome appears in a variety of forms and can be so mild that few, if any, organ symptoms are manifest. According to the American Heart Association, there is "no single conclusive test for diagnosing" Marfan syndrome. Its most obvious traits include above average height, slender elongated limbs, long fingers and toes, flat narrow feet and hammer toes, abnormal curvature of the spine, stooped shoulders, protruding or sunken breastbone, unusual joint flexibility, a long narrow face, and full or blubbery lips. While Lincoln and Trout had some of the characteristics of a marfanoid body type, the fact that both lived well beyond the life expectancy of people with Marfan syndrome or MEN 2B is the principal challenge to their having suffered from either malady. It is not possible to confirm a diagnosis of Marfan syndrome on physical characteristics alone; only through DNA testing might evidence be found to resolve the issue conclusively in both cases (Schwartz 1964, 490-495; Boritt 1983, 213-229; McKusick 1991, 280; Harrison 1998, 2131, 2192-2193). Thus Trout's physical appearance and his perception of it need to be taken into account in trying to understand what drew him into friendships with handsome younger men and made him camera-shy.

Bill's sensitivity to male beauty is apparent in his correspondence with Don Smith, in which he frequently refers to his young GI friends as "lads." The wartime letters to Smith, with whom he had a platonic relationship since Smith (as a teenager) first came to the Trout house to listen to Bill's large collection of classical-music recordings and to play the piano for him, read like courting-letters—though Smith's chaste interests in girls and his naiveté seem to have made him unaware of the fact. Trout closes his letter of 29 April 1944 by telling Smith that his mother "sends her best wishes. From me you must surmise what goes out to you in the way of illegitimate affection and hopes for luck." And he ended a letter written a few days later with: "Of my own feelings, thoughts, and wishes, you must, if you care, make surmises by reading between the lines." At the time of their correspondence Bill was in his mid-thirties, Smith in his early twenties.

There is evidence that Bill may have felt a romantic attraction to good-looking young men, though no first-hand evidence that he ever acted on it. Several of the people I interviewed said they suspected he might be gay, and one who had been his pupil at Gap School in the late 1930s reluctantly admitted he had "heard rumors" that Bill liked boys too much, which his wife, sitting in an adjacent room during the interview, interjected were "not true." Such rumors may have been no more than the whispered speculation about people who do not marry made by those suspicious of others who are "different." Whether the rumors were true or not, this exchange suggests that Bill might have been the object of idle talk, something not unusual in rural and small town communities, particularly if the victim of the gossip does not "fit" the community's norms. Bill may have remained closeted all his life, but in a curious comment made in a letter of 7 May 1944 to Don Smith, he hints at what may have been a romantic encounter, saying that Massenet's *Manon* always elicits strong emotions in him, "bringing back one November afternoon, one of the few times in my life when I have been completely happy ... But to pursue that theme would be to betray too much I would never have you know." We may never know with whom, if anyone, he shared that November afternoon listening to an opera about lovers kept apart by family, social conventions, and their own weaknesses and missteps. But in this confession and others in letters and in such poems as "Cliché," "Lonely wanted but companionship," and "Onset" there are hints that Bill's loneliness grew out of not finding someone with whom to share a romance, a love relationship made impossible by his obligations to his mother and his own reluctance either to risk rejection or to express feelings considered "unnatural" by the society of his day, which prosecuted same-sex relations under a statute passed in 1917, and though declared unconstitutional in 1980, was not repealed by the Pennsylvania legislature until 1995. Moreover, there are subtle indications in his letters and poetry which when taken together suggest he may never have experienced the type of affection and love he desired.

Trout's handsome and sophisticated cousin Elford Caughey (fig. 9) referred to as "L" in Bill's letters—with whom he corresponded frequently and on at least one occasion visited in Boston—was a harpist with the Boston Symphony Orchestra in the Koussevitsky years. There is also evidence that Caughey visited Bill in Gap. "L" seems to have had a male companion named Watson whose imminent induction into the military in July 1942 depressed Caughey because, as Bill reported to Don Smith, "he ["L"] will be alone during the hot summer days" and forced to play Esplanade concerts of "mediocre music" to "callous audiences." In a July 1943 letter Trout tells Smith "L" was worried because Watson was out again on an Atlantic convoy.

According to the 1900 Census, Elford's father, Charles E, was of Irish descent and listed as a coal merchant who owned a house free of mortgage. The 1910 Census lists him as a clerk in an iron company, and in the 1930 Census as shipping clerk in a hardware factory. Elford's mother, Clara, was a homemaker. His older sister, who was born in 1898, became a schoolteacher. Born in Bellevue, Pennsylvania near Pittsburgh, in 1904, Elford, when he was eighteen, went off to the New England Conservatory of Music and according to information on his class card studied there from 1923-1927. His principal instrument was the harp, but he also studied organ and voice. The BSO Fact Sheet he completed for press purposes provides personal and educational information about him. He played with the BSO and the Boston Pops beginning in 1925-26, and then from 1928-1951, and was also an instructor at Boston Conservatory. He took poetry writing as a special student from 1937-1940 at Harvard with Robert Hillyer (1895-1961), whose *Collected Verse* won a Pulitzer Prize in 1934. A copy of Hillyer's 1939 collection of poetry *In Time of Mistrust* inscribed to Elford Caughey is among Trout's books. According to the May 25, 1939, *Harvard Crimson* Caughey received "the Harvard Monthly prize of $50 for the student in an advanced English composition course showing the greatest literary promise."

From the 1930s to the early 1950s Caughey published poems on a regular basis in newspapers, small literary journals, and magazines, among them *The Virginia Quarterly Review*, *The New Yorker*, *Harper's Magazine*, *The Atlantic Monthly*, *American Mercury*, and *The Saturday Evening Post*. Although he wrote in a variety of forms, Caughey, like his teacher, was primarily a lyric poet whose work is in meter and often rhymes. Not surprisingly, music is the subject of several of his poems, as in "No Music Now" (1942), "The Harp" (1944), "Symphony" (1949), and "The Singing Dark" (1949). Typical of his pastoral poems are "Nocturne Above Derry" (1943) and "The Haymow: Winter" (1943). "To A Dreaming Dog" (1942) may have been inspired by the Russian Wolf Hound Alice Trout Smith recalled Caughey owned. His "Animal Kingdom" (1943) is set in the jungle of some South Pacific island and combines animal imagery with the tools of war—planes, tanks, guns, and a submarine. In poems like "Futility At Dawn" (1939), "Wound" (1943) and "The Man in the Field" (1943) he treated the themes of troubled personal relationships, lost love, and loneliness. Contemplations of time and the transience of life, interests he shared with Bill, are central to "The Silent House" (1943), "The Poem" (1948), and "Afternoon in Summer" (1953).

After leaving the BSO in 1951 Caughey continued living in Boston until his death in August 1963 at the age of 59. He apparently never married, and as his will and probate records show, he "purposely omitted" his sister, Mrs. Helen C. Weiss, his only sibling, from receiving anything from his estate, leaving the bulk of his assets to his two nieces and a married woman friend of thirty-two years. Bill Trout was not mentioned in the will. Caughey's apartments, according to the Boston City Directories, first on the Fenway and later on Westland Avenue, held his sizable collection of rare books, illuminated manuscripts, and prints, including etchings by Schongauer and Rembrandt, mentioned by him on his BSO Fact Sheet.

Bill made frequent references to Caughey in his letters to Don Smith, suggesting that he and his cousin kept up an active correspondence. For Christmas

1941, Elford sent him a recording of Edna St. Vincent Millay reading her poetry. There are only hints that the cousins discussed poetry in their letters, as in one to Smith from July 1943 in which Bill tells him "L" is doing some writing at the urging of the *Atlantic* editor. He praises "L" in an October 1943 letter to Smith not only for his musical knowledge and talent but also says "he beats me on the ground I am native to, books." We may never know whether Trout shared any of his verse with his cousin or asked his advice or help with publishing it, but it seems unlikely given what he wrote to Smith on 3 March 1945: "You tell me to write about music, and I remember that you used to mock my ignorance: L induces me to write about books, and then laughs at my ignorance and bad taste." Don Smith once visited Caughey in Boston and seems to have come away with the impression that he was "a playboy." But in his letter to Smith of 8 May 1943 Trout insists: "Nothing could be further from the truth. At bottom he is an unassuming, wholly generous and tolerant person, serious to the core, a fastidious and exacting artist, and a most loveable person." Clearly, Bill liked and admired Caughey though politically they disagreed—his cousin held FDR "in horror" according to Bill who loved and admired the President. Elford Caughey and William Trout lived in vastly different worlds, one cosmopolitan, and the other utterly provincial. And yet their correspondence and apparently infrequent meetings may have helped to reassure Bill that he was not alone in his affectional preference, and may also have helped sustain him spiritually and intellectually in the alien atmosphere of Gap. A colleague at Millersville, Louis Jennings, recalled that Bill once told him his best friend was a musician, presumably Caughey.

During World War II Bill carried on regular correspondence with at least half a dozen GIs, several of whom had been his pupils. Over the years, he made close friendships with a number of young men, among them one named Jim, who, as mentioned earlier, worked at Lukens Steel before being drafted. In his letters to Don Smith, Bill wrote about Jim (whose last name he never mentions) frequently and at some length, early on describing him as "six feet three of bone and sinew" with "a deeply hidden vein of Gallic melancholy ... a remarkable talent for drawing and painting, and a stroke of poetry that is oddly in contrast to his rather overwhelming masculine virility and passion for hunting and ski-ing and the outdoors." As with some other young men Bill befriended, Jim, an orphan, had a "rather unhappy" home life.

Jim began writing to Trout after being drafted into the army. In a letter of 29 June 1943, Bill didn't disguise his pleasure in telling Don Smith that a week doesn't go by without a letter from Jim, "very typically James-ian and aptly illustrated with original, mordant, humorous, and often ribald drawings." He tells Smith in another letter that Jim has artistic talent and that wanting to foster it, he has been writing to art supply companies in several cities to get pastels, paper, and other materials to send to him. In a letter postmarked 31 January 1944, he describes to Smith the "unforgettable four-hour interim, with drinks in abundance and dinner" he and Jim spent together in Harrisburg during a layover before he shipped out to the Pacific. They had not seen each other for months, and Bill said that when Jim swung his "magnificent length off the train" he did not recognize him because his face seemed "aged and lined and very thin." When Jim saw him in the crowded station, Bill relates, "he grabbed my hand and let out a 'wohoop'—Very flattering to an aging jerk." With dinner they drank Old-Fashioneds. Then they "rambled around the Capitol, which he [Jim] had never seen, stopping occasionally for more alcohol." Jim told him about his military training and "mainly about a girl—There is a one and only." Finally, they "went reluctantly to the station," and Jim left, after which Bill says he spent a "rather desolate" half hour waiting for the train back to Gap. But "Most shattering," he admits, "was the haunting sense I had as he left—that I wouldn't see him again ... it was the same premonition I had about Hookie." Throughout the war Bill mentions to Don Smith the letters he received from Jim, and in one of 29 April 1944 tells Smith Jim is "my only really faithful friend and much loved comrade"; but as with so much in Trout's life, there is no documentation about the fate of his friend or evidence that they resumed their friendship after the war.

Trout's war-time letters to Don Smith reveal the personal worries he experienced concerning the well-being of his brother and soldier friends but also his empathy for the suffering of others on the home front whose loved ones were also in the military, as is apparent from a story he tells Smith in a letter of 3 October 1943.

> The other day at work I almost burst into tears. Goldy, the North Carolinian who helps me, has a son—a corporal—in England from whom he has not heard for over a month. Like most of his class, Goldy is rather inarticulate, but he does confide his troubles to me. The other day I ran across a scrap of paper on which he had written and re-written his son's name, "Corp. Alonzo Golds." The terrible thing about all this is that for every man in uniform there is at home at least one person who doesn't sleep well, who knows what is meant by the cliché, "a heavy heart."

"This year," he goes on to say, "all the beauty [of autumn, his favorite season] carries the hidden sting, has become ominous, the elaborate stage-setting for Heart-break House" (perhaps a reference to George Bernard Shaw's 1919 play *Heartbreak House* about the unwillingness or inability of members of British society on the eve of the 1914-18 war to understand the meaning and material consequences of such a conflict), and ends by saying: "This damned war obliterates everything, even sex."

It was not only the death of his former student "Hookie" Bair that plunged Bill into despair, but the deaths of other young servicemen such as the sons of fellow Lukens workers whom he did not know personally but saw photos of—among them Dan Dobbs' son, a nineteen-year-old tail gunner on a bomber, and "the Manship boy" he describes to Don Smith as "incredibly young, handsome to the point of positive beauty," which a three-quarter length picture of him in uniform confirms is no exaggeration. Fred Manship, Jr., whose photograph Bill saw in the *Lukens Plate*, the company newspaper, was killed in North Africa in May 1943 at age nineteen. He had started at Lukens as a messenger boy before working in the mill, where Bill intimates he had seen him. Trout dropped other hints in his letters about his sexual orientation. He asks Smith in a letter of 6 June 1945 whether he recalls the gossip about Ludwig II of Bavaria (reputedly a homosexual) and Richard Wagner, and also notes that his "worthless and magnificent favorite, Hart Crane," while in France, "was chasing sailors in Marseille when he should have been writing verse in Montmartre"—a bit of "teacherly," not moral, censure.

Though much of what Trout wrote to Don Smith (fig. 10) concerned news from home and intellectual matters, particularly music and literature, on several occasions he chides him about his prudery and chastity. "But don't let purely intellectual affairs interfere with love," he advises Smith on 8 May 1943 "no spiritual enthusiasms, no lofty flights of the mind, can equal the supreme delight of going to bed with a beautiful and naked human being. Don't sneer at sex, me lad, for lust and liquor are the only wholly satisfactory delights, spring-fleeting tho they be." When Smith enrolled in a language program paid for by the army at the University of Nebraska, Lincoln in the fall of 1943, Bill teases him in a letter dated 3 October 1943, saying: "What terrific luck you have—university, in uniform, among a bevy of virgins (presumably), and with a diet to make a civilian grind his teeth (false). You'll be lucky if you emerge from the place with your chastity unimpaired; don't go out alone or you will be raped—It's odd what a number of girls are willing to give their 'all' for their country; that 'all' is so frequently given that in time it must be terribly threadbare." "Long pondering on life and the paths that lead to the grave has convinced me," Bill tells Smith in a letter postmarked 20 March 1944 "that of the two absolute 'good-s' in life, the greatest possibly—is the pleasurable sensation attained by the uninhibited friction of two healthy naked bodies." (I think that it is telling that in two of these letters Trout doesn't use the feminine pronoun to refer to the sexual partner.). He said the other "good" is alcohol. Shocking, and some might say sexist, as such hedonistic statements may seem, they do reflect the usually unspoken realities of life and coming-of-age experiences and interests of GIs and young men in general during the period, who decorated footlockers or bedrooms with Betty Grable and Rita Hayworth pin-ups. Writing to Smith on 3 March 1945, he reminds him that the English poet John Donne, "in his young days, celebrated 'loves sweet Part, Variety,' and warned against a 'dangerous constancie.' And somewhere else he asks, 'Who e'er rigg'd faire ship to lie in harbours?' "

By telling Don Smith *carpe diem* (make the most of every day) and to take Herrick's advice to gather rosebuds while you may, Bill (then in his mid-thirties) had come to recognize the transience of temporal things, his own missed opportunities, and the inability and dangers of trying to revisit the days of one's youth, as he warns in such poems as "Du Temps Perdu" and "Not we the white wind-flower." His seeming hedonism was also rooted in his knowledge of and fondness for the poetry of Catullus and François Villon, the prose of Marcel Proust, and the music of Maurice Ravel, all four of whom he valued for their celebration of the senses, of sensation. Nor should one forget Trout's interest in the music of Richard Wagner, who professed that the fullest reality of love is possible only within sex, from which "all other love is derivative." Then, too, Millay, who burned her candle at both ends, and whose poems Trout had been reading for more than a decade, had written many poems, particularly sonnets, about her love affairs, some of them adulterous.

In spite of his erudition Bill was no ivory-tower academic or sentimental poet but a man who knew the hard realities of life and accepted people blemishes and all. While he guarded his privacy, he was not unapproachable. He was understanding and accepting, particularly of the young; and they responded to him with affection and trust. As his letters to Don Smith testify—whether it was the soldier who revealed in a letter "shocking" things about his dreams; the Lukens men "absorbed in sex, liquor, money, and gripes" and "adore finding someone who listens with not-altogether-feigned interest in how many pieces of ass they can compass in one night"; the "seventeen-year-old, who had borrowed Bill's antiquated Plymouth to take his girl to a carnival" and stretched out on his sofa at three in the morning telling him "the delights of a moonlight summer night" (James Cauller confirmed he was the lad, and even remembers the name of his date that night); or the eighth-grade boy who asked Bill to go to a horse show in New Holland—all knew they could trust Mr. Trout and confide in him. And he also relates in a letter to Don Smith, the time in a local tap room when Bob—"a kid I used to have in school, a nineteen-year-old veteran of Guadalcanal"—introduced him to "Waltzing Matilda" by singing it to him "very softly, with never a glint of amusement in his deep blue eyes that had looked on so much that was terrible." Years later, as his Christiana pupil William Axe recalled, Bill taught the song to his class. Another hint that Trout occasionally spent time with young men in area bars comes in a letter to Don Smith of 7 May 1944, in which he says: "In other ways Ephrata can be very productive—Ephrata and the surrounding towns; I could … [Trout's ellipsis] but I won't try to corrupt you."

William Trout was a deeply sensitive man. We know from his letters that classical music had the power to move him to tears. And more than one student remembers that when he played music in class or recited certain poems, tears would well-up in his eyes and sometimes run down his cheeks. A measure of his humanity and sensitivity is found in a poem he wrote about a Millersville colleague, Harold Weirich, a tall, handsome man in his thirties who joined the biology faculty in 1958, the year Trout came to the college. Only because Bill told me in the 1970s the story on which the poem is based was it possible to identify its subject:

> The teacher of biology—a former marine,
> Who had survived the worst of Guadalcanal—
> Said one day, in talking quietly
> About his dead father, whom he loved,
> That he thought foolish, bad, criminal
> The sot convention that men must not weep.
> And as he talked, with cold profanity,
> The tears brimmed, and were allowed to fall.
> (He will not know my gratitude, in the deep
> January blackness, the cold, between
> The daylight desert and the bleeding grove,
> Where broken branches cry, begging pity.

But the teacher was still young, had yet to learn
The obscurity where time's dull henchmen sit,
Feeling the bitter salt to ridge and burn,
Because the years have dried the saving thread
Of shallow Lethe that would lull the dead.)

Clearly, Trout was an uncommon man with a very common touch. As photographs document (figs. 13 and 14) and former students confirm, he was no victim of fashion: he always wore a dark blue suit, white shirt, a dark tie, and black shoes from his early days as a teacher until he retired. I have a vivid memory of seeing Bill from a distance striding like an apparition, or a figure drawn by Edward Gorey, head down, across campus to the library on a bleak mid-winter day, clad in a long black top coat, its collar pulled up against the cold, and a high-crown, broad-brimmed black hat pulled down low, carrying books clasp tight against his chest under his right arm. He was spartan in his diet. Former Gap and Christiana pupils remember his lunch on most days consisted of brown bread and coffee. And William Axe recalled that once when he and his wife visited Bill and his mother in Gap and were asked to stay for a meal, they were served good bread, cheese, and homemade soup.

To some children in the elementary and middle grades at Gap school who did not have Mr. Trout as a teacher and knew him only as the rule-enforcing Principal, he seemed "scary," as Rhoda Hostetter Clemens and a few other of his pupils recalled. One of his high school students at Octorara told me a boy Trout had never taught once referred to him as "Spooks." Yet most former pupils and colleagues commented that students sought him out, and as seen in a photograph taken surreptitiously by one of them, Emory Phillips, on the grounds of Christiana School (fig. 11), more often than not it was young men who surrounded him in conversation. Those young people who looked for any excuse to be around him, found Bill interesting—perhaps charismatic or even exotic—someone very different from their other teachers, neighbors, or family members. Lewis Simmons, who was his seventh and eighth grade pupil at Christiana from 1946-48, recalled: "After I moved on to high school, I would stop and talk to him while he was waiting for the 4:20 PM bus" back to Gap. "We talked about politics mostly, since he knew I was interested in U. S. history at a young age." Another Christiana pupil, Hab Butler, said of Trout in an email: "He was smart as a whip, created a learning environment with appropriate doses of discipline and recognition and caused most of us to have a lot of fun. I'd often visit with him on Friday or Saturday nights at his home in Gap. Those visits were a little akin to a graduate course." Dennis Rittenhouse mentioned visiting Trout at home and recalled borrowing his 1948 Ford sedan to transport flowers to decorate the Christiana Fire House for the Junior Prom. Mary Lou Kenworthy, who had Trout as a teacher at Christiana in the early 1950s, alone or with friends often visited him at home, arriving to find other students there or showing up when she was leaving. "Like a trip to Mecca," she said, students and service men came back to see their former teacher in his classroom or home. A 1968 Millersville graduate wrote, "Mr. Trout was the kindest professor I ever had—he demonstrated humanity when others remained distant." As part of an oral history project undertaken for Millersville University's sesquicentennial, Betty Curtis, one of those interviewed, noted that "many students emulated [Trout's] walk, his talk, everything. They just loved him. He was a sensational teacher." She was right about students emulating Mr. Trout. As an undergraduate I switched to unfiltered Camels because they were his brand, and carried my books clasped next to my chest as he did.

Certainly part of what drew young people to him was that he really listened to them, not just the things they said but with apparent sympathetic understanding of their motives for saying them. Bill had a particular faculty for listening, which is apparent from the recollections of those who came into contact with him. Obviously, for young folks part of the fascination with Trout was that they heard things not mentioned let alone talked about around the family dinner table. As Mary Lou Kenworthy remembered, "You could discuss anything with Mr. Trout; no subject was too far out or off limits. It seemed like he knew everything. Mr. Trout told us of things that we would encounter in our lifetime; he said Social Security would be running out and that the middle class would no longer exist, there would be the rich and the poor. He told us this over a half century ago; if you think he was wrong, just look around." When Don Smith was sent to an Army foreign language school at the University of Nebraska during World War II, Trout suggested he study Spanish on the grounds that after the war it would be a useful language as Latin America rose to greater prominence in terms of U. S. involvement in the Southern Hemisphere. Smith, however, was assigned to a German program, not one in Spanish.

Like Emily Dickinson, Bill liked children, and they liked him. Lamenting the end of the school year, he tells Don Smith in May of 1945: "I have a weakness for kids, even at my advanced age [he was only 36]—I miss the stimulation, the amusement, and the exasperation." Bill's fondness for children and their closeness to nature, with which he, as did Walter de la Mare, associated them, is suggested in his poem "Garden Toad":

> He stood tiptoe, and coaxed with short finger
> The contumacious latch of the whitewashed gate,
> And entering solemnly, he only lingered
> To push with both hands—then turned, gravely elate.
>
> Between the lilac bush and the parsley bed
> He ventured on, past the onion rows,
> Where here and there, lifting a high head,
> A seeding globe reared its tranquil pose;
>
> On the right, a staked forest of tomato green
> Was lamped with scarlet. But to the path's end,
> He stalked, where under the thorned gooseberry sheen
> Squatted, pigeon-toed and warty, the sleepy friend.

He captures something of the mystery and magic this garden has for a boy so tiny he has to stand on tiptoe to unlatch its gate and, negotiating the towering onion stalks and a "forest" of tomato plants, goes to meet his friend under the gooseberry bush. It is a glimpse into childhood, or the memory of it, that brings to mind themes also found in the work of Walter de la Mare and Forrest Reid.

John Bryer, Norma Patterson, William Axe (who visited Trout frequently at home from his teens well into manhood), and other pupils remember that he introduced them to such classics of literature as Washington Irving's *The Legend of Sleepy Hollow* and Robert Louis Stevenson's *Treasure Island* by reading fiction and poetry to the class each day for twenty or thirty minutes after lunch. He also worked hard to interest James Cauller, Axe, and other young visitors in classical music and opera, in part by translating French and German arias as they listened to his many recordings or to Met Opera broadcasts on Saturday afternoons. Trout also had a particular fondness for two of the Kendig boys, Robert, one of his high school students, and his little brother Glenn. Writing to Jean Rentz in July 1953, Bill tells her his home is "occasionally invaded by a contingent" of students from Christiana. And in an undated letter to her from the early 1950s reports with obvious delight: "Glenn Kendig and I have become rather fast friends; he writes me wonderful 'letters' consisting of A B C in endearing hieroglyphs." While he was a first and second grader, Glenn not only visited Trout in his classroom after school but also spent time at his home, and remembers Bill took him on "field trips" to a local feed mill, lumberyard, and beekeeper. He also bought him a model train set, thus initiating Kendig's life-long interest in railroads. Whether a recollection of his own childhood or the observation of a child at play, Bill's poem "Boy with a Kite" further documents his imaginative observation of children.

Out in the March wind blown and rolled,
Anchored to kite-string, angled, leaning,
You move sedately in this cold,
Against a slope of southern greening.
Wind in your hair, and you a veering
Weather-vane horse that cannot roam,
The Easter twilight, chill and nearing,
Rolls up the kite-string and draws you home.

But as with many of Trout's poems, philosophical reflections are present even when he observed children at play, as is the case with "Sic Transit":

Into evening's resolute chill
Rises the urchin's shrill yell,
As up to spangle-star the ball
Curves, suspends, and starts its fall,
Then the hurtling bodies streak
The twilight.
From the hemlock's peak
The cynic starling bends an eye
Scornful—crassly, utterly.

Now the street lamps, bluish-white,
Bite the dusk with harsh spite;
Cut the smoke of burning leaves
That eddying, slowly rising, weaves
Forms essentially as sound
As these that wrestle on the ground.
Incuriously earth's shoulder turns,
To hoist the rude funeral urns.

The poem's title comes from the Latin phrase *Sic transit Gloria mundi* ("Thus passes the glory of the world"; or more freely interpreted as "Worldly things are fleeting"), and may have been originally adapted from "How quickly the glory of the world passes away!" from Thomas à Kempis' *The Imitation of Christ*, Book I, Chapter 3, in which the fifteenth-century monk asserts that we are all deceived by both our senses and our "ardent pursuit of learning." Trout's poem is filled with imagery reminding us of the transitory nature of life and material things. He sets the poem in the "chill" of evening and repeatedly reinforces the closing of day with the words "twilight" and "dusk"; relates how the ball rises, "suspends, and starts its fall"; describes the movement of smoke as dead leaves are burned; suggests the passage of time and the passing of youth as "the earth's shoulder turns" in predictable rotation; and with the hoisting of funeral urns acknowledges the inevitability of death. Emily Dickinson used *Sic transit Gloria mundi* as the first line of a witty and light hearted poem, in which while accepting the passing of all fame and things material, she celebrates in her song-like cadences the achievements of famous people (and by implication ordinary folk) and seems to recommend that all of us take *carpe diem* (seize the day) as our credo.

In her senior year in high school, Norma Patterson, who had Trout as a junior high teacher in Gap, wrote an essay about him titled "A Peculiar Character, Whom I Liked," which she has kept for over sixty years. In it she describes his physical appearance, his early arrival and late departure from school, his excellence as a teacher, his approachability that drew students to him, and concludes: "Although he was rather peculiar and had strange ideas, you could have considered it a privilege to know him because his friendship was something that most people appreciated." In a similar vein, William Axe told me Trout was "A study in what we thought we should be like. We wanted to emulate him."

Responding to a question posed in the "What Do You Think Of It" column of the Coatesville High School newspaper in 1927 about the qualities students looked for in a teacher, Bill replied: "Knowledge of subject, impartiality, self control and cheerfulness are the qualities I admire most in teachers." As a teacher he embodied those qualities himself. Dennis Rittenhouse recalled how much he learned from Trout in Latin I at "little Christiana" school and how disappointed he and his fellow students were when they moved the following year to the consolidated high school at Octorara, where they had to take Latin II with a different teacher—a "dry, boring, and redundant" experience—because Mr. Trout was not certified in the subject. "We all loved him," Rittenhouse wrote, "held him in high esteem, and respected him for his knowledge and his sense of fair play in disciplinary situations." By all accounts a master teacher, he inspired his talented or committed students;

encouraged and nurtured the slower ones; urged all of them to ask questions; and as a no-nonsense disciplinarian believed that serious infractions should be dealt with swiftly, including the occasion paddling of a loutish pupil (bent over the desk at the front of the classroom to receive ten swift strikes with a bed-slat, as Jim Cauller recalled). Gail Gibson Kowalski, who was a student in Trout's English class at Octorara High School in the 1950s wrote: "He was a remarkable teacher … and I have credited him with my love of literature/reading so many times through the years. He was such a gentle person, soft spoken, who truly loved teaching. His physique was such that some of my classmates poked fun at him," but he pretended not to hear it, and "just kept teaching." Her brother, Fred Gibson, who graduated in 1958, wrote in an email that on commencement night a group of students went to Trout's home "to bid him goodbye. It brought tears to his eyes as he was quite reclusive and couldn't believe we did this." He was a demanding but inspiring and compassionate college teacher. Rita Bechtel Smith wrote of a Friday in December of 1958 when she missed her ride home from Millersville for Christmas vacation "because I was sitting in Mr. Trout's [freshman composition] class writing a paragraph on 'A November Cornfield.' I had to rewrite that paragraph many times until Mr. Trout accepted it. How proud I am of that paragraph!"

Even a year after leaving Octorara for Millersville, Trout was one of two teachers both senior girls and senior boys said was their favorite teacher according to the 1959 yearbook, in which it was also noted: "Mr. Trout may have moved on to bigger and better things, but he's still in the heart of our average girl." Bill told me in a letter postmarked 31 October 1971 that he "adored" the essayist William Hazlitt because he was "angularly crotchety, fiercely individual, gifted with the severely lonely personal viewpoint, and with the genius of phrase to match the vision." It was therefore fitting that the students in his 1962 Essay class at Millersville gave him as a gift when the course was over a copy of Herschel Barker's biography of William Hazlitt as a token of their affection and appreciation of him as a teacher. The inscription they chose to write in the book is a quotation from Michel de Montaigne, another of Bill's favorite essayists (whom Virginia Woolf calls, along with John Donne and Sir Thomas Browne, "the keepers of solitude"), which expressed their feelings about their teacher and captured succinctly the sentiments of many of his students: "His thoughts have a high aim, though their dwelling be in the vale of a humble heart." Both the gift and the sentiments probably made the shy and self-effacing Trout uncomfortable since he did not think he deserved such recognition. Louis Jennings, his colleague in

Millersville's English Department and later the University's dean of humanities, said Bill was brilliant and hungry for knowledge, possessed detailed information on many authors, which he willingly shared, and while polite and unassuming would at times "let you know in a very nice way that you were an idiot."

While most of his poems are serious, and not a few are dark, students and friends remember Bill as having a sharp wit and a marvelous and sometimes wicked sense of humor. In a self-mocking comment on school teachers, he quotes a passage from Arnold Bennett's *Old Wives' Tales*, which he was reading at the time, in a letter to Don Smith postmarked 19 January 1942: "Miss Chetwynd, simpering momentarily, came forward with that self-conscious, slightly histrionic air, which is one of the penalties of pedagogy." Further along in the letter he relates that he and his mother "roared over" Bennett's description of Fossette, an old French poodle in the novel who is reduced to being carried around in a basket because she can no longer walk: "When everything was done that could be done for the aged virgin in the basket—." In the same letter he mentions reading Walter Pater's *Marius the Epicurean*, and says of the book: "At 18 it would have seemed the gospel of intelligent conduct of life from the lips of a high priest; at 33 I find it the too-pretty maundering of an Oxford professor, whose grasp of the workaday world (a la the New Yorker) comes from a frigidly unbending exchange of civilities with an over worked char woman." He relates an amusing incident to Don Smith in a letter of 3 October 1943: "Yesterday I went to make a blood donation (!) only to discover I must wait till the 22nd. Joe the crane runner [at Lukens Steel], threatened to denounce me to the F.B.I. for subversive activities, averring (wholly without justification) that my blood was an unholy combination of alcohol, nicotine, caffeine, and printer's ink."

Both Bill's whimsy and interest in spiders are apparent in his lighthearted close to a letter of 14 January 1945 sent to Bud Cauller, a former Gap pupil then serving in the military, in which he reports: "Jake, my favorite centipede in the cellar, has fallen into evil ways – he has discovered the [empty] beer bottles contain ample (from the insect viewpoint) malt for a good drunk, so instead of being the acute commentator on life in general (below stairs) to which I am accustomed, he has degenerated, in his hoary years, into a besotted old reprobate who hiccups at me from the asbestos-covered furnace pipe." Describing the demands made on him by household chores and teaching duties, Bill pokes fun at himself in a letter to Don Smith of 21 April 1945, claiming that "The Trouts' home – the neighbors say – is the abomination of desolation (see Jeremiah, ... or Isaiah), the House of Usher, and the locale of a de la Mare tale of eeriness and decay. But I don't listen, except to Schumann's wanderer in the woods...." His Christiana colleague, Jean Rentz, recalled him cracking jokes but never himself letting on they were jokes or laughing at them. She said that outside of school both colleagues and students found Bill funny and students in particular were clearly entertained by his witticisms. In a letter he sent her in the 1950s, Bill typed a quotation from an essay in E. M. Forster's *Abinger Harvest*, calling it a "clever" observation on Marcel Proust:

> A sentence begins quite simply, then it undulates and expands, parentheses intervene like quick-set hedges, the flowers of comparison bloom, and three fields off, like a wounded partridge, crouches the principal verb, making one wonder as one picks it up, poor little thing, whether after all it was worth such a tramp, so many guns, and such expensive dogs, and what, after all, is its relation to the main subject, potted so gaily half a page back, and proving finally to have been in the accusative case.

Trout had a limited interest in popular culture that did not extend to pop music or Hollywood films but did include selected light fiction and a fondness for cartoons, particularly those of George Price (1901-1995), an American cartoonist who began working for *The New Yorker* in 1929 and continued well into his eighties producing work which also appeared in other magazines. Price represented what one writer calls the "Swiftian tendency" in modern humor, which given Bill's affection for Swift's *Gulliver* and other comedic works of social criticism may help explain his enjoyment of Price's cartoons. Price created concise visual and verbal commentaries (some of which, as one writer observed, "would be sad if they weren't so funny"), by combining remarkable draftsmanship with none-too-subtle irony in situations in which mix-ups are taken to a deeper level of confusion, thereby making him, as Robert Coates observes in his Forward to *George Price: An Album of Cartoons* (1951), "a satirist as well as a humorist." Bill owned three books of Price's cartoons, all published between 1943 and 1955, which he gave to his student Byron Detwiler in the 1960s. But as he told Detwiler, his favorite cartoon was one from William Steig's 1942 collection of drawings *The Lonely Ones*, which shows a wild-eyed, crazed-looking woman holding a rolled-up umbrella in front of her and captioned: "Mother loved me—but she died." The drawings in *The Lonely Ones* satirize personal neuroses; or as Wolcott Gibbs points out in the Introduction to the book: "Steig offers us a series of impressions of people set off from the rest of the world by certain private obsessions, usually, it seems, by a devotion to some particularly disastrous clichéd thought or behavior." In his 7 October 2003 *Guardian* obituary of Steig, Christopher Hawtree quotes John Updike, who wrote: "Steig's cartoons do not only deliver a joke but make us reflect upon the nature of reality. There is a psychological and philosophical resonance in Steig that has long set him apart" from other cartoonists, which may account for Trout's appreciation of his humor.

Years after having him as a teacher students remembered Bill's sense of humor in class and the wit he showed in grading our less-than-stellar freshman essays (one-paragraph compositions were written in class each Friday in the first semester; three-to four-paragraph essays written outside of class were required every Friday of the second semester, sometimes with a separate sheet attached on which we justified our punctuation). Dianne Danz recalled one essay she wrote for Trout which had been red-lined half way through before he stopped, drew a tomb stone, and wrote (knowing she was Catholic and had four years of high school Latin): "*Requiescat in pace* [rest in peace]. She showed great promise as a writer. **F**." Danz went on to take all of the advanced elective courses Trout taught, and over time earned A's and B's on tests and essays. On one of my weekly essays written on a Friday in April, I wrote at the top of the page—thinking to impress the teacher I so admired—the first two lines of Robert Browning's "Home-thoughts, from Abroad": "O to be in England / Now that April's there." Bill's response was: "What Hitler said in 1940."

From these examples, one can understand why Bill's wonderful sense of humor tickled his students and friends but may sometimes have been lost on less-discerning minds. Only occasionally does his wit come through in his verse, as in "Lark Descending" and here in "Commencement," a poem that documents his occasional use of literary references, and does not hide his contempt for pomp and pretense and having to dress up in academic regalia and parade across campus for graduation ceremonies in Lyte Auditorium:

> Come, Gulliver, the strain is arduous, but
> Be circumspect; summon commonsense;
> Here is a scurvy dukedom in Lilliput,
> And with these scuttling here we can dispense—

Mere Lilliputian (to an eye serene),
Minute, noxious, but not worth a bean.

As you stand there, foolish in the black
Ridiculous robe, recall that grazing roan
In the June meadow; and when you go back
This afternoon, salute the charlock-strewn
Green fastness, where that knowing one will stare
Distastefully, scenting Yahoo air.

In its biting satire, this poem reflects Bill's discomfort, even contempt, for academe. Employing references to Jonathan Swift's *Gulliver's Travels*, he equates the college to a vile duchy in the mythical kingdom of Lilliput, populated by a race of miniature people and ruled by an emperor who has designs on a neighboring kingdom and maintains his autocratic rule by playing one political faction off against another. He likens the inhabitants of academe to "mere" Lilliputians. Over time "Lilliputian" has become synonymous with the diminutive, trivial, petty, which is apparently Trout's intended verdict on academics ("these scuttling here") in his characterization of them as "Minute, noxious, but not worth a bean." Feeling "ridiculous" in his academic gown, he recalls the roan horse he saw grazing in the June meadow (a reference to the Houyhnhnms, the wise and virtuous horses who rule by reason the country Gulliver visits on his fourth and final voyage). These horses or Houyhnhnms (which in their language means "the perfection of nature") rule a race they call Yahoos, who are deformed and debased creatures resembling human beings. But in typical self-deprecation Bill acknowledges that because of his own shortcomings and his association with the Lilliputians of academe, the "grazing roan" is sure to stare at him "Distastefully, scenting Yahoo air."

No matter how troubling, dark, or depressing some readers may find Trout's poems, they do not represent the image he presented to students and others who were acquainted with him. Normally young people do not seek out or hang around a person who is gloomy, which suggests Bill did not come across to them as negative or morose.

He needed solitude for reading, writing, and contemplation, as well as time to prepare for his teaching duties, which he took very seriously. His conscientiousness is reflected in the proverbial midnight oil he burned correcting students' quizzes and tests and filling the margins of their essays with useful and lengthy suggestions for improvement, not generic or impersonal comments dashed off just to get the job done. He was a "night owl" who stayed up into the wee hours, something confirmed by Glenn Kendig who remembered as a child being impressed when Trout showed him the three alarm clocks in his bedroom he needed to wake himself. Clocks, which Bill saw as machines that control, regulate, constrain, interrupt, pester, rob people of freedom and remind them of their mortality, appear in several of his poems, among them "Unplanned Obsolescence," "Omitted," and "Winter Afternoon."

In her poem "The Soul selects her own Society," Emily Dickinson affirms her intention to live in virtual seclusion from the world. Though admitting to Don Smith in a letter of 20 March 1944 to his "constitutional shyness," and taking care to guard his privacy, Trout never sequestered himself the way Dickinson did (at least not until the last decade or so of his life); though he probably agreed with her assertion in "Never for Society" that one is best served by cultivating one's own society, by acquaintance with "the Man within." His shyness is confirmed by his Christiana pupil Lewis Simmons, who recalled that he didn't stand with his pupils for the annual class picture and is further documented by the way he averted his eyes or turned his head from the camera in most English faculty photographs in Millersville yearbooks. When Bill resigned from Octorara High School (fig. 13) to join the English faculty at Millersville his colleagues planned a dinner honoring retiring faculty. Knowing he would be reluctant to attend such an affair, to which some sixty guests had been invited, the organizers asked his friend and former colleague Jean Rentz to sit next to Bill at the head table to help put him at ease. During the meal, she recalled, he leaned over and whispered in her ear: "I don't know why I came. It is barbaric having people watch one eat."

On the other hand, former students recall how he welcomed their visits to his home and always seemed sorry to see them leave. Drawing on memory and imagination, Bill in a poem records the end of one such visit from students to his home in Gap that ends on an eerie note of foreboding as, dredged from the unconscious, the shadowy figures of two children approach.

> Now the sky fades, and the light upon the water
> Changes, darkens in the approach of evening.
> Gone townward now at last the young laughter,
> The supple bodies, and the snatch of singing.
> Across the brittle fields that sink to winter,
> Cold-sharpened faces, showing structural bone,

Elfishly vanish; and the scarlet sweater
Dwindles. The silent watcher is alone—
Alone, where the naked elms, through black branches,
Discover, on the hill-slope, fading in the dusk,
The white barn, the gray sky that arches
November's diminished world. A dry leaf rustles.—
And these two shadowy children, with frosty breath,
Laughing and coming—these are Age and Death.

And I, too, can affirm the pleasure Bill took in my afternoon visits over the course of a decade in the 1970s, and the sincerity of his regret when it was time for me to leave. With that Lincolnesque right hand of his, he delivered a long and firm hand shake at the kitchen door when we said good-bye, the press of which I can still feel more than thirty years later, and which brings to mind Thomas Carlyle's description in *Reminiscences* (a copy of which Bill owned) of leave-takings from his aged father: "Even at every new parting of late years I have noticed him wring my hand with a tender pressure, as if he felt that one other of our few meetings here was over" (Carlyle 1881, 4). In letters to Don Smith, Bill mentions visits from friends, among them Paul Rostock, whom he calls "my good German friend," a Gap resident and mechanical engineer at Lukens Steel who shared his classical records with Bill and spent Sunday afternoons with him listening to recordings.

But for the most part Trout's Gap contemporaries remember seeing him around town only when necessity required: walking to school; waiting for the bus or trolley; or going to the store, bank, or post office. However, Glenn Kendig recalled that when as a child Bill took him on one of their "field trips" to a feed mill in the neighboring town of Intercourse, everybody there knew him, further indicating that while a homebody, Bill was no stranger even to folks in nearby towns, probably because of his reputation as an excellent teacher and because he taught them or their children. It was only later, after his mother's death and his retirement that he became profoundly reclusive.

Yet even in his mid-thirties Bill was a lonely man concerned about growing old, as he sometimes admits in letters. Some twenty years later he confesses to a Millersville class (with his characteristically self-effacing manner, but with a touch of humor) at the beginning of a lecture on Millay's poetry: "Most of us, laboring under mental handicaps, poverty, the necessity of earning a living, and the imperative demand that we live amicably with our fellows, rarely enough find another person with whom we can feel at ease. So we must make the concession and turn to literature." The psychoanalyst Carl Jung says in his autobiography that both as a child and in adulthood he felt himself alone. "If a man knows more than others," he observes, "he becomes lonely," which may have been as true of Trout as of him. What Jung discovered in his own childhood, Bill also seems to have realized about himself: "Loneliness does not come from having no people about one, but from being unable to communicate the things that seem important to oneself, or from holding certain views which others find inadmissible." And equally true of both men is Jung's assertion that "no one is more sensitive to companionship than the lonely man ..." (Jung 1973, 356).

His solitary interests and constant care of his aging mother, together with the need to hide his radical social and political views and sexual orientation, tended to make Bill secretive and protective of his privacy. It seems that by middle age he had already developed a split personality and had adopted a persona, a mask, that Jung describes as "a functional complex that comes into existence for reasons of adaptation or personal convenience, but is by no means identical with the individuality" (Jung 1971, 464-465). To which Bill responded in a marginal note, "Wear it long enough—and see." In one of his letters to Don Smith he admits to his "phobia," "a horror of being dissected, even by people to whom I am devoted," and insists that Don destroy his letters. "If I ever discover that you're using these insane dissertations as psychological experiments in the realms of the abnormal," he tells Smith in a letter of 4 May 1944 "— if I ever learn that you aren't secretly destroying the evidence as soon as read, I will," he jokingly threatens, "permanently wreck your chances at Carnegie Hall. I know quite well what I must sound like on paper...." He once told me he did not like people "poking and sniffing" at him and admitted that while he admired the novels of Jane Austen, "would not have stayed five minutes in a room with that woman" because she would have exposed all his faults, foibles, and deepest secrets. Yet her scrupulous attention to details of the material culture, social structure, and customs of her world along with her perceptive insights into the psychology of her characters account for his appreciation of her work. A letter of 6 June 1945 to Smith reveals much about how Bill confronted the world:

> One accedes to conventions because it is the only way to live in a difficult world; you grow a protective carapace, and within that, believe it or not, the personality continues to grow and attain its destined shape. Those who do not grow the carapace shrivel and die in a climate to

> which they could never become inured in a thousand years. Everyone would remold the world nearer his heart's desire; that being impossible, he takes the next most sensible way. That is only intelligent. Daily I must teach things I secretly shudder over, but what else is there to do, and why spend thought on what really isn't worth it?

"Late, late I have come to be convinced," he says in a letter to me of 2 May 1971, "that the token submission does not mean impoverishment of spirit, confession of servility; it merely means determination to avoid waste of energy in combating unworthy antagonists." Bill's letters and poems reflect the resignation of a disillusioned but persistent idealist. His reclusive nature and willingness to make the "token submission" may have been rooted in experiences in early manhood and were likely fed by Melville's assaults on the corruptions and hypocrisy of conventional American society and its authority figures in such novels and short stories as *Pierre; or The Ambiguities*, *The Confidence-man*, and "Bartleby, the Scrivener. A Story of Wall-Street." In congratulating Don Smith in 1944 for completing his first year of military service, he recalls: "I remember how I revolted, against enforced conventions, social usages, a social pattern to which I supposedly belonged, and how bitter I was over the futility of revolt." What form his "revolt" took and against which "enforced conventions" may never be known. Yet this admission gives a clue to why he marked the page of his first edition of *Bolts of Melody: New Poems of Emily Dickinson* (1945) containing the poem "Tell all the Truth but tell it slant," and may also provide a clue to understanding his poems, particularly those whose meanings are not apparent.

Trout lived both literally and figuratively on the edge of Gap, and even after moving to Lancaster kept to himself, sending his brother Frank, after their mother's death, to the public library or the library at Franklin & Marshall College for books or to copy articles. He often spoke to me of "living to one's-self," which was actually the title of an essay written in 1821 by William Hazlitt. In his copy of the *Essays* in the Modern Readers' Series, Bill marked the passage in which Hazlitt explains his approach to living, and which can also be taken to explain Bill's approach to life.

> What I mean by living to one's-self is living in the world, as in it, not of it: it is as if no one knew there was such a person, and you wished no one knew it: it is to be a silent spectator of the mighty scene of things, not an object of attention or curiosity in it; to take a thoughtful, anxious

> interest in what is passing in the world, but not to feel the slightest inclination to make or meddle with it. It is such a life as a pure spirit might be supposed to lead, and such an interest as it might take in the affairs of men, calm, contemplative, passive, distant, touched with pity for their sorrows, smiling at their follies without bitterness, sharing their affections, but not troubled by their passion, not seeking their notice, nor once dreamt of by them.

Bill may also have found a kindred spirit in John Cowper Powys (1872-1963), a British man of letters who wrote poetry, novels, nonfiction, and was a noted lecturer in both the United States and Britain. The example of Powys' search for personal identity may well have influenced Bill's own quest. Powys' works reflect a particular affinity with the natural world—its landscape, weather, and wildlife—tinged with mysticism and pantheism. He respected small-shopkeepers, farm-laborers, and factory-hands but not "financiers." He had a keen interest in the personal and historical past, and in his unusually frank *Autobiography* (1934) describes his view of life and the origins of his shyness and self-doubts, of being convinced he was an "awkward," "graceless," "ugly-mug fool," who abhors organized sport and prefers reading to games. He reveals his sympathy and respect for African Americans; his insights into child psychology, particularly the innocence *and* the cruelty of children; his remarkable memory and vivid imagination; his sensitivity and sensuality; his manias, phobias, fetishes, and erotic fantasies, including "gazing at slender-ankled girls." His appreciation of male beauty included admissions of boyhood crushes and furtive glances at pretty boys and handsome classmates in the pool changing room. "Yes," he insists, "for all misfits, and 'funny ones' in the world Nature is the only refuge." Later he expands this "refuge" saying:

> O books, O book-shops, O libraries, how, all my life, have ye, like great Nature herself, fed the desires and nourished the feelings that the stupid brutality of a false morality would fain stamp out. For in books, and in books alone, save for the indulgent solitudes of Nature, can the individual soul disport itself in sweet security, and laugh at the moral censor.

In addition to the poets and tragedians of ancient Greece, particularly Homer and Aristophanes, Powys' favorite writers (some of whom were on Trout's list as well) included Shakespeare, Charles Dickens, Dostoevsky,

Thomas Hardy, and Walter de la Mare. Having traveled throughout the United States from 1905 to the mid-1930s and finding much to like there, he nonetheless believed that to be "a genius in America is twice as difficult as elsewhere" because of the society's emphasis on materialism, standardization, conformity, and "rugged individualism," which he says opposes "all things in life that can be described as poetical or philosophical," nature among them. "The Earth is not a mother to an American," he maintains. "She is a tool shed, a smithy, a tank, a malevolent but sublime volcano, out of which so much Horse-Power calculated in terms of so many dynamos or kilowatts is forced to erupt." Questioning the importance the average American gives to science, technology, and utility, he insists that, "Mysticism and Sensuality are the things that most of all redeem life"; yet he found these undervalued in the United States, particularly by men. In consequence of this utilitarianism, Americans of "genius"—among whom he lists Walt Whitman, Herman Melville, Edgar Lee Masters, Theodore Dreiser, Vachel Lindsay, and Edna Millay—had "to develop a sort of protective chain-armour" (perhaps like Trout's "carapace"?) or "be driven to suicide" (Powys 1934, 86-87, 259, 127-128, 203, 112, 169, 510-511, 451-457, 542-543).

Powys also explains his "suspicion of the Great World, and those who ascend to eminence," and like his father, an Anglican clergyman, has a "solitary pride, a pride that need[s] … neither applause from the world, nor a place of authority" in it. "Ambitious young men," he admits, "were sealed books to me." He goes on to observe: "The grand secret of enjoying yourself with a free heart is to get rid of ambition, rid of even the most trifling competitions with other poor devils. We must have a pride in simply being ourselves outside and beyond any conceivable competition" (Powys 1934, 158, 567). Among the many books Bill recommended to me was Powys' *A Philosophy of Solitude* (1933), written during the years he lived in the United States. In it he advances a philosophy of "metaphysical introspection" as a way to live an independent life free of the spurious values and demands of modern society.

Some of the essay topics Trout assigned when I was his student in freshman English—"living happily alone in a crowd" and "the fact of individual sin"—reflect his view of life. His feelings of alienation and loneliness stemming from a need to hide his passions and beliefs comes out in a poem freighted with anxiety, perhaps born of fear of a chance discovery of his deepest secrets. What word or deed by "Lonely" (presumably Bill) in seeking companionship produced an "appearance" that created so violent a reaction that he is forced to leave home? And in his reference to Lethe, the mythological river that flows through Hades, whose water brings loss of memory, oblivion to those who drink from it, he acknowledges still being haunted by memories of the past and sees life's affronts and disappointments annulled only by death.

Lonely wanted but companionship;
Monster innocent, how was he able
To know appearance would dash the wine glass down,
Crash back the chairs, and overturn the table,
Send the guests flinging doors and leaping through
The nearest window? How could lonely know
That Lethe indolently moves to brew
Conclusively earth-reason's overthrow?
In vain, from sill he quaverlingly calls,
"Come back; I'm going now—not to return."
Leaving Fernwood, the house knee-deep in bracken
That stirs a little, as he looks sadly back—
The last glance at home's impossible walls—
He sees white faces peering through the fern.

Chapter 4
Imaging Nature

Planting trees and growing vegetables and flowers were interests Bill's mother shared with his paternal grandmother, Mary Elizabeth Bitzer Trout, who lived with Alice and her sons, subsisting on her Civil War widow's pension and the sale of produce from her garden, until her death in 1929. Alice Trout continued Thomas Bitzer's practice of planting trees on the property, particularly Japanese and Chinese chestnuts, the fruit of which they sold at Coatesville market. Dr. C. John Bryer, a veterinarian in Gap who had been a pupil of both Mrs. Trout and Bill, and who as a youth was a frequent visitor in the Trout house, remembered that the property had flowerbeds enclosed in stone walls and that Mrs. Trout planted many trees, including sycamores, white pines, spruce, and such exotics as an American linden and two ginkgoes. Trees figure prominently in many of Bill's poems. In a letter to me at the end of October 1971, he typed the following poetic memory of his mother, saying about it: "A quarter of a century old [ca. 1946], this jingle of the worst; and yet it was so deeply felt, and so much I wanted it to be something."

If there are trees in heaven,
She will be happy there;
The merest sapling, even,
Will make the streets more fair.

The hickory and the holly,
The sycamore, the fir,
Adjacent grow, and shyly
Bow to her,

As, stooped by age and illness,
She moves beneath their leaves,
And touches their bark to bless them
With gypsy sorceries.

Part Eve, part hamadryad,
She is grateful to retain
A few loves—and her willows,
Trooping in April rain.

Though not typical of Trout's nature poetry, this particular poem does bear the marks of those British poets Robert Ross calls the Neo-Georgians (to differentiate them from the Georgian poets, ca. 1910-1922), whom critics characterized as the "drenched in moonlight school of poetry" and "misty-eyed lark-lovers." The poem's cataloguing approach to nature, mawkish sentimentality, and adoration for trees (to say nothing of its very un-Georgian resurrection of stilted Victorianisms like "With gypsy sorceries / Part Eve, part hamadryad"), reminds one of such Neo-Georgian poems as J. C. Squire's "The Birds" and John Freeman's "I Will Ask" (Ross 1965, viii, 221-223, 231-233).

A good deal of Trout's work can be categorized as nature poetry (though not of the Neo-Georgian stripe); some of it growing out of specific childhood memories; some of it mood pieces; some of it metaphoric or symbolic; much of it layered with philosophical reflections on time, the meaning of life, death, and the relationship of humans to the universe; but none of it is merely a celebration of nature. Many of his nature poems suggest a relationship between the transience of human life and the cycles of the seasons. Unlike the Romantic and Transcendentalist poets, Trout did not look to nature for spiritual renewal or as a place of escape from the urban-industrial world. And in this regard he also differs from such Georgian poets as Harold Monro (whose verse he must have known if for no other reason than from his purchases from the Poetry Book Shop and Alida Monro's letters and occasional gifts of her husband's books), who saw the countryside as a source of regeneration for the harried urbanite (Grant 1967, 208-209).

Like E. E. Cummings, Trout created a type of nature poetry, which Michael Webster says rejects "the Romantics' religious veneration of nature as teacher, guide, and nurse" while *not* adopting the distanced objectivity of such modernist poets as Wallace Stevens and Marianne Moore, those dispassionate observers of the natural world. In a 1959 article Robert Langbaum describes "The New Nature Poetry" as taking as its subject matter not landscapes but animals "with a consciousness of their own"—which Webster takes further by saying, "animals have feelings of their own which may or may not have a relation to ours"—and focuses on "the mindlessness of nature, its nonhuman otherness." Because of the "nonhuman otherness" of their nature—their shunning of human emotion—Langbaum claims that Stevens (in poems like "The Snow Man" and "Thirteen Ways of Looking at a Blackbird") and Moore (in "A Grave," "The Fish," and "The Plumet Basilisk") are the most representative practitioners of the new nature poetry (Webster, 2000, 109; Langbaum, 1959, 324, 327, 331-334).

Both Cummings, as in "here's a little mouse) and" and "Me up at does," and Trout use animals as subjects. Bill did recognize, as in his crow poems and "In Brief," where a muskrat struggles to free itself from a steel trap, that animals have feelings of their own. In these poems we see a kinship with Richard Wilbur's "The Death of a Toad" and Richard Eberhart's "The Groundhog," poets whom Langbaum also counts as examples of the new nature poetry, though they differ I would argue in important ways from modernists like Stevens and Moore. Webster's observation that the "ecological sense of an animal's right to be in the world and of the profound connections between animal and human consciousness that should exist, but often do not, lie at the heart of many of Cummings' nature poems" and might be said to inform Trout's nature poetry as well (Webster 2000, 111, 116). Whereas Cummings focuses on single natural elements—the moon, stars, trees, rain—Trout often takes a micro-landscape—a vegetable garden, flowerbed, meadow, or field—as his subject, which reflects the human geography of southeastern Pennsylvania with its small farms whose fields are separated by hedgerows, not by stone walls as in Frost's New England. The micro-landscapes Trout created in poems like "Garden Toad," "Near the neglected orchard home-keeping," "Behind weathered pickets, and thrusting through," "Elderberry," and "Summer Ending" might well be taken as further evidence of his home-centeredness, his domesticity, and confirm his belief that the universe can be found in a grain of sand and philosophical questions explored in things familiar and close at hand.

Wallace Stevens and Marianne Moore were urbanites whose emphasis on style, metaphor, and symbolism intellectualizes and "aestheticizes" the natural world but in the process lead us into seeing it from different perspectives, albeit with little or no emotional engagement. Theirs is a "cosmopolitan" approach to nature in keeping with the formalism of High Modernism. Louis Untermeyer observes that Stevens cared little for content. The "cool elegance" to which he aspired in his arrangement of words and phrases creates an air of detachment, leaving his works without passion or even a trace of emotion. In a similar vein, Untermeyer sees Moore's verse as "intellectual dissertations in the form of poetry," in which "everything is rigidly planned, distorted, squeezed into protesting structures; nothing moves freely, nothing is spontaneous or without strain." She "delights" in the "eccentricities of design," he maintains, using "astringent," "cerebral lines" to construct her passionless "essays" disguised as verse (Untermeyer 1923, 324-325, 327, 363-367). There is something clinical, scientific in the way Moore—who studied nature in classrooms and through books rather than living close to it—treats her exotic creatures: lizards, a mongoose, cobra, and Sahara field-mouse. Stevens and Moore wrote "nature" poetry for the denizens of the concrete and steel, the asphalt and plate glass world of urban America, who went to zoos, read *National Geographic*, or saw nature from trains, highways, or footpaths in parks. Cummings and Trout, on the other hand, lived close to nature from childhood and had an intimate and personal association with it. Bill spent much of his life in a rural setting. Cummings as a child explored Norton's Woods in Cambridge, Massachusetts and as an adult roamed the nearly three hundred acres of woodland on his family farm in New Hampshire. Thus both were more attuned than either Stevens or Moore to the rhythms of nature in which intuition and emotion are more important than the material, rational, and empirical, which drives the mechanized, institutional routines of society whether commercial and industrial or academic and cultural (Parekh 1994, 63-66).

Bill sometimes saw in nature's creatures (as in "There at the wood's edge, in the pitted snow"), the seasons, and the weather analogies, parallels, or allegories of human experience; a characteristic one also finds in such poems by Robert Frost as "West-Running Brook" and "October." In "Light Snow" Trout suggests, as Frost does in "Tree at My Window," that there is a connection between inner and outer weather:

The snow that fell by night reveals,
On the hills, the fields and clearing
That are not plain in summer; steals
Secrets from autumn's sly wearing.

Crooked rectangles under the low
Gray sky are softly sheathed
In washed wool, and cobalts flow
And undulate as though they breathed.

Mind peers out of flesh, and ponders
Whether its weather can betray
New terrain—minor wonders—
Inlay, in some similar way.

Though there is more of Wordsworth in Frost's poetry than in Trout's, both poets acknowledged their admiration for the work of Thomas Hardy and shared his tragic view of life. But while Trout did not see nature as benign, neither did he seem to see it simply as "red in tooth and claw" as Frost seemed to in poems like "Design" and "Pod of Milkweed" (so different from Trout's "Milkweed") in which the poet describes a Darwinian struggle among butterflies made "intemperate" by the plant's nectar. For Trout, as in "Crow" and "One Pheasant," man is regarded as far more cruel than nature's creatures because he kills for sport, not out of the need to survive. The "dimpled spider, fat and white" of Frost's "Design" is not the benign inquisitive arachnids of Trout's poems "Two" and "Ambiguity." Even allowing for the occasional darkness of Frost's pastoral verse, there is more sunshine than shadow in his nature poetry than there is in Trout's. Such Frost poems as "Going for Water," "A Nature Note," "A Young Birch," and "The Pasture" are expressions of pure joy in nature (not necessarily a bad thing) without a trace of melancholy, regret, or philosophical reflection. Even his more philosophical nature poems—those with a homespun moral like "The Tuft of Flowers," "Mending Wall," and "The Road Not Taken"—are essentially positive in outlook. Nostalgia, which is so much a part of Frost's nature poetry, is less pronounced in Trout's. As Henry Steele Commanger observes, the New England Frost wrote about—a place of crumbling stone walls, weathered houses, abandoned farms, rocky pastures left to old men and women by the young people who have moved away—had been chronicled earlier by novelists like Mary E. Wilkin and Sarah Orne Jewett (Commanger, 1950, 66-67). Much of Frost's poetry explores the landscape, customs, and character of New England, marking the poet as a regionalist, albeit one who also explores universal themes. Trout's nature verse though also rooted in rural America, does not carry the mark of identifiable regionalism.

As noted earlier, Bill admired the verse of the Georgian poet Ralph Hodgson, whose view of nature combined realistic attention to detail with mysticism, and often voiced concern for modern man's estrangement from the natural world. Hodgson along with Walter de la Mare, and W. H. Davies were exempted from the sharp criticism leveled against other Georgian poets by such *avant-garde* poets and critics as Edith Sitwell (Ross 1965, 173).

Georgianism, as Robert Ross points out, was not a poetic movement. It did not represent a commitment to specific subject matter or a shared style. Rather, it was "a state of mind held in common by poets of divergent aims and methods ... it was an attitude more spiritual than intellectual." Georgianism accommodated the nature poetry of W. H. Davies, Edward Thomas, and Ralph Hodgson; Walter de la Mare's "haunting evocations of the far-away and the strange"; the sometimes-brutal realism of Rupert Brooke, John Masefield, Lascelles Abercrombie, and George Bottomley; and the truth-to-life war poetry of Wilfred Owen, Siegfried Sassoon, Robert Graves, and Isaac Rosenberg. On the poetic political spectrum, the Georgians were Centrists, moderates, committed to rooting out the "vices" of Victorian "lushness," "enervation," and literary diction. In their truth-to-life realism they adopted contemporary language, strengthened representation by incorporating details based on the five senses, and spurned sentimentalism while not abandoning human values and personal emotions. Some of them sought to make poetry more dramatic. For the most part, they favored blank verse or fixed forms—meter and rhyme—to free verse, and rejected the effort of the poetic Left, the *avant-garde* to make poetry more intellectual, obscure, esoteric, and impersonal (Ross 1965, 116-126).

Edward Thomas (1878-1917) came late to poetry, having spent most of his career writing prose and criticism. Robert Frost, who became one of his closest friends, encouraged him to concentrate on writing verse. Trout took as themes for many of his poems those Matthew Hollis says were pursued by Thomas: "country characters," "the elemental conditions of the weather and the seasons," "the spaces in which the human and the natural worlds intersect," and "the power of memory and of childhood." Both poets had a "power of recall" that went beyond objects and events. So keen were their senses that they could give expression to remembered sensations as Thomas does in "Digging" and "The Mill-Water" and Trout does in "September Noon" and "Cold twilight still—but life begins to stir." As Louis Untermeyer observes, Thomas "caught the magic of the English countryside in its unpoeticized quietude. Many of his poems are full of a slow, sad contemplation of life and a reflection of its brave futility"—lines underscored by Bill and characteristic of his verse as well. Thomas' "constant search for neglected loveliness," as in "Tall Nettles" and "Bird's Nests," is equally true of Trout, as seen in poems like "Wild Chicory," "Weed," and "Before the Sale" (Hollis 2011, 196, 205; Untermeyer 1962, 214).

Trout owned copies of Ralph Hodgson's (1871-1962) *The Last Blackbird, The Skylark, Collected Poems*, and two chapbooks sent to him by Hodgson's widow. What he valued in this British poet, in addition to his craftsmanship, was his humanitarianism and love of nature, particularly his sympathetic rendering of animals in lyrics written in the simple language of everyday speech.

In "The Sedge-Warbler," Hodgson's focus on the sounds of nature heard in "early summer moonlight"—the sedge-warbler's low lisped song that swells to shrill chatter, "the crusing fern-owl's cry," and "a beetle's nearing drone"—bring to mind Trout's own attention to the sounds of the countryside. In "The Last Blackbird" one finds Hodgson expressing concerns about the threat human beings pose to nature, concerns Bill shared. "The blackbird piping from the hill, / His insolent wild eye—its yellow rim— / His coaly vest and yellow mandible—" are threatened, as are other creatures, by hunting and the destruction of habitat, which brings to mind such Trout poems as "One Pheasant," "Crow," and "Entre Chien Et Loup." It is likely, given his love of birds, that Bill relished Hodgson's "Hymn to Moloch," written in 1921 during the campaign in Britain for the Plumage Act, which is a biting attack on those who make their living killing birds to supply the ladies' hat industry with feathers, the market for which in the first decade of the twentieth century, the high tide of the plumage fad, saw over fourteen million pounds of exotic feathers imported into the United Kingdom. W. H. Hudson, another writer Bill admired, campaigned for the passage of the act, as did Virginia Woolf in her somewhat ambiguous essay "The Plumage Bill," which blasted men whose lusts for hunting, profit, and women decked out in feathers turned sport into commerce, while ignoring market demand by giving a rather mild reproof to the beauty-loving woman of fashion who merely wanted to look lovely by wearing a "lemon coloured egret in her hair."

Both poets went beyond the sensuous in their treatment of nature. They freighted their poems with imagination and insight; with social and philosophical questions readers ought to ponder. They found in nature, as Hodgson does in "The Linnet," and Trout in poems like "Weed" and "Wild Chicory," that though, as Hodgson says "the world's a sham, and life a lease / Of nightmare / Where all is vain and vanity is all / a linnet and a hawthorn hedge / Still wants explaining and accounting for." In an unsigned review in *Time* magazine from 30 March 1959 (which Bill taped in his copy of *The Last Blackbird*) of Hodgson's *The Skylark and Other Poems*, the reviewer reported that Hogdson lived "a long life of deeper privacy than most poets ever dream of," the last years of which were spent in a "shabby farmhouse" outside of Minerva, Ohio, whose postmaster said of the town's "spooky" and "mysterious poet": "Oh, he's a brilliant man all right. But such a funny fella. He just sits out there and writes and writes." John Crowe Ransom said Hodgson's "Eve" and "The Bull" are "great, wonderful poems that will live forever." But T. S. Eliot in the fourth of his "Five-Finger Exercises" disparages his friend Hodgson for what he considers pandering to popular taste with what he believed was "light" verse adored by "all waitresses" to the determent of his own "serious" poetry. Hodgson's obituary in the November 4, 1962, *New York Times* (a copy of which Trout kept in one of his scrapbooks), quotes one of Robert Hillyer's reviews of his work, which zeroed in on those qualities Bill likely admired most: "Mr. Hodgson is also musical and impassioned, with the true mystic's love of animals and birds and the world of nature, and a horror of what man has made of his Eden … The simple delicacy of his phrasing is almost miraculous." Edna Millay also praised Hodgson in a 1921 letter to Elinor Wylie (Macdougal 1952, 138).

Trout's "Blacksnake" is a poem that carries meaning beyond its description of nature and can be read on several levels, showing that beneath its beauty lurk temptations as well as dangers or unpleasant surprises:

> Among the dark purple, dense
> Violets, the bland gold
> Of dandelions, by the fence
> Above the ditch, from fold on fold
> Of gleaming black, he raised his head
> And stared at us. We looked, and fled.
>
> So strange, among the smell of green,
> He glistened there, burnished new,
> Lithe, and of a loathsome sheen;
> He reared wedge-head and stared us through;
> The subtle cleft flicked probing out,
> Cleaving the warm air like a shout.
>
> Pell-mell fear sped our bare feet
> And legs abbreviate; but even
> Then one felt a god's retreat—
> Retreat of rebel pitched from heaven—
> Had been invaded, sun-slope where
> He oiled his flesh and combed his hair.

The rhyme scheme, action verbs, and strong, vibrant colors contribute to its musicality. It contains imaginative turns of phrase such as the snake's tongue "Cleaving the warm air like a shout" and appeals to olfactory senses in "the smell of green." Along with careful attention to descriptive detail are biblical allusions and a veiled reference to lost innocence. There is something both eerie and delicious about this poem. Concealed unsuspected among the golden dandelion and purple violets (in Christian symbolism the former represents one of the "bitter herbs" of the Passion and the latter the humility of Christ) lurks beauty of a different sort, the "burnished," shining, glistening, sinister, but oh so appealingly tactile, beauty in black. The very words used to describe the snake are redolent with temptation like the serpent in the Garden of Eden and appeal to the sins of the flesh (Ferguson 1961, 30, 40). There may have been no symbolism intended in Trout's choice of flowers here. However, that the snake is likened to a "rebel pitched from heaven" cannot be mistaken for any one other than Lucifer, who led the revolt of the angels against God's authority. And although a serpent or snake can convey multiple symbolic meanings depending on the culture or context in which it is presented, in Trout's poem where its sensuous qualities are enumerated, it seems to be a symbol of temptation or sexuality, or as Jung points out can relate to abnormal stirrings in the unconscious (Cirlot 1962, 272-277; see Jung 1956, *passim*). The individual words and phrases that Bill underlined in D. H. Lawrence's "Snake" reveal a close reading of the poem and, although it is uncertain when he read it, hints at how it may have influenced his "Blacksnake" and "Some flagged corridor of exit—more."

As is so often the case in Trout's poetry, there is a Proustian quality about "Blacksnake" in its evocation of the senses, what Bill once wrote to Don Smith as Proust's "cult of sensation." It is also Proustian in that like much of Bill's non-nature poetry it deals with time and memory—"the remembrance of things past." Though not in the least derivative, the poem also brings to mind the way Emily Dickinson images reptiles, as in her "Sweet is the swamp with its secrets" and "A narrow fellow in the grass," two of her eight poems about snakes, all of which present them as suspect and threatening. But both his poem and her "narrow fellow in the grass" testify to their economy of means in creating that distillate of an emotion that is the essence of good poetry.

Bill and his mother loved wildlife and enjoyed feeding and observing birds, as their copies of Audubon field guides testify. In a letter of 3 March 1945 he tells Don Smith that his mother "limps around polishing the kitchenware and coaxing the birds, which have come back this year in droves – the morning is an unbelievable hubbub of calls, like a disorderly orchestra tuning for a symphony that never occurs. Somewhere an oriole has nested, probably in the elm, and thrice a day he makes an exotic appearance, the flash of color and the clear notes causing cacophony among the starlings, wrens, robins, song sparrows, and plain sparrows.... Such is life on Tobacco Road." But as a poem recording bird watching on a Sunday morning in autumn makes clear, Bill's nature poems involve something more than just observing wildlife.

> Near the neglected orchard home-keeping,
> Assenting only—in the Sunday morning's
> Autumn sun, and almost half asleep—
> To watch the finch flock, angle to a shore
> Of brooding weeds, intently feed, and go
> Southerly: the narrow mind is so.
> Unrewarding, those Pascalian spaces,
> Where universes vagabond at Will;
> Barren the sub-perceptions, interlaced
> By the lithe dancers. Stauncher is the chill
> That musingly recedes, kindly to leave
> A half-numb honey bee upon the sleeve.
> So the dull tenant house-keeps—and death's door,
> By grudging cleft, the known avers once more.

The Trouts had bird feeders in Gap and at their Lancaster apartment, as did fellow bird-watcher Edna St. Vincent Millay at Steepletop, which may in part account for qualities in her nature poetry that Bill appreciated. A measure of the Trouts' affection for and identity with nature's creatures was revealed by his student Ellen McCulley, who recalled that during a visit to their Gap home with some of her high school friends, "a mouse was continuously playing on the floor" of the parlor, and seemed not to have concerned either Bill or Mrs. Trout.

Trout was not an amateur naturalist like Emily Dickinson who roamed the countryside around Amherst with her dog Carlo collecting botanical specimens, creating a herbarium, and spending hours tending the exotic plants, ferns, and wildflowers that filled the conservatory her father had built for her. After she secluded herself in the mid-1860s the grounds of the Dickinson homestead; the conservatory plants; the nature essays published by Henry David Thoreau, James Russell Lowell, and Thomas Wentworth Higginson; and the Hudson River School and Luminist landscape paintings her brother Austin and his wife collected were the principal sources for Dickinson's nature poetry. Some of her nature poems carry symbolic meaning or spiritual/

religious significance; others are word paintings intended to record her fascination with nature's creatures and her love for natural beauty. While many of Trout's and Dickinson's nature poems are "dark" (as Higginson called hers), both poets also show us nature's brighter side, as Dickinson did in "I'll tell you how the Sun rose," "Nature—the Gentlest Mother is," and "A Bird came down the Walk" (St. Armand 1984, 188-190, 198, 200-202, 250-251, 256-257). However, with few exceptions, "Abendrot" among them, even Trout's brighter evocations of nature like "Summer slowly takes its leave," "Summer Ending," "October Morning," and "Behind gray weathered pickets, and thrusting through" are rendered in autumnal light and muted hues.

Because Bill lived close to the land his poems about nature grew out of both unconscious empathy with the environment and conscious and focused observations of its creatures, moods, and rhythms. Thus his way of seeing was not merely clinical or scientific. Though based on tangible, palpable reality grounded in the knowledge of botany and ornithology necessary to teach public school science units, his nature poems are also a product of attentive looking and imaginative realism. That his observations of nature are so tellingly accurate is a function of his sensitivity, his unusually keen eye, and his knowledge of birds and plants gleaned both from seeing them on a daily basis and from the well-thumbed books he owned on American wild flowers, common weeds of the United States, and Audubon field guides. The accuracy of his observations of plants, birds, weather, and landscape combined with the imaginative, and at times mystical, manner of conveying it in his poems and letters helps explain his enthusiasm for the writings of both Forrest Reid (see Chapter 8) and W. H. Hudson, particularly Hudson's *Afoot in England* (1909/1939), a book he often urged me to read for its marvelous evocation of rural England. Like Trout, Hudson was a perceptive student of plants and animals, particularly birds and wildflowers, and possessed sensitivity to topography and weather that resulted in some of the most telling descriptions of the English countryside and its villages. His knowledge came from extensive walking tours in all parts of England, during which he spent hours watching the behavior of birds, thus becoming familiar with their songs and habits.

Trout's way of seeing may also owe something to his reading of Marcel Proust. For as Harold March points out, "Poetry, obviously, is much more than a matter of rhythm; it is a way of seeing. And Proust saw like a poet. He was not content with surface resemblances and disparities; he always struggled to get at the 'profound, authentic impression,' and relate it to something else." Trout, like Proust, had an "extraordinary acuity of vision" (March

1948, 245, 238). There is also something Proustian at work in Trout's nature poems that grows out of the "remembrance of things past," as is the case with his "Elderberry":

> Bending above the meadow stream,
> In June, the elderberry spread
> Its gypsy disks of white and cream—
> Wine-scent prodigally squandered—
>
> Where sunfish, sucker, catfish bred
> In pools swirling darkly there,
> Where the blue kingfisher dived and fed,
> Indolent in orient air....
>
> Now fifty years have gone in dust
> Futility; yet to a room
> Vile with narrow-eyed mistrust,
> Drifts back the scent of elder-bloom.

The few poems in which snakes, particularly copperheads, figure in Trout's poems hint at another side of his view of the natural world, one confirmed in a letter of 15 July 1945, in which he tells Don Smith, slightly tongue-in-cheek, that the devastation of his garden by Japanese beetles confirms "my natural pessimism and hostility to Nature." In trying to understand Trout's view of nature, it may be helpful to keep in mind Herman Melville's observation in his novel *Pierre; or The Ambiguities* (1852): "Say what some poets will, Nature is not so much her own ever-sweet interpreter, as the mere supplier of that cunning alphabet, whereby selecting and combining as he pleases, each man reads his own peculiar lesson according to his own peculiar mind and mood." Similarly, Emily Dickinson held an ambivalent attitude toward nature, which she saw as beautiful, "bountiful and inviting" but also, where snakes, thunderstorms, and volcanoes were concerned as duplicitous, "unpredictable and potentially ruthless" (Munge 1975, 160-163).

Yet in their poems in which spiders are the subjects both poets take a positive view of nature. In poems like "The fairest Home I ever knew," "The Spider holds a Silver Ball," "A Spider sewed at Night," and "The Spider as an Artist," as Levi St. Armand observes, Dickinson sees the spider as an industrious craftsman, artist, and even "a metaphor of the poet herself" (St. Armand 1984, 32-36). Rather than viewing arachnids simply as creatures to be feared and squashed, Trout in "Demonstration," "Ambiguity," and "Two" considers them from a philosophical/psychological perspective, perhaps as Jungian archetypes of the "collective unconscious." He knew from his reading on symbolism, that through the ceaseless spinning of its web and the killing of prey the spider represents both the creative and destructive power necessary for the stability of the universe. Its web, whose spiral shape resembles a wheel (the Wheel of Transformations) in the middle of which the spider lurks, symbolizes the negative aspect of the universe (Cirlot 1962, 289-290, 49). While for Dickinson arachnids are industrious, ingenious, and playful "insect artists," for Trout, as in "Demonstration," they represent dexterity, skill, volition, and purposefulness or seem to be enigmatic carriers of cryptic messages containing psychological insights or philosophical lessons gleaned through the regressive probing of memory into the "collective unconscious," as suggested by Carl Jung (see Chapter 5).

> No fancy: rather admonitory fact,
> That from the cornice-crevice nine feet toward
> Tradition's heaven, launches the poised act,
> Composedly accented, clearly scored
> For withering demonstration: entrails provide
> A quarry adequate for patient skill,—
> And the small spider hangs before the eyes,
> Studying one who is devoid of will.
> —Out of centrality, psyche, soul,
> Mind, perhaps, can be spun the lean
> Transit of the terror, not at all
> Terror for the being that is whole;
> Faith flings its tough tenuity between,
> To prove enigma candid as the wall.

Trout, like Thomas Hardy, recognizes the kinship of people and lower animals: "They known Earth's secrets that know not I," Hardy says of night insects in his poem "An August Midnight"; while Bill in "Ambiguity" observes:

> The small, fawn-colored spider from the high corner,
> Come to traverse tentatively my sleeve,
> Might be surmised a cryptic courier,

If one were but adroit enough to weave
Potentiality into design,
To put the esoteric to sturdy use;
One might conjecture a token to divine
Some secret embassage; but there I lose
All direction, sadly.—Carefully,
I snare Arachne, and send her on her way.

Trout here combines an ordinary observation with philosophic musing and a clever play on words in referring to the arachnid as Arachne, the girl in Greek mythology turned into a spider for presuming to challenge the goddess Athena to a weaving contest.

The diminutive held a particular fascination for Bill. He often took small creatures—ants, spiders, crickets, wrens, toads—as subjects, as in the poem "Two," which not only records his concentrated observation of the tiny creature but his willingness to share his bedroom with it and ponder their relationship:

Overhead the pale-brown, small
Spider weaves his web, the frail
Hostelry; but down the wall
He sometimes ambles, stops to hail—
Seems to hail—the dim eyes
That stare at him. Curiously
He stares back, but enterprise
Calls him to more hazardous
Inquisition. He goes obliquely
Scuttling widdershins, up, over
Crevice and crack, till on the ledge
Of the window-top, he cons demur,
Spying downward, from the edge,
To where the dim eyes upward peer.
Scornful, he knows that nothing like
His nimble genius huddles here,
For abruptly he is gone.
Below remains the aimless dust,
That the bitter west wind, probing through
The crannies, pushes in little rolls

Along the floor. With slant thrust
The lamp penuriously doles
Penumbra in the far purlieu
Of bed and book-shelf. No being is drawn—
Revenant-slow or spider spry—
To query with mocking How—or Why.

Interest in small creatures was something Trout shared with Emily Dickinson, who took bees, caterpillars, butterflies, spiders, and small birds as subjects (Mudge 1975, 20, 214). Likewise, E. E. Cummings, wrote poems about mice, bats, porcupines, bees, all sorts of birds, and perhaps most famously one about a grasshopper whose sudden, undirected, erratic leap is captured not so much verbally as by the poet's idiosyncratic spelling, spacing, punctuation, capitalization, and rearrangement of words. As Michael Webster claims, Cummings' "animal poems focus on small, less powerful creatures that often function as stand-ins for the poet's own persona of 'small eye poet' "—a reference to his practice of using a lower case "i" to refer to himself, much as Emily Dickinson, who as a nineteenth-century woman may have felt her powerlessness, identifies herself in "I'm nobody! Who are you," and as Bill did through his repeated self-disparagement and insistence that he is just a country schoolmaster (Webster 2000, 111).

Typical of the way Trout selected flora and fauna was the specificity of his choices—finches, wrens, red-wing blackbirds, blue jays, ash trees, chestnuts, sycamores, shell-bark hickories, particular varieties of apple trees—and often the most proletarian and least "romantic" of nature's creatures—crows, starlings, groundhogs. Sometimes the plants he chose for his poems, the anemone in "Du Temps Perdu" and "Not we the white wind-flower" for example, carry symbolic significance in a more formal literary sense in keeping with the theme and tone of the poems. (In Greek mythology the anemone sprouted where the blood of the beautiful Adonis fell; in Christian symbolism it stands for the blood of Christ and martyrs; and in popular culture it represents eternal love.) But more often the plants and flowers he selected, though they too sometimes have social implications, would be considered by many people common weeds: dandelion, stag horn sumac, milkweed, skunk cabbage, and Queen Anne's lace, as in the poem "Weed":

As our ancient car climbed the hill,
And topped the sunny, windy rise,

We confronted the infinite, brooding and still—
The dense blue of July skies.

And single against enormous light,
A tilted disk of Queen Anne's lace
Swung serene, enchanted, white
Drenched, drenched in cryptic grace.

No gloss was needed: each aware
That the other saw and understood,
We passed the weed, swaying there,
Evangel, in peopled solitude.

Bill's philosophic interpretation of the plant differs from William Carlos Williams' formalist reading in his poem "Queen-Ann's Lace," which he sees in impersonal terms of size, shape, color, and composition. Although both poets capture a moment in time, Trout gives significance and nobility to plebeian plants—as with the Queen Anne's lace which he likens to the Gospels, the bringers of good news—whose promiscuity and ability to survive poor soil and attempts at eradication make them the bane of farmers and suburbanites. While in "Weeds" Millay records the pleasure she found in daisies and sorrel, the "worthless weeds" and "bastard" flowers "Cursed by farmers thriftily," Bill sees them as marginalized members of society with whom he identifies. Such plants are the unappreciated, the uncared for, the unwanted, and often the unnoticed, metaphors for those who must struggle to survive, but at the same time, in the way they brighten roadsides, are a manifestation of the divine—the botanical equivalent of an Epiphany—as he intimates in "Wild Chicory":

In the gray gravel-dust mixed with the brown field-dust,
In the acrid, blue-gray exhaust from the motors.
In the parching west wind and the pitiless August sunlight,—
The blue wild chicory grows by the highway,
Dips on the slopes of the ditches.

Asterisk of sapphire on its lean, almost denuded stem,
Unwithered in a weather parching harshly,—
This deplorably proletarian weed, humiliatingly promiscuous,
Seen near at hand, is sadly representative of humanity,—
But seen at a distance, is a tranquil vista of lagoon,
Sweeping in calm curve, unassailable.

And seen in memory: efflorescence singly regal,
A star-wheel of sapphire, it swirled, at first slowly,
Passing from the clear stain of pale-blue lake water,
    through the plumbless depths of the true stone,
Then whirled swiftly on, into serene turquoise,
And stilled slowly, through sapphire, to the blue wild
    chicory of the roadside,
But transformed now,—a festival of epiphany.

And just as the Lancaster painter Charles Demuth (1883-1935) used flowers from his mother's garden for his exquisite modernist watercolors, so Trout painted the contents of his mother's flowerbeds in words—daffodils "Cool, clear, yellow, reticent, poised" and crocus like blue Etruscan cups, and as in this poem, dahlias threatened by Jack Frost:

"Frost tonight," you said, and took
From the dish-bench drawer the great pair
Of treasured shears. "Put down your book
And carry for me." (On the stair
The robber crept, but I obeyed.)
Across the autumn overlaid
With mantling cold, you went; shears snipped
Deep crimson dahlias, mop-heads made
Of lemon light, flutings tipped
Rose and cream. I could not see
Over the color heaped on me.

While Emily Dickinson favored the bright colors of spring, and particularly summer's yellows, Bill's palette is essentially the earth tones of autumn—bronze, russet, umber, rust, gray, and shades of brown, which he uses in this poem to document his mother's garden as it slips into autumnal hues:

Behind gray weathered pickets, and thrusting through,
Flocked the chrysanthemums, old gold and copper,
Smoky Burgundy, and a very few
Fringed stars, white, enigmatic clarity.
An umbered drift, they murmured in the muted
Dim November, charcoal and purple smudged.

And a white Leghorn bobbed a scarlet comb
Under the russet apple tree, and scratched,
And peered, and pecked. A reek of garden loam
And frosted cabbage stalks touched dankly
The cold nostrils; but smouldering,
The bitter flowers confidently murmured.

In some of Trout's poems the weather is likened to human moods or emotions, while in others he explores the kinship of man and creature and his own personal identification with maimed nature, as in such poems as:

There at the woods' edge, in the pitted snow,
Timidly lurching, dragging a broken wing
The green briar caught, sidled the black crow—
Even in this dark world a pathetic thing.
Fearful, that black one huddled under the oak,
Under the stubborn leaves' whispering stir,
As the February night, like gray smoke,
Came secretly on, swift and sinister.
A dusk confrontation: so we stared
Each at the other, brothers, and each bearing
A little truculently his ugly wound;
There in a sibilant quiet tensely shared,
We stared and waited, each coldly fearing
The lonely night and the mist along the ground.

But not all of Trout's nature poems are based on first-hand observation. Just as he showed no interest in sports, so Bill did not hunt, an activity common among rural males, including his older brothers Charles and John, who are seen in family photographs with guns and hunting dogs. Some of Trout's poems about the victims of hunting appear to be based either on encounters he had as an adult or on childhood memories, of which "One Pheasant" seems to be an example. In it we see no scene of carnage—the shot and its echo have passed; there is no writhing victim or blood-drenched ground—only silence, "indefinite down," and bronze leaves stained to rose. The colorful ring-neck noble in bearing in his Grecian-plumbed helmet, "lies shattered" as his mate conceals herself in the grass waiting for the killer to pass. Except for the implied sound of the "hunter's heavy boots," silence, softness, subtlety, and sorrow characterize the poem. One senses a note of regret for the shattered beauty and quelled vitality of the flamboyant, strutting, phallic pheasant in contrast to the curt disapproving dismissal of the man, who is reduced to a pair of boots:

> Where the frost has powdered
> Heavily the brown
> Surrendered leaves, and scoured
> The air, the indefinite down
> Of the struck pheasant drifts and blows,
> And blood has stained the bronze to rose.
>
> Phallic, male, the helmet
> Grecian-plumed with jet,
> This vitality, quelled,
> That could flamboyantly fret
> The processional of October, lies
> Shattered, past the last surprise.
>
> And the slight brown hen, crouched in the thatch of grass,
> Waits for the hunter's heavy boots to pass.

That crows appear in a number of Trout's poems, including some of his most memorable ones, may be because of their acknowledged intelligence; association with magic, darkness, and death; their stark contrast to the beauty of song birds popular with so many nature poets; their reputation in literature as "outlaws" (ugly-ungainly-noisy-thieving-unreliable-carrion-eating pests); and because Bill thought of them, as he tells me in a letter postmarked 31 October 1971, as "the Hazlitts of the bird-world—Charlotte Mew's 'wise old rooks.' " Although among the most social of birds with their own kind, crows are wary and shy, and it may be that Bill identified with them as outcasts because he too was shy and saw himself as awkward, unable or unwilling to "fit in," and as having an "ugly face."

Because of its color and habits attributed to it, the raven in Christian tradition is a symbol of the Devil, and, because of its association with certain hermit saints, also symbolizes solitude. A raven is the companion of Wotan, ruler of the gods in Richard Wagner's *Ring* cycle operas, and the bird that accompanies the souls of slain heroes to Valhalla. There is a sizable body of mythology, folklore, and literature associated with the crow with much of which Bill was likely familiar. Among some cultures the crow is associated with magical powers; its image is the principal motif on shaman rattles of Northwest Coast Indians. In the legends of a number of cultures, including the Indians of the American Northwest Coast, the crow is a "trickster," the animal equivalent of the irreverent Till Eulenspiegel of Middle Low German folklore (and the subject of one of Richard Strauss' tone poems, which Bill knew from radio broadcasts and recordings), who played pranks on craftsmen, the clergy, and other "respectable" people, exposing their vices, hypocrisy, and foolishness. Till rejected conventional mores and paid for it with his life.

In Edgar Allan Poe's poem "The Raven," the bird, a traditional symbol of ill-omen, perches on a bust of Pallas Athena, the Greek goddess of wisdom, in the chamber of the lonely and melancholy narrator who reads old books of "forgotten lore" and mourns the death of his beloved, much as Bill occupied his time both before but particularly after his mother's death. Trout's poems, letters, and many of the notes he wrote in the margins of his books testify to the persistent memory of his mother. Just as in "The Raven" Lenore's chair raises painful memories of the narrator's lost love, so in poems like "Come back, come back, across this wind," "A Dry Leaf," and "Infringing the stricture that flowers must not be mentioned" objects like a "scarlet robe" "blue-gray scarf" and a "time-battered chair" are reminders to Bill of his mother. Another possible source of his interest in crows is "The Raven," one of the pieces in Franz Schubert's song cycle *Die Winterreise* (Winter Journey). In his copy of Schubert's vocal works, Bill starred or circled several lines of the song, including: "Raven, bird of ill design, / Wilt thou leave me never?" And then there are the crows depicted in the work of some of Bill's favorite painters: Bruegel's *Hunters in the Snow* (1565) and van Gogh's *Wheatfield with Crows* (1890)—the last painting the artist completed before shooting himself—in which a narrow path disappears in a field of golden wheat over which a flock of crows flies close to the ground into a dark and brooding sky.

Just as "There at the wood's edge, in the pitted snow" probably records a chance encounter with a wounded raven, so his poem "Crow" likely owes its origin to his stumbling upon the decomposed carcasses of a victim shot from its perch in an elm tree. He sneers at the notion that a creature possessing higher intelligence would kill another creature for sport:

> Now here is a dead bird beneath the elm;
> The eyes have dried and sunken, and the feathers
> That dared the whimsicalities of weathers,
> Gales and snowing airs, to overwhelm,

Fell to the sporting creature with the gun,
The speculative and cerebrating one.

Even the maggots have deserted this,
And left it washed by winter now and faded;
Yet these three violets do not feel degraded
To unfold here the purple complexities
Dabbed with white. Soft airs of April freak
The shattered wing, nudge softly the parted beak.

Burglar crow, how coarsely here you lie,
The clenched claw faded, and the withering skin
Draws across a skeleton white and thin,
While over the valley, in the upper sky,
A flock-mate flaps, but still you do not stir—
Sated explorer, fooled philosopher.

The beauty of its imagery—the trinity of blue-and-white violets (in Christian symbolism the flower of Christ's humility) growing among the bleached bones, the gentle nudging of the beak by the soft spring air—together with the marvelous internal and end rhymes and the philosophical issues it raises—make this one of Trout's most satisfying poems. Like Richard Eberhart's "Groundhog" and the dead mouse wrapped in a leaf and placed in the ground in Cummings' poem "mouse)Won," Trout's decomposing crow, fertilizer for the violets, will in time, like all of us, become one with the earth. But the violets pushing through the bird's skeleton and the reference to the gentle April breeze also refer to the cycles of life and to death and rebirth—to life in death.

Trapping was common among rural and small-town residents of Lancaster County. Bill's information about it probably came from them, specifically his brothers and friends like the teenage William Axe, whose family depended on trapping muskrats to supplement their income. According to Axe, Bill questioned him in detail about the technical aspects of trapping and hunting, which appear to form the basis for several poems, including "In Brief":

Trapped by the steel, and now to die
In winter woods knee-deep in snow,
The furred four-foot does not cry
To wind racing, to stars slow.

At fur and flesh and ligament
It sometimes gnaws, but then desists,
Huddling stilled, courage spent;
Gnaws again, since life persists.

Booted trapper, with club and sack,
Wades the snow before sunrise,
And the trapped, a little shrinking back,
Raises comprehending eyes.

It is not surprising given his fascination with time and transience that Trout's nature poetry often deals with the seasons and is frequently redolent with self-reflection, often tinged with a certain weariness or melancholy that bring to mind lines from another of Bill's self-confessed favorite poets, Robert Burns: "Come autumn sae pensive, in yellow and gray, / And sooth me wi'tidings o'nature's decay." But the following Trout poem has an unmistakably modern tone, ending with what may be a veiled and darkly humorous reference to Bill's resort to alcohol (Four Roses whiskey in this case) to soothe his sorrow:

Summer slowly takes its leave
Contentedly, assignment done;
The fine tautness of the weave
Shimmers in the flooding sun,—
In the west-wind, urging caravans
Of cloud-dazzle moving grandly,—
In cornfields, aged and crisply dried
To brown and amber, stiffly standing
Rectangular on every side,
As though each raised a wrinkled hand.
—A sleepy red—not so much red
As rust—clings and fumbling flows
Along the fence, where stoops its head
The last pink September rose.
The next breeze will rob the bush
Of the fragile disarray of age.
(Here a train crashes the hush—
Purposive life's uncaring rage.)
We pass the gate, thinking to slake

Sleepless grief's immortal thirst
With other roses, no less dust.

As with Emily Dickinson in a poem like "As imperceptibly as Grief," Trout was unusually adept at evoking the moods of nature and describing the subtle variations in the weather and landscape occasioned by the change of seasons in "March" and "Light Snow," but particularly by capturing the time when summer begins slipping into autumn, as he does in "September Noon," and in one of his most beautiful and nuanced evocations of nature, "Summer Ending":

Late in August the jays come nearer,
To clamour morning at the very eaves;
The stooping sunflower grows no higher,
But arches its disk and swells its seeds.

Beetled-harried, over the arbour,
Grape leaves curve like sieves of brown;
Densely scarlet or streaked with amber,
Tomatoes drag the vine-stems down.

Cabalist spider-webs glint and shimmer,
As morning climbs from the clinging mist....
But western fire sinks to umber,
And the ship of summer begins to list.

Like anyone who lives close to nature, Trout had no need of calendars to tell him when autumn has arrived. It is well to remember that his early years were lived before the passage of the Time Act in 1918 set standard time zones in the United States and established Daylight Saving Time, a provision of the law dropped the following year. After World War II local laws and customs determined Daylight Saving Time until the passage of the Uniform Time Act of 1966. For Bill not a calendar date but remembered smells, sounds, and sights were the true "Signs" of the change of season.

Signs that could be named official, formal,
Arriving at a fore-warned date, and always within a few
Vagrant days, this side or that: those signs we knew so well
That mind accepted, abstractedly alerted, but staying semi-dormant.—
From the long doors of the packed tobacco shed,

Pungency slowly flooded, a coarse drug that gripped the throat;
And from the kitchen—murmuring, stirring always now—there drifted
Spice-smell of catsup boiling, a scent of Latin red.—
The indolent Jersey raised the head and stared, when the evening call
Sounded diminished, under a mackerel sky.
And children's hands were stained by juice of walnut hulls, high
Up the wiry wrists. Along the creek
The wild asters banked in a turquoise wall.—
But conclusive somehow, confirming finally the sun's calm retrogression,
Were your words, as you came back from the pump under the grape arbour.
(Almost as though you told the hard luck of a nearby neighbor,)
You said—and it was the winter theme of a known music—
"Now the wrens have gone."

By October frost has done its work and days grow shorter, as Bill notes in "October Morning."

Fitfully, the rooster's crow,
In the long washes of the wind
Shrills. The crooked black gum glows
Raggedly, by rigor thinned.

Seed-wings from the maple whirl
Sibilant on the scaling slates;
And sycamore sends leaves to skirl
Across the porch. The slow sun waits,

Rising late in pale gold,
Soberly above the hill.
—Stirring, settling, all grow old,
These, and the heart's patient mill.

Arriving later in summer than other insects, crickets are also among the last we hear as the days shorten and the nights grow chilly as late autumn anticipates winter. The subtlety of this seasonal transition figures in the poems of Emily Dickinson ("Nature, the Gentlest Mother is" and "My Cricket"), and in Trout's "Fourth Act," and in this short poem:

Immemorial cricket, in the long
Autumn grasses underneath the sill

Of the south window, persists to throb and shrill,
Around the clock, his minor, metallic song.
Rackety organ grinding a tiny tune
Unheeded, still this miniature creaking
Is almost lost in the vast chorus, speaking
The grave cadences of October noon.
Small, black, shining—quizzical face
Philosophic, the cricket has become
Sibylline, as the leaf's down-drifting grace,
Foreboding, as the white oak's somber drum:
Cruel caricature, that maddening whirr—
Cassandra crying, crying in vain, like her.

He likens the tiny creature to a philosopher, ancient Roman texts of wisdom and prophecy, and finally says that its "maddening whirr" is like the Greek prophetess Cassandra, whose warnings of misfortune were disregarded. In cultures from Europe, to the Middle East, to Asia, crickets symbolize harmony, protection, or good luck, and since crickets molt, are also, as in China, linked to death and resurrection or transformation, which helps explain the presence of cricket amulets found in ancient cultures. Crickets are also associated with the subconscious, introspection, and heightened intuition, which may well have some bearing on Trout's taking them as the subject of several of his poems.

Trout's prose depictions of nature are as poetic as his verse. A letter of 29 April 1944 to Don Smith contains a paragraph in which he did his best to paint for the homesick soldier as true and poetic a picture as possible of what the young man would remember about spring in Lancaster County.

> Here the countryside is in the tender but relentless grip of spring. The sky is the delicate blue you remember; willows are fountains of green; the maples in the yards are yellow-green; those in the woods are coral; wheat and rye fields are emerald, and the ploughed land is three shades of brown. And across the valley the hills are misty lilac. Forsythia flourishes with its flamboyant color, and the scanty hyacinths are purple and pink; and this year there are thousands of daffodils, reminiscent of Herrick and Shakespeare. The plum trees begin to look like the ebon mistress of Genghis Khan fluttering fans of white; and the bees stray back, one by one, to the pear trees. One has the feeling that there should

> be no spring this year [because of the war]; but nature, as always, is oblivious of man's trouble.

Writing to Smith six days later (7 May 1944) he treats him to the wonders of an unusually lush Lancaster County spring, making references to classical music and Greek mythology.

> These Maynights [sic] are eerily beautiful, too, like nothing so much as Brahms's Die Mainacht [May Night], full of spellbound witchery; the young leaves are pale in the soft, evanescent light, the white lilacs are ghostly, and the few stars sparsely dusted across the sky seem to proclaim that their wanton sisters are elsewhere sleeping with the immortal gods or lapped in some mortal Endymion's [in Greek myth a beautiful youth loved by Selene, the goddess of the moon, and caressed by her as he slept] shepherd's cloak.

But Bill could also capture the transition between winter and spring as in "March":

> March brooms the empty countryside
> And litters all the gutters
> With chattering waste, and far and wide
> The silly sparrow stutters.
>
> Incredibly, immortally,
> The fountains of pure light
> Drench desolation handsomely
> With diamond-dazzling spite.
>
> And every winter-besomed tree
> Is stitched against the blue,
> Traced with entrancing clarity,
> Shrewd as a witch's brew.
>
> Is needed but one other thing
> To pitch us into fright—
> A small boy tethered to a string,
> And tugged at by a kite.

Trout sometimes saw spring as gaudy and out of place for one who had suffered loss and sorrow, or as in time of war, as he tells Don Smith on 7

May 1944, saying: "spring is a pageant, ironically, never more so, I think, than this year, when – if I notice – it is only with a stab of grief for the ones who don't see, for those who never will see. One feels traitorous, first; then angry, that this year spring should come, [quoting Millay's "Spring"] 'like an idiot, Babbling and strewing flowers.' " The spring of 1944 saw no let-up in American casualty reports as Allied forces island-hopped across the Pacific toward the Japanese home islands and General Mark Clark's forces in Italy slogged away against stiff German resistance, causing Bill to worry about his young GI friends and bringing back memories of those he had already lost, making the "spring pageant" seem inappropriate as he, with a twinge of guilty regret, describes it to Smith.

> Were there ever so many flowers? This morning after a night of rain the world is gray green, and the few tulips burn like candles. Lilacs have outdone themselves; the bushes sag with great masses of purple and white, and the fragrance, that I have loved so long as I can remember, makes the air heavy and delirious and nostalgic with memories one would rather not recall. Last night's rain has scattered the cherry blossoms; this year it was with a vengeance, 'the white riot of the cherry tree'; but I was not tempted, like Housman's 'Shropshire Lad', to go about the woodland ride 'to see the cherry hung with snow'... Even my pear tree this year didn't stir me much, tho she outdid herself, an exotic Lilith [according to medieval Jewish folklore Adam's first wife, a demonic female] seducing Adam. The aged trunk, the bewitching antique shape, the garlands and strands and ropes of milky blossom, the heavy, honey-like perfume, and all the golden bees of Hybla [a town in ancient Sicily known for its bees and honey] swarming in the flooding sunshine: even the seductions failed this year. Allie's [his mother] Judas tree along the drive also was moved to resurrection this year, and stands even now a minor miracle of mauve and purple strands. Massed, they are a fearfully exciting thing; you are almost forced to believe in black magic. I saw them one spring at Gettysburg, against the gray rocks [of Devil's Den and Little Round Top, that Civil War scene of carnage]; it was a shattering experience, and I have never since been wholly sure this pagan spirit of mine wouldn't at some time desert its stooped and sallow be-spectacled shell and go forth some moonlight night to dance in unholy rites on the hills outside of Gap....

He expresses similar sentiments about spring in the poem:

> Worse than winter's villainy
> For solitary grief to bear,
> This unrestrained effrontery,
> Seasonal and cavalier,
> Assails with flashing irony
> The head bent in cold aversion,
> In silent hate of luminous spray,
> Of color dazzling into blur.
> Japonica, scarlet couched in green,
> Scorches; and the stiff design
> Of the narcissus, poised between
> Larch and forsythia, gloats malign.
> Only the dandelion, low
> And sober, slows hate's overflow.

Emily Dickinson wrote more than a hundred poems about summer. And as Jean McClure Mudge observes: "Summer for her was the season of apex, a noon or high time of great promise, and in retrospect, profound despair" (Mudge 1975, xiv). But Robert Rentz, the principal of Christiana School during part of Bill's tenure there, and a friend, remembered that in their debates over which season is the best, Bill always insisted on fall because it mirrors the waning of human life. Autumn is a season he loves, Bill tells Don Smith in an October 1943 letter. And he would no doubt have agreed with Millay's final line in "The Death of Autumn"—"Oh, Autumn! Autumn ! What is the Spring to me?" Imaging autumn to Smith in a letter of 26 September 1943, like something a Regionalist painter of the period might have created, he describes it as: "cool and golden and scarlet and brown, with fawn-colored shocks of corn drenched in windy sunlight, the meadows tangles of chalky blue asters and goldenrod and stag-horn sumac." Writing to Smith on 13 November 1943 he says: "Here too it is late fall," and then quotes a quatrain from Archibald MacLeish's poem "Immortal Autumn," in which MacLeish calls fall "the human season":

> But now in autumn with the black and outcast crows
> Share we the spacious world: the whispering year is gone:
> There is more room to live now: the once secret dawn

Comes late by daylight and the dark unguarded goes.

Trout frequently set his poems in the fall or winter, as he does in "September Noon," which captures the mid-day atmosphere of early autumn.

The wrens have gone: that stuttering no more stirs
The clear airs of morning; the last of nine
Once fledglings has departed. The green burrs
Nestle prickly in the grass; a scent of wine
Drifts from the arbour; the warm garden smell
Lies in layers beneath a heavier sun,
Throbbed through at noon by the cricket's rackety swell.—
The saunter into autumn has begun.
And through this opulence that drugs the sense
With wafts of odor and the cool burning
Of scarlet tomatoes and the dense dye
Of goldenrod, under this brooding sky
Of cobalt blue, glides the shadow whence
All grief is born, remorselessly returning.

As Levi St. Armand points out, to Emily Dickinson the sun "was a living representation of the deity." Although her sunrises among them, "The Day came slow—till Five o'clock" and "I'll tell you how the Sun rose," are dazzling feasts of color and sparkling light, it was the end of day that most fascinated her. "Each of her sunset poems [and there are many of them] was a "sketch" or "study from nature," according to St. Armand, "that tried to be as faithful as possible to particular conditions of local character and color without sacrificing the imaginative quality that separates an effective composition from a mere servile imitation." For her a sunset, he claims, "was not a profane but a sacred experience." Indeed, her sunrises and sunsets are freighted with religious meaning (St. Armand 1984, 264-269, 276; Wolff 1986, 289-294). Trout's nature poems have the same qualities: they are true to the observed realities of nature, are rendered imaginatively, carry meaning beyond corporal reality, and, though they are not informed by religion the way Dickinson's are, do have a spiritual, mystical quality of the kind found in the novels of Forrest Reid.

For the most part Trout did not share Dickinson's reverie in sunrises and sunsets. With few exceptions, "Abendort" for example, he took neither the beginning of the day nor its shining end as subjects for poems but instead used other, less dramatic, times of day to set the tone or mood for his poem. He, like E. E. Cummings, preferred setting poems at gloaming, when the quality of light is truly magical, ethereal, as in "Hawk in February," "There at the woods' edge, in the pitted snow," and in

Cold twilight still—but life begins to stir
Upon these fields; at evening, light lies longer,
Lengthening winter's abrupt diameter,
Summoning home a little later the throng
Of croaking crows, pouring from the clear
And gelid north. The naked elms release
A barely perceptible sigh, relax, confer
Stealthily, the frost about their knees.
Pausing in the presence of this wonder,
Initiated so punctually once more—
The numbed, muttering god, stirring under
The sleeps of Orcus, stumbling the Stygian shore—
Man briefly dares to ponder how old grief
Can be transmuted to the green leaf.

As is so often the case in Trout's verse, subtlety, nuance, economy of means are reflected in his phrasing and choice of words to create a subdued mood: "life begins to stir," "light lies longer / Lengthening," "release / A barely perceptible sigh, relax, confer / Stealthily." Bill's preoccupation with death finds its way into the poem with references to Orcus, a god of the underworld who in the afterlife torments evildoers and those who break their oaths, and to the Stygian shore, a synonym for the dark, gloomy, and forbidding banks of the river Styx in Hades.

And yet as here in "December Evening," he renders the memory of a winter sunset as a banquet of sumptuous colors, pungent aromas, and distinctive sounds rendered in memorable turns of phrase, and delicious rhymes and varied rhythms.

Lighted by winter sunset, bitter blue
And smeared orange, when purple shadows lay
North and northeast, a shroud spread for the day,
We dug and scrounged, piercing the brittle sheath
To find the apples, tawny brown in hue,
Buried in the snow; then warmed them with our breath.

The first taste was strange wine, along
The quivering tongue, a sting that twitched and sang
In the jaw-muscles, a Moorish-gypsy tang;
The teeth ached in their sockets. Meanwhile
Night swooped. The Leghorns clucked their evensong
In the chicken-house, and settled in roosting file.

From Trout's interest in the visible world we must now turn to that of the invisible world, the realm of the unconscious, which he explored with equal singleness of purpose but with different motives.

Chapter 5
The Search Within

Just as Henry David Thoreau quipped that he had "travelled a good deal in Concord," so Trout might have said the same of Lancaster County. He made few trips beyond the county line. We know he had been to Boston at least once; to Coatesville and Washington, D.C.; at least twice to Philadelphia; several times to Harrisburg; to visit his brother Frank in Maryland; and to Gettysburg—a visit he mentions in a letter to Don Smith and alludes to in the poem "Encounter"; another example of his fascination with time and memory, in which he and his mother survey the battlefield from Little Round Top, a key to the Union line at the Battle of Gettysburg.

In the chill wind of a sunny May,
On the high hill from which one saw
Blue hills beyond, orchards that lay
White with blossom, in the flaw
Of gay valleys here and there,—
You brushed back your blown hair.

That was a land where men had died
In agony—blood and oath—
And laughing Cosmos had complied—
Feigning Law and clouding Truth—
In mocking deference to man's lust.
Hence murmured there unquiet dust.

So many careless years had passed,
One might have thought the dust become
Cancelled, impotent at last,
Homeless, in its final home.
But you—aging, worn, wise,
Wordless—heard with seeing eyes.

Almost four decades later, here—
In the grim lapse of a loitering year—
I long to understand
The wisdom musing in your eyes,
Wisdom that grasped some Enterprise,
Wisdom that fused May's flowering land
And the dust's death-cries.

Here he rejects the notion that war is glorious or heroic or waged for noble purposes by dismissing such slaughter as a consequence of "man's lust" justified by the spurious appeals to Law and Truth allowed by the "laughing Cosmos," which makes humanity its plaything. Yet he wants to understand the lesson his mother "heard with seeing eyes" that allowed her to grasp both some "Enterprise," and through her wisdom seemed to settle the unquiet dust of the killing fields, by reconciling "May's flowering land" with the "death-cries" of those killed in the battle. And here again, as in "Crow," Trout reprises the irony of death in the midst of blooming life. The lesson his mother learned from the silent voices of the dead soldiers, which he attempts to grasp, suggests the Jungian idea of the "collective unconscious." But like Emily Dickinson, whose trips beyond Amherst were few—though some were more protracted than Trout's—he was, as this poem hints, often a sojourner in the landscapes of the mind.

Bill's poetry documents an interest in the inner life and introspection characteristic of modern art stretching from Poe, Hawthorne, and Melville through Proust and the Symbolists to Eliot in literature, and to Gauguin, van Gogh, Munch and the Expressionists in the visual arts. The first direct evidence that Bill was interested in psychology is a reference he makes to Sigmund Freud (1856-1939) and Carl Gustav Jung (1875-1961) in a 1943 letter to Don Smith. Over the years he purchased many of the major works of Jung in addition to the two volumes of his letters and several monographs on the Swiss psychiatrist and founder of analytical psychology—in all, twelve heavily underscored and annotated volumes. He tells his former student Betty Curtis in a letter of 19 October 1977 that he has been reading Jung for "a quarter of a century, a resource." His study of Jung seems to be part of an effort to make sense of the human condition, his own personality and experiences, and a quest for the spiritual to fill the void left by loss of faith in conventional religion.

In the Prologue to his autobiographical *Memories, Dreams, Reflections*, Jung says his life was "a story of the self-realization of the unconscious.

Everything in the unconscious seeks outward manifestation, and the personality too desires to evolve out of its unconscious conditions to experience itself whole" (Jung 1973, 3). Trout no doubt saw in Jung's ideas a means of discovering his own identity through self-knowledge. In his poem "August Evening" Bill, recalling his mother via Jung's process of "regression" (resuscitating reminiscences),gives us a glimpse into the way he used Jungian analysis in writing poetry. But in the end he questions the comfort it provides.

> These rashly impulsive raids into the past,
> No matter how painfully plotted and mapped, step by step,
> On paper, in code—the plan memorized then, and the paper
>   destroyed—
> Are they ever rewarded in such way that, even fragmentarily,
> The venture is justified?
> —You came at sunset around the bend of the woods-path,
> While, from the south edge of the town, whistled its good-bye
> That trolley car—your vehicle of necessity,
> In which you had been prisoner for an hour,
> In the lag-end heat of the day,
> Dazed by the smell of sweat, the smell of August dust, by
>   the level glare.
> But here, among leaf shadows,
> Your face—a taut, gray mask of fatigue, worry, and grief—
>   your face:
> You looked, you saw, and, loyally, the smile (so-known)
>   came back.
> Stopping beside a spreading bracken fern,
> You stretched your hand in welcome.—
> But now the treasure, thieved thus from the past,
> Alters to ache, and blurs the groping mind.

During the 1960s and 1970s, as documented by dated marginalia, Bill was reading and rereading Jung's works. And it may be at this time that many of the poems with psychological content were written, as a comment dropped in a letter to me of 11 June 1971 suggests: "Self-scrutiny imposed during the three years and 196 days [the period since his mother's death] has revealed to me only abyss—the dark chaos of moi." It is apparent from the types of markings he made in books—ranging from underlining, to Xs, to asterisks and stars, to single or multiple vertical lines to written notes—which of Jung's ideas most interested him and the level of importance he attached to them. However, he did not swallow Jung whole as his many marginal notes questioning, criticizing, doubting, or dismissing certain pronouncements by the Swiss psychiatrist testify. Bill would have agreed with the claim of H. Stuart Hughes that while Jung "understood things about history, religion, and mythology that escaped Freud," he "was unable to express what he had learned in an unambiguous form." But he would probably have accepted only part of Hughes' final judgment that, [Jung's] "mind was profoundly confused, and his writings are a trial to anyone who attempts to discover in them a logical sequence of ideas" (Hughes 1958, 160). Some of Trout's marginalia testifies to his frustrations with the way in which Jung presented his ideas.

Nonetheless, Trout accepted Jung's assertion that the unconscious has two dimensions—the "personal unconscious" and the "collective unconscious." The personal unconscious, which is not merely the repository for suppressed instincts or desires as Freud stressed, but contains "lost memories, painful ideas that are repressed" [deliberately forgotten], and "sense-perceptions that were not strong enough to reach consciousness" obviously captured Trout's interest. What also made sense to him was Jung's assertion that "certain psychic contents or images are derived from a 'material' environment ... while others, which are no less real, seem to come from a 'spiritual' source which appears to be very different from the physical world." Key to Jung's psychology was the notion that "the human psyche is not a self-contained and wholly individual phenomenon, but also a collective one," and by psychic awareness, paying attention to dreams, one can recognize the connectedness we all share in the experiences of life across time and cultures. Thus what he called the collective unconscious—"which lies at a deeper level [than the personal unconscious] and is further removed from consciousness"—consists of primal instincts and patterns of thought in the human psyche going back eons and taking the form of archetypical images or motifs—things to which cross-cultural symbolic meaning are attached, e.g. water, cave, mother, father, old man, certain animals and plants, and so forth—that are universal and transcend time and place. It is by dredging up these archetypes in the "*individuation process*" that leads one to personal wholeness, one's own identity, by integrating the unconscious and the conscious (Jung 1953, 144-145, 124-125; Jung 1960, 346-353).

J. E. Cirlot explains Jung's archetypes as "an epiphany, that is, the revelation of the latent by way of the recondite: vision, dreams, fantasy, myth."

He goes on to say, "they are the fruits of the inner life perpetually flowing out from the unconscious, in a way which can be compared with the gradual unfolding of creation" (Cirlot 1962, xxxiv). As Jung explains in "The Phenomenology of the Spirit in Fairy Tales" (in *Psyche and Symbol*) fairy tales are a rich source of the archetypes found in the collective unconscious. The inability to assimilate content from the unconscious into the conscious and thereby achieve psychic wholeness, he maintains, is "owing to the lack of apperceptive concepts that would 'grasp' them. That is why it is extremely important to tell children fairytales and legends, and to inculcate religious ideas (dogmas) into grown-ups, because these things are instrumental symbols with whose help unconscious contents can be canalized into consciousness, interpreted, and integrated." He goes on to say that "Myths and fairytales give expression to unconscious processes, and their retelling causes these processes to come alive again and be recollected, thereby re-establishing the connection between conscious and unconscious." Failure to make this connection, he insists is the root of neuroses, "groundless phobias and obsessions" from hypochondria to "intellectual perversions suitably camouflaged in social, religious, or political garb" (Jung 1959, 169, 180).

Jung's views may in part explain the presence in Trout's library of Joseph Jacobs' *English Fairy Tales*, Lloyd Daly's *Aesop Without Morals*, and *The Oxford Dictionary of Nursery Rhymes* edited by Iona and Peter Opie, in addition to Antoine de Saint-Exupery's fable *The Little Prince*. On 11 June 1945 Bill mentions in a letter to Don Smith that he is busy comparing his English version of *Grimm's Fairy Tales* with one in German that Elizabeth Rostock, a Gap friend, had lent him. In his copy of Stechow's book on Bruegel, Bill taped Elizabeth Bowen's "Enchanter Centenary of the Brothers Grimm," an article published in *The New York Times Magazine* on September 8, 1963. Being able to recognize and come to some understanding of archetypes requires knowledge of mythology, folklore, and comparative religion and helps explain Trout's wide-ranging intellectual interests as reflected in his library, letters, and poetry.

Bill owned Lewis Carroll's *The Hunting of the Snark* and an illustrated edition of *Alice's Adventures in Wonderland* and *Through the Looking Glass* annotated by Martin Gardner. These stories are rich in symbolism and as such are fertile ground for Jungian research and analysis. Both of the Alice tales are cast as dreams at the conclusion of which Carroll places a poem ending in the line: "Life, what is it but a dream?" By going down the rabbit hole or stepping through the looking-glass Alice enters the realm of Jung's collective unconscious, which is filled with archetypes, examples of opposites like the Red Queen and the White Queen, the Sphinx-like Cheshire Cat and the Caterpillar, a symbol of transformation (death and rebirth—worm to butterfly). Alice's adventures can be seen as a process of self-discovery, achieving wholeness—what Jung calls "individuation"—by reconciling opposites, the conflicting elements of her nature.

For Jung dreams are the reflection of the dreamer's personality, *not* wish fulfillment as Freud maintained. Bill seems to have accepted this view as well as Jung's idea that dreams do not express themselves in logical, causal ways "but always in the language of parable or simile." That for Jung dreams are "an extraordinarily effective instrument of education" also struck a responsive chord in Trout, who wrote in the margin of Jung's *New Paths to Psychology*, that dreams are a means of "reinforcing that which one could not recall when one is in the waking state." As Jung points out, "... we know that dreams generally compensate the conscious situation, or supply what is lacking ... a principle that also applies to the interpretation of myths." The content of dreams, Jung says, contrast/complement the content of consciousness and are particularly "vivid" when the "one-sided" consciousness threatens "the vital needs of the individual." Both dreams and myths, he insists, have many possible meanings and "the same apparently limitless interchangeability of figures." What he calls "the big dreams," which come at the three critical stages of life—early youth/puberty, middle age, and "within sight of death"—are revealed through the archetypes that inhabit the collective unconscious (Jung 1953, 23-27, 104-105; Jung 1960, 247-253, 291-292; Jung 1956, 390).

Bill read Jung in order to achieve self-understanding, what Jung calls *individuation*, and in the process his poetry (which was one means to this end) was influenced by the quest as his poems "Intuition," "Compulsion," "Individuation," "Unprofessional Psychiatry," and "Onset" testify. "The aim of individuation," Jung claims, "is nothing less than to divest itself of the false wrappings of the persona [the mask one creates and presents to the outside world in order to live in accordance with societal norms and assumptions without questioning them] on the one hand, and the suggestive power of primordial images on the other." Individuation means the "more complete fulfillment of the collective qualities of the human being" by becoming the "unique being he in fact is" through "fulfilling the peculiarity of his nature," which Jung insists "is vastly different from egotism or individualism" represented by the persona. As part of the individuation process—which does not simply follow a linear progression but is a matter of moving forward and slipping back over an extended period of time (perhaps a lifetime)—"it is essential for a man to distinguish between what he is and how he appears to himself and to others...." As Jung puts it, "The dissolution of the persona is therefore absolutely necessary for individuation," and thus it is impossible to achieve individuation "by conscious intention, for conscious intention leads infallibly to a conscious attitude, which excludes whatever does not fit with it." Only through the "assimilation of the unconscious" can individuation—"coming to self-hood or self-realization"—be achieved, Jung concludes (Jung 1953, 156, 171-174, 193, 284-285). As his later poems suggest, Bill recognized that merely growing a "protective carapace" (Jung's "persona") within which to allow his personality to "grow and attain its destined shape"—as described in his letter of 6 June 1945 to Don Smith—may not be enough to achieve selfhood.

Jung explains the way a person achieves self-knowledge or individuation in terms of "progression and regression." He defines progression, as "a continuous process of adaptation to the environmental conditions," to society, while regression is "an adaptation of the inner world." He goes on to explain that man "can meet the demands of outer necessity in an ideal way only if he is also adapted to his own inner world, that is, if he is in harmony with himself." Through regression, Jung says, the racial memory is probed, "springing" images "from the life, the joys and sorrows of our ancestors." Such imagery, according to Jung, takes the form of symbolic archetypes "found in the mythologies of all ages and peoples. The sum of these images constitutes the collective unconscious, a heritage which is potentially present in every individual." Regressive probing, Jung points out, leads to maternal memories, and goes on to assert: "The golden haze of childhood memories arises not so much from objective facts [though these are present in much twentieth-century poetry, including Trout's] as from the admixture of magical images which are more intuited than actually conscious," a characteristic also found in Trout's verse. Regression can lead even deeper into the "prenatal stage" and non-human life forms, which may in part explain Trout's musings in his spider poems (Jung 1960, 39-40; Jung 1953, 78; Jung 1956, xxix, 329-330, 335, 408).

Evidence of regression can be found in Trout's poems, among them "Return," "Through the Shadows of the Shadowless," and "Recurrent dream: I stand knee-deep in reeds." Based on his 1930 essay "Psychology and Literature," Jung might consider these poems "visionary modes of artistic creation" in that the experience that furnishes the material for them is not familiar. In Jung's words: "It is something strange that derives its existence from the hinterland of man's mind...We are reminded of nothing in everyday life, but rather of dreams, night-time fears, and dark, uncanny recesses of the human mind. The public for the most part repudiates this kind of literature, unless it is crudely sensational, and even the literary critic finds it embarrassing." The creator of visionary art has "distinct leanings toward the occult," Jung observes, and "is in touch with the night-side of life." He goes on to point out: "The poet now and then catches sight of the figures that people the night world—spirits, demons, and gods; he feels the secret quickening of human fate by a suprahuman design, and has a presentment of incomprehensible happenings in the pleroma," the totality of divine powers (Jung 1966, 90-91, 93, 95-96). Not only did Bill tell Don Smith of his "pagan spirit" and interest in "black magic," but poems like "Individuation," "Doppelgänger," and "Unseen" also suggest his acquaintance with the "night-side of life."

Although Jung acknowledges that works of art originate in a variety of ways, he believed that in the process of creating art the unconscious is activated. While some works of art are the product of a conscious intent to produce an intended effect, others, he insists, originate in the unconscious and may have a "strangeness in form and content" and "can only be apprehended intuitively"—they are "bridges thrown out towards an unseen shore." In his 1922 lecture "On the Relation of Analytical Psychology to Poetry" Jung rejects Freud's reductive method, which is centered on biological causes. By focusing on the personal unconscious rather than the collective unconscious—thus incorrectly treating the "conscious contents which give us clues to the [personal] unconscious" not as "true symbols" but mere "signs or symptoms of the subliminal processes"—Freud's approach, Jung says, treats the artist or the work of art as diseased. True symbols according to Jung come from the collective unconscious—"a sphere of unconscious mythology whose primordial images are the common heritage of mankind"—and are intuitive ideas, "attempts to express something for which no verbal concept yet exists." Jung reminds his readers of Gerhard Hauptmann's assertion: "Poetry evokes out of words the resonance of the primordial word." The "unconscious activation of an archetypal image" from the collective unconscious, Jung says "makes it possible for us to find our way back to the deepest springs of life" (Jung 1966, 66-80). The process of writing poetry was one way Trout sought these deep springs of life that would lead him to self–realization. Another was through the analysis of dreams.

That dreams were the source of a number of Trout's poems is suggested not only by the use of the word *dream* in titles, but also by internal evidence, as in:

Recurrent dream: I stand knee-deep in reeds,
In lake-edge shallows, in an evening light;
A dank coolness and the smell of water-weeds
Constrict the breath; and there—across—the white
Walls, spires, domes dreaming sleep,
Yet summon the dream-thing, call, from the Deep.
I know the city empty. Strangely, I know
Each room slyly deserted; that fountains play
For Nobody; there no noisy crew
Of boys crouch at marbles; no woman prays
In a dark church. Yet the dream-thing strains
Toward the far whiteness, the mocking Unexplained.

In a letter to me written at 2 A.M. on 3 May 1974, Bill confirms that dreams are a source for some of his poems: "In a dream, a gentle serpent elevated slowly its head from a coil at my feet, and—slowly, delicately, with slender jaws—took a crumb of bread from my hand. I have thumbed eight volumes of Jung, and frenetically applied 'active imagination,' but—enigma." Perhaps in an effort to make sense of this dream, Bill followed Jung's recommendation and recorded it, though in verse, not prose:

Some flagged corridor of exit—more,
An arched doorway, a stone step descending:
The dream was imprecise. Then from the floor
Rose from coil the flat head, shyly bent
On the unswaying stem. How prospered craven,
Neighbored nearly by that somber wedge?—
But gentle eyes were malachite and grave,
As courteous supped from palm a crumb of bread.
Incredulous of any slackened thew
In the grim pursuit, wake wavers, half-dismayed,
Half-wanhopeful. From what fissure poured
That fluent evil, an adjunct evil brewing?
And yet—a crucified? and thence a sword?—
Waiting, wake steadies, tremor half-allayed.

As noted earlier, serpents carry many symbolic meanings. Clearly, this is not the same sort of reptile found in the poem "Blacksnake." Or is it? Its shyness and "grave" but "gentle" eyes and the "courteous" way it takes the crumb of bread from his hand suggests healing, sublimation, the feminine side of man, or any number of other meanings, which accounts for Trout's difficulty in interpreting it. And yet the "unswaying stem" and the "somber wedge" carry phallic overtones. That the dream elicited a sense of foreboding in Bill is apparent in the final lines in which he questions the source of "That fluent evil, an adjunct evil brewing?"

There are likely multiple sources for Trout's interest in dreams. His Millersville student Dianne Danz recalled that in class he often talked about dreams and once recommended she read *Footfalls on the Boundary of Another World* (1860) by Robert Dale Owen (1801-1877),in which she reported him saying, "the author believed that in sleep, all boundaries disappear and we can wander in the future as easily as we do in the past when we are awake." Owen was born in Scotland, and in 1825 accompanied his father, Robert Owen, to the United States to help him found the cooperative community of New Harmony in Indiana. One of the rationalist reformers of the 1830s who stressed solutions to social evils rather than peddling lurid descriptions of vice, as many of his contemporaries did, Robert Dale Owen actively supported women's rights, birth control, universal education, and the abolition of slavery. He served several terms in the Indiana legislature before being elected to the U. S. Congress (1843-1847). While serving as an American diplomat in Italy, he became a spiritualist before writing *Footfalls on the Boundary of Another World.* Also not to be ignored as a possible influence on Trout's interest in dreams is the work of Edgar Allan Poe. Steeped in popular antebellum reform tracts, particularly those by evangelical temperance crusaders, and newspaper articles about violent crime, Poe, according to David Reynolds, drew on their dark and sensational rhetoric to create "images of perversity and terror" he used in his stories and poems, among them "Spirits of the Dead," "Dreams," "A Dream within a Dream," in which he asks "Is *all* that we see or seem / But a dream within a dream?"; and particularly "Dream-Land," in which Poe says he has reached a land "Haunted by ill angles only," a place "Out of Space—out of Time" (see Leopold 1940; Reynolds 1988, 44-45, 70).

Trout's search for self-knowledge led him to *Psychological Types*, one of Jung's most important books, and possibly his most famous, though *Modern Man in Search of a Soul* is probably better known among the general public. Jung drew on mythology, religion, philosophy, literature, and case studies from his years as a clinical psychiatrist in describing psychological types. While acknowledging the existence of individual differences, he identifies two types—extraverted and introverted—each containing its own secondary or subtypes. The interests and attention of the extravert Jung points out, "are directed to objective happenings, particularly those in his immediate environment." On the other hand, the introvert orients himself not by objective data but by "subjective factors." What we know of Bill's personality seems to place him among the introverts, albeit with individual differences allowed for by Jung. The general characteristics of the introvert according to Jung include: "extreme sensitivity," mistrust of the new and the strange, and resistance to change. The "Introverted Thinking Type," according to Jung, is "strongly influenced by ideas, though his ideas [as distinct from the extravert's] have their origins not in objective data but in his subjective foundation," and in which intuition and feeling figure prominently in his perceptions. He tends to be impractical, non-competitive, and have a "horror of publicity." He tends to shut himself off from outside influences: "Thus his isolation gradually increases," Jung notes; to which Bill responded by writing "Happily" in the margin. The introvert "thinks his withdrawal into ever-increasing solitude will protect him from the unconscious influences," Jung observes, "but as a rule it only plunges him deeper into the conflict that is destroying him from within"—to which Bill wrote "True" in the margin. But Jung's assertion that introverts are poor teachers is not true in Trout's case; though Bill's self-image may explain why he made no marginal response to Jung's claim (Jung 1971, 334, 373-380, 383-384, 386-407).

According to Jung "Neurosis is self-division"—the inability of an individual to "harmonize nature and culture [the complexities of modern civilization] within himself"—and is not explainable by Freud's "one-sided and exclusive" sexual theory (Jung 1953, 18-19, 27). Among the topics Jung discusses in his exploration of ways for dealing with neurosis in order to gain both self-knowledge and psychic wholeness that received the most attention from Trout (measured by his marginal notes and underlining) are: religion, "a persistent attachment to the dead," ghosts or spirits, a "mother-complex," "an unbearable sensitivity" that leads to a "feeling of inferiority," the need to balance introversion and extraversion, the need to integrate the conscious and the unconscious, the limitations of cognition/intellect/reason, and the importance of feeling/intuition/instinct (Jung 1960, *passim*). As is apparent from his letters, Bill appears to have had a tendency to experience negative emotional states, which combined with his shyness, self-consciousness, and low self-esteem seem to confirm him as neurotic, though this was probably not apparent to most of those who knew him. The obvious interest he took in those parts of Jung's writings that deal with neurosis (phobias, obsessions, compulsion, and so forth) is pretty compelling evidence that he recognized himself as neurotic. These topics also provide clues to the content of his poems, particularly those in which the subject or purpose may not be immediately apparent. There are at least eighty of Trout's poems that appear to be directly traceable to Jungian ideas and are particularly tough going for anyone not steeped in Jung's writings, and because of the way Trout condenses his ideas, uses symbolism and metaphor, unusual or archaic words, literary references, and coding. Among these more inscrutable poems is:

> Over the black line of a cloud island
> That inked the brooding dawn, the white burst
> Of a planet poured, and hushed the querulous Why
> With a cold opiate.—Appeasing thirst,
> Appeared a revenant so long forgotten
> That neutral Third forsook the trembling brim,
> Left the white fire, to study that besotted,
> Made drunken by an almost Missa hymn.
> Though Third was ignorant of the planet's name,
> He gathered revenant and pharos-blaze
> Into reprieve's prospect, unashamed,
> Knowing verbal-cipher for those rays
> Imported little.—But the acrid First
> Cried, "Fools," and the pretty scene dispersed.

The frequency with which Bill refers to his own aging in letters, even when he was only in his thirties, may explain his interest in Jung's discussion of the consequences of trying to carry the psychology of youth into adult life. It also sheds light on his closeness to students and young male friends and what they confided to him, thereby allowing him to live vicariously through them. James Cauller told me that when he was a teenager he often wondered why Bill took such an interest in him and why he wanted to know about his "little escapades" and why he was so keen to hear all the details of the kinds of "trouble" he and his friends got themselves into. As his students and young friends moved on with their lives, leaving Bill to his books and records, teaching, yard work, and the care of his mother, he was no doubt conscious of his missed opportunities, disappointments, and the sorrow of loss—of the "awful brevity" of experience and of having slept before evening, as Walter

Pater put it. As Jung observes, "for many people all too much unlived life remains ... so that they approach the threshold of old age with unsatisfied demands which inevitably turn their glances backward" (Jung 1960, 401). To which Trout responded in the margin: "The revenge of the unlived life." No wonder he found Proust so appealing, savored Millay's poems, particularly "First Fig," where she speaks of burning her candle at both ends. But the possibility of renewing his own youth through friendships with boys and young men also meant having to accept that as they grew up they would also grow away, which may explain both his attachment to the writings of Forrest Reid and why he identified so closely with the Marschallin in Richard Strauss' opera *Der Rosenkavalier*.

In his 1926 lecture "Spirit and Life," Jung observes that while "the 'living being' is the quintessence of the life of the body, so 'spirit' is the quintessence of the life of the mind," but suggests that the two may not be as separate and distinct as one may think; for, he insists: "Everything is mediated through the mind, translated, filtered, allegorized, twisted, even falsified by it." As "psychic experiences" manifesting themselves through affective, emotional means, the spiritual "cannot be proved to exist in the external world and cannot be understood rationally," thereby showing, according to Jung, that "our conscious mind does not express the whole of our human nature; it remains only a part" (Jung 1960, 326-327, 329, 332). Jung's examination of the origins and nature of religious beliefs, which he addresses often in his writings as a manifestation of the spiritual, was no doubt of interest to Trout in his own search for a faith to replace his rejection of conventional Christianity. He also found in Jung validation for his rejection of materialism and the uncritical acceptance of the narrow empiricism of modern science. Like Jung, he spurned the "gospel of materialism," which sees life as a function of matter and energy and claims that all psychic activity is physiological in origin, can be explained by mere "biochemical processes." Jung insists that

> one should never forget that science is simply a matter of intellect, and that the intellect is only one among several fundamental psychic functions and therefore does not suffice to give a complete picture of the world. For this, another function—feeling—is needed, too. Feeling often arrives at convictions that are different from those of the intellect, and we cannot always prove that the convictions of feeling are necessarily inferior. So we have every reason to grant our intellect only a limited validity.

Both Jung's assertion that emotions play an important part in the search for knowledge, particularly self-knowledge, and his insistence that psychology and philosophy are indissolubly linked resonated with Trout (Jung 1960, 280, 318, 343).

And as his marginal notes in Jung's books show, Bill also recognized a connection between the importance of symbols in Jungian psychology, specifically related to archetypes, and the Tarot. "*Symbols* are not allegories and not signs," Jung insists, "they are images of contents which for the most part transcend consciousness." He goes on to point out: "A symbol is an indefinite expression with many meanings, pointing to something not easily defined and therefore not fully known." And he even goes so far as to assert that symbols "express something that is little known or completely unknown." In his Commentary on *The Secret of the Golden Flower: A Chinese Book of Life* (a book Trout owned), Jung points out that the language of the conscious and the collective unconscious are different: "Therefore it is necessary to have the magic of the symbol which contains those primitive analogies that speak to the unconscious. The unconscious can be reached only by symbols, which is the reason why the process of individuation can never do without the symbol" (Jung 1956, 77, 124, 222; Jung 1962, 107). In his copy of J. E. Cirlot's *Dictionary of Symbols* Trout underlined the observation that a "symbolic connotation" in no way "annuls the material and specific validity of an object or action," that it does not render invalid "literal or historical meaning." When analyzing symbols, Cirlot observes, it is necessary to recognize: "Nothing is meaningless or neutral: everything is significant … the quantitative becomes qualitative in certain essentials … everything is serial … series are related one to another, and the components of each series are related as to meaning" (Cirlot 1962, xiv, xxxvi).

In many of the Jung books Trout owned, but most numerously in *Symbols of Transformation*, he noted in the margins how what the psychologist says relates to specific Tarot cards, for example the image of the Hanged Man. According to Arthur Waite: "The Tarot embodies symbolical presentations of universal ideas, behind which lie all the implicits of the human mind," which are truths "imbedded in the consciousness of all, though they have not passed into express recognition by ordinary means" (Waite 1959, 59). There can be no doubt that Jungian psychology had a profound impact on Trout's thought and poetry, particularly in his later years, in part because of its usefulness in understanding the Tarot. As Cirlot points out, "the Tarot cards comprise an image (comparable to that encountered in dreams) of the path of initiation," and that according to Jung they portray the "two different, but complementary" struggles faced in life by human beings: that involving others in the course of one's social life and calling, and the other with one's self "involving the process of individuation." What is more, Cirlot observes, the manner of these struggles relates to whether the personality of the individual is primarily extraverted or introverted (Cirlot 1962, 310). "After long, I begin to discover companionship in the Tarot, although I am less intuitive than a frying pan," Bill comments in a letter to me written at 3:50 A.M. on August 4, 1972. References to Tarot cards, of the Juggler for example, appear in a number of Bill's poems and have direct implications for aspects of his personality or experiences. But perhaps nowhere are these references more apparent than in "Two Ways," a poem that contrasts those people—symbolized by the Knight of Swords—who give their lives to the pursuit of success as measured by possessions, status, and power and those—symbolized by the Fool—who approach life not as a matter of accumulation and competition but as a means of feeding their imagination and enriching their inner life, the spirit, in harmony with nature and their fellow human beings, and are rewarded for "Eluding prudent servitude"—failing to adhere to the values of the dominant culture—with contempt and chastisement.

The Fool runs all the world's ways,
Eluding prudent servitude,
Watches the Jerseys drowse and graze
Knee-deep in meadow solitude
Of June, and sprawls to spy a school
Of nimble minnows. Profound Fool.

The Knight of Swords rides by, intent
On worldly business of import
To State and Fate, and proudly bent
To arrogate a princely sort.
Fool elevates his long spoon
In salutation. Knight flouts the loon.

Another June, while slipshod Fool
Communes with willows by the creek,
A pilgrim halts beside the pool
To scoop a palm meager, meek.
Fool draws from script a crust, elate
To share it with dismounted Hate.

There is some variation in the iconography and interpretation of the Fool in the Tarot deck. However, he is generally seen as symbolizing the spirit in search of experience (particularly that gained through intuition, the senses, or the flesh), a seeker after mysteries and enlightenment. He is preoccupied with musings and imagination, oblivious to earthly realities—a dreamer. He is imaged by Waite as a carefree youth striding through the mountains, face to the sky, accompanied by a dog and carrying a script (a wallet in which he carries his unused knowledge) at the end of a long pole, and unaware he is about to step over a precipice (representative of a "leap of faith"). Knights in general in the Tarot symbolize practical, confident, decisive men of purpose, with the Knight of Swords carrying the added meaning of direct action and aggressiveness (Cirlot 1962, 105-106; Rakoczi 1954, 27-28; Waite 1959, *passim*). Whether the poem is a philosophical observation on Trout's part, a rendering in verse of a key Tarot concept, a comment on the artist in relation to society, or a personal statement of how he sees himself in relation to the world is open to interpretation. The references to watching Jersey cows in a meadow, a school of nibbling minnows, and willows by a creek are common images found in Trout's poetry obviously referring to things he had known since childhood and to his connection to the land.

Among his books are several on magic and six on the Tarot. And he owned at least four complete Tarot decks, two of which he gave to Byron Detwiler in the 1960s; the others Frank Trout gave to me. The notes William Snyder took in Trout's Essay course at Millersville State College in 1963 document that three times during the summer session class Bill discussed the suits and trump cards of the Tarot deck and their relationship to symbolism in literature, and recommended books on the subject, further documenting his interest in the Tarot and the importance he attributed to it. On at least one of my afternoon visits to 920 Elm Avenue, Lancaster, I saw a Tarot hand Bill had laid out on the kitchen table, something Jeannette Dillman, the private-duty nurse who cared for Mrs. Trout in her final year, also remembered seeing. It may be through using the Tarot that he tried to make contact with his deceased mother, an idea that may have been suggested by other books he read.

As H. Stuart Hughes observes, "Even more than [Henri] Bergson, Jung turned increasingly toward mysticism in the course of his long life. And it is fair to say that his intellectual bent gave him a sense for the ambiguities of history, which was closer to that of the true historian than Freud's" (Hughes 1958, 156). That Jung recognized the importance and usefulness of telepathy, parapsychology, numerology, alchemy, magic, spirituality, and Eastern Philosophy (particularly as found in the *I Ching*, a copy of which Bill owned) for understanding humankind may have led to Trout's study of these subjects and to the incorporation of insights gleaned from them into his outlook on life and his creation of poetry. Among his books on the occult is Israel Regardie's *The Middle Pillar*, in which this founder of modern Western occultism made an assertion Trout may have found congenial: "Analytical Psychology and Magic comprise in my estimate two halves or aspects of a single technical system ... so psychology and Magic comprise similarly a single system whose goal is the integration of the human personality"—precisely what Bill seemed to be searching for and struggling to achieve (Regardie 1945, 16).

"Beginning in the 1850s," as R. Laurence Moore points out, "spiritualism became vastly popular in this country...Americans in astonishing numbers studied the reputations of a growing roster of professional mediums and crowded into séance rooms of those they judged the best." Among those with interest in spiritualism and the occult were such luminaries as the abolitionist William Lloyd Garrison, the journalist Horace Greeley, the novelist James Fenimore Cooper, and John Roebling, the civil engineer hired to build the Brooklyn Bridge. "Against the belief that nothing existed in the universe but matter," Moore explains, "spiritualists waged a steady, though confused, battle." They sought to "demonstrate the independent existence and endurance of spirit ... to prove that there was some life beyond this one." According to Levi St. Armand, Emily Dickinson's interest in spiritualism and the occult is important to understanding her thinking and therefore to understanding her poetry. In letters to friends she mentions, among other things that document knowledge of spiritualism, a conversation with her brother Austin about "the Extension of Consciousness," by using a "spirit pen" (*planchette*), a device employed by psychics in automatic writing and alchemy. She read occult fiction as well as Sir Thomas Browne and Robert and Elizabeth Barrett Browning, whose poetry held a special place in her affection. Among her poems that suggest acquaintance with spiritualism and the occult are: "Trust in the Unexpected," "Strong Draughts of Their Refreshing Minds," "The Poets light but Lamps," and "A Word made Flesh" (St. Armand 1977/1978, 345-357). Given Trout's enthusiasm for Dickinson's poetry and his own interest in spiritualism and the occult, it is probably safe to assume that he knew these poems and may have recognized their author's acquaintance with spiritualist ideas and practices. Based on his poems, letters, and the books he owned and annotated, it seems reasonable to conclude that, like Dickinson and John Cowper Powys, Bill's thought occupied the borderland between realism and spiritualism and is given voice in his poems.

In "Shiver of sudden gooseflesh raced the spine," a person (presumably Bill) sitting alone on a snowy evening becomes aware of the presence of a spirit in the room.

> Shiver of sudden gooseflesh raced the spine
> And scattered in a twitching of the nape.
> Seeing the snowfall swarm the trumpet vine,
> Hearing a silence whispering "Escape,"
> And "Saved," incredulous, we breathed, and turned
> Shaken, to catch at causal commonplace,
> Stirred the soup, and blessed the fire for burning
> Loyally, plodding its steady pace.
> But flickered at the window-ledge a flurry
> Of junco wings; a triad of smooth heads
> Bobbed over seeds the snow was hurrying
> To hide, the lean supper before bed-time:
> Warned by the Three, deceived became aware
> Of shadowy Presence in the usual chair.

Who is the "shadowy Presence in the usual chair" whose presence is signaled by a twitching in the neck and the fluttering juncos at the window feeder? Is it Trout's deceased mother, some other relative, or a malevolent spirit, as the whispered words "Escape" and "Save" suggest? Though they may have secondary symbolic meaning depending on their type and color, birds are generally symbolic of spiritualization and may according to culture or context be interpreted as symbolic of the human soul. Whether this poem records a conscious event Bill experienced or a dream is uncertain. But there seems to be no doubt that the poem "Unseen" deals with an ancient malevolent spirit, though its exact origin and nature remain a mystery.

> Under the shadow of that island we shall never go again,
> Let its elms feather never so alluringly in the hot July,
> Bending to dip green finger-tips in the smooth stream;
> We shall not there propel the clumsy boat, nor in those
>   dark waters drop the bright fly;

For the redwing whistle from far off across the dappled
fastness,
A call that flutes over green cascading, over dark water,
over amber stubble-field,
Is a primitive portent, as now to our grief we guess—
We know—having weathered-out one storm that up from behind
that island lurched suddenly and reeled.

The deceitfully whistling redwing was seductive emissary
Of That which dwells and glides and gloats under the elms,
among straggling hawthorn and witch-hazel—
Something that was here before the Algonquin wandered, dully
aware, bluntly wary—
Spirit that had stared malignly at a spawning tepid tide,
and even then began to spin the evil spell.

This poem contains references to things suggestive of Jungian archetypes and to the dangers with which the unconscious is fraught. In myth and legend the Red-winged Blackbird is connected to primal feminine energies and to Cancer, the sign of the Zodiac under which Trout was born, July 17, and to which an allusion is made in the poem. The bird's whistle is called a "primitive portent" by the poem's speaker, who has already experienced a "storm" associated with this island, where a malignant spirit dwells and spins evil spells. We are told the "deceitfully whistling redwing was seductive emissary" of this spirit that has haunted the island—"before the Algonquin wandered" the land. It is unlikely that we will ever know whether this poem had its origins in an actual life experience or came as a dream out of the unconscious.

Of particular interest are two books Bill owned (*Why I Believe in Personal Immortality* and *Raymond, Or Life and Death With Examples of the Evidence for Survival of Memory and Affection After Death*) written by Sir Oliver Lodge in the years after the 1914-18 war, when interest in contacting those killed in the conflict was in vogue, which may have led Bill to make similar attempts to contact his deceased mother. In *Why I Believe in Personal Immortality*, a book containing sections on psychical research, clairvoyance, and methods of communication and mediumship, Lodge asserts "that individual character and memory do persist" after death and that because "the mind can act independently of bodily organs," it is possible under certain circumstances to have "telepathic communication with those who have survived the death of the body," a claim Dr. Charles A. Mercier exposed as unscientific, winning May Sinclair's applause, but also her criticism for his views on telepathy and clairvoyance (Lodge 1929, 19-20, 75; Boll 1973, 257). Bill underlined and made marginal notes, including references to Jung and Stewart Edward White, on nearly every page of Lodge's book, which dated annotations testify he was reading in 1970-71.

In the mid-1970s Bill read *The Job of Living*, *Anchors to Windward: Stability and Personal Peace-Here and Now*, and *The Stars Are Still There*, all published in the 1940s by the American author Stewart Edward White and based on material "channeled" to him by his wife, which White believed provided valuable information for the interpretation of daily life. White also describes how achieving a meditative state could help facilitate "channeling" with a "medium." Bill's skepticism about White's ideas is apparent by such repeated marginal comments as "All the weary abstractions" and "Always the abstraction – nothing concrete." However, it is important to note that some of the books Trout owned (including these by White), mostly those published after his mother's death, contain her initials, A.G.L.T. (Alice Gray Livingston Trout), and a date. Might Bill have believed that writing her initials in books would serve something like a talismanic or perhaps a telepathic function, a way of keeping open communication with her? Some books with her initials contain messages. For example, a volume on the painter Pieter Bruegel the Elder has a dried maple leaf taped to its fly leaf and this message: "11.1.77 (All Saints' Day) a.m., mardi, My dear, it struck my shoulder as it fell." He also wrote two poems ("Near All Hallows" and "Past All Hallows, past All Saints") relating to All Souls Day—the day of remembrance and prayer for those who have departed this life. Among his poems that allude to making contact with the dead is this one addressing his mother, hinting at his confessed "tippling" and admitting being a prisoner of maternal love. He wrote:

> Not knowing what to do, I wait,
> And drug the mind, and move the hands
> Through trivial tasks, to dissipate
> The flocks of phantoms, rising fast
> Out of the black swamps of the past,
> Those drearily revolted lands.
> Not knowing well to wait, I pray,
> In silent wordlessness, in haste,

Since there, gaunt upon the way,
Madness lurks, in ambush crouched,
Twinned with terror, slyly couched,
While death runs laughing through the waste.
I pray to you alone, because
I never knew another good;
Your beauty made my proper laws;
Your charity was stars and sun;
And in your steady light was run
My destined course of servitude.

At the core of spiritualism is the belief that at death the personality of the deceased is transferred to another plane of existence with which communication from the world of the living is possible through a medium. Such contact between the living and the dead is the subject of some of Trout's poems, among them "With supplicating eyes, the dead return" and "You seem to come between the page."

It may be that Trout's study of Jung encouraged an interest in other areas of knowledge that went beyond the confines of empirical science and rational thought. Jung says he uses the term irrational "not as denoting something *contrary* to reason, but something *beyond* reason, something, therefore, not grounded in reason." He goes on to observe: "Practical psychology stirs up many problems that are not susceptible to rational solutions, but can only be settled irrationally, in a way not in accord with the laws of reason" (Jung 1971, 454-455). One of these is the concept of synchronicity, the inexplicable coincidence of a psychic experience and an actual event. Another is unexplained events or phenomena. Bill owned the one-volume edition of *The Complete Books of Charles Fort*, a 1974 reprint of books published between 1919 and 1932; however, there is no record that he read Fort before he purchased the collected edition. Charles Fort (1874-1932) gathered data from newspapers, scientific journals, and other periodicals from all over the world on anomalous phenomena—poltergeist sightings, levitation, reports of unidentified flying objects and extraterrestrial events, strange objects found in unlikely places, or animals living outside their normal range—which are ignored or dismissed by most scientists. His books report on objects and occurrences normally referred to as occult, supernatural, and paranormal. An interest in such phenomena may explain why Bill read so carefully, but not uncritically, Charles Berlitz's *The Bermuda Triangle* (1974) in which the author explores not only the unexplained disappearance of ships and planes in the Atlantic Ocean between Bermuda and the Bahamas but time-space warps and unexplained phenomena in other parts of the world and at different times in history.

The first documented indication that Bill wrote verse is in a letter to Don Smith dated 20 March 1944 in which he self-effacingly admits: "... if I try to ride my peculiar and innocent hobby-horse, I turn out stuff that is a combination of Ella Wheeler Wilcox and E. A. Guest and I regard myself with horror and revulsion." In an October 1945 letter he tells Smith: "... my secret vice of trying to make verses never leaves me, much as I am ashamed of it; the lesson of EAR's [Edwin Arlington Robinson] Amaranth doesn't sink in." (Robinson's poem describes the disappointment, frustration, and failure of mediocre poets, composers, artists, and others who refuse to recognize their lack of talent and who continue to pursue their muses or professions in the face of public indifference, resign themselves to their mediocrity, or in utter despair commit suicide.) Although he did not share his poetry with Smith or discuss its content or the reasons he began writing verse, in the 1970s, as he told me, writing poetry was for him therapeutic, which suggests that his later poems differed significantly from those he had written in the 1940s and '50s. And in a letter to me of 30 May 1971 he explains that by writing "a journal, by free association ... [of] whatever bubbles to the surface of the cloacae—of the psyche" he had found a means of "psychic catharsis," a way of "draining the abscess" and "cleansing the Augean stables." But he goes on to say, that trying to learn to know oneself through "verbal externalization" was "a horrible process, dreadful, and frequently very, very dangerous." In other letters to me he refers to his poems as "insane doggerel," a "batch of imbecile jingles," and "psychiatric records—secret[s] of the confessional." Although Bill's poems are often self-referential, they embody what many people experience in their quest for self-knowledge or inner peace. A work that captures the essence of such struggles is "Search":

Along these gross corridors
I quest and stumble, fumble and grope;
Distant, muted, all mortal wars
Shrink in bruit, dwindle in scope,
In contrast to my restless search,
High and higher; the stairs grow steep,
Crumble, and accumulate

Obstacles to the blinded touch.
Here the skeleton watchmen sleep—
Drowsy espials sleeping late;
But I creep on, not caring much
Except that on and on I creep,
Since ahead the shadow goes,
At whose side only is repose.

Bill also deals with the process of self-exploration metaphorically using striking imagery in this short poem:

The day's imperative history
Lies always in, toward unexplored
Terrain of mountain, swamp, and mist,
Of forest, and of storm untoward.
Dimly the outer days go by
Like shadows on a sea of wheat,
The cloud shadows cast from high,
Remote dazzle.—All defeat—
The gleaned grain of mythic sheaves—
Lies in, in land of talking leaves.

The truth of Jung's claim "All that I experience is psychic" seems to have been acknowledged by Trout, as was the need to penetrate the "obscurity and darkness" of our being if one wishes to achieve completeness, individuation. Failure to engage in self-examination, Jung says, leads over the years to "stagnation and desiccation of the soul. Our convictions become platitudes ground out on a barrel organ, our ideals become starchy habits; enthusiasm stiffens into automatic gestures." Thus Jung believes that "If we should risk a little introspection, coupled perhaps with an energetic attempt to be honest for once with ourselves, we may get a dim idea of all the wants, longings, and fears that have accumulated down there [in the unconscious]—a repulsive and sinister sight" (Jung 1960, 353, 389; Jung 1956, 357).

Bill's belief in the necessity of understanding the spiritual and instinctual elements of his psyche was no doubt predicated on Jung's insistence that: "A psychology that satisfies the intellect alone can never be practical, for the totality of the psyche can never be grasped by the intellect alone." He also accepted the truth of Jung's assertion that our fantasies are our own but that the physical and spiritual passions are "brothers-in-arms" and "a being without opposites is completely unthinkable." Having read the *I Ching* Trout was familiar with the Taoist idea of two complementary forces at work in the universe: the dark, passive female principle represented by the *yin* and the active, bright male principle of the *yang*. The idea of opposites, which so fascinated Bill and informs so much of his thought and poetry, includes: good/evil, cognition/intuition, materialism/mysticism, nature/spirit, rational/irrational. The quest for self-knowledge and psychic wholeness involves recognizing the dark side of one's being—what Jung identifies as "shadow," by which he means "the 'negative' side of the personality, the sum of all those unpleasant qualities we like to hide, together with insufficiently developed functions and the contents of the personal unconscious." Yet even the shadow has a duality according to Jung: it "is on one side regrettable and reprehensible weakness, on the other side healthy instinctivity and the prerequisite for higher consciousness." To "live without self-deception or self-delusion," Jung points out, involves the recognition that self-knowledge, "wholeness" comes only when a person knows the two sides of his nature—both "how much good he can do, and what crimes he is capable of" (Jung 1953, 29, 32-34, 53, 94, 65n).

As his lecture on Goethe's *Faust* testifies, Trout drew on Jung in his college classes. Following his discussion of Faust's "yearning for the remote, the unusual, the unattainable" in his quest for "the ultimate in personal growth," which plunged him into the abyss, Bill quotes Jung to make Goethe's poem resonate with his twentieth-century students: "Man conquers not only nature but the spirit also, without realizing what he is doing." Jung said that *Faust* "awakened in me the problem of opposites, of good and evil, of mind and matter, of light and darkness. Faust … encounters the dark side of his being, his sinister shadow, Mephistopheles, who … represents the true spirit of life…" (Jung 1973, 235). The Jungian image of the "shadow" symbolizing the primitive or instinctive side of the personality with all its negative connotations leads Bill toward self-knowledge in poems like "Search."

But such self-examination is fraught with danger, as Jung warned and as Bill found out. In the mid-1960s he offered advice on what to avoid in writing poetry to one of his Millersville students and a fledgling poet, William Snyder, after reading a poem of his about turning one's eyes inward. In Snyder's words, Bill cautioned him: "Don't mess with your unconscious. Let it alone. If you poke around in it, there's no telling what kind of horrors you will stir up." However, in a letter to me postmarked 20 November 1971 Bill ventures: "A broken word of acrid wisdom: study yourself, learn to know yourself, and do not be shaken by the enormities that the psyche is capable of casting up during the unbroken succession of storms that seem to be human life." This was the course Bill followed himself because he understood the need for self-analysis, as the passage from Michel de Montaigne's essay "Of Solitude" he quoted in a January 1971 letter to me suggests: "The greatest thing in the world is to know how to belong to ourselves." Writing poetry was one way for Trout to try to know himself.

Jung's writings were an important source, but not the only one, for Trout's interest in non-cognitive approaches to knowledge. His interest in intuition, spiritualism, and other alternatives to reason and empirical science as ways of knowing are important to understanding the man and his poetry. To know one's self, Jung argues, means reexamining our unquestioning faith in rationalism and science, which disparage and dismiss the value of myth, dreams, parapsychology, and the instinctual in achieving personal wholeness. "Rationalism and doctrinarism," he is convinced, "are the disease of our time; they pretend to have all the answers." The more they dominate us "the more impoverished life becomes," Jung insists. The approach to education taken by Western societies he believes bears much of the blame for keeping people from achieving self-knowledge and realizing their potential because education "promulgates the old generalizations and says nothing about the secrets of private experience"; it leads people to look for external rules and regulations and teaches "idealistic beliefs or conduct which people know in their hearts they can never live up to" any more than can those in authority who preach such things knowing that "they themselves have never lived up to these high standards and never will" (Jung 1973, 300-302, 330). Such views would have struck a responsive chord with Trout, who repeatedly lamented his forty years of teaching as nothing more than "mental prostitution" and help to explain his willingness to challenge the conventions and unexamined beliefs of the dominant culture—to get young people to question what was taken for granted by mainstream society—that so impressed them and led some, like his Gap pupil Norma Patterson, to say that while he was "rather peculiar and had strange ideas … it was a privilege to know him."

The specificity, clarity, and vividness of the images found in so much of Trout's poetry suggest that his mind or thought processes were photographic in nature. And there is also ample evidence that the inspiration for some of his poems came from family snapshots. Jung maintains that "the psyche consists essentially of images"—some "acoustic," others "visual," and still others of "feeling"; consequently, "we live immediately only in the world of images," many of which are archetypes, ever shifting, translated, filtered symbolic elements of spirit and instinct found in the collective unconscious. "The years when I was pursuing my inner images" Jung recalls, "were the most important in my life—in them everything essential was decided" must have had a powerful influence on Trout and encouraged him to search his own past (Jung 1953, 76; Jung 1960, 322-333; Jung 1973, 192-193, 199). Not surprisingly, many of Bill's poems appear to incorporate aspects of Jungian psychology, including the use of archetypical imagery and color symbolism. Even without its title, "Unprofessional Psychiatry" suggests its roots in Trout's study of Jung:

> Strangely familiar in the inner landscape
> The untameable horrors grow—the fiend unseen
> That tilted bright day from the horizontal,
> And turned the summer fields to fever's dream
> Of mouthing madness; too, the desolate ape,
> Dragging cerements, uttering his primitive call.
>
> These wax familiar as the days shorten
> Into life's autumn.
> Then shall the fiend be tame,
> At last, to carry faggots for the fire
> And water from the well? Even this same
> Ape of madness become Lob that, for
> His bowl of cream, is effort that does not tire?
> Creatures of grief and horror, of fear and shame,
> Sometimes grow household beings, with humble names.

Poems like this one with its eerie mood and unsettling monster may come out of Trout's reading of Jung or may be traced to the influence of other poets or fiction writers. In all likelihood such poems have multiple sources. The imagery of his "horror" poems may owe something to what David Reynolds calls "the voyeur style" of antebellum reform tracts, penny newspapers, police gazettes and trial reports, and popular literature, that contained "titillating descriptions of debauchery and seduction," sensational crimes, "psychopathic states," "perversity," and nightmare visions that found their way into the work of such major writers as Poe, Melville, and Hawthorne, all authors Bill knew well (Reynolds 1988, 85, 44-45, 70, 225, 236-237, 124, 133, 178, 258). Responding in a letter of 11 October 1943, to Don Smith's apparent confession of "relish[ing] movie thrillers," Bill admits that "for an hour a day I sit reading murder thrillers (Ellery Queen!) to Allie [his mother], and we both relish them." He relates to Smith in a letter of 29 September 1945 that on a sleepless night he read a "masterpiece," Jules Barbey d'Aurevilly's *Les Diaboliques*. Barbey d'Aurevilly (1808-1889), whom Mario Praz calls a "Holy Father of the Decadents," was a French novelist, short story writer, and literary critic who held reactionary political views, and was a dandy and a favorite of fin-de-siècle decadents. In spite of his vehement Catholicism, his writings are characterized by their sadistic and licentious content in which "pleasure and horror are closely intertwined," à la Marquis de Sade (Praz 1933, 311-314). Of *Les Diaboliques*, a collection of six stories, each about a woman (a classic fin-de-siècle femme fatale) who commits violent crimes or acts of revenge, Trout says: "Style of a perverse, panther-like, eerie grace-world-weary, aching with beauty, electric with those frightening overtones we all catch sometimes but can never articulate. And the story! A revolting and breathless and magnificent tale of human horrors. The man is a devil. But what a devil. Gilles de Rais [a wealthy French nobleman, occultist, sodomite, and serial child-killer hanged in 1440 for ritually murdering between 80 and 200 boys and girls] writing fiction." These short stories (in keeping with the prevailing interest of the times in Satanism), as Jean Pierrot points out, "depict the devil's influence in an interiorized form, acting not upon the world of perceptible phenomena but directly upon the human consciousness, thereby leading some of those so assailed to choose the path of evil" (Pierrot 1981, 90). Such literature fits with Trout's interest in the macabre, black magic, the occult, and the Tarot mentioned in his letters as well as his interest in Jung's idea of the "shadow," the dark side of the human personality. But there were likely other literary sources (as will be discussed in more detail in Chapters 7 and 8) that contributed to Bill's writing of ghost and "horror" poems.

According to F. O. Matthiessen, most of America's poets active from the mid-nineteenth century into the mid-twentieth can "in the broadest terms ... be described as descendants of Whitman or as descendants of Poe" (Matthiessen 1950, xxvii). The horrifying elements in some of Trout's psychological poems, among them "Unprofessional Psychiatry," "Compulsion," "Onset," and "Invasion," one might speculate owe something to Philip Freneau's (1752-1832) poetry ("The House of Night—A Vision") or Edgar Allan Poe's (1809-1849) crime and detective stories ("The Black Cat," "The Murders in the Rue Morgue," "The Tell-Tale Heart." "The Pit and the Pendulum") and verse ("The Sleeper," "Dreams," "Spirits of the Dead," "The Bells"). As with Poe, Trout's "horror" poems reflect the psychology of dream states through the uncertainty of the shadowy scene or setting, the inclusion of repugnant creatures and monsters, and an atmosphere of eerie uncertainty heightened by strange and ominous noises. It is the ambiguity of the threat and the seeming isolation and helplessness of the victim that make Trout's "horror" poems so spooky, as in:

> Nothing is safe. No corner of the dwelling
> Defends in such expedient degree
> As would permit the hunted to repel
> The Wheeling Monster, crafty in Its glee.
> Out of the dry darkness of the attic
> The Bat drops, fanning Its webbed crescents;
> And up the cellar stairs, the scaly Rat
> Hops. A Warning atom shrills ingress.
> Slide no useless bolt. Do not cast
> Frenetic confidence in bar or key.
> No subterfuge remains where dread can hide.
> Declining flight, the victim now abides
> The gloating climax, —But, until the last
> Foul invasion, memory's wings are free.

In "Threat" Trout builds tension by evoking an eerie mood with "failing light," the sound of wind and spinning leaves, "furtive noise," menacing silence, and a "rat beneath the stair":

> There is someone strange near the house tonight.
> The rat beneath the stair,
> The wind abroad in the failing light,
> The leaves on the crisping air—
> By stealthy movement, furtive noise,
> By silence menacing,
> Each reveals it is aware
> Of malignance that deploys
> Its gliding force, encircling
> Our center of despair.
>
> We so not speak the word of fear;
> We turn the usual task
> With wonted hands, but hearts veer
> To the question each must ask.

A stranger is at the door tonight.
The first flakes swirl, the last leaves spin;
Hand in hand fly wind and light. . . .
Already the foe has stolen in.

In poems such as "Unprofessional Psychiatry," he refers to the "Creatures of grief and horror, of fear and shame" who populate his "inner landscape" and threaten to drive him mad. Nightmares possibly associated with a sense of guilt or shame and perhaps related to his sexual orientation threaten his mental stability in poems like "Onset."

In sleep or wake, appears the fiend,—
Who knows where born, how subtly armed?
By wile and craft, he has gleaned
Venoms with which the outland swarmed.

He is timeless: in five decades
The vileness has not altered more
Than the visage of this Prince of Shades—
This spiritual carnivore.

Worse than his withering of the quailing
Prey, he darkens love, and sends
The spirit to grope, faltering, failing,
Where ultimate loneliness attends.

But love can win—and not its first
Victory: across the waste,
The timeless fiend, in time immersed,
Wavers before love's patient haste.

To interpose the rose that holds
A pentecostal power. Thus
Spirit is steadied, and emboldens
To wait love's charity and grace.

And yet for all of its imagery of ogres, torture, and suffering the last two quatrains of the poem offer hope and comfort. The "spiritual carnivore" can be vanquished by a "pentecostal power," which in time will bestow "love's charity and grace." But even more frightening is "Compulsion" (a poem freighted with the symbolism of carnal lust and suggestions of illicit desire and congenital weakness) in which an ape (a Christian symbol associated with the devil and eroticism), one of a number of fiends to appear in Trout's poems, terrorizes its victim. Who or what does this fiend represent? Might it be another manifestation of Trout's struggle with his repressed homosexuality?

> The ape that rides the shoulders and sucks the brains
> Out through the skull's fissures—that grossly lewd
> Lampoon of seemliness only refrains
> To reach repletion, because his line is bred
> Illicitly of man's seed; gourmet, bent
> On sipping all, on savouring the strangled wail
> Of the wretched ridden, he does not wish soon spent
> His delectation; gliding the pleased tail
> About the victim's neck, he clucks in glee
> To palate creation's insufficiency.

The expression of mental anguish, even terror, in these poems, and particularly in "Invasion," contain images of Trout's tormenters that call to mind the demons representing the follies and vices of humankind depicted in the paintings of Hieronymus Bosch (1450?-1516), specifically in his triptych *Temptation of Saint Anthony* (Gibson 1973, 140-150), an image Bill knew from a book on Bosch he owned.

> They glide and slide, they slink and peer,
> They titter at the latch, and then
> They nudge the door, to bob and leer—
> This spawn of quagmire, marsh, and fen.
> And then they push and crowd, invade,—
> Obscene pollutions, all the stench
> Of treachery and ambuscade:
> The helpless self must stare and blench,
> And stare in horror; can not lift
> A limp arm in his defense
> Against this shoaling, loathsome drift—
> Time's malignant recompense.
>
> Is there no hope? And is it doom
> Foregone and final, that must fall,
> To such a foe, love's taintless room,

That now should be but grief's bare hall,
Whitened wall and floor of stone?
With a last despairing groan
Can love not kill, and so atone,—
Destroy, and be once more alone?

A number of Trout's "horror" poems can also be read as "confessional poems," a topic explored in Chapter 9, in that they reveal his personal anxieties, sense of guilt or shame, self-doubts, phobias, frustrations, loneliness, hidden desires, and deepest secrets, albeit coded or wrapped in metaphor and symbolism. They represent his application of Jungian psychology in an attempt to achieve self-knowledge, individuation.

In discussing Emily Dickinson's poem "One need not be a chamber – to be Haunted," Domhnall Mitchell raises an issue that may contribute to our understanding of Trout's "horror" poems by noting, "there is no essential difference between the ghosts of the world and the ghosts of the mind—it may seem as if external ghosts have internal origins and that internal ghosts have external origins ..." (Mitchell 2000, 54). Yet both Dickinson and Trout focus on "the interior drama of the mind," which can be more terrifying than any external threat. But whereas Dickinson's horrific imagery seems to owe something to her fascination with sensational journalism and the reform literature of her day, as David Reynolds asserts, Trout's has other origins (Reynolds 1988, 433-438). It is difficult, if not impossible to determine if such poems came from Trout's conscious imagination or were manifestations of his unconscious in the form of dreams or nightmares he may have been trying to interpret using Jungian methods. One suspects that the origins can be found in both. As noted earlier, there is direct evidence that the genesis of the poem "Some flagged corridor of exit—more" was a dream Bill had in 1974. Other poems—"The Price of Sleep," "Communication," and "In dream, a voice, like that of some glib guide"—not included herein clearly had similar origins.

We also know from Trout's letters to Don Smith, accounts from several of his former students and friends, and from the poems themselves (for example "Through the ebbing fumes of midnight wine") that Bill drank alcoholic beverages on a pretty regular basis, perhaps in part to relieve his loneliness and the pressures that came with his responsibilities as both a full-time teacher and the sole care-giver for his mother. In a favorable response to the news that Don Smith had taken to drinking a "little beer" with his army buddies, Bill says in a letter postmarked 1 November 1943 that even though *The Rubáiyát of Omar Khayyám* "has fallen into disrepute, I still think the wine quatrain [which he quotes] the best thing that has been written on the subject." He then tells Smith: "The things I love are [because of the war] practically non-existent—whiskey and gin. Rum—on which I could subsist—sells for exorbitant prices that I can't pay. So I don't drink too much alcohol, but live on strong coffee ... and cigarettes...." It may well be that the strange dreams or nightmares he turned into poems were due partly to sleep-deprivation (we know he stayed up late at night), to alcohol consumption, and to the books he read, including Jung. Yet Bill's drinking, which some might see as "a problem" given the number of people who mentioned that he "liked his beer" or "liked his liquor," does not seem to have interfered with either his teaching or his writing. Nor did any of my informants mention ever seeing Bill "in his cups." Nonetheless, concern about heavy drinking is given voice in "Street Scene" when he comes face to face with a victim of demon rum.

There in the dingy, bitter
Street of dirty snow,
What could have been fitter—
Life dragging slow—
Than the spreading fungus nose, the greasy
Cap, the eyes bleared and boozy?

Clumsy, stumbling feet
Stopped, then shuffled by.
(Once the mouth was sweet,
Young.) Like a shrill cry
Came the demonic, jibing prod:
"There, but for the Grace of God. . . ."

Not a few of his books, but mainly the Jung volumes, contain large coffee stains and burn marks from fallen ashes or dropped cigarettes that are as likely to have been caused by concentration on the text, to jotting marginal notes, to arthritic hands in later life, or to dozing off momentarily as to the effects of alcohol.

In a lecture on *The Rubáiyát of Omar Khayyám* (a work that deals with the effects of time on man and the transience of things temporal) that Trout gave to his Millersville World Literature classes, we get some insight into his views on alcohol. He pointed out that Omar said what eight hundred years later the American psychologist and philosopher William James observed, "the exaltation derived from religion and the exaltation derived from alcohol are basically the same." He then read a long passage from the "Mysticism" chapter of James' *The Varieties of Religious Experience* about the effects of drugs and alcohol on consciousness, concluding his discussion of the mystical side of the Persian poet by stressing two points: "for Omar, wine was the key that momentarily unlocked the door that the Dervish howled without; and, second, that no confirmed addict of alcohol or drugs ever produced a body of enduring work." And then as a sort of postscript, adds: "And, musical or not, if you have ever been subjected to the experience of the last five quartets of Beethoven, you will understand that William James's 'requisite stimulus' to an awareness, however teasingly fleeting, of those 'entirely different forms of consciousness' may be something other than vodka or morphine—in fact a 'requisite stimulus' more to be depended upon and less destructive to the nervous tissue."

Although liquor and morphine are depressants not stimulants, Trout was right that like music they could affect one's consciousness and dreams. A letter to Don Smith of 13 November 1943, suggests that Bill may have thought about experimenting with illegal drugs. "There is a point on the avenue back of the [Lukens Steel] mill," he explains, "where, they say, you can procure 'snow' if you know the right word. I am tempted to have a whack at the 'drowsy syrops [Old French spelling] of the East.' " Smith apparently expressed disappointment that Bill would consider taking cocaine. In a reply to him postmarked 13 December 1943 Trout thanks him for "that scrap of paternal advice about my slight deflection from code." But he goes on to say, "you mistook the motive, which was not an attempt at bohemianism, but just an effort to escape a little from the general damnation of existence," which he pleads resulted from his "own pathetic failure to 'measure up' and the general hellishness of existence." He assures Smith there was little danger that he would become an addict since "the stuff is vilely adulterated, the dangers of procuring it are [not] exaggerated, and there are a couple of people who might be embarrassed by any stew I might get into." He then ends the topic on a testy note by telling Smith not to "ever again anger me [by] trying to make me think anybody does or ever did 'look up to me' as you so artlessly (or cruelly) phrase it."

There are other factors to be considered in piecing together the genesis of Trout's inward-looking and "horror" poems, as well as those that take more serious psychological disturbance as their subject. Evidence exists that some members of his family may have suffered serious emotional instability. Several former Gap students remember that late in her career Mary Livingston's strange behavior in the classroom (something Alice Trout Smith referred to as "fits") led her pupils more than once to summon another teacher and may explain the timing of her retirement. According to Alice Trout Smith, during his freshman year at Penn State Bill's brother John suffered a nervous breakdown and came home to Gap to recuperate. Many years later, after Bill's death, John, who was in his eighties, drowned himself in the Octorara Creek. John's teenage grandson also committed suicide. The poem "Autumn/Watching" mentions a suicide forty years earlier that "tainted / Thus the family." Bill admits to Don Smith in a letter of 13 November 1943: "The encroachment of age" and "a general hopelessness ... have combined to make me suicidally depressed...." In the poem "Let us leave him in the hallway, go in, and shut the door," the subject is unsympathetically accused of "neurotic shifts of mood from gloom to laughter," which seems to suggest that Trout knew someone, perhaps even himself, suffering from manic-depressive illness. And in the poem "Not knowing what to do, I wait," Trout writes: "Madness lurks, in ambush crouched." In a letter to me of 30 May 1971 he says he was stricken "with horror that my childishness has permitted you to see the wretched jingles" [his poems], the product of "the vagaries of senility," and closes by quoting Shakespeare: " 'let me not be mad, kind Heaven.' But Heaven has not been kind either to Lear nor to me." What appears to be a memory (or dream, perhaps) of an attempt to haul someone off in an ambulance to the psychiatric ward is the subject of "Removal Manqué." (Manqué comes from the French *manquer*, to fail, and indicates frustration in the fulfillment of one's aspirations or talents.)

These try to tug the mind-sick from his chair—
Two white-starched healers, male and female, glib,
Briskly canting. What household Judas dares
Admit this oily Adam and his rib?
The motor, murmuring docile at the door,
Discreetly bends to baffle, if it can,
The window titillation peering, pouring
Avidly across the winter rain.
Mind-sick is desperate; but when resistance
Slumps in crumbling terror, then the twisted
Mouth invokes the Gone.—As in the past,
At every crossroad crisis, grace invests

> Chaos with calm, summarily dismissing
> Rib and rib-cage, Judas boarding last.

While poems like this and the "horror" and dream poems as well, may have multiple sources, there can be no doubt that they owe something to Trout's study of Jungian psychology.

The early twentieth-century intellectual climate of opinion in which Trout grew to manhood, including the revolutionary impact of Albert Einstein's theory of relativity (1916), called into question the idea of fixed laws of nature such as the determinable reality of time and space outside of individual consciousness, and led other physicists to assert the impossibility of the orderly sequence of cause and effect, thereby casting doubt on many of the certainties underpinning the values and beliefs of Western society. These theories influenced the thought of nonscientists, among them the artistic and literary champions of Modernism, as well as Carl Jung, who in a series of dinner conversations between 1906 and 1912 discussed relativity with Einstein. As Charlene Burns explains, collaboration with the Nobel Prize physicist Wolfgang Pauli, whose quantum theory held that energy radiates discontinuously in fixed units, played a significant part in shaping Jung's concept of synchronicity (Burns 2009). As discussed elsewhere in this study, Bill was fascinated, indeed preoccupied, with time. His interest in the nature of time, in transcending or escaping from it may explain his careful reading of *Man and Time*, a collection of essays edited by the anthropologist Joseph Campbell, which contains contributions on time in relation to art, death, and science; to Islamic, Indian/Hindu, and Christian thought; as well as one by Jung on synchronicity (Campbell 1957).

The last chapter of Jung's *The Structure and Dynamics of the Psyche*, titled "Synchronicity: An Acausal Connecting Principal," is based on historical research, case studies, and personal experiences from which he arrives at a definition of synchronicity, which he says is the meaningful coincidence or equivalence of a psychic experience (a dream, vision, premonition, etc.) and a physical state or event that has no causal relationship. Therefore, such experiences "cannot be a question of cause and effect but of a falling together in time, of simultaneity." Thus, Jung argues, there are some states of mind or temporal events or experiences for which there is no apparent cause "because causality is bound up with the existence of space and time and physical changes" (Jung 1960, 441, 435, 443-447, 531). Like dreams, synchronistic events, Jung was convinced, were a means by which a person could reach beyond his consciousness to the deeper order and wholeness found in the collective unconscious and thereby achieve self-realization, individuation. Reading Jung may have been one way Trout sought to understand what he himself was experiencing, a means for pursuing his search for self-knowledge, or a way to communicate with his deceased mother. Through studying parapsychology he might come to an understanding of such supernatural phenomena as clairvoyance, telepathy, and apparitions, which are not based on materiality and verifiable using reason or scientific methods. Poems like "Onset," "Compulsion," "Individuation," and "Encounter," for example, relate to his interest in this aspect of Jung's work. It is also worth noting that the Society for Psychical Research in London, to which one of Trout's favorite writers, May Sinclair, was elected a board member in 1914, (see Chapter 7) began serious investigation into extrasensory perception (ESP) in the early 1880s.

Many of Bill's poems, among them "Time now to thumb the page's edge," "North of the old orchard, the house shambles," "An abrupt click, a scornful, spinning whirr," and "And still she sings, the Marschallin" take time and memory as their theme. The poems apparently based on family photographs—"See, on the right, there just in the corner," "They," and "Remembered"—suggest his attempt to stop time in words as a camera freezes it in photographs.

Finally, part of what attracted Trout to Jung was the Swiss doctor's breadth of knowledge. Jung, as H. Stuart Hughes tells us, "came to psychoanalysis steeped in philosophy, literature, and history" and had "imbibed the tradition of [the philosopher] Nietzsche, of [the historian] Burckhardt" and the writings of the ethnologist and student of mythology, J. J. Bachofen (Hughes 1958, 156). His interdisciplinary approach to analytical psychology—drawing as he did on Western and nonwestern thought in archeology, philosophy, ethnology, mythology, literature, visual art, music, history, and religion—obviously appealed to Bill. Jung's broad interdisciplinary and rich multicultural research led him to the realization that the "discontents" of modern Western Civilization are traceable to its "loss of connection with the past" through its disregard of history and its unquestioning faith in the idea of progress based on innovation and technology and the belief that the future will be better than the present. Furthermore, Jung observes that all man's achievements in science and technology have merely given him "a wealth of useful gadgets" while ignoring, even disparaging, the needs of the spirit (Jung 1973, 236-237). That Trout shared such views as these is evident in his correspondence, teaching, and poetry, not a little of which is informed by his rootedness in the land, his personal past, and a knowledge of history and literary tradition. But as will be seen in the following chapter, his life and poetry were deeply influenced not only by his study of the humanities and behavioral sciences but also by the visual arts and music.

Chapter 6
Seductive Masters: Visual Art and Music

The painterly quality and sensitivity to color in Trout's verse suggest he was knowledgeable about the visual arts; and though he never mentioned visiting an art museum, one suspects he may have availed himself of opportunities to tour such institutions on those few occasions when we know he went to Philadelphia, Washington D.C., and Boston. However, what he knew of art may have come mainly through reading and reproductions. Among the books he gave me in the 1970s were illustrated volumes on ancient Greek sculpture; the prints and drawings of Albrecht Dürer, Rembrandt, Francisco Goya; two on the Dance of Death (one of which was by Hans Holbein and included his Bible woodcuts); two on the paintings of Hieronymus Bosch; three on the paintings of Pieter Bruegel the Elder; and two on Vincent van Gogh. It is likely he owned other art books that he either sold or more likely gave to friends or students. Scattered through his poem "...il en faut peu ..." are references to Giotto, Bruegel, and van Gogh. In the poem "Apparition" he mentions the cypresses in van Gogh's paintings as well as knowledge of his self-portraits. And in another poem, "Doubtful Solstice" (not included herein), he refers to one of Botticelli's mythological paintings. Henry Adams (1838-1918) commissioned the sculptor Augustus Saint-Gaudens (1848-1907) to create a funeral monument for his wife, who took her own life, which Trout made the subject of his poem "Adams Memorial":

In that city, visited infrequently and now almost forgotten,
In the vast formal graveyard, guarded by the nondescript employees of the State,
The great bronze stands—
Not great in size; really, one was surprised,
One paused in silent astonishment to see how little space it occupies,
There in its protective hedge of evergreens and holly.

And here, between midnight and dawn, on the last day of June,
In the humid quiet, where only the alarm clock ticks and a distant car
skids on the asphalt,
And one's ears buss dimly,—
The memory of that hooded face
Returns:

And with a long tremor of resignation, of surrender, of the acceptance
of the essential release into dust,
Of the determinate quenching of the querulous and waspish, accursed
consciousness,
The being kneels, touching with timid finger the green hem of the robe;
And the bronze soars,
Towers like a vast shadow, protective,
A defense, conceived in a human mind, born of a man's hand,—
Rears itself, as silent surrogate for whimpering human frailty,
To dare the dread,
The infinite, the eternal nothingness.

What no doubt appealed to Trout as he knelt at the *Adams Memorial* (1886-1891) in Rock Creek Cemetery in Washington, D. C. was how Saint-Gaudens achieved the desire of Adams, who found the Christianity of his day hollow, to have the monument capture the spirit of Eastern philosophy, particularly the concept of Nirvana—the absorption of the soul at death into a state of transcendent enlightenment and internal peace through the extinction of all desires and passions. Trout records the memory of his reaction to the sculpture, its impact on him rather than its appearance, its aesthetic qualities, or its intellectual significance. Since Bill had read *The Education of Henry Adams* he would have been aware of Adams' own reaction to the statue and his observations on the "vacant-minded" tourists who sought only an explanation of its "meaning" and regarded it as "a figure of despair, of atheism, of denial" and a waste of money (Craven 1968, 385-387; Adams 1918, 329).

It is easy to understand Trout's interest in the Northern Renaissance artist Albrecht Dürer if one looks at his portraits and particularly at his self-portraits, including his drawing *Self-Portrait Naked* (ca.1503), the first nude self-portrait in Western art. Fascinated with his own personality, Dürer was not only meticulous in his realism and attention to the detail with which he rendered the physical features and captured the individuality of his sitters, but was unusually adept in revealing their psyche, as with *Self-Portrait* of 1498 in which his vanity is apparent in his facial expression, elegant quaff, and costly clothing; while in his *Self-Portrait* (1500) his vanity becomes blasphemous in portraying himself in the pose and likeness of Christ. Like Dürer's self-portraits, many of Trout's poems are autobiographical, and while they may not contain descriptions of his physical appearance they do reveal much about his personality and psychology. Dürer's woodcuts of the Passion of Christ are also masterful depictions of emotional states of mind, not only in his recording of Christ's facial expressions and body language but also by the faces of soldiers and onlookers distorted by hatred as they mock him on the way to Calvary. In such allegorical works as Dürer's engraving *Melancholia I* (1514), the obsessive stare of the brooding figure, like the crazed look of *Oswald Krell*, painted in 1499, reveals deep psychological disturbance.

According to Michael Levey, Dürer "seems always to have been haunted, and fascinated, by the freakish effects of nature," and late in life "dreamt a terrifying dream of the earth inundated by roaring waters pouring from heaven, a vision so frightening that he could exorcize it only by recording it in writing and by a sketch"—*Dream of Waters Descending from the Sky* (1525). While there is no way of knowing whether Trout had seen Dürer's watercolor sketch or read his account of the dream, the record of the nightmare is in keeping with Bill's practice of recording his own disturbing dreams. What is more, he would have found Dürer's prints and drawings filled with Jungian archetypical images like those in his 1513 engraving *The Knight, Death, and the Devil*. In addition to the characters named in the title the print includes a horse, dog, lizard, snake, skull, and blasted and barren trees. Contributing to the emotional impact of Dürer's prints and drawings was the shading and modeling he used to create a wide range of tonal gradations through skillful and sensitive hatching and crosshatching (closely set parallel and crisscrossed lines). In his copy of Wolfgang Stechow's book on Pieter Bruegle the Elder, Bill taped reproductions of *The Knight, Death, and the Devil*; Hans Holbein the Younger's woodcuts "The Plowman" and "The Young Child" from his *The Dance of Death*; and four Japanese prints.

Dürer was also fascinated by nature, particularly its oddities. He did a watercolor of a walrus in 1521, a woodcut of a rhinoceros in 1515, and got sick and died when he traveled to Zeeland to sketch a beached whale. The intensity of his observation, not only in the way he rendered his own face and those of others, but also in his studies of nature go deeper than mere verisimilitude (thanks in part to his technique), as his watercolors *Young Hare*

(1502) and *Great Piece of Turf* (1503) testify (Clark 1969, 148-156; Levey 1975, 67-68, 196-197, 170-171, 173). The imagined smell of the moist loamy soil in which the common weeds (among them cock's foot, creeping bent, plantain, hound's-tooth, and withered dandelions) of Dürer's little corner of the universe are rooted, reminds one of Trout's circumscribed landscapes (a flowerbed, a section of vegetable garden, the bank of a meadow stream) and the lowly plants he imaged—Queen Anne's lace, wild chicory, violets, goldenrod—with such affection, sensitivity, and truth to nature in rendering the textures, colors, sounds, and odors of the natural world in poems like "Behind gray weathered pickets, and thrusting through," "Blacksnake," and "Summer Ending."

A number of twentieth-century poets have taken Pieter Bruegel the Elder's paintings as subjects for poems, and at least four (recently Joseph Langland in 2000) have given verbal renderings of his *The Hunters in the Snow* (1565). The appeal of *Hunters* for William Carlos Williams, as with other modernist poetic readings of Bruegel's works, is in its formal qualities. In his "The Hunter in the Snow," Williams begins by looking at the subject "overall," then to the "icy mountains" in the background, to the returning hunters and their dogs and the inn-sign and figures around the fire in front of the inn, to the "pattern of skaters" in the middle distance, and finally to "complete the picture," the "winter-struck bush" the painter placed in the right corner of the foreground. While Williams' reading of the painting is primarily compositional in its presentation of details in order of visual importance, his interpretation also addresses the issue of time, specifically, as David Wyatt explains, his rendering the sequence of visual imagery, thereby transforming a "'spatial' into a temporal one" much as he does in his poem—"The Great Figure"—of a fire engine speeding down a city street on a dark and rainy night, which inspired Charles Demuth's 1928 painting *I Saw the Figure Five in Gold*. Demuth captures visually Williams' "sense of sequentiality" by diminishing the size of the fire engine's number as it disappears down the street. In contrast to Williams' interest in the present moment, John Berryman in his poem "Winter Landscape," shows more concern for the duration of time through references to history and an hour glass and the repeated use of certain words ("returning" and "return"), with bringing out the brooding quality of *Hunters*, and by inviting us to contemplate universal issues of life and death, of permanence and decay rather as Keats does in his ode "On a Grecian Urn" (Wyatt 1977, 247, 250-254, 257-259, 260). Walter de la Mare's poem "Brueghel's Winter," which Trout marked with a star and underlined its final sestet in his copy of the poet's *Collected Poems*, also stresses the brooding mood, bleak landscape, and inhospitable weather in *Hunters* by focusing on the painting's earth tones and by the imaginative realism of his diction in describing its weather and landscape: "Jagged mountain peaks and skies ice-green," "wild cold," "freezing quiet," "ink-black shapes." But it is an idea de la Mare hints at in the final sestet, particularly in the last two lines—"Give more than subtle hint of / Who squandered here life's mystery"—that Trout turns into his poem "Intimation (Bruegel)," the title of which refers to de la Mare's indirect suggestion which may reflect Bill's sense of his own inadequacy, failure, and, perhaps, guilt.

I

They troop nearer, the winter trees,
Stalking down the snowy hill,
Pilgrims prodigal unfeed
By benefice, except the will
Born in that wide heart: they come
To lead a shabbier pilgrim home.
Under snow the valley sleeps,
Its biped citizens withdrawn,
Domesticated brothers deep
In stable straw—all drowse-yawning,
Careless of misery.—Only these
Proffer arm-crook, the holy trees.

II

Here none heeds. Everywhere,
We can wander undisturbed.
Intently brooding, the wintry air
By no shrilling bird is stirred,
Though birds in naked trees may seem,
From their dream, to scan our dreaming.
These villagers, and birds, and hills
Snow-sheathed, the very hunting-hounds—
A world it is that fusing fills
Our microcosmos: each abounds,
Interpenetrating; so
Does Hither, through the Other, go?

Trout uses the hunters as metaphors for pilgrims who "come / To lead a shabbier pilgrim home." They are "unfeed," without land and by implication poor and of no account in society. He identified with those who suffered social or economic injustice, as well as with those who suffer spiritually. He personalized the experience of the painting (Everywhere, / We can wonder undisturbed.) and in recognizing a kinship between the still and silent birds that "seem / From their dream, to scan our dreaming," as well as the villagers, hills, and "the very hunting hounds" that fuse and fill "Our microcosmos." Trout sees Bruegel's painting as a dream world suspended in time like the sign suspended on a single hook. The scene reaches across time to fuse with Trout's "microcosmos" in a way that recalls Jung's concept of the collective unconscious.

Yet another key to understanding Trout's Bruegel poem lies in the symbolism of the inn or tavern sign that hangs precariously ajar above the straw fire. The sign contains an inscription "Under the Stag" and an image of St. Eustace, identified by his principal attribute, a stag with a crucifix between its horns. Eustace, a Roman officer who converted to Christianity, encountered such a stag while hunting and was told by Christ (the figure on the cross) that he would suffer many misfortunes, but that God would not abandon him. In time he and his family were martyred for their faith. Eustace is sometimes shown accompanied by hounds. He is the patron saint of hunters. Bill was a hunter of a different sort in the sense that he was searching for self-knowledge and trying to find a way to inner peace by ridding himself of his private demons, as references to himself in poems as a seeker or searcher testify. It is also significant that the body of a red fox, traditionally a symbol of cunning and guile and of the Devil, hangs from the back of one of the hunters. Finally, though shown nowhere in Bruegel's painting, Trout mentions "Domesticated brothers deep / in stable straw," a reference to the animals shown in Renaissance paintings of the Nativity. In Wolfgang Stechow's book *Peter Bruegel the Elder* (1968), a copy of which Trout owned and underlined, the point is made that *The Hunters in the Snow* is one of the artist's "Months" series and probably represents December, thus accounting for Trout's references to the Nativity. Or might Bill have seen the martyrdom of Eustace as another instance, as with Job, of God allowing even those who believed in him and did his will to suffer? Such a view that saw the Christian God as cruel and indifferent undermined both his faith and that of Emily Dickinson. Yet given the Christian symbolism Trout attributes to it and the fact that he both likens the hunters to "Pilgrims prodigal" and "unfeed" who have "come

/ To lead a shabbier pilgrim [himself perhaps] home," suggests that he saw in this painting something (perhaps the relentless passage of time arrested) that was comforting to him or might help resolve his own self-doubts and assist him in his struggle to regain lost faith, or at least give him solace in his unbelief. I know from conversations with Bill that this painting was one of his favorites.

Trout, always sensitive to matters of time, apparently relished this scene frozen in time by Bruegel, where "none heeds" his undisturbed wandering through the "intently brooding" landscape and the silence of "the wintry air." And he may have sensed that his, and by extension our, "microcosmos" through the collective unconscious shares something with "These villagers, and birds, and hills," in asking whether something "Interpenetrating" "Does Hither, through the Other, go?"

Rembrandt's prints and paintings of Biblical subjects and van Gogh's of landscapes and humble objects and people interested Trout. Then, too, their life experiences resonated with him as well. Though successful and prosperous early in his career, Rembrandt later suffered a reversal of fortunes and went deeply into debt, becoming something of a social outcast. The subtle tonal gradations in Rembrandt's prints and painterly canvases result in marvelously atmospheric effects that obviously appealed as much to Trout as the subject matter. Anyone who images the elderly as Bill does in his poems would cherish Rembrandt's sensitive and caring depiction of old people.

Vincent van Gogh, whose brother supported him financially, never enjoyed either economic security or professional recognition during his lifetime. The son of a clergyman, he worked for a time as a lay minister among the impoverished coal miners of Belgium, not unlike Trout's five years spent teaching among the rural poor on Welsh Mountain. Like many of the people E. A. Robinson chose as subjects for his poems, van Gogh was an eccentric and a failure by the conventional standards of middle-class society. He took as subjects: miners, peasants, prostitutes, village folk, a postman, a doctor, and humble objects like pieces of furniture, paperback books, and his own boots, as well as flowers. Vincent's temperament and personal habits put people off; even his brother found him nearly impossible to live with (Rewald 1978, 40-41). His unconventional lifestyle put him on the margins of mainstream society, a situation with which Bill could identify. Many critics and members of the public couldn't make sense of his wild paintings with their shocking nonreferential colors and violently slashing brushwork. And there was no market for his paintings in his lifetime. Like Trout, van Gogh was an avid reader, particularly of realist novels with a strong social or moral content, among them those of George Eliot, Charles Dickens, and Emile Zola, at least two of whom were authors Trout admired—Dickens and Eliot. Among the books he included in his still life paintings were those of the Goncourt brothers, Maupassant, and Zola, choices that no doubt reflect what he was reading and document his commitment to Realist/Naturalist literature (Pickvance 1984, 35). Van Gogh's illness, which resulted in periodic stays in a mental hospital, led to worries about his psychological health, a personal concern Bill apparently shared as occasional references in his letters suggest.

Perhaps what in part attracted Trout to Rembrandt and van Gogh were the many self-portraits in which they examined their changing physical features and plumbed their own inner beings, much as Bill did repeatedly in poems that explore the evidence of life's experiences and his personality, psyche, and unconscious. In addition to numerous portraits of ordinary people, van Gogh painted more than thirty-seven self-portraits, many of them during the last five years of his life. While in many of these he was experimenting with color theory and brushwork techniques, in them he also left a record of his varied moods and insights into his personality (Pickvance 1984, 34-35, 171, 213). For someone like Bill who was so deeply interested in psychology and psychoanalysis, and whose poems give glimpses into his own psychological state, van Gogh's numerous self-portraits must have held a particular fascination. Recognizing how portraits can reveal things about a sitter's personality may have contributed to Bill's reluctance to being photographed.

Not only are van Gogh's portraits and self-portraits explorations of human psychology, so too are such paintings as *The Artist's Bedroom at Arles* (1888)—which can also be read as biographical since it was the artist's private space—and *The Yellow House* (at Arles, 1888), in both of which his use of color was intended to express the happiness and optimism of the period when he hoped to form an artists' colony with Paul Gauguin at Arles, in the south of France. But as in *Night Café* (1888), he used color symbolism to explore the dark side of the human personality, as he told his brother: "I have tried to show that the café is a place where one can ruin one's self, go mad, or commit a crime"—an allusion to the dark side of the human psyche that so intrigued Bill.

These paintings, as well as examples of the subjects listed above, were among the color reproductions in one of the books on van Gogh Trout owned and annotated. As John Rewald maintains, "It becomes clear from van Gogh's own commentaries that each subject he chose to paint released in him specific emotions or associations of ideas which he sought to express by means of composition, of simplification, and especially color. Thus every one of his canvases has a spiritual content, crystallizing a genuine feeling. They are laden with meaningful allusions, reminiscences, mediations, and even forebodings—are pregnant with repressed compassion and tenderness, evangelical fervor or pagan ecstasy" (Rewald 1978, 210-211). No wonder Trout found van Gogh's paintings so appealing, since many of the same impulses and means informed his poems, whether the subject was a landscape; a season; a memory; or a person, animal, or dream. In "Apparition" Trout recalls van Gogh's self-portraits, the cypresses (among both pagans and Christians associated with death) in his landscapes, and alludes to their shared concern with emotional stability (Ferguson 1979, 30).

> Strangely, the Van Gogh cypresses appeared,
> Swiftly, in a rigorous arrest
> Radiantly gleaming out of mere
> Nothingness,—by what serene behest
> Imperiously signalled? Across the air
> Of lapsing summer, a long wave of peace
> Swept in, foamed, receded—some mute prayer
> Tranquilly answered.
>   The spirit—on its knees,
> Its humble knees—remembered a mad face
> On savage canvas, and was stilled by grace.

But for all his interest in visual art and artists and his love of words and literature, it was music, I believe, that was William Trout's real passion and touched him most deeply—was his greatest solace and source of joy—or as he puts it to Don Smith in a letter of 2 September 1945, is "my seductive master." Reflecting on the power of music after hearing a recording of J. S. Bach's concerto for two violins, he tells Smith in a 1943 letter: "Suddenly for no reason you are rapt; identity falls away and fear with it. You wander in a moon-world, the antique world of old tales; you climb above the timberline, above the snow line, and wander ankle-deep in shale and the cold arrows thru you. A kind of odd peace, and the exultation of a sound pattern. And then it's all over, and you feel like the drunkard walking in the gutter at dawn. Like Caliban [in Shakespeare's *The Tempest*] you 'cry to dream again.' "

Bill's taste in classical music included vocal, chamber works, orchestral, keyboard (particularly piano), and opera. Clues to his listening habits and musical interests are provided by his taped and battered copy of *The Oxford Book of English Verse, 1250-1900*, in which (from 1936 through 1939) he noted in the margins the month, day, and year of the performance and the names of composers and works he was apparently listening to on the radio while reading poetry. Similar dated jottings are found in other of his books, including his copy of Thomas Hardy's *The Dynasts*. Sampling these notations gives us some idea of the variety of music Bill heard on the radio. On 1/22/39 he listened to Rubenstein's "Quintet for Woodwinds, Op. 55, in F Major and noted its movements and instrumentation. It appears that he was a regular listener to a radio program called The Music Hall, where on its 1/29/39 broadcast he recorded hearing Beethoven's Leonore Overture No. 3, the *Liebesnach* from Wagner's *Tristan und Isolde*, and Ravel's *Rapsodie espagnole*; the 2/5/39 broadcast included Alexander Glazunov's "Elegie" (for violin and piano), songs by Eric Korngold, and Rachmaninov's Piano Concerto No. 3. He wrote down the names of the pieces Arturo Toscanini conducted on his NBC Symphony Orchestra's all-Sibelius program of 2/18/39: The Second Symphony, *The Swan of Tuonela*, *Finlandia*, and *En saga*. In 1940 Toscanini led the same orchestra in a radio broadcast of Sibelius' Symphony No. 4 and *Pohjola's Daughter*. It may have been through these radio concerts that the foundations were laid for Bill's interest in the Finnish composer's works, recordings of which he purchased. His interest in the music of Richard Strauss was nurtured by the frequency with which Toscanini and guest conductors programmed his tone poems in the weekly NBC Symphony broadcasts, to which Bill apparently was a regular listener.

While some of Toscanini's NBC Symphony programs were devoted to excerpts from operas (mostly Wagner and Verdi), his repertoire was drawn mainly from the tried-and-true-symphonic literature, focusing on Haydn, Mozart, and the nineteenth-century warhorses—lots of Beethoven, Mendelssohn, Brahms, Wagner, and Tchaikovsky—salted with some Rossini, Berlioz, Debussy, and Respighi; more sparingly peppered with Ravel and César Franck; but rarely seasoned with Stravinsky, Prokofiev, Shostakovich or such modern American composers as Roy Harris, Samuel Barber, and Aaron Copland. Radio audiences were more likely to hear "new" music from guest conductors and particularly from Leopold Stokowski, a champion of contemporary music, after he began sharing the podium with Toscanini. Stoki included works by six American composers in his eight NBC Symphony broadcasts in 1941-42, and later introduced listeners to the work of Gustav Holst, Paul Hindemith, and Vaughan Williams, composers—

along with Mahler, Bartók, and Berg—Toscanini never conducted. NBC Symphony concerts were aired on Saturdays from 10:00-11:30 P.M. until the 1942-43-season, when the broadcasts were moved to Sunday afternoons at 5:00, just after the New York Philharmonic concerts aired from 3:00 to 5:00 on CBS (Horowitz 1987, 130-131, 133, 173, 262; Frank 2002, 43-114). With the Metropolitan Opera radio broadcasts Saturday afternoons and at least two symphonic concerts aired on Sundays, Trout's weekends gave him a feast of classical music. But there was more.

In 1936, I. A. Hirschmann and his wife Hortense Monath founded the non-profit New Friends of Music to give chamber music concerts in New York's Town Hall featuring masterpieces of chamber music, as well as neglected or unfamiliar works, and *Lieder* recitals. Beginning in 1938 these live concerts were carried on radio. Marginal notes in his books document that Trout tuned in to these programs. On 12 February 1939, for example, he heard a Haydn trio and several of the composer's quartets on the New Friends of Music broadcast. With the 1940-41 season, the works of modern composers began to share the program with Beethoven, Brahms, and other Old Masters (Weber 1983, 44-47). But the New Friends had to compete for Bill's attention with other offerings since their programs also took place on Sunday evenings.

Other dated jottings Bill made in books document how important listening to music was to him and also chronicle the range of his musical taste. Many of these notes don't specify whether he was listening to the radio or to one of his many phonograph records. Although his enthusiasm for composers changed over time, a sampling of these book notations tells us something of the range of his taste in classical music: Verdi's *Aida*, J. S. Bach's Cantata No. 3 (1/29/39) and Cantata No. 126 (2/12/39), "Cleopatra's Air" from Handel's *Julius Caesar* (2/5/39), Haydn's Quartet in C Major, Op. 20, No. 2 and Bach's Mass in B-Minor and one of his sonatas for flute and harpsichord (2/5/36), and an unidentified work by the contemporary British composer Michael Tippett.

That Bill's taste in classical music was somewhat more adventuresome than that of many middle-brow concert-goers and those in the radio audience may well owe something to his cousin Elford Caughey, who gave him phonograph recordings and kept him abreast of the Boston Symphony's repertoire in letters and through copies of the Orchestra's programs. As a member of the BSO during Serge Koussevitsky's tenure as its music director, Caughey was in a good position to comment on a wide range of symphonic music and perhaps make recommendations to Bill as to what was worth listening to and perhaps acquiring on disk. In contrast to Toscanini's preference for canonical compositions, Koussevitsky performed the Old Masters and was a champion of modern European and American composers whose works were a regular part of BSO programs. He also commissioned works from Ravel, Prokofiev, Hindemith, Stravinsky, Berg, Bartók, Roy Harris, Copland, Samuel Barber and George Gershwin. During the 1930s and '40s he was an acclaimed conductor of Sibelius' symphonies and tone poems, and in 1932-1933 led a Sibelius symphony cycle. On 16 October 1931 he conducted the U. S. premier of Gustav Mahler's Ninth Symphony. The BSO under Koussevitzky gave the first live radio orchestra concert, broadcast in 1926 on NBC. Such live BSO broadcasts under his baton continued until 1951 (BSO Broadcast Archives). Whether Trout was able to receive these broadcasts in Gap is not certain, but what we do know is that his cousin kept him abreast of what the BSO was playing.

Bill enjoyed sharing with Don Smith news of the Boston Symphony sent by his cousin Elford, including information about programs and an amusing story about Igor Stravinsky arriving at a BSO rehearsal with Nadia Boulanger (one of the foremost teachers of music composition in the twentieth century) following on behind carrying the great man's suitcase. In a letter of 1 November 1943 Bill relates to Don Smith that "L writes dismally of the [BSO] programs: Eine Kleine Nachtmusik (which I adore, to his scorn), the Pastorale [Beethoven's Sixth Symphony], a Berezousky symphony, Rimsky's[-Korsakov] Cappriccio, something called Prairie by one of K's [Koussevitsky's] white-haired boys, the Berlioz [Symphonie] Fantastique." Caughey played both the celesta and the harp in performances of Schostakovitch's Fifth Symphony "together with the Russian's first, and a symphony by [the American composer] Wm. Schumann," Bill tells Smith in a letter of 13 November 1943. In another, postmarked 31 January 1944, he mentions works by Mussorgsky and Grieg, reports to Smith that Caughey "raved" about Debussy's *Iberia*, and says he received a recording of C. P. E. Bach's violin concerto as a gift from Elford. Responding to an inquiry Smith had apparently made about the contemporary American composer Lukas Foss, Bill enclosed in his letter of 7 July 1945 a clipping about Foss taken from a BSO program Caughey sent him.

To Smith's query whether Bill had heard a recently released recording of a Prokofiev symphony, he responded on 11 November 1943 that he had not, and goes on to list those works currently occupying his attention: Brahms' Fourth Symphony and his Second Piano Concerto, songs by Robert Schumann, the overtures to Weber's operas *Oberon* and *Der Freischutz*, and closes by saying he "longs" to have Smith listen with him to "the last 30 minutes of Act I and the trio from the last act of Rosenkavalier." Early in June 1945 Bill writes Smith that he is enjoying a recording of Bach organ music played by Albert Schweitzer (the medical missionary and authority on J. S. Bach), lent to him by his Gap friend Paul Rostock, and the last of the Beethoven quartets, of which he says: "Oh, that such things can exist in such a world...." He ends a letter of 11 June 1945 by telling Smith he wishes he were there to "enjoy a feast of Mozart and Ravel, Sibelius and Strauss." In a letter of 21 April 1945, he jokes with Smith about robbing his father's bank [Mr. Smith was President of the Gap National Bank] to buy the new Eugene Ormandy (Philadelphia Orchestra) recording of Richard Strauss' *Symphony Domestica*, and a month later tells Smith he has been listening to Strauss' *Death and Transfiguration*. The works of Hugo Wolf, an Austrian generally regarded as one of the finest composers of *Lieder*, is mentioned in several of Bill's letters to Don Smith.

Trout's record collection is another source of information on his knowledge of and taste in music and helps to document how his taste changed over time. He owned several recordings of Manuel de Falla, among them a 78-rpm of his popular Spanish songs. While he does not mention in his letters listening to disks of the works of such *avant-garde* composers as Stravinsky, Schoenberg, Berg, and Shostakovish, he did own the Pierre Monteux recording of Stravinsky's *Rite of Spring* and a five-disk set of ballet music that included works by Prokofiev, Khatchaturian, Stravinsky, and Bernstein. He mentions to Don Smith in an April 1944 letter that he listened to and tried to like the music of George Gershwin because his brother Frank and Lukens friend Jim were enthusiastic about him, but "except for some bits of Porgy [and Bess], Gershwin doesn't touch me; and for a real expression of the times, I'll argue for Harry James, Tommy Dorsey, Count Basie, Dinah Shore, Dwight Fiske, Eddie Dochin, and the little jingles they sing to me this week, vending Chicklet's Candy-Coated Chewing Gum, as I sit grimy and weary [from working at the steel mill] on a stool by the radio, drinking coffee and waiting for the news broadcast." Linking the greats of Big Band jazz and the "perky" Dinah Shore with a Chicklet's jingle reflects Bill's dim view of contemporary American society and its popular culture. He admits to an inability to appreciate jazz, saying: "I am ... self-conscious and ill-at-ease in your swing-band night clubs." The few 78-rpm recordings he gave me together with the approximately one hundred 33-rpm disks (including many works for the piano) he gave in the late 1960s to Byron Detwiler (his former student and later a member of Millersville's French faculty) are an important source of our knowledge of the composers and types of music Bill liked. However, as he aged his musical interest seemed to focus on the songs of Schubert, Schumann, Wolf, and Richard Strauss; Beethoven's *Missa solemnis* and the Third, Sixth, Seventh, and Ninth symphonies; and the late Beethoven string quartets, of which he owned multiple recordings by different chamber groups. After telling him early in the 1970s that I frequented record stores, he would apologetically inquire that "should I happen to find myself in a record shop, might I be so kind as to look for...." These requests included, among others, Lotte Lehmann singing Verdi and Wagner arias; Kirsten Flagstad performing Wagner, Brahms, and Grieg songs; and recordings of Beethoven's symphonies and late quartets. In a letter postmarked 17 February 1971 he thanked me for the recordings, saying: "Luckily you were not present when I played the Lehman record, for I wept, a sight that must have been revolting. But the sound of that voice—so beloved—seemed to dislodge memories that became an unbearable avalanche. 'Dich teure halle' [an aria from Wagner's *Tannhäuser*] swept over me like a spring storm. All one side was entirely new. I have not yet dared the Flagstad." And it was the legendary 1933 recording of Strauss' *Der Rosenkavalier* with Lotte Lehmann (Marschallin), Maria Olczewska (Octavian), Elizabeth Schumann (Sophie), Richard Mayr (Baron Ochs), with Robert Hager conducting the Vienna Philharmonic that Bill listened to in his last years.

While there is no evidence Bill ever made music (save for the passing remark he drops in a letter to Don Smith, postmarked 22 May 1943 that he "fingered" out Schubert's *Rastlose Liebe* on the piano), there is no doubt he read it. His library contained many books on music—composer's biographies, among them Mozart, Beethoven, Rossini, Tchaikovsky, Mussorgsky, and Ravel; monographs on the symphonies and quartets of Beethoven; books on music history and theory; books on Wagner's operas and libretti for those of Mozart, Verdi, and Puccini; and scores for Beethoven's *Missa solemnis*, symphonies, and late quartets; Schubert's songs; and his favorite opera, Richard Strauss' *Der Rosenkavalier*. His Beethoven, Schubert, and Strauss scores are heavily annotated, taped and tattered from frequent use—testaments to his careful and painstaking effort to understand the technicalities of composition. He was obviously an active not a passive listener who seems to have followed the score as he listened to his many recordings. The notations and other marks he made in his two Schirmer's Library of albums of Franz Schubert's songs leave no doubt about which were his favorites (though he seems to have liked many of them) and useful to our understanding of Trout the man and the poet. Among those marked which give insights into his personality and way of life are: "Wandering," "The Wanderer," "Wanderer's Night Song," "Solitude,"

"My Abode," "Serenade," "Yearning," "The Recluse," and "Parting." Those that reflect his interest in death and the macabre include: "The Erlking," "Litany for All Souls' Day," and "Death and the Maiden." Human cruelty and the violation of nature expressed in "The Trout" remind one of Bill's crow poems, "In Brief," and "One Pheasant." Three songs are marked with tape tabs, suggesting pieces he listened to frequently: "In the Red of Evening," "In Spring," and "An die Musik" ("To Music"), which Bill mentions in several letters as his favorite Schubert song.

Every morning at Gap Centralized School Trout would gather students in grades 5 through 8 in the wide second-floor hallway to sing songs, as Rhoda Hostetter Clemens, one of his eighth-graders remembered, as did Don Smith, who sometimes played the piano for the song-fest portion of what Clemens called "opening exercises." Following the singing they would salute the American flag. On Fridays during the school year, Norma Patterson recalled Trout telling his Gap classes the story of the Met opera to be aired on Saturday afternoon and urging them to listen. As a teenager, Don Smith played the piano in the Trout dining room; and after learning Beethoven's "*Waldstein*" *Sonata* at Bill's urging, one of his Christiana students remembered going to his home to play it for him. William Axe, John Bryer, and James Cauller mentioned that as teens Bill tried to interest them in opera. Bill's college lectures contain references to specific operas or classical pieces, and students also recall that he sometimes played classical recordings in class.

Paul Rostock, a German-American who was one of Bill's few close friends in Gap and shared his enthusiasm for classical music, frequently spent time with him listening to phonograph recordings, as his son Eric recalled. Eric Rostock also remembered his father, who was an engineer at Lukens Steel in Coatesville, where there was a good record shop, taking recordings (among them one of Brahms' Double Concerto, which became a favorite of Bill's) to Trout's house, where they listened to them together. They also lent records to each other. In a letter written to Don Smith on 26 August 1945, he says that Paul Rostock visited him and they talked until midnight about "Spengler and Bach, Goethe and Faust, ducks and gypsies, Brahms songs and the ways in which marriage interferes with a man's career." One evening early in September of 1945 Rostock showed up with Bach and Beethoven recordings, Bill wrote Smith, telling him they spent four hours listening to music. His niece, Alice Trout Smith, recalled stacks of classical and opera records next to the Victrola in Trout's living room and remembered that her uncle's favorite singers were the Italian soprano Amelita Galli-Curci and the

German-American contralto Ernestine Schumann-Heink. Later it was Lotte Lehmann who moved Bill to tears. He also liked the Swedish tenor Jussi Bjoerling enough to buy several of his recordings, urging Don Smith in a letter of 10 June 1944 concerning a Bjoerling recording: "you must hear [it] for the voice, not for the music." Sometimes having to work at the steel mill on Saturdays he tells Smith means missing parts of a Met opera broadcast or the entire opera. After hearing the April 8, 1944, opera broadcast of Puccini's *Tosca*, he lets Smith know he heard

> irregularly thru the muddling fumes of my secret and protracted tippling, the Met's "Tosca". In spite of the fact that with advancing years my affection for opera suffers from prolonged lapses of interest, I can still be pleased and even mildly enthusiastic over parts of "Tosca": Tosca's voice offstage in the first act calling, "Mario, Mario" always seems like the irresistible onset of that one passion of late youth, the one that matters, when age knows and youth can; Scarpia's diabolic baritone weaving its sinister obligato thru the Te Deum; the "Vissi d'arte" can be a splendidly emotional moment; and the two arias of Mario in the last act – the E lucevan le stelle and O dolci mani were the first Tosca music I ever heard, on Gigli's old record; and then the old thrill of the third act prelude, with the shepherd lad's husky, throaty contralto, and all the bells of Rome chiming through the dawn.

Trout's letters of the early 1940s to Don Smith frequently mention his fondness for Ravel's music, including the Piano Concerto for the Left Hand, which he insists Smith "must listen to" and the "untarnished sparkle and freshness" of his *Alborada del gracioso*. In a letter to Smith of 19 January 1942 he mentions hearing a Philadelphia Orchestra broadcast that included Haydn's Symphony in G and "Ravel's Albordado [del gracioso], the latter in all its (to me) untarnished sparkle and freshness. Ravel is much to my taste (don't laugh; I'm learning)," he tells Smith in a September 1943 letter, and then ticks off seven of the composer's works he says he is listening to "pretty constantly as opportunity offers," and also mentions having bought recordings of two Schumann song cycles. Bill again conveys his enthusiasm to Smith in a letter of 3 October 1943.

> But I do like Ravel. [Le] 'Tombeau'[De Couperin] glitters, like most of Ravel; there is not much humanity in it, a kind of sparkling mask that may hide anything—but I like it. And I always thrill to the tumul-

> tuous controlled climax of 'Daphnis' [Et Chloe]. In [Ma] Mere l'Oye the sad wandering little Hop-o-my-Thumb, and the twittering birds that eat the crumbs, always delight me. I think the Fairy Garden section is a wonderful shimmering unforgettable piece of orchestration. Do you know the piano pieces, 'Valses Nobles et Sentimentales'? Of course La Valse, with its reckless daemonic whirl, is irresistible; and I am shallow enough to like the wistful 'Pavane' [pour une Infante défunte].

And in November 1943 he writes Smith: "Ravel doesn't age—for me: he seems to say that it is futile to feel, emotion is wasteful and useless, this surface sensation, this equable temper, this play with glittering, shimmering sound will suffice."

It is difficult to reconcile Trout's enthusiasm for Ravel with his lack of interest in jazz. Ravel drew inspiration from such Symbolist poets as Verlaine and Mallarmé; from Impressionism, Pointillism, and Cubism in the visual arts; and was eclectic in the composers and musical styles he looked to when creating his own compositions. A student of Gabriel Fauré, he found in composers like Chabrier, Rimsky-Korsakov, Mussorgsky, and Borodin rich sources of inspiration. Arnold Schoenberg's chromaticism and twelve-tone music interested him as much as did the orchestral works and songs of George Gershwin and American jazz and its African-American musical sources. When he visited the United States he made a point of frequenting jazz clubs in Harlem. The small-scale compositions of the seventeenth and eighteenth centuries also held a fascination for him. Basque by origin, he was drawn to all things Spanish, as works such as *Rhapsodie espagnole*, *Alborada del gracioso*, and *Boléro* testify. According to Vladimir Jankelevitch, "Ravel's music ... is always more or less a kind of pastiche." As his letters to Don Smith make clear, it was the sensuousness created by varied rhythms (dances like the Malaguenña, Boléro, Habañera, and Tango); by the ever-changing atmosphere of fevered dancing, perfumed gardens, and the nocturnal languor of Ravel's tempos and attraction to unusual instruments; by his penchant for uneven rhythms and asymmetric time signatures; and by the rich instrumental color of his orchestration that together made his music so appealing to Bill. Perhaps it was also the varied musical landscapes created by Ravel that drew Trout to him (Jankelevitch 1959, 8-9, 11, 16-17, 55-56, 124-126, 128, 132-133, 152-153, 46, 94-95, 99, 119).

It was what music said to him emotionally and philosophically through both its content and its formal qualities that seems to have mattered most to

Bill. What he had gleaned from Marcel Proust about "music as a means of communication," he found in classical music, particularly in the songs of certain composers, among them Schubert, Mahler, and Richard Strauss. A Schumann *Lied* ("Waldesgesprach") and Beethoven's last quartet provided inspiration for his verse. The memory of a melody and the happier times it brought to mind comes through in his poem:

Out of the past the voice that sang
"Du bist die hexei lorelei"
Rings again, as once it rang—
Rings again in memory.

Across the early autumn fields,
The rising sweep, the silver curve
Lift the wand such sorcery wields,
Sting to ecstasy the nerve

We thought had withered. Here among
Disease and terror, fear and death,—
Clear and steady, lingering long,
It rings—silver, with bronze beneath.

Throughout adulthood Bill was drawn to the life and works of Beethoven. The years of financial security and fame, when rich patrons supported his work, royalty paid him court, and a circle of friends gave him companionship and affection, began coming to an end for Beethoven in 1814. One by one his patrons died or abandoned him. Deafness compounded by problems with his eyes isolated him from people and increased both his loneliness and irascibility, which in turn alienated friends and acquaintances. In the face of declining commissions and repeated bouts of debilitating illness that kept him from working, his finances were further drained by a series of lawsuits and family quarrels. His poverty reduced him to living in cramped and squalid quarters. And his insensitive and ungrateful nephew Karl, whose guardian he was and whom he loved, hurt him deeply with his irresponsible behavior and indifference to his uncle's feelings. It was during the terrible years 1824-1826 (he died in 1827) that Beethoven wrote his last five string quartets. In July 1826 Karl tried to commit suicide, which filled Beethoven with grief and guilt. He was urged to leave the "wagging tongues" of Vienna and take Karl to the estate of his rich brother Nicholas Johann at Gneixendorf in Lower Austria.

In spite of frequent rows with his brother, Beethoven stayed at Gneixendorf from September 29 to December 1, 1826, during which time he finished his last complete composition by replacing the final movement of his B flat quartet, Op. 130. He left for Vienna on December 1 after a bitter quarrel with his brother. Riding in an open cart (his brother refused him the use of his closed carriage) in the teeth of inclement weather aggravated Beethoven's illness and no doubt contributed to his death four months later (De Marliave 1961, 197-218).

As scholars have noted, Beethoven's late quartets are fundamentally different from his earlier ones. The late quartets arc more subjective and intensely emotional; in the range and subtlety of the feelings they exhibit they are seen as expressions of the composer's inner consciousness. The loneliness, agony, and despair Beethoven experienced during the years in which he worked on the late quartets are apparent in the music. And in their complexity and the manner of their writing they are different from any of his other works. They are so deeply personal, enigmatic, and even obscure that they do not make easy listening, as some commentators have pointed out (De Marliave 1961, 219-224, 228). That Trout found in the late Beethoven quartets something that spoke to his own struggles, sorrow, and disillusionment, while taking comfort in the way Beethoven expresses his and even concedes a glimmer of hope in his final quartet, is apparent from the fact that he owned a number of recordings of these works and listened to them frequently over the years, and particularly in the last years of his life. What is more, he read and annotated De Marliave's book on them and studied his copies of the Eulenburg edition of the scores, in which he made notes on tempi, key changes, and other compositional matters as well as reflections on emotions expressed, such as "Smiles through tears" and "Longing for human intimacy unattainable." Bill owned a copy of J. W. N. Sullivan' *Beethoven: His Spiritual Development*, which he underlined, annotated, and filled with post-it notes containing references to the composer's life and works as well as to his own mother and family members. In his last five string quartets, as Sullivan points out, "Suffering no longer plays the part it did in the attitude of the young Beethoven," and that at the end the composer reached a "final serenity" (Sullivan 1960/1927, 168, 173), which Trout interpreted in his own way by writing at the bottom of the page: "Submission to suffering, because creation issues from that suffering." And yet no doubt thinking of his own suffering and that of others, Bill asked: "But what of those who are unable to create?" Clearly, he had doubts about his own poetic creativity.

Beethoven's last quartet, No. 16 in F major, Op. 135, is a retrospective piece, one that looks back over the composer's life from the happiness and confidence of the first movement, to a sparkling and vivacious second, to a third of deeply brooding tranquility, to a finale of peaceful resignation that begins with the musical question "Muss es sein?" (Must it be?), and is answered: "Es muss sein!" (It must be!). Yet one should not read too much into the grave opening of the final movement, to give it a metaphysical meaning or philosophical weight the composer may not have intended; for though the quartet speaks of weariness and impending death, it is also, as Sullivan observes, "the work of a man who is fundamentally at peace … a man who has known conflict, but whose conflicts are now reminiscent" (Forbes 1970, 1010, 975-977; Sullivan 1960/1927, 169). Beethoven's final quartet was one of Bill's favorite pieces, a work he listened to often late in life, suggesting his own search for inner piece, and which he uses as the theme for a poem describing how the music consoles him in his loneliness and sorrow and offers some hope that in death he might be reunited with his mother.

As though the May earth gathered silently, and folded quietly away—
Sheathed in leaf mold, fixed in clay, and over the stilled thing neatly drew
        the seamless green—
Poor misery unapt, unable to do more: so it is that the irascible,
That German in Vienna—his personal bizarreries so comforting to dull
    mediocrity—
Speaks in this Sixteen.
How—good God, but how—how did he know
Thus to gather mortal weariness, sick to death,
Sheathe it drowsily in May,
And fold it thus away, under the clover and the chalky yarrow. And yet,
Humanly, to whisper some blurred murmur, not quite intelligible
To an ear sinking slowly into sleep,
Some half-hint of a possible awakening
To the known face to the touch of the dear hands?
But here is "Muss es sein?"

Trout and the Finnish composer Jean Sibelius (1865-1957) shared certain personality traits which influenced their creative work and may help explain Bill's interest in his music. While Sibelius valued the solitude of country living and had a genuine love of nature, which informed so much of his

Figure 1 Village of Gap and Surrounding Area, 1951

Figure 2 Charles Edgar Trout

Figure 3 Alice Livingston Trout

Figure 4 William Trout as an Infant

Figure 5 William Trout at Age 18

Figure 6 Alice L. Trout, Frank Trout, and Mary Livingston, ca. 1919

Figure 7 William Henry Brown, ca. 1900

Figure 8 Centralized Public School, Gap, Pennsylvania

Figure 9 Elford Caughey, 1936

Figure 10 Donald Smith on Leave, Southern France, 1944

Figure 11 William Trout & Students on Christiana School Grounds, ca 1955

Figure 12 Frank Trout in Trout Family Living Room, Gap, 1958

Figure 13 William S. Trout, 1957

ENGLISH

Front Row: Dr. Mary A. Brightbill, Mr. Joseph E. Rhen, Mrs. Margaret Woodbridge, Dr. Lynwood S. Lingenfelter, *chairman.* *Middle Row:* Mr. R. Shields Metzler, Mr. William F. Diller, Mr. William Trout, Mr. Charles E. Cumpston. *Top Row:* Mr. Louis G. Jennings. *Absent:* Mr. Earle M. Hise.

Figure 14 Trout with English Department Colleagues at Millersville, 1959

music, his conducting engagements, foreign travel, and socializing with writers, composers, artists, and musicians gave his life a cosmopolitan quality not shared by Trout. They both suffered from loneliness, melancholy, and periodic bouts of depression, were acutely self-critical and haunted by self-doubt, all of which informed much of Trout's poetry and Sibelius' music. Both were drinkers, Sibelius going so far as to call alcohol "the only friend that never lets one down"; however, while Trout seems, for the most part, to have confined his "tippling" to home, Sibelius, whose drinking was apparently more serious, drank at home, and when he was young, engaged in boozing bouts with friends in hotel bars and restaurants. While Bill was frugal and lived a spartan life, Sibelius could not manage money and was constantly in debt (Barnett 2007, *passim*).

The agonies of life and the mystical qualities in nature were given musical expression by Sibelius. And while his orchestral works combine heroic affirmations, epic majesty, and haunting evocations of the natural world with deeply personal revelations of the composer's psychology and philosophical musings, Sibelius insisted he was "not a literary musician" and rejected assigning programmatic interpretations to his symphonies. The Fourth Symphony is his most personal and introspective work and certainly his least accessible (Barnett 2007, 211-213, 227, 229). Although Sibelius wrote a good many short, lighter pieces, the evidence suggests it was his symphonies and symphonic poems that appealed most to Trout. He tells Don Smith in a letter of 10 June 1944 that the finale of Sibelius' Second Symphony "is rather like being strapped to the bridge of the Queen Mary in a North Atlantic storm."

Growing out of the Finnish landscape and mythology, Sibelius' orchestral compositions express by purely musical means man's relationship to nature, the mysteries of life and death, and lament the transience of beauty and happiness. Steeped in the Finish landscape—its lakes, meadows, marshes, forests, mist, northern light, and sounds (among them the cries of swans and cranes)—gleaned from his travels around the country and daily walks in the countryside near his home north of Helsinki—Sibelius created seven symphonies all different from the work of any of his contemporaries and each of them unique. The melodies of his Fifth Symphony are informed by the crisp air, morning haze, and scent of the Finnish soil, and by the memory of the plaintive cries of swans, which he describes in his diary: "Just before ten to eleven I saw sixteen swans. One of the greatest experiences of my life. Oh God, what beauty! They circled over me for a long time. Disappeared into the hazy sun like a glittering, silver ribbon. Their cries were of the same woodwind timbre as those of cranes, but without the tremolo ... Nature's mystery and life's melancholy! The Fifth Symphony's finale theme." *The Oceanides* (1914), a tone poem the New York critic Olin Downs called "the finest evocation of the sea which has ever been produced in music" might be taken as the Nordic equivalent of Debussy's *Le Mer* (1903-1905). The longest of his tone poems, *Tapiola* (the domain of the forest god in Finnish mythology), evokes the "Northland's dusky forests, / Ancient, mysterious, brooding savage dreams" wherein "dwells the Forest's mighty God, / And wood-sprites in the gloom weave magic secrets"—themes certain to appeal to someone like Trout who was interested in myths and fairy tales. He owned a recording of *Tapiola*, which he tells Don Smith in a letter of 21 July 1945 he had listened to the night before. Many of Sibelius' shorter pieces for piano, voice, violin, and small instrumental ensembles take birds, flowers, trees or the seasons as themes. But his later works about nature are more conceptual than descriptive. The texts for his songs were drawn primarily from Nordic and German poets (Barnett 2007, 13, 45-46, 75, 103, 155, 192-193, 244-245, 308, 250, 242, 321, 262, 269, 272, 329).

The dark colors of Sibelius' music—reflecting his Nordic melancholy—call to mind Trout's poetic earth tones and "soft sorrow." But also like Trout's poetry, much of Sibelius' music is deeply personal and reflects changes in his psychological state. Many of his compositions, like many of Trout's poems, are not literal representations of the natural world containing programmatic elements or borrowings from everyday life like those found in works by Strauss or Mahler as they are remembrances or echoes of the soul. As Sibelius confided to his diary in 1910, a symphony is "an inner confession at a given stage of one's life" (Barnett 2007, 213). Likewise many of Trout's poems also take the form of confessions or statements of belief. Nordic austerity, rhythmic discipline, economy of means and formal compression, and the modification or outright abandonment of sonata form for what some critics call "rotational" or "cumulative" development combine to create the hypnotic effect of Sibelius' organic symphonies, and may help explain their appeal to Trout's appreciation for craftsmanship, love of nature, stoicism, and mysticism (Ross 2007, chap 5).

In his mid-thirties, Trout was also attracted to the works of Gustav Mahler (1860-1911), who like Sibelius wrote music that changed traditional orchestral composition and challenged both critics and audiences to rethink their ideas about the symphony. Mahler believed that the symphony "must be like the world [and] contain everything," while Sibelius "admired its strictness and the profound logic that creates an inner connection between all the motifs" (Barnett 2007, 185). Clearly Bill found both approaches to symphonic composition congenial since together they reflected his belief in the reciprocity of the rational and the intuitive and confirmed his own view of the centrality of the supernatural in the universe.

Mahler's symphonies contain many references to nature and everyday life in the countryside, among them birdcalls, cowbells, and sleigh bells. His Third Symphony is an all-encompassing vision of the universe and what nature has to teach humankind. It explores the great questions of existence and seeks answers to life's contradictions. The first four symphonies he wrote were based thematically on songs, some containing song phrases, others actual songs. There is a connection between Schubert's songs (which Bill knew well) and those of Mahler. As with Schubert, poetry-inspired lyricism was a part of Mahler's very being from an early age. He was a skillful versifier who modified lines of the original poems or created entirely new lines of his own to substitute for the originals as the need arose. And just as childhood memories informed his early compositions, so too did such memories form the basis of many of Bill's poems (Kennedy 2000, 33-34, 110, 124-125).

Both Mahler's music and Trout's poetry are autobiographical. For both men unhappy experiences in childhood stayed with them for life and left marks on their creative work. Their works grew out of their life experiences and reveal their inner lives, their psychology. Mahler's symphonies, particularly the early ones, contain musical memories of childhood: march tunes and rhythms of a military band, the hurdy-gurdy of a street musician, "Frère Jacques" (a French children's nursery tune), *Ländler* dance-tunes, folk-tunes learned from Slavic servant girls, songs sung by patrons in his father's tavern, and a klezmer band—all of which bewildered many concert-goers and which critics thought inappropriate in "serious" music. From childhood Mahler knew the folk-poetry collected by Achim von Arnim and Clemens Brentano in the early nineteenth century for their anthology *Des Knaben Wunderhorn* (The Youth's Magic Horn), whose poems inform his symphonies and from which he selected humorous, bitter, sad, playful, eerie, and macabre poems as text for his song cycle of the same title. As we have seen, Bill's library documents his keen interest in fairy tales and folk poetry.

As with Trout, Mahler's attitude toward religion was complex (he converted to Roman Catholicism from Judaism while retaining a deep-seated pantheism and being influenced by Oriental philosophies, perhaps Taoism among them), and his symphonies testify to both his struggle to free himself from the vicissitudes of life and find peace, and his life-long quest for spiritual enlightenment, a search that also engaged Bill to the end of his days and finds expression in his poetry. Mahler was a tortured soul and much of his music, but particularly his Sixth Symphony and his Ninth with their alternating expressions of hope and despair, reflect his angst and preoccupation with death, a preoccupation found in much of Trout's poetry as well. As Michael Kennedy observes, Mahler's "is music of exultation and hope, of fatalism and optimism, of anguished questioning and universal affirmation, worldly-wise and world-weary." At the core of all his works Kennedy insists is "conflict." His symphonies reflect what Bruno Walter, his protégé and close friend, describes as "the tragic existence of man" together with "that longing for fulfillment that search for answers to his questions about life, which always haunted him." And Mahler himself said: "Music must always contain yearning, a yearning for what is beyond the things of this world. Even in my childhood, music, for me, was something mysterious that lifted me above the world." We know from Trout's correspondence that music had a similar effect on him and that it was the purely musical aspects of Mahler's work (including the lyricism of the words/poetry in vocal texts) apart from its "content" that most appealed to Bill and may have left its mark on his poetry. Mahler's symphonies are tonal, psychological, and spiritual journeys of immense complexity that inspire reflection and contemplation. Through frequent key and tempo changes, varied rhythms, shifting timbres, and rich orchestral color his symphonies elicit both powerful and subtle emotions, from joy to anguish, soaring optimism to utter despair, turmoil to tranquility (Kennedy 2000, 1-8, 106-107, 110; Walter 1966, 122, 138).

Like Trout, Mahler, as Bruno Walter notes, was "a man deeply absorbed in cosmic problems, poignantly aware of the sorrows of humanity," whose "gaze was turned inward." Both were subject to bouts of depression, in part the result of personal tragedies and in part from their "agonized effort to find sense in human life." Trout's search for self-knowledge can be likened to what Bruno Walter calls Mahler's "unrestricted drive for self-revelation." Both men had a "religious cast of mind" but suffered a crisis of faith, trying to reconcile the evil and suffering in the world with the idea of a good and omnipotent God, and spent their lives searching for something to replace organized religion (Walter 1966, 160, 163, 145-146, 143). The Third Symphony, which Mahler said is about "my *personal* emotional life (in the form of what things"—flowers, animals, night, angles, love—"tell *me*"), ends in a "celebration of transcendent reconciliation" (of persistent earthly pain and divine love) in what one critic called the "hymnic splendour" of a chorale, "a prayer without words," reflecting Mahler's profound attachment to life (Franklin 1996, 49, 71, 29, 73). As Bruno Walter observes, "Music has … an incomparable power of drawing us toward the spiritual [and] also sows the seeds of faith. In its highest manifestations, it is mysteriously related to religion," something, as noted earlier, Trout acknowledged to Don Smith when he heard a radio broadcast of Toscanini conducting Beethoven's *Missa solemnis* and on first hearing Bach's *Saint Matthew Passion*. Both men found consolation in music for their pain and loneliness, Mahler by creating it and Trout by immersing himself in listening to it (Walter 1966, 150-151).

Bill confesses to Don Smith in a letter of 29 April 1944 to the "willful extravagance of buying Mahler's *Das Lied von der Erde*, "long a desire." He purchased a recording of the live performance of the Vienna Philharmonic led by Bruno Walter. In a long paragraph in a letter of 7 May 1944 he treats Don Smith to a sensitive and eloquent description of Mahler's *Das Lied von der Erde* (The Song of the Earth), saying of the German adaptations of Chinese poems by Li-Tai-Po, Tchang-Tsi, and Mong-Kao-Jen "to my delight" used as sources for the work's text:

> The resignation, the quiet acceptance of transitoriness of earthly beauty and mortal happiness, the fleeting of youth, the calm delight in wine and the poppy of oblivion… are transmuted with startling impact into the Western medium of music; the melancholy is Occidentally heightened and intensified—almost unbearable at times. My favorite [of the six poems Mahler used] has always been the second song, 'Der Einsame im Herbst' [The Lonely One in Autumn]. Even through the murk of the German you sense the drifting mists of autumn, the brittle grasses, the fading lotus blossoms on the brimming pools, the pale fleeting sunlight, the loneliness of the deserted heart.

By 15 July 1945, he admits to Smith he has grown "fanatical" about *Das Lied.* In a letter of 29 September 1945 he tells him: "The last section I think I could sing without notes, if I had a voice. That magnificent and resigned farewell to the beauty of the earth has no counterpart that I know, and with the approach of age, one grasps it with terrible clarity."

Bruno Walter saw *Das Lied von der Erde* as Mahler's "most personal utterance," and "more subjective than any of his previous works" (Walter 1966, 140-141). Mahler had begun the piece in 1907 and completed it in 1909 at a time when his doctors had already told him of his fatal heart condition. *Das*

Lied (what some scholars call a symphonic song-cycle), with its songs about male friendship, combines the sensuousness of earthly life with feelings of loneliness, a sense of transcendence and dissolution without any certainty of religious immortality. In a letter penned early in 1909 Mahler wrote: "What nonsense it is to let one's self be submerged by the brutal whirlpool of life; to be false, even for a moment, to one's self and what is above ourselves." Just as Beethoven's final quartet and Sibelius' Fourth Symphony end on a note of peaceful resignation, so in *Das Lied*, as Walter says, in spite of the sadness at departing this life, "Earth at the leave-taking shows a face of tender loveliness" (Walter 1966, 173-174): "The dear earth everywhere / blossoms in spring and grows green again! / Everywhere and eternally the distance shines bright and blue! / Eternally … Eternally." No wonder Bill found it "magnificent" and with "no counterpart."

That the passage of time, partings, the transience of earthly things are mentioned often in Trout's letters, help explain the music and literature he found most appealing, and informs the tone of much of his poetry. He asks Smith in a March 1945 letter if he remembers Walter de la Mare's poem "Music," and then quotes its third quatrain:

> When music sounds, all that I was I am
> Ere to this haunt of brooding dust I came;
> While from Time's woods break into distant song
> The swift-winged hours, as I hasten along.

But nowhere did Trout experience Time's poignancy and bitter-sweetness more than in his beloved *Der Rosenkavalier*, with whose principal character he so obviously identified. In one of the Marschallin's first act arias, Strauss adapted a line from François Villon—"Go, seek the snows of yester year!"—the implications of which would not have been lost on Bill. He understands the Marschallin when she tells Octavian: "Time is a strange thing. When one lives for the moment, time means nothing at all. And then, of a sudden, one is aware of nothing else. It is all around us, even! Oh, often I hear it flowing, irrevocably. Often I get up in the middle of the night and make all, all the clocks stand still"—lines Bill quoted in German in a letter he sent Don Smith in December of 1943. As Beth Hart points out, the relationship between the Marschallin and her teenage lover Octavian is the struggle to reconcile "the longing for symbiosis and oneness with the equally powerful drive for individuation." Bill knew what the Marschallin means in her duet with Octavian in which she foresees the inevitable end of their relationship by telling him, "everything disperses like mist and dreams." She senses that like sand through an hourglass, everything slips away; that in life nothing lasts forever; that everything has its season and only by finding inner resources can one "face life's ultimate loneliness." He also grasped the meaning of her admonition to, "hold and take, hold and relinquish" and her warning that those who do not "will be punished by life and God, and God will have no pity on them." But he also knew from experience that no matter how firmly knotted the strings of partings or death may be tied, they always leave threads dangling in the breeze. As he tells Smith in a letter, it is the aria at the end of the first act, when the Marschallin (who is in her thirties, as Bill was when he first heard the opera on a Saturday Met broadcast in January of 1939) realizes Octavian, her seventeen-year-old lover, will one day leave her, that Bill takes as the theme for his poem:

> And still she sings, the Marschallin,
> As on that afternoon of snow
> A January long ago;
> Magicks the grimness that between
> Summons pain and shame in vain,
> And then rebuked, withdraws its bane.
>
> And we sit here, limp hand, slack jaw,
> Remembering "in die Kirchen gehn";
> The fiddles sighed exquisite pain,
> And youth's bland edict, smiling law,
> Ironically evoked the flower
> Of resignation from the hour.

The poem captures something of what he confesses to Don Smith in a letter postmarked 31 January 1944: "The end of the first act, with the Marschallin saying [at the moment she accepts that she and Octavian must part] those trivial things about going to church ['in die Kirchen gehn'] and driving in the Prater and visiting her old uncle, while the music is saying all the yearning, caressing things that lie beneath—is there any love music more tender and moving." Some of the sopranos who have sung the Marschallin have taken a tearful, clinging approach to portraying this woman who is being deserted by her lover; others have conveyed a somewhat bitter reaction to the boy's "betrayal," but Lotte Lehmann's "maternal" approach to the role, as Beth Hart characterizes it, is convincing in the way she consoles the youth's bruised ego in the first act—by assuring him, "I do not wish to torment you, my darling. I'm saying what is true, saying it to myself [that they will part] as well as to you"—and in final trio in the last act urging him, as a mother does a child reluctant to leave home, to go to Sophie, for whom his love the older woman reads in his eyes. Lehmann's portrayal of the Marschallin was certainly one reason for Bill's devotion to the work of this gifted artist. The psychologically complex character of the Marschallin is, as Hart observes, a mirror held up to the audience so that they might find in themselves the strength to accept graciously what in life cannot be changed. It is the diametric opposite of what Mann's Aschenbach does in his pursuit of Tadzio or Dylan Thomas' advice on aging and death, "Rage, rage against the dying of that light," in his poem "Do not go gently into that good night." The Marschallin's letting go of the summer of life and accepting life's approaching autumn is an affirmation of Jung's views on the stages of life that would not have escaped Trout (Hart 1999, 420-429).

And of the opera's end, when the Marschallin does "cherish him in the right way" by leaving Octavian with Sophie, his new young love, Bill describes the emotional impact for him in a letter to Don Smith: "Over it all is the mask of worldliness, of over precise and weary civilization; but behind the mask are all the shabby, loveable, passionate truths of the human heart. From the time, in the last act when the Marschallin takes the chair proffered by Octavian until the final curtain, I don't even make an attempt to behave like a normal human being."

In a letter of 10 June 1944, Bill urges Smith to listen to the complete *Der Rosenkavalier*, saying "It remains one of the few reasons one occasionally feels compensated for the sordidness and hatefulness of life; and it holds, suspended as in crystal, all the passion and ecstasy, all the degradation and humiliation of love, the unbelievable joy and the wrench of loss and the slow pain of resignation."

Chapter 7
Literary Interests — British and European

The authors of both fiction and poetry whose work Trout chose to teach in his college courses, as well as the content of his lectures and letters, reveal much about his philosophy of life, values, literary tastes; his search for self-knowledge; and his own approach to the content, technique, and style of writing poetry. However, considerations of space and available documentary evidence do not allow all of his literary interests to be explored here in equal depth. But mention must be made of his fondness for Charles Dickens, of whom he said in a letter to me of 20 June 1971, "in spite of his faults," he has, "as [G. K.] Chesterton notes, a fecundity that is matched only by Shakespeare and Chaucer." We know from other letters that he read Dickens novels to his mother in her old age, as she had read them to him as a child. The remainder of this chapter explores Trout's principal British and European literary interests.

Bill was drawn to writers whose fiction or poetry addressed psychological and philosophical issues and grew out of lived reality and deeply felt personal emotions. For more than a decade, beginning in the mid-1960s, he carried on a correspondence with Professor T. E. M. Boll of the University of Pennsylvania. Boll was delighted Bill shared his interest in the British author May Sinclair and surprised, as Bill told me in a letter of 1 August 1971, that his "affection and admiration [for her went] back to 1924, no less," while he was still a high school student. He owned copies of all Sinclair's novels, as well as her collected stories and verse and her two philosophical works, *A Defense of Idealism* and *The New Idealism*. The underlining in Trout's copy of her *The Dark Night*, which deals with aging, illness, and death, as well as questions of faith, testifies to his careful reading of her work. He also had a file folder containing both her journal articles and articles about her. He gave three of Sinclair's letters found in secondhand copies of her novels to Boll, who had started the collection of her papers at Penn; a gift acknowledged in Boll's critical biography of the writer.

May Sinclair was a feminist committed to women's suffrage who served briefly in an ambulance corps in World War I. An early advocate of psychoanalysis, she gave financial support to the Medico-Psychological Clinic of London, and in 1914 was elected to the board of the Society for Psychical Research, whose members investigated various manifestations of parapsychology. She read papers at psychological and philosophical conferences. In her two-part article "Symbolism and Sublimation," published in 1916, she analyzed the theories of Freud, Adler, and Jung and concluded, as Boll points out, that while Freud "revolted and depressed," Jung "consoled and encouraged." Trout often wrote Sinclair's name or initials in the margins of his Jung volumes indicating where the psychologist and the novelist shared common ground. Yet unlike Freud and Jung, Sinclair believed that sublimation was "the only effectual form of self-assertion and redress" and that both "underrated the value of repression, which at some period must have been of advantage to the race." Yet the principal character in her 1907 novel *The Helpmate* insists: "That there is no spirituality worthy of the name that has not been proven in the house of flesh," an observation sure to have attracted Trout's attention. She also thought that while Freud had failed to link psychoanalysis and psychotherapy, "Jung had built that bridge with his discovery of the function of the symbol," a view central to explaining Trout's interest in Jung and obviously influential in his thought and poetry. As Boll puts it: "The core of meaning running through May Sinclair's novels is a person's progress toward becoming an individual self ["individuation"] against the forces outside the person, such as family, class, and convention, and inside the person, such as racial, heredity, and singular forces." In addition to philosophical works, novels, poetry, and criticism, Sinclair wrote short fiction, including horror, ghost, and occult stories (Boll 1973, 256-259, 82-90, 104-105, 108-109, 193, 140-141).

May was the only one of the Sinclair children for whom there is no baptismal record. Though she later became interested in Buddhism, her father's alcoholism, problems with family finances, the horrors of the 1914-18 war, the experience of caring for her ill and aged mother, and the deaths of three brothers all contributed to her religious doubts and growing agnosticism (Boll 1973, 24-26, 39, 61, 115). Her life experiences, intellectual interests, and loneliness must have made her seem a kindred spirit to the brilliant and deeply sensitive high school student, and later schoolmaster, trapped in the isolating world of Gap, which for Bill may have seemed the equivalent of Edwin Arlington Robinson's "Tilbury Town."

As will be discussed in the next chapter, Trout held Robinson in high regard as a poet. Sinclair's article, "Three American Poets of To-Day"—E. A. Robinson, William Vaughn Moody and Ridgely Torrence—(published both in the United States and in England in 1906), Bill says in an August 1971 letter to me, "made EAR known and appreciated in England." He also notes that the two of them "once stood for almost an entire night on Brooklyn Bridge, talking." Not only did Sinclair cherish her friendship with Thomas Hardy—another writer Trout admired—she also had close ties to the Imagist poets and gave financial support to Ezra Pound, who was not among the poets Bill admired. But the same cannot be said of Charlotte Mew, a poet who ranked high in Trout's literary pantheon. Sinclair, an early supporter of Mew, in time hurt her deeply by rejecting her love and then telling others about Mew's lesbianism (Boll 1973, 82-87, 103-110; Boll 1970, 453).

Bill had known Charlotte Mew's verse since 1934 when he ordered copies of it from Harold Monro's Poetry Bookshop in London, where not only were books sold but also published, particularly the work of modern poets. Regular poetry readings were held there featuring such contemporary poets as Rupert Brooke, W. B. Yeats, Walter de la Mare, T. S. Eliot, Ezra Pound, Edith Sitwell, and Robert Graves, as well as Harold Monro (Grant 1967, 75-86). Trout's book purchase initiated a decades-long correspondence with Alida Klementaski, Monro's assistant and later his second wife. They exchanged Christmas greetings over the years, wrote each about their old houses (hers, Haise Farm near Chichester in Sussex, was nearly two hundred years old and stood on a site occupied by a house since 1209), and discussed books and writers. In 1961 Mrs. Monro sent Bill, as a New Year's present, a copy of *Poems Penyeach* (1927) containing fifteen poems by James Joyce, explaining: "It is the only edition in which these poems of Joyce appeared & for which the Poetry Bookshop was joint publisher with Shakespeare & Co" (the Paris bookshop owned by Sylvia Beach and frequented by the likes of T. S. Eliot, Ernest Hemingway, Scott Fitzgerald, and Gertrude Stein). She came to the United States in the summer of 1963 to lecture on "Harold Monro and the Poetry Bookshop Circle" and sent him a note thanking him for sending her "those lovely roses—you could not know it, but those dark red ones are my favorite flower—they are simply lovely & I have them in my room at [Hilltop House in Devon, Pennsylvania where she was staying] & they have opened during the night & are making a wonderful show this morning." She had sent Bill a printed invitation to attend her lecture at Drexel Institute of Technology in Philadelphia, writing at the bottom of the card, "Do come!"

He didn't. And she never got to meet her "old friend" as she called him in her letters. Both championed the poetry of Charlotte Mew.

Mew's life was tragic, a chronicle of poverty, adversity, illness, and death—three siblings died in childhood, then her father, next her mother (long an invalid for whom she cared), and finally her beloved sister, Anne. Poems such as "Expecto Resurrection" and "To A Child in Death" written years after the their deaths record her lingering grief. Later two other siblings were committed to mental hospitals—her sister Freda and brother Henry, who suffered from schizophrenia—which may in part account for her asylum poems, "Ken" and "On the Asylum Road." Like Trout, she had low self-esteem. When Alida Monro met her for the first time at a reading in the Poetry Bookshop and asked, "Are you Charlotte Mew?," she was told, "with a slight smile, 'I am sorry to say I am.' " She suffered rejection by the two loves of her life and paid dearly not only for her sexual orientation but for ignoring society's norms by cropping her hair, wearing tailored men's clothes, smoking in public, and using strong language. Though never explicitly addressing her lesbianism, she encoded her verse to express the pain of concealing her sexuality, as in "The Farmer's Bride" and "Saturday Market" (Fitzgerald 1984, 16-17, 43-47, 48-49, 169, 184-186, 189-189, 191-193, 206, 150, 128, 133).

Like Ralph Hodgson—for whom Bill once confessed "a life-long, profound, and unchanging devotion to the work of one of the few significant figures in 20th-century literature"—Mew was so demanding in her poetic technique that only a small number of her poems were published in her lifetime. She apparently destroyed many poems, leaving only a handful to be published after her suicide in 1928 (Monro 1953, vii-xviii). The central themes of her poetry—developed through interior monologues—dealt with loss, isolation, disillusionment, disappointment, sexual longing, and death. She never subscribed to the conventions of the Modernists, preferring to adapt traditional diction and metrics in unique ways. Her free-rhyming verse resembles the manner of speech, resulting in changes of meter within the line, something Walter de la Mare, the consummate metrical purist, did not approve. As with Mew's poems, some of Trout's don't scan with the regularity and purity found in de la Mare verse. "Hers is the distillation, the essence of emotion," Louis Untermeyer observes, "rather than the stirring up of passion." And he goes on to say: "Her most remarkable work is in dramatic projections and monologues" filled with "fantastic pathos" and "powerful meditation." "Apart from her other qualities (not the least of which is her control of an unusually long and extraordinarily flexible line)," he concludes,

"Miss Mew's work is a series of triumphs in condensation" (Fitzgerald 1984, 122, 164; Untermeyer 1962, 158-159).

In her friendly, chatty letter of 10 January 1954, Monro tells Bill not only about her hobby breeding and showing miniature Poodles—she sent a photograph of herself with two of them to him in 1964—and a recent visit with the poet Ralph Hodgson, but also about her lectures, broadcasts, and literary tours reading Charlotte Mew's poetry, as well as relating her efforts with editors (alas unsuccessful) to get Mew's stories published. Her postscript mentions that she hoped to publish a book the following year on the Poetry Bookshop that would include information on Mew and other writers associated with it, and closes by saying: "It is refreshing to know there are still people alive [an obvious reference to Bill] to whom poetry, real poetry means something." Bill tells me in a letter of 12 August 1971 that Mew had "an intensity and a rhythmic lyricism rarely equaled." He mentions in one of his wartime letters to Don Smith that he keeps the last line of Mew's poem "Smile, Death" tucked in the corner of his bedroom mirror: "And we will not speak of life or believe in it or remember it as we go" (from *The Rambling Sailor*, 1929).

Something of Mew's circumspection and wish to obscure meaning through coding seem to inform some of Bill's poems, as in the following one which may be an encrypted admission. It addresses things about himself that he felt a need to conceal but wanted to acknowledge, but only if wrapped in ambiguity. He hints at unspecified temptations, desires, of a hunger for companionship but rejects "Convention's … frugal charity," which he likens to a "crowded hostel" with a leaky roof and reeking of 'other armpits'," and instead dons a mask beyond which he can still hear shrill cries "hinting" other possibilities. It is the assertion of the quiet nonconformist living to himself but paying a price for it by having to hide those ideas, needs, and desires that run counter to social conventions.

Since contiguity is, at a pinch,
Conceivable, though named improbable,
Age, thereby, is not constrained to blench,
Forswear, conform, if intuition lobs
Some lure a little down the way, leading
Into the pool of shadow. Who shall say
The lobbed allure is less than science? Need
Hungers for company; then why stay?
And stay for what? Convention's providence

Proffers a frugal charity, provides
Only a crowded hostel, viscid with reek
Of other armpits—and the roof leaks,—
Though mask be donned, beyond the mask there cries
A shrill unknown, hinting further skies.

Goethe's *Faust*, as noted earlier, is important to understanding William Trout the man and the poet, as a number of the issues addressed both in his letters and his reading of Jung suggest. In a lecture on Goethe's great drama, he says: "Faust learned that to find his soul, he must maintain the thirst for all experience, including all experience of evil, so called. He must hope only for new experiences, and each day new experience." Thus, he observes: "Faust learned that the will to live is not educated by experience." To which he adds parenthetically: "That is, by the way, a basic idea underlying Proust's great novel, The Remembrance of Things Past—that we are basically unteachable, that we endlessly repeat our errors." Perpetual dissatisfaction—the Romanticist idea that "the worth of life lies in the pursuit, not the attainment," being always "miscellaneous, indefinite, unfinished"—Trout observes is essential to salvation, though not of the conventional Christian type. As he points out, the play ends with Faust's soul being borne away by angels who drown out the voice of negation, Mephistopheles, with their chant, "Whoe'er aspires unweariedly / Is not beyond redeeming," which must have given Bill some comfort and perhaps a little hope. Faust's experience of transcending time and space, not only time past but the future—something addressed by Jung's collective unconscious and his views on synchronicity—also engaged Trout's imagination, and may have reinforced his interest in the Tarot and the occult.

It was psychological and philosophical issues that in part drew Trout to Thomas Mann, particularly, as he tells Don Smith in a letter of 11 June 1945, to *The Magic Mountain*, which he says "is a warmer thing, more human, if less as artistic achievement, than Proust: Proust is so objective, the striving after some reality is so alien to him; but Mann recognizes and dignifies a need that Proust would look on as a genuine but rather limited manifestation of the mind ... You must read this book. No[t] the least of its charms is its discussion of Castrop's discovery of music." This novel, published in 1924, examines German bourgeois society in the years before World War I, and in the process explores, among other matters, questions related to sickness and health (particularly the relationship between disease and artistic creativity), life and death, culture versus civilization, democracy versus authoritarianism, intellect versus emotion, mysticism and the supernatural, man's relationship to nature, and "forbidden" love (Heilbut 1996, 401-402, 410-411). Throughout the novel philosophical debates take place between Settembrini, who represents the secular humanism of the eighteenth-century Enlightenment with its optimistic belief in progress, rationalism, liberalism, and pragmatism, and Naptha, who is hostile to modernity and an apostle of violence and reactionary radicalism. The two men compete to convince Hans Castorp, the novel's hero, to accept their particular world-view. In the end, though more inclined to Settembrini's philosophical views, he rejects both.

A central theme of the novel is the nature of time, a topic we know interested Trout and informs much of his poetry. "At least as much as Proust's masterpiece," Anthony Heilbut insists, "*The Magic Mountain* is about the movement of time" and employs a greater variety of types of time than did Proust in *Remembrance of Things Past* (Heilbut 1996, 416, 545). Although the topic of time runs throughout the novel, it receives its most extended discussion in the "By the Ocean of Time" section, where its varied manifestations appear in relation to literature and music. "For time is the medium of narration," Mann claims, "as it is the medium of life. Similarly, time is the medium of music; music divides, measures, articulates time, and can shorten it, yet enhances both at once. Thus music and narration are alike, in that they can only present themselves as flowing ..." (Mann 1927, 683). But as the discussion of time in relation to storytelling and music goes on, the characters examine differences in the nature of time.

Music also plays an important part in Mann's fiction, particularly in *Doctor Faustus* and in *The Magic Mountain*, in which the sanitarium patients each evening listen to gramophone recordings of *excerpts* (which Mann sees as rather bourgeois) from operas by Mozart, Offenbach, Gounod, Verdi, and to Schubert's songs (Heilbut 1996, 37, 403; Mann 1939, 800-818). Hans Castorp's favorite Schubert *Lied* is "The Linden-Tree" because of its association with memories of a classmate, Pribislav Hippe, his first love. Mann modeled Hippe (a blonde schoolboy whose "eyes were a grey-blue, or a blue-grey ... like the hue of far-distant mountain ranges") on the object of his own childhood love, a blonde-blue-eyed classmate named Armin Martens. The song's lyrics tell of a linden tree on which were carved "words of love I made" and under which were had "sweet dreams" of love for "a beloved companion" recalled in later life. In a masterful example of his skill at innuendo and concealment, Mann says that trying to understand what "The Linden-Tree" "meant" to Castorp "is a truly ticklish endeavour; requiring great delicacy of emphasis" to avoid doing "more harm than good" because "the love felt for such a creation is in itself 'significant': betraying something of the person who cherishes it...." But in the end, without ever naming Pribislav Hippe as "the object of love" that causes Castorp to take stock "as to the ultimate propriety of his love for the enchanting *Lied*," Mann intimates that it grew out of "forbidden love" (Heilbut 1996, 408-409, 418-420; Mann 1939, 155-159, 818-822). The perceptive Trout, who marked "The Linden-Tree" in his copy of Schubert's song scores, would have understood Mann's inference.

Mann was knowledgeable about classical music and opera, particularly that of Richard Wagner, in addition to holding the works of Richard Strauss and Evard Grieg in high regard. As Heilbut observes, he found in the elements and methods of musical composition, and "particularly Wagner's leitmotifs, a method of organizing experience" that gave a symphonic quality to his stories and novels, something Mann himself acknowledged, saying that from early in his career he had a "deep inward affinity" for music and "a tendency to apply its techniques" to his own art form. According to Heilbut, Mann's "prose becomes symphonic in its never-ending series of climaxes and cadenzas" (Heilbut 1996, 37, 64-65, 71, 74, 108, 517). As will be discussed later, Trout had recognized, years earlier, the direct influence of music on Mann's fiction and no doubt saw it as well in the novels of E. M. Forster, something the British writer made explicit.

Mann met Gustav Mahler after the premier performance of his Symphony No. 8, and modeled the physical appearance of Aschenbach in *Death in Venice* on the composer. Inscribing a copy of one of his books he sent to the composer, Mann wrote: "To Gustav Mahler: In whom, as I believe, I recognize the most serious and holy artistic will of our era." While listening to Tchaikovsky's Sixth Symphony, the *Pathetique*, which he describes as a work "inclining to the overly sweet," Mann "intuited the 'depression of a boy lover' " (Heilbut 1996, 235, 247, 253, 395, 556). Perceptive as he was, Trout may well have drawn a similar conclusion from listening to his recordings of Tchaikovsky and from reading his copies of "*Beloved Friend": The Story of Tchaikowsky and Nadej von Meck* by Catherine Drinker Bowen and Barbara von Meck, and from Herbert Weinstock's biography of the composer. Thus Mann and Trout shared similar interests in music that included a number of the same composers. What is more, in sections of the novel the atmosphere or mood is colored by suggestions of Wagner's operas *Tristan and Isolde* and *Tanhausser. The Magic Mountain*, Trout told his Millersville classes, is "perhaps the most important novel of our century." In it, he observes, Mann suggests how both those "who have the gift of seeing" and those "who have the gift of creating" can become reconciled to "a purposeless universe: accept the disease from which you suffer—learn to use it—and take your delight from the form imposed upon chaos by the artists who work with so little reward, work perhaps especially for such as you." But he does not clarify for his students that the "disease" which troubles Hans Castorp is not tuberculosis but repressed homosexuality.

In recommending Mann's *Death in Venice* to Don Smith in a letter of 6 June 1945, Bill calls it "a beautiful and very disturbing story on a theme generally designated as 'questionable,' a small masterpiece you will never forget." Disease, decay, and death and their relationship to art and creativity recur in Mann's fiction, including his novels *Buddenbrooks* (1901), *The Magic Mountain* (1924), and the *novella Death in Venice* (1911). Given Trout's obsession with time and its effects, and that even in his thirties he thought of himself as "old," what he might have found in *Death in Venice* of particular relevance to his own life, in addition to the theme of forbidden love, was Mann's exploration of the psychological experiences of aging, a theme explored by David English (English 2008). Set in Venice, the Byzantium of the West, with its associations of exotic beauty, decadence, and decay, Mann describes the flagging artistic creativity, loss of a sense of personal worth or purpose, feelings of futility and hopelessness, diminished physical energy, loneliness, and a longing for emotional attachment experienced by his principal character, the aging Gustav von Aschenbach, who had lost his wife and children as well as the ability to continue the passion of his life, creative writing. Contrary to Carl Jung's admonition not to extend the expansive goals and practices of youth into the autumn of life, advice Trout appears to have followed, Aschenbach goes to Venice to recapture the inspiration and creativity he had as a writer earlier in life, where he succumbs to another youthful practice, falling in love, and is besotted by the beauty of an adolescent Adonis whom he stalks through the streets of the city. He makes repeated trips to a barber in an effort to give himself a more youthful appearance by styling and dying his hair and by the application of cosmetics to mask his age-lined face in a pathetic attempt to expand a relationship with a boy named Tadzio, whose half-smile acknowledgement of the old man had precipitated Aschenbach's infatuation. The *novella* is filled with symbols of death, another theme that we have seen fascinated Trout: the stranger Aschenbach sees at the Byzantine-style mortuary chapel in the old Munich graveyard early in the story; the unlicensed, Charon-like (in Greek mythology the boatman who ferries the souls of the dead across the river Styx to Hades) gondolier who rows Aschenbach to his hotel in a Venetian gondola, "black as nothing on earth except a coffin" (shades of Arnold Böcklin's painting *The Isle of the Dead* [1880], a black-and-white photograph of which inspired the artist, and Rachmaninov's 1909 symphonic poem of the same title); the leering, vulgar red-headed leader of a troupe of street singers who invade the grounds of the hotel; and finally to Tadzio himself standing on the shore pointing out to sea, a reference to the god Mercury who guided the dead to the banks of the Styx (Mann 1936, 378-437).

But it is Mann's *novella Tonio Kröger*, a story on one level that treats the joys and sorrows, the yearnings and aspirations, and the crushing disappointments and bitter disillusionment of youth, Trout assigned to students and explicated in a Millersville lecture, and in the process gives us important insights into his own personality or psyche, as well as a revelation of the life experiences that shaped his own self-image and contributes to the tone of much of his poetry.

The character Tonio Kröger, Trout explains, is not just about the psychology of the artist. "A closer examination reveals that the human value of 'Tonio Kröger' lies in its being a scrutiny not alone of that strange human being—the practicing writer—but of every human being who, through some chance or through some ironic jest of nature, enters life bearing a physical or a mental trait [in Tonio's case repressed homosexuality] that diverges from the so-called normal, a trait that seems to prevent his assimilation into the aggregate of society." Interestingly, Trout digresses in the lecture to tell the story of Philoctetes in the *Iliad*, a man with a mysterious and stinking wound that never heals, who, though he inherited the magic bow the god Apollo gave to Hercules, was abandoned on an island by the Greek army bound for Troy. Two twentieth-century writers who took an interest in the legend of Philoctetes with its idea that "genius and disease, like strength and mutilation, may be inextricably bound up together," were Andre Gide (whose writings Mann admired) and John Jay Chapman, who like Philoctetes and Tonio, Bill observes, "stood at an angle to the morality of society." Is this perhaps a cloaked confession on Bill's part? Gide's 1899 play, *Philoctetes*, was a reworking of Sophocles' drama of the same title, and while there is no evidence that Trout read Gide's work there is no doubt that he knew of both Gide and Chapman. Like Mann, who dropped hints about his homoerotic desires and whose adolescent love for a fellow student was the basis for *Tonio*

Kröger, Trout may have been hinting at his own homosexuality. Another autobiographical parallel he underscores is that Tonio, a classic introverted personality in the Jungian meaning of the term, suffers from a "sense of isolation and inferiority" and from the "unreciprocated feelings" for his "normal" classmates, the beautiful Ingeborg Holm and the handsome, athletic Hans Hansen (his boyhood love), both of whom are extraverts and heterosexuals. Like Tonio, Bill was a very bright and serious student. As Mann tells us, Tonio often asked himself: "Why is it I am different, why do I fight everything, why am I … like a stranger among the other boys?" To this question Bill offers one answer in noting that Tonio, unable to shed his bourgeois sensibilities, is accused by his friend Lisaneta of being "a Bohemian with a bad conscience," "a *bourgeois manqué*"—of straying off into art—a charge Bill might have thought applied to him as well—a failed bourgeois and would-be poet. Judging from his letters, the marginal notes in his Jung volumes, and his poems, Trout was, as Mann says of Tonio, "looking within, into himself, the theater of so much pain and longing." What Tonio says of himself seems equally true of Bill: "I stand between two worlds. I am at home in neither, and I suffer in consequence." But what he doesn't share with his students are his thoughts on Tonio's final observation about himself which brings the *novella* to an end: "But my deepest and secretest love belongs to the blond and blue-eyed, the fair and living, the happy, lovely, and commonplace" (Mann, 1936, 88, 110, 96, 131-132).

The appeal of Mann's work to Trout and the high esteem in which he held it is summarized at the end of his lecture on *Tonio Kröger*. The encyclopedic range of Mann's interests that saw him address political issues, moral and philosophical questions, music, psychoanalysis, and more impressed him. The ability of Mann to "perform his exposition of a character's psychology" without resorting to "textbook" analysis won his praise, as did Mann's skillful use of "dualism" (spirit versus material, normal versus abnormal, complex versus naïve, illness versus health) and irony. He valued the fact that Mann created characters willing to ignore convention, to "cast the old aside," and try new things. Bill's knowledge of music and awareness that Mann shared his love of it led him to suggest that the structure of *Tonio Kröger* "is based on the structure of the sonata: anticipation, exposition, variation, recapitulation." He believed that Mann "brought to perfection the symphonic novel," a novel "constructed as a symphony for a large orchestra." And finally, Trout says that he had "always been arrested by Mann's interest in the occult; in his essay—'An Experience in the Occult'[1923]—he makes it plain that he believes in the authenticity of some spiritualist mediums and in their findings." He might also have noted Mann's fascination with the strange and the macabre, an interest the two also shared.

But what Bill did not tell Don Smith or his Millersville students, though he dropped hints about it in discussing *Death in Venice* and *Tonio Kröger*, was that Thomas Mann was homosexual as were two of his sons and a daughter. Though some friends and members of his family knew of his sexual orientation, Mann, who was married for fifty years and fathered six children, had to repress any open expression of homoerotic desire both in keeping with the social conventions of the day and because paragraph 175 of the 1871 German constitution criminalized homosexuality. What is more, Mann learned from the publicity occasioned by the 1908 Eulenberg case—in which many wealthy and powerful men were ruined by being implicated in a homosexual clique at the Kaiser's court—that one's career and reputation could be destroyed by revelations of one's homosexuality (Heilbut 1996, x, 14, 40, 210). As a result Mann was, for the most part, circumspect about his sexual orientation and repressed the urge to act on it by sublimating his homoerotic desires in his fiction. Two volumes of Mann's letters were translated into English and published in 1971, but his diaries, which contain unequivocal proof of his homosexuality, were not published in English until 1995, years after Trout's death. Nonetheless, the hints Mann dropped in his novels and short fiction about his sexual preference would not have been missed by any fellow traveler, particularly one as sensitive and discerning as Bill.

As an adolescent, Mann fell in love with at least two of his classmates and throughout his life, though he also had erotic feelings for men in their twenties, was primarily attracted to adolescent males. At age seventy-five he wrote, "That the adoration of 'godlike youths' surpasses that for everything feminine and arouses a desire comparable to *nothing* in the world is my axiom." Anthony Heilbut makes a convincing case that Mann's "sexuality animates his fiction." There are intimations of homoeroticism in *The Confessions of Felix Krull*, *Joseph and His Brothers*, and *Doctor Faustus* (novels Trout owned), and, Heilbut maintains, "*The Magic Mountain* was fundamentally a narrative of desire"; indeed, "a novel about forbidden love." At the age of fourteen, Mann fell in love with his classmate, Armin Martens, an infatuation that served as the model for Tonio's crush on Hans Hansen in *Tonio Kröger*, as Willri Timpe, another of Mann's adolescent heartthrobs, was for Hans Castrop's love for his schoolmate Pribislav Hippe in *The Magic Mountain*. Like Tadzio—the "long-haired boy of about fourteen" with "honey-coloured ringlets" and the face of a Greek god—whom Gustave Aschenbach falls in love with in *Death in Venice*, Hippe and Hans Hansen are blond-haired beauties, as was Mann's classmate Armin Martens. Tadzio's beauty is, however, compromised by imperfect teeth, which are "rather jagged and bluish, without a healthy glaze," suggesting sickness and reminding us of a variation on the legend of Philoctetes (Mann 1936, 396, 404). When he was twenty-four, Mann met the Ehrenberg brothers, Paul and Carl, who were also in their twenties, and fell in love with the former, with whom he may have had a sexual relationship. Writing to their sister, Mann tells her: "Through his personality, Paul is the dearest fellow, but Carl has music on his side, the art which I pursue amorously because of the unrequited love in my heart." Might a similar devotion to music have underpinned Bill's sense of unfulfilled love? Certainly his letters suggest it. When Mann was seventy-six, the great love of his life was Franz Westermeier, a nineteen-year-old waiter who was unaware of Mann's feelings for him. In his late seventies Mann wrote in his diary of the impossibility "that any young man could love me." Yet as Heilbut points out, "his pessimism dated from adolescence" and is reflected in his fiction; for his characters—Tonio Kröger, Hans Castrop, and Aschenbach—all experience unrequited love, just as Mann did with his schoolmates, waiter, and perhaps Paul Ehrenberg. "Mann's career," Heilbut observes, "may be read as a tale of profound erotic disappointment, and its diversion into and projection onto the widest range of disparate subjects. The loss informed his lifetime of melancholy" (Heilbut 1996, 14-17, 38-39, 52, 56-57, 120-124, 340, 247, 265, 433, 502, 452-454, 401, 406, 408, 45).

The tone of Trout's letters to Don Smith and some of his poems suggest a similar source—erotic disappointment—for the expressions of self-deprecation, melancholy, loneliness, and fatalism found in them. Living with his mother all of her life and being her sole caregiver for twenty-five years, from the time he was thirty-three until he was fifty-eight, seems to have robbed Bill of the opportunity of experiencing the joy and satisfaction of reciprocated romantic love with another human being. No wonder Mann's work held such a strong attraction for him. He may well have seen himself in disappointed love affairs in Mann's fiction. But the longing that comes across in Bill's poetry had other sources as well.

In his search for faith, meaning in life, and inner peace, Trout read voraciously, including C. S. Lewis' *Surprised By Joy*, a "spiritual autobiography" as Lewis called it, that accounts for those factors leading to his recovery of the "joy" he had experienced as a child in the wonders of the world and its mysteries, and which led to his eventual acceptance of Christianity at age thirty-one. Lewis, who edited *Essays Presented to Charles Williams* (1947), was a champion of Charles Williams, an author Bill seems to have focused on in the 1960s and '70s. He owned seven of Williams' novels, including *Many Dimensions* (1930), *Greater Trumps* (1932), *Shadows of Ecstasy* (1933), and *All Hallows' Eve* (1945). Like May Sinclair and Walter de la Mare, Williams wrote ghost stories, a genre that interested Bill. Williams also expressed a kind of religious mysticism that attracted him. The rich theological insights and metaphysics of Williams' writings obviously appealed to Bill as well, though his marginal notes testify to skepticism about some of the author's conclusions. Apparently Bill was not among those put off by Williams' interest in the occult and black magic, or by his belief in the continuity of the spiritual process, the existence in a single spiritual realm of the living and the dead as Bill's poem "With supplicating eyes, the dead return" testifies.

Trout owned all of Walter de la Mare's novels and eight volumes of his poetry, including his verse for children, all of which he praised in letters and conversations. He also filled five pages of one of his scrapbooks with quotations from de la Mare's book *Behold, This Dream* (1939). A poet of the "inner life," who described himself as one of the "visionaries, the introverts, whose eyes are set inward," de la Mare's philosophic symbolism and interest in nursery rhymes overlap, as Vivian de Sola Pinto observes, in poems that drew on the tradition of English medieval ballads, popular song, and the poetry of William Blake, Samuel Taylor Coleridge, Edgar Allan Poe, and Christina Rossetti (Pinto 1951, 122-124). Like de la Mare—a writer whose novels, short stories, and poems reflect Jung's theories of archetypes and the collective unconscious—Trout believed that the imagination, whose source is the unconscious, is a surer path to reality and truth than pure reason. Bill had known de la Mare's work since 1927 (his senior year at Coatesville High School), when he first read "The Listners," as he wrote on the last page of his copy of Russell Brian's *Tea With Walter de la Mare*. Brian, a neurologist with a keen interest in literature who had corresponded with de la Mare since 1942, wrote summaries of their conversations over tea from 1951 until the poet's death in 1956. It is interesting to note how closely de la Mare's topics of conversation parallel both themes found in Trout's poetry and the subjects that most occupied his study of Jung. The principal topics of what de la Mare called these "tea-talks" were: memory, time, childhood, ghost stories, apparitions, dreams, the unconscious, telepathy, intuition, obsession, and imagination (Brian 1958, *passim*). As with de la Mare, dreams play a central role in Trout's poetry and reflect both the bright and the dark side of life and the human personality.

The characters, settings, and moods of de la Mare's prose and poetry drew Trout to him, as did, Bill said, his skillful use of meter. The difficulty de la Mare's fictional characters have in communicating or relating to each other; the presence in his poetry of ghosts, spirits, revenants, the dead, travelers, and pilgrims; and the pervasive sense of difference or alienation, of isolation and loneliness may have influenced the themes and tone of Trout's poems as much as his own life experiences. Both de la Mare and Trout were preoccupied with death, though neither in a morbid way. This preoccupation is part of their interest in the human condition—a recognition that death and the dead are part of our lives, though neither poet apparently held a religious or specifically Christian belief in life after death (McCrosson 1966, *passim*). Both Jung's concept of the collective unconscious and Charles Williams' ideas about a single spiritual realm of the living and the dead, as well as a hint of de la Mare, seem to underpin Trout's poem:

> Now a light along the room
> In April dawns; now the call,
> Muted, of white cherry bloom;
> Now a shadow, on the wall,
> Of the naked ash bough, moved
> In the chill northwest gale:
> Since all of these you knew and loved,
> Now for me they do not fail.
> Instinctively I choose, reject,
> Guided surely by a power
> I may not doubt, may not suspect—
> Final, in a final hour.
> Legacy: by these I know
> Whereof, and how, and why I go.

Bill shared de la Mare's interest in ghosts. In commenting to his Contemporary Poetry class on de la Mare's poem "The Ghost" he said, according to Dianne Danz: "The shadowy world impinges so directly on the consciousness that we cannot afford to ignore it," which may be why he took such a manifestation of the spirit world as a "double walker," a paranormal look-alike of a person (perhaps in this case Bill himself) regarded as a harbinger of misfortune or death, as the subject for his poem "Doppelganger," which may also have been inspired by *Der Doppelgänger* (The Double), one of his favorite songs by Franz Schubert.

> Who is this stranger, in these wonted rooms—
> Shuffling and old, shaking, white-haired and bent?
> Before I am aware of him, he looms
> Out of the shadow, and stares as through he meant
> To speak, but found no words. Who is he—
> This harmless haunting, this pitiably dazed,
> Hopelessly lost thing, roaming aimlessly
> His fire-circle, and evidently crazed?
> Eluding him, I steal out of the room
> Because I do not know that face of doom.

Norma Patterson, one of Bill's seventh- and eighth-grade students at Gap, remembered him telling ghost stories while teacher and pupils ate lunch in the classroom, and Rhoda Hostetter Clemens' brother Abe recalled hearing other pupils say Mr. Trout told "scary stories." He gave poetic voice to such tales in "Ghost Story."

> Around the house the summer night
> Quivered as the crickets whirred;
> But even the small bat's goblin flight
> He noted absently, and stirred
> Slack hand to turn the page.
>
> Above, he seemed to hear the slow
> Rocking chair sway to and fro;
> And stop. He then heard cross the floor
> And pause before the stubborn door
> The shuffling feet of age.
>
> The door tugged free, and closed again.
> (Some ancient sentry of the brain
> Alerted, called in primitive tongue.)
> Annoyed but heedless, he read on.
> Upon the banister
>
> A groping hand had come to rest.
> The uncertain foot in the loose shoe

Faltered, then the stair-tread pressed.
Slow steps came down in darkness, through
His consciousness of her.

Six months dead, and yet she comes,
Just as so many times she came;
She comes, and in three seconds more,
What will stand in the stairway door?
The wry flesh tugged the bone....

And then the headlights of a car
Swept the window; a laughing shout
Revoked the being on the stair,
Cancelled the dread solution out,
And gave the dark its own.

The unusually acute powers of observation possessed by both de la Mare and Trout, though neither is merely descriptive, are demonstrated in their renderings of nature. They also focused on the miniature, as de la Mare does in poems such as "Titmouse," "The Moth," "The Snail," and "The Snowdrop," while Trout zeroes in on a patch of garden or flowerbed; on a single flower; on a toad, cricket, snake, ant, or spider. The fascination with the diminutive may also in part explain de la Mare's interest in and empathetic understanding of children. Midgetina, the principal character in his novel *Memoirs of a Midget*, lives isolated from people of common size, spending long solitary hours in the woods making friends with little creatures—caterpillars, spiders, birds, and flowers—and reading folktales and fiction thereby feeding her imagination, honing her uncommon powers of observation and reflection, and freeing her from conventional society. De la Mare was a prolific writer of poetry for and about children, much of which is found among Bill's books.

In the summer of 1971, Bill gave me the bulk of his library, hundreds of books he called his "orphans" (others were given to me by his brother Frank after Bill's death). The emotional experience of boxing up his books comes through in a letter of 11 June 1971 in which he makes the apologetic admission that "it would be difficult—and boring, to you—were I to say how much support I owe to these companions, faithful across the vicious and dreadful decades." Sometime before I carted off the boxed-up books, he wrote a poem that acknowledges Jung's admonition not to cling to the things of youth during the autumn of life and reflects a resigned acceptance of having to give up his books, some of which were his mother's and had been at the very center of his life for so long. Among the memories that came back to him as he packed the boxes was one about a barefoot Aphrodite, his mother reading to him in the kitchen while preparing meals, canning, or doing other chores.

> Like the house of childhood, if one be unwise
> Or mad enough, there to make return,
> These books that, decades long, undid the eyes
> And the dull heart, sadly are discerned
> Dwindled—deities to kitchen tasks
> Fittingly condemned: Aphrodite
> Barefoot, and, in patched apron masked
> With grease, totes the scullery debris.
> No. They are now a lumber valueless.
> Pascal, Paul, even Euripides,
> Stratford land-holder, Spengler, and Carrel
> And all the other saviours; grim-lipped,
> Box them for exit. A single quality
> Inly remains—the conjectured desert-well.

Among his "orphans" were a number by Forrest Reid (1875-1947). He wrote to me on 8 August 1971 saying that "Reid is almost unknown" and that to find copies of his works he had to "get them through Blackwell [in Oxford, England], and then second-hand." He characterizes Reid's writing as possessing: "Strange sensitivity, lightness of touch, delicacy—but [with] Gaelic second-sight, wit. The Tom Barber books [there were three with this boy hero] and the two autobiographical ones [*Apostate*, 1926 and *Private Road*, 1940] I think that you will adopt," he tells me in a letter of 12 August 1971. In a letter of 15 February 1977 he says of Reid: "A companionably sensitive person—sensitivity gratefully balanced by clear-sightedness and sardonic irony, which can at times be savage." Asking if I had yet read *Uncle Stephen*, he went on to say: "But much of Reid I read under cruel pressures; hence my mind divagates [sic]." [Denis] Bracknel [1947] I recall as almost unbearably sad. The two autobiographical ones are masterly, and his study of De la Mare (they were friends) says all that is needed."

Trout admired Forrest Reid both for his style and subject matter. Born in Belfast, Reid lived there all his life, save for his student years at Cambridge University, where he met and became friends with E. M. Forster who encouraged his literary ambitions. He wrote critical studies of William Butler Yeats and Walter de la Mare, who became a life-long friend. The history and landscape of Ireland together with his early and life-long interest in ancient Greece (he published a volume of poems he translated from the *Greek Anthology*) and his rejection of Christianity made Reid what one writer called "a genuine pagan." His dream-like fiction, a blending of history, memory, fantasy, and mysticism, has the quality of optical illusions and reflects his ability to depict the psychological element of the Ulster countryside. The "strange sensitivity, lightness of touch, delicacy" Bill found in Reid's writing comes from his visual and emotional immersion in the beauty of Irish countryside, as Reid explained in a letter to a friend: "… Ireland is more spiritual," he wrote; "it is more remote and imaginative, with a kind of light that never shone anywhere else…." It is the subtlety and sensitivity of his descriptions that give a magical quality to his landscapes, as in the "moon worship" scene in *The Bracknels*, and so won Trout's praise. Responding in a letter to E. M. Forster's approval of *The Bracknels*, Reid makes a point about nature with which Bill would have agreed: "That is to say the visible world is not everything, there are deeper and more hidden things touched on, and above all there is a sense of beauty, both of material beauty, & of spiritual beauty, without which, I confess, no book is of much interest to me." Themes of youth, nature, the supernatural, time, and memory are found in all of Reid's novels (Taylor 1980, 1-2, 61-63, 79-81, 173, 21-22, 29, 49, 54-57, 62).

"Forrest Reid loved boys, wrote about boys, and wanted to write about nothing else," Brain Taylor maintains. But unlike the British artist Henry Scott Tuke (1858-1929), who painted beautiful nude adolescent males swimming, sunning themselves on secluded beaches, and sometimes looking longingly at one another, Reid, as Taylor puts it, "desensualised" his boy heroes. However, when Reid dedicated his *Garden God: A Tale of Two Boys* (1905) to Henry James, whom he admired, James refused to acknowledge the honor, perhaps because woven into this "idyllic" tale of friendship cast in a "supernatural" setting was a note of "subdued eroticism," which according to Brian Taylor was conveyed more by the "lyricism" and "sensuousness" of the writing than by any overt depiction of homoerotic desire. Certainly boys and boyhood were central to his novels, and were in part a way Reid sought to relive his own childhood through his boy heroes and to express his "longing for an ideal companion": but as Taylor explains, there is so much more to these stories. He points out that Reid, who had not "outgrown" his interest in the activities of childhood and spent a lot of time with boys, several of whom were devoted to him, had a genius for "divining the thoughts and attitudes of small boys, a genius, which, in various ways, is at the heart of his finest writing." His were not books for boys but about them. Walter de la Mare observed that his *Pirates of the Spring* (1919) was a novel for adults about the "psychology of school-boys." Reid said it was his "conviction that the years of childhood, boyhood, adolescence are the most significant." He believed: "The spirit of youth is not merely bright and vivacious; above all, it is not merely thoughtless and noisy. It is full of curiosity; it is healthy, and it is morbid; it is animal, and it is spiritual; sensual, yet filled with vague half-realized yearnings after an ideal … it is spirit of life itself...." The boy heroes of Reid's novels are sensitive and misunderstood by unsympathetic parents or other adults around them; they pursue their own inner lives; they are dreamers who live in worlds of their own imagining and to whom "marvelous things" happen. Reid's novels reveal his life-long search for affection and lasting companionship, something he gives voice to through a character in *Brian Westby* (1934): "Happiness is only made by affection. Nothing else in the long run matters" (Taylor 1980, 2, 17, 174, 38, 40-43, 89, 93-94, 73, 71, 86, 126, 134-135, 151, 181, 64, 27, 150, 155; Wainwright and Dinn 1989, *passim*). With such sentiments Bill would have agreed.

The skill and imaginative realism used by Forrest Reid in depicting childhood in part accounts for why Trout found his fiction so appealing. Bill had spent many years observing children in the classroom and on the playground, and like de la Mare, Forrest Reid, William Blake, and Christina Rossetti (a volume of whose poetry he gave to his young niece, Alice Trout Smith), he was just as comfortable as they were in the world of children, as his friendship with the young Glenn Kendig and other youngsters who sought his company testifies. And he seems to have shared with Reid and de la Mare a sense of nostalgia for childhood and regret at its passing. While only a few of Trout's poems actually take a child as subject—"Boy With A Kite" and "Garden Toad" for example—others of them—"Blacksnake," "The Book," "Forecast," "Then and Now," and "Sur Le Noël" among them—take childhood as a theme and are probably based on his own early experiences, the exploration of which is in keeping with the importance Jung attached to the regressive probing of such memories. It is worth pointing out that except where the child is either his deceased sister Susanna or his mother, all the children in Bill's poems are boys. And like Reid Bill, as some of his poems reveal, was trying to discover by dredged-up childhood memories and self-analysis what might have gone wrong with his life, just as Reid did as Brian Taylor observes in claiming: "The whole of *Apostate* is given over to this nagging question ..." (Taylor 1980, 177). Also like Reid, Trout, as suggested in his letters, craved the companionship of an ideal male friend.

Nature plays an important part in Reid's novels, including his love of animals, whether his pets, or creatures of the woods and fields that find their way into his fiction, and which he always treats with affection and "a recognition and acceptance of the animal's own life." As we have seen, Bill's nature poems show he held a similar attitude toward animals. "Reid's descriptions of natural beauty," Taylor observes, "always say something about its human observers; far less about any possible intrinsic aesthetic," an observation apropos of Trout's treatment of landscape in such poems as "Light Snow," "September Noon," and "Cold twilight still—but life begins to stir." As Taylor points out, a sense of the supernatural runs through Reid's work, as he himself admitted in saying that the supernatural "was inseparable from my conception of reality." He had a particular talent for spiritualizing a landscape or scene through depictions of light and the unusual settings in which his boy heroes find themselves. Taylor observes that Reid added "depth" to the "visible landscape" by "opening dream passages through it, dreams and visions, which do not make the visible world faint but intensify and add to its richness and nearness." Dreams are the source of many of Trout's poems and also figure prominently in Reid's fiction as Taylor's assertion makes clear: "The relationship between dreaming and reality was always a fascinating one for Reid." Fairies, angels, and ghosts populate Reid's dream landscapes. Taylor suggests that this interest in spiritualism and the occult may owe something to the research Reid did for his book on William Butler Yeats. The fascination with the supernatural and ghost stories Reid and de la Mare shared, may in part account, along with the tales in German *Lieder*, for the "scary" stories Trout told his pupils and for the appearance of ghosts, revenants, and changelings in his poems (Taylor 1980, 75, 104, 177-180, 85, 96, 81-82, 130, 182, 150-153, 134).

Manifestations of Trout's obsession with time and memory are found in many of the documents he left behind, among them his letters and book marginalia, as when he marked a line in his copy of Eugene O'Neill's *Strange Interlude* in which Nina, the daughter of Professor Henry Leeds, thinks to herself, "... the only life is in the past and future ... the present is an interlude ... strange interlude in which we call on the past and future to bear witness we are living...." That many of his poems grow out of personal memories or explore the nature of Time—among them "Let us stop Time forever at ten o'clock," "Time now to thumb the page's edge," and "Burn now the calendars, and halt the clocks"—I think is one of the keys to understanding his fondness for Forrest Reid, and may also have been influenced by his reading of Reid's Tom Barber trilogy and his autobiographical works. Trout no doubt recognized in Reid what Brian Taylor makes explicit in saying: "Like Proust, Reid knew the power of literature to invoke the appearances of the past, to reconstitute in character and in landscape those longings to which the nostalgic temperament is prone" (Taylor 1980, 176-177, 3).

One of the most lasting literary influences on Trout was the work of Marcel Proust (1871-1922). When Bill first read Proust is uncertain, though his letters of the early 1940s contain frequent and extended discussions of his work. As late as the mid-1970s he urged me to take a full year to read *Remembrance of Things Past*, whose "narrator or hero"—as E. M. Forster points out in his 1943 essay "Our Second Greatest Novel?"—"more or less resembles Proust himself … who grows up with his mother and grandmother—the only characters displaying human integrity," something with which Bill could identify (Forster 1951, 224). Then, too, Proust's interest in music; his fascination with intuition, the subconscious, mysticism; his views on the nature of Time, seeing it both as external/chronometric and internal/psychological and considering ways of escaping from it; his belief that heredity is a "constantly recurring" pattern of ancestral conduct; his view of homosexuality as an act of nature for which a person is not responsible; and the way he guarded his privacy were all matters that not only appealed to Trout's intellectual interests but also touched him personally and may provide insights into his poems, including "Heritage" and those dealing with time and memory. The reason for Bill's devotion to Proust is explained by Harold March's insightful observation: "Prerequisite to the enjoyment of Proust is a preference for the overtones of experience to experience itself. Proust writes for introverts. If the reader wants action and events he is sure to be disappointed, for all he will get will be the careful exploration of an inner world" (March 1948, 228-229). Like much of Trout's poetry, Proust's *Remembrance*, as E. M. Forster observes, "is full of echoes, exquisite reminders, intelligent parallels, which delight the attentive reader … For all its realism, it has about it something of a day dream. It plays about with time" (Forster 1951, 224-225).

The polar opposites of intellect and feeling appear in the temperament and the approach to knowledge of both Proust and Trout, and with both the latter tended to win out in the end. Trout's hostility to materialism may in part owe something to the three types of reality explored in Proust's works: material reality, that perceived by our senses; intellectual reality, the perception of the world created by thoughts; and "transcendent reality," which is "intangible" and is reached through "involuntary memory." A chance sensation—a smell or odor, a sound, a taste, the feel of some object, a certain quality of light—can bring on a cascade of associations—an "involuntary memory"—out of the unconscious where forgotten or imperfectly registered memories are stored which link the past and present, creating a living or continuing past brought to life in all its emotional nuances. Such moments of the past are not merely remembered but relived. Henri Bergson's (1859-1941) concept of intuition and his idea of duration, Harold March observes, are related to "Proust's sense of the continuing past," which may in part account for Trout's interest in Bergson's philosophy (March 1948, 139, 146-147, 195-197, 211, 215-217, 221, 245-247). The importance of memory, the past, the flow of time, and the transitory nature of life found in such poems as "Encounter," "North of the old orchard, the house shambles," "Before the Sale," and "They" are also central to Virginia Woolf's fiction, particularly in her novels *Mrs. Dalloway*, *To the Lighthouse*, and *The Waves*. As with Woolf's novels and short stories, Trout's poetry is not only about the experiences of life but also about the experience of living. It is contemplative; it values understanding over action, and so while informed by intellect also draws on emotion and intuition.

This living or continuing past not only complements the Jungian idea of the collective unconscious, which so intrigued Bill, but also an idea Jung floated in a 1952 letter to the English psychologist John Raymond Smythies, who authored many papers on extrasensory perception. Trout underlined this passage in Jung's letter to Smythies: "The question is, in short: shouldn't we give up the time-space categories altogether when we are dealing with psychic existence? It might be that psyche should be understood as *unextended intensity* and not as a body moving with time. If there is no body moving in space, there can be no time either and that would account for the 'elasticity' of time" (Adler 1975, 45).

Some of Trout's poems record an "involuntary memory" prompted by music, as is the case with "Out of the past the voice that sang," which relates how a chance hearing of "The rising sweep, the silver curve" of a Schumann song during a time of illness and sorrow "Sting to ecstasy the nerve / We thought had withered." In other cases the "involuntary memory" resulted from a visual event, which is the source of the poem "Easter."

A pink candy rose on a silver leaf;
Daffodils (we called them cups-and-saucers);
Hyacinths, pink, white, purple—

A thick sweetness in the warm room:
Outside, the April wind on green hills
And dark purple ridges, under a pale blue
Easter sky, fluted and called, shaking a loose pane.

(A little island of child-memory,
Bright in the sea of mid-life loneliness,
Appeared suddenly out of numb grief,
Because you showed me, in a tinsel box,
A pink, spun-sugar rose upon a silver leaf.)

According to Harold March, involuntary memory is a means of escaping time—getting beyond the everyday world of change, desire, sorrow, decay, death—because the past moment and the present are coterminous and "tomorrow is made from yesterday, and cannot greatly differ from it" and allow one to experience the ideal forms of beauty, peace, freedom. It is not an active life but a contemplative one that makes this heightened insight or consciousness possible (March 1948, 68, 108-110, 139-140, 214-215, 225-229).

Trout discusses some of Proust's most important ideas and images in a letter to Don Smith of 18 July 1943. He tells him that he has been re-reading for at least the fourth time the last two volumes of Proust.

> He's very tonic just now, with his calm disbelief in anything except the reports of the senses. Love, friendship, moral codes, character as an enduring thing—he sees it all as subject to the erosion of Time, and satisfies himself with making a cult of sensation. He has infinite power to delight me in the insouciance with which he disrobes the soul of a duchess or charts the moral decline of a valet. And I love the wholly impersonal scientific curiosity with which he invades the Paris underworld with his little net, stirs the fetid depths, brings his slimy wriggling little monsters to the light, studies them, and tosses them gently back to slither away into the putridity from which he hauled them. I never tire of his style, even when it smothers you (paradoxically) under oceans of boredom.

A year earlier (4 July 1942) Bill had shared his enthusiasm for Proust in telling Smith that the writer suggests:

> If the human race hadn't learned speech so soon, it would have discovered music as a means of communication and expression. He means to

> say that experience, being filtered, analyzed; externalized as speech is transformed and becomes something entirely different; but that music is direct and true communication, is the experience itself projected and made accessible for those who can hear. With his resources of language and subtlety of thought, Proust makes this intelligible, and I should quote, but you read it with the genuine thrill of discovery—it is like a new and unsuspected world—I am fast learning to live a little in his world and to understand slightly, and it is like becoming acclimated to life in a new medium, on another planet; it is like a vast mountainous country that one must explore and map with crippled precision but with mounting and enthralled excitement. You only realize how crudely you have been schooled, how blindly you have blundered thru the world, how brief a time is left to learn a little about the puzzling and mysterious human personality.

But nowhere is the impact of Proust on Trout more directly, albeit briefly, acknowledged than in his letter to Smith of 22 May 1943, in which he goes so far as to say of Proust: "He isn't a book—he's a way of life … One could almost say he is a religion—godless, creedless, but as passionate and undying as earth-worship."

Many of Trout's poems deal either directly or indirectly with issues of memory and time, some originated with childhood memories or recollections based on family photographs; others record specific times of day, the changing seasons, or the physical changes in people or objects brought on by the passage of time, as is the case with a poem that takes as its subject the small stone house (the original Bitzer home) up the hill from the Bitzer-Trout homestead, where William Henry Brown lived.

> North of the old orchard, the house shambles
> Earthward; in angles the sloping porches hold
> Damp mats of leaves faded; the door stumbles
> Ajar vaguely, to admit the manifold
> Inquisitive cavalcades of rain and sleet,
> Of mist and frost and snow, to wander through
> The lank rooms. That ever human feet
> Here dragged or danced, the witnesses are few.
> And yet, and yet, to one who comes in faith—
> Renouncing time's treason and the allure

Of somnolent senses—infrequently is shown
Plane displaced by plane, a sudden, sure
Radiance,—life in dazzling depth,
Beyond the tyranny of weathering stone.

In a similar vein is "Before the Sale," a poem written either about the time the Trouts sold their house in Gap and moved to Lancaster or recorded later as a memory of the preparation for the sale before the move. It tells of layers of time folded and laid away, of the slow and inevitable decay of all things, and carries Proustian overtones with which anyone who has cleaned out the family attic can identify. "Before the Sale" is both beautiful and moving without succumbing to maudlin nostalgia.

At last almost anonymous—here
Dispersal sleeps, orphaned and dispossessed,
In the dim garret. Fragile, yellowed, sere,
The wedding veil once was carefully pressed
And laid in this small box; that pitcher holds
Its own handle and four maple seeds,
Gale-driven under the eaves; from these folds
Of childish stitching scatter the small blue beads....
Dynastic time surcharges the thick walls,
Saturate inscrutably in drowse,—
Scant joy, much grief. Out there a robin calls
Deliriously, but irony cannot rouse
The gray residual dust: two centuries
Leave of passions but frail warranties.

Both "Before the Sale" and "North of the orchard, the house shambles" bring to mind the "Time Passes" part of Virginia Woolf's novel *To the Lighthouse*, which centers on the Ramsays' unoccupied summer beach house. It is a record of the effects of neglect and decay on the house and its contents: the changing light of the seasons in its abandoned rooms; the sprouting of weeds and self-seeding flowers in its untended garden; the sound of wind, creaking floors and windows, and scampering mice no ear hears that together marks the passage of time during the ten years the house stood empty.

Yet Bill recognized the dangers of dwelling in the past, as is apparent from his poems "Not we the white wind flower" and as here in "Du Temps Perdu."

One dare not picnic in the Past,
Or ramble undirectedly;
Too many places are nefast,
Since they are thronged by derelict
And exiled revenants, wild for home,
Sly to possess what host may come.

You think to pick the anemone
Swaying by the gray rail fence;
You kneel and reach—and learn what glee
Opportunity can dispense.
Heart staggers, brain dims,
And upward swirl hell's dissonant hymns.

Do not dispose your sandwiches,
Or think to cool your tepid wine,
By creeks where childhood expeditions
Felt only sunfish tug the line;
There a kelpy tosses mane,—
And you will not come home again.

Trout's preoccupation with Time is a central concern in much of his poetry. He recommended to his students J. W. Dunne's *An Experiment With Time* (1927), which he describes to a Millersville class as, "a small unobtrusive volume that carries enough concentrated dynamite to disturb your peace of mind for some months—a book that had its influence on such men as John Masefield, William Butler Yeats, John Buchan, J. B. Priestly, and others." Dunne's book reports the results of experiments he conducted on dreams, and advances the theory that the past, present, and future are all present in the human consciousness at once but are not apparent because of the concrete, linear way we think when awake. However, based on his experiments he believed that in sleep we have what he calls "precognitive dreams" as the unconscious mind roams freely in the past, present, and future at the same time, and that by recording one's dreams and comparing them over time, one can experience the simultaneity of time—be as it were both inside and outside of time.

Trout's obsession with Time, which owes so much to Proust and Jung, may in part explain his interest in the work of other writers of fiction and poetry, and, as we have seen, to such composers as Gustav Mahler and Richard Strauss, who also ruminated on transience and the nature of Time. In a 1943 letter to Don Smith, he quotes the final quatrain of Elinor Wylie's poem "Let No Charitable Hope," which he likens to "a gay brittle laugh heard in a dark street":

> In masks outrageous and austere
> The years go by in single file;
> But none has merited my fear,
> And none has quite escaped my smile.

And in a bitter-sweet passage in his last wartime letter to Smith (27 January 1946) expressing how happy he is to learn that Don is coming home—though he knows that as one who has seen Europe he will not find Gap or him so interesting any more—Bill wrote, quoting from Shakespeare's *Richard II*, Act III, Scene 2: "I am too old to think one can 'call back yesterday, bid time return.' But do you remember ED [Emily Dickinson] saying":

> The things that never can come back are several—
> Childhood, some forms of home, the dead;
> But joys, like men, may sometimes make a journey
> And still abide.

Bill taught himself French so that he could read both the Sand-Flaubert correspondence and George Sand's (1804-1876) novels and journals in the original. He tells Betty Curtis in a letter of 1 March 1970 that since his mother's death and his "leaving the mental prostitution of school teaching," he has read only works in French, "since the challenge of the language is a sort of drug for the loneliness." And in his letter of 19 October 1977 to Curtis, he mentions having "finished the eleventh volume of the letters of my old friend George Sand." Years earlier he told Don Smith in a letter of 27 January 1941 that he likes Sand better in old age and in her journals than in the "tears and turbulence" of her novels, adding: "But then she loved so verbosely and so often! Enough to wreck anyone's nervous system." His library contained two complete sets of Sand's novels, one in English the other in French, as well as collections of her letters, journals, and several biographies and monographs. At Bill's request I borrowed a French edition of the Sand-Flaubert correspondence (he had the letters in English translation) from the University of Minnesota Library and he photocopied and began reading them during the Christmas holidays of 1971 while I was in Lancaster County visiting my parents. He had written some months earlier telling me why he wanted the letters: "It is that the old woman says things there that comfort oddly—someone has been near her before." He also collected in two large ring binders anything related to Sand's life: photographs, clippings from newspapers and magazines, postcards, photocopies of letters, cartoons, and other ephemera. He owned two copies, both in French, of Georges Lubin's picture book, *George Sand En Berry* (1967), with photographs by Robert Thuillier, which he filled with marginal comments in French and English.

Trout seems to have been drawn to the intimacy and close observations of nature that characterize Sand's descriptions of the flowers, birds, insects, and landscape, (as in her novel *Valentine*) of Berry, the province in which she was reared and lived for most of her life, and to her sympathetic interest in people, particularly peasants. She was critical of the restrictions on liberty imposed on people by the Catholic Church. Her writings address the need to grant women greater freedoms and rights and document a commitment to social reform and equality among the classes that had not been realized in the years since the French Revolution of 1789.

A staunch champion of representative government, she rushed to Paris from her country home at the outbreak of the Revolution of 1848, where she wrote political tracts supporting the republican cause and founded her own newspaper, printed by a workers' cooperative, which championed the rights of the proletariat and the peasantry. Frightened by street violence and the demands of the working classes, the bourgeoisie gave moderate republicans and conservatives control of the National Assembly, which paved the way for the election in 1851 of Louis Napoleon as president of the Second Republic, who the following year assumed autocratic powers and established the Second Empire, taking the title of Napoleon III. In a letter of 30 September 1848 to her friend Giuseppe Mazzini (1805-1862)—an Italian patriot who wanted to free his country from foreign rule and unify it under a republican form of government—she laments the defeat of the radical republican cause in France, telling him: "The majority of the French people are blind, credulous, ignorant, ungrateful, malicious and stupid. In a word they are mostly bourgeois" but refuse to recognize the sovereignty of "the people," which is based on the right to universal suffrage. Her fictional works address social problems and won for her the admiration of Russian intellectuals and writers, among them the novelists Ivan Turgenev (1818-1883) and Fyodor Dostoyevsky (1821-1881) and the political philosopher Michael Bakunin (1814-1876), the theorist of anarchy (Doumic 1910, 255, 260; Blum 1994, 45, 82; Robertson 1952, 21, 53, 74, 86; Lucas 1930, 165; Brower 1975, 174, 191-192).

As we have seen, Trout sympathized with Sand's social and political values. During one of my afternoon visits he mentioned that her novels introduced Western ideas of social justice and equality through fiction, which kept them from being banned or censored by the Tsarist government, and helped prepare the way for political and social change called for by Russian intellectuals in the years after 1840. But it seems to have been Sand's character and values and how they were manifested in her life and work that most impressed Bill, and in her old age perhaps reminded him of his own mother. On the fly-leaf of his copy of *Correspondance de George Sand* he wrote a translation of what Pauline Viardot said of her to the Russian novelist Ivan Turgenev: "I consider that people do not say enough about her kindness. However rare genius may be, such kindness is rarer still...." And on the book's title page he translated Turgenev's comment to Gustave Flaubert (1821-1880), her friend and fellow novelist, after Sand's death: "What a heart of gold she had! How completely devoid she was of any sentiment which was petty, mean, or false...." Bill saw these same qualities in his mother.

Trout's interest in Gaius Valerius Catullus (ca. 84 BC-ca.54 BC), a poet of Republican Rome, and the fifteenth-century French poet François Villon reveal a different aspect of his personality. He owned a copy, in Latin, of Catullus' *Carmina*, an anthology of 116 poems, some of them to or about friends; others rude or obscene invectives aimed at former friends, fellow poets, politicians and other public figures; and, most famously, erotic ones mainly about women but also some revealing homosexual proclivities. In contrast to Virgil about whom he had little good to say either as a man or a poet, Robert Graves praised Catullus for constantly varying his meters, not letting "metrical difficulties thwart the plain sense of a poem by driving him to clever periphrasis," and sticking to short poems rather than penning epics with "boring passages" (Graves 1962, 43). All these are things with which Bill no doubt agreed as his underlining of the passage suggests. Dates in the margins of his copy of *Carmina* document when he read the poems, which are heavily marked-up. On the last page of the book he taped and labeled a sprig of "Olive leaves from Sirmio," the site of the Catullus family villa on Lake Garda near Verona, Italy, and dated it 8-30-63. There is no record of how Bill came by this little souvenir, though it is safe to assume that it was a gift brought back from Italy by someone who knew he enjoyed reading Catullus.

A French writer quite different from Georges Sand with whom Trout had a long-term fascination was the lyric poet François Villon (1430-1463). Louis Jennings, one of his English Department colleagues at Millersville, who also shared his love of classical music, remembered that Trout spoke frequently about Villon. References to and quotations from Villon are sprinkled through his correspondence as early as the 1940s. Bill owned several biographies of Villon as well as books of his verse in both French and English. The macabre elements in Trout's poetry may owe something to his reading of Villon.

In a Millersville lecture on Villon, Trout explains what he admired in the poet's work. He calls the "Ballade of Dead Ladies" "one of the towering, soaring poems of all literature, for its verbal melody; ... it is great in the texture of its shimmering fabric woven of a subtle rhythm and a succession of words chiming with overtones and connotations; great in the evocation of each of the images" of the ladies. In assessing the strengths found in Villon's verse he says that concreteness is "always a quality of the best poetry," and went on to insist that: "Nothing in genuine poetry is abstract or vague." Concreteness in poetry, he observes is partly due to "the image chosen" and partly to "the diction in which the image is conveyed," and in both regards Villon was a master. He praises his lyricism, defining it as "what happens when imagery and rhythm and sense marry together, and the verse moves inevitably" producing a "singing quality." Further insight into what Trout meant by this is found in marginal notes in his French edition of Villon's poems, where he says of the "Ballade Pour Pier Notre Dame": "Apart from piety and exquisite tenderness: his vivid phrase ... the curiously processional effect of the meter and of the construction of the stanzas." He also notes "the extra line and the extra foot lend themselves to a chant in their balanced, slow rhythm." Thus Villon's craftsmanship and adherence to form was something he admired. Just as Bill enjoyed ghost stories, so Villon's excesses—his sexuality and violence—fascinated him. Nor did the attraction end with his taste for the macabre. It was Villon's range—"All emotion. All feeling. From brutal lust to the most delicate and veritable filial love" from "reckless abandonment" to "strong, simple tender religious passion" as well as all ages and classes of people from the good and noble to the scum of society are found in Villon's verse. "There is in Villon," he told students in his World Literature classes, "the range of life's experience, without which no poet can claim the highest place, no matter what his gifts."

Trout knew well the Elizabethan and Jacobean poets—Spenser, Sidney, Greene, Webster, Marlow, Herrick—and once told his Millersville student Dennis Simmons that he reread all of Shakespeare's sonnets every year. Bill's copy of the Yale facsimile edition of Shakespeare's plays is heavily underlined and annotated; and the presence of dates in the margins testify to his rereading it several times. It was "that perverted, bloody, but magnificent masterpiece - Tourneur's *The Revenger's Tragedy*" (a Jacobean play now attributed to Thomas Middleton), that was currently occupying his attention, Bill tells Don Smith in a letter of 31 January 1941: "It is bitter, ironical, intense, fantastic," he explains, "but written throughout with a crackling brilliance in the poetry, a unique harmony, and a coruscated, fretted, daring originality." He was immersed in Robert Burton's *The Anatomy of Melancholy* (1621) when he wrote to Smith on 22 May 1945, which he notes contains "unique medical lore, Latin quotes, bizarre anecdotes, sexual analysis." In his nearly nine hundred page tome Burton, an author not lacking a sense of humor, covers, in a sometimes serious sometimes satirical tone, not only the nature, types, and causes of melancholy but digresses into discussions of, among other subjects, digestion, goblins, theology, astronomy, astrology, and geography. Writing to Smith in September of the same year, Bill tells him he has taken up Victor Hugo's *Toilers of the Sea*, saying it is "a good story, a wonderful evocation of the atmosphere of the sea," as a "vacation from Burton," which he is still plowing through.

The amount of underlining and number of marginal comments, many of them skeptical or critical, in Trout's copy of Sir Thomas Browne's *Religio Medici* (1643) testify to the care with which he read the thirty-year-old physician's wide-ranging interests: his observation, born of introspection, that "We carry within us the wonders we seek without us: there is all Africa and her prodigies in us"; his admitted superstitions, among them a belief in witches; his confession that "sturdy doubts and boisterous objections" challenge his religious faith; his profession that where Jews are concerned "Persecution is a bad and indirect way to plant religion"; his support for the execution of two women accused of bewitching children; his recognition that there is a dark side to human nature and that "I feel sometimes a hell within myself," that "Lucifer keeps his court in my breast," and that "we are all monsters"; his conviction that "no man can judge another, because no man knows himself"; and his belief that "there are many pieces in this one fabric of man," including the "private and domestic enemies" we carry within ourselves. Much of this must have sounded familiar to Bill, who read Jung and engaged in his own self-examination. While Trout rejected Browne's religious beliefs and royalist politics, and labeled many of his speculations and conclusions as "lofty flights," "mordant farce," hypocritical sludge," "cant," "incomprehensible," "idiotic," or just plain "mad," there can be no doubt that he recognized the important contribution this small volume made to the work of literary figures from Coleridge and De Quincey, to Emerson, Thoreau, and Melville, and to the modernists, among them T. S. Eliot and Virginia Woolf, who credited Browne with being among the first writers to explore the "consciousness of one's self," "brooding solitude," the mysteries of the soul, and the sublime.

But it was John Donne who probably had a more profound influence on Trout's outlook on life and on his poetry than any of the other early English writers. In a letter to Smith in January 1941 he calls Donne "a great man" whose poetry he reads "over and over." And two years later he tells Smith he is reading Donne's poems "for the 300th time." By September of 1945 he confesses to Smith: "Donne is still a bible." The Donne edition he used was the 1941 complete poetry and selected prose edited and with an introduction by Robert Silliman Hillyer, the Harvard professor and poet with whom his cousin Elford Caughey studied poetry.

Trout began his Millersville lecture on Donne by dismissing as "not true" the textbook's (*The World in Literature*, edited by Robert Warnock and George K. Anderson) characterization of his poetry as "odd bits of learning and excessive intellectual refinement" in "a crabbed, whimsical style that cramps the emotion into bizarre forms." "The style," he counters, "is simply a reflection of the mind: Donne's mind was an eternally questioning mind, torn first of all between the flesh and the thinking apparatus, torn second by philosophical tortures"—an apt description of Trout's own mind. Saying that Donne's mind was one "that dialectic intoxicated," and though admitting the complexity and difficulty of his poetry, Trout goes on to call his style "conversational—the dialogue of the mind with itself. It is intimate speech that does not only rely on tradition, but creates its own tradition as it goes along. The phrasing is short and closely fitted to the voice; the expression (thought) makes sudden leaps, those freely associative leaps that you yourself make when you really meditate—leaps that are usually plain enough to you, but which would be incoherent babbling to a reader of your thoughts, especially to the ordinary inattentive reader."

Trout rejected the labeling of Donne's poetry as "metaphysical," which he calls "a useless word, with so many spurious overtones that the term seems to have no meaning at all—and no critic should use it." Pointing out that the literal meaning of the word metaphysics (something beyond the physical/ material world) has to do with "our conception of existence," "the universe," or "the place of man in the universe," he objects to the use of the term metaphysical "to refer to the unusual metaphor by which ideas widely apart are brought together—the kind of metaphor that the sixteenth and seventeenth centuries called conceit." True metaphysical poetry, he insists, is that of Lucretius (whose poetry was based on philosophy, particularly that of Epicurus), Dante (poetry as religious/spiritual journey), and, more recently, Robert Bridges (philosophical reflections on the nature of art and the human soul).

According to Trout the "prevailing mood" of Donne's poetry is the "clash between an emotion and the speculative mind," seasoned with "cynicism." This and Donne's speculations on "the mystery of time," "the purpose of life," and "the enigma of death" helps to account for Bill's life-long dedication to this poet and does much to aid our understanding of his own verse. "Always in the background of Donne's thought," he observes, "lurked death," something that might also be said of Bill. And when he reminded his students that Donne "was tortured by the passing of time," he is also speaking of himself. In explicating Donne's poem "Love's Infiniteness," which he explains to students is somewhat like the Marschalline's situation in Strauss' opera *Der Rosenkavalier*, Bill is acknowledging, as was Donne, a recognition of "the old and trite truth, that human relationships must either move or perish."

And just as Donne could not accept the dualism of body and soul, so Trout can be seen as expressing his own beliefs when he observes: "The body, Donne concluded, is not simply evil, the spirit good; sense simply a corrupter and a misleader, the soul pure and heavenward aspiring. Man is body and soul, and neither attribute can be complete without the other. To separate them absolutely is heresy, alike in love and in religion." The issue of the separation of the outer from the inner world was a problem with which many modern poets struggled; hence their interest in John Donne.

Thomas Hardy (1840-1928) was another of Trout's favorite writers who explored humanity's relationship to the universe in his novels and poems. The prose and poetry of Hardy made a deep impression on Bill, no doubt in part because he and Hardy shared a similar worldview and because each explored both the outer and the inner world in their poetry. They moved easily within the spirit world, the natural world, and the commonplace realities of village and rural life. Though he owned well-thumbed copies of all Hardy's novels (as well as a collection of his short stories, his collected verse, *The Dynasts*, and *The Famous Tragedy of the Queen of Cornwall*), Bill's favorite Hardy novels were *The Return of the Native*, *Tess of the d'Urbervilles*, and *Jude the Obscure*. The main purpose of his novels, after telling a good story, Trout explains in a lecture, is for Hardy to convey his "view of man," which "sees man as a sport of Nature, a chance grouping of atoms, his so-called mind a transient phosphorescence, a sad accident, since consciousness has merely added to man's misfortune by making him aware of his doom." He observes: "Hardy never discovered a way to explain the riddle of the universe; and he never discovered a way to numb his mind to the pain and anguish, physical and mental, that the race of man must endure." Bill also seems to have gone to his grave without solving the same riddle. Perhaps thinking of himself and his own childhood experiences, which appear to form the subject of many of his poems, Bill says of Hardy, "he was as acutely sensitive to human suffering—and animal suffering—as he had been when as a child he watched the birds and the snails, the toads and the snakes, the spiders and the sheep and the wild ponies of Egdon Heath."

Writing of his approach to subject matter, Trout points out: "Hardy believes man to be a transient ephemeron. First by showing man as a microscopic ephemeron, a puppet jerked to and fro at the whims of the Eternal Will, the Unconscious, the Immanent Unreckening, the Great Foresightless, as Hardy names in the Dynasts." And then in contrast he "shows men and women as heroic figures of self-sacrifice, courage, endurance, and sensitivity to beauty, figures subjected to unmerited suffering and humiliation by the whimsical or uncomprehending Destiny that jerked them to and fro." Using "The Three Strangers," which he maintains is "a model of what a short story should be," Trout says it illustrates Hardy's traits as an author: "the use of coincidence"; "the omnipresence of Nature as environment, as actor in the story, and overpowering symbol"; "exact, minute description"; and "the apotheosis of the indomitable spirit of man." He also, as Vivian de Sola Pinto points out, extended "the boundaries of poetic sensibility by an expression of new types of beauty and significance which he found in the ugly and the commonplace," as Trout does in poems like "Crow," "In Brief," "Autumn/Watching," and "Country Sale" (Pinto 1951, 40). Both poets were equally at home exploring the spirit world, the realities of rural village life, and the spiritual crisis of modern humanity.

Noting that Hardy was "always raising questions supposed to be beyond discussion," Trout says he gave up writing novels after the public outcry over *Jude the Obscure* (which raises issues of same-sex bonding, undermines traditional assumptions about gender roles, and exposes middle-class exploitation of the working classes), and focused on poetry, Trout claims, because he "still held ideas that he knew ran counter to the opinion of the reading public; but common sense told him that he could say in verse what he could not think of saying in prose"—which may also have guided Bill in writing poetry. He then enumerates the characteristics of Hardy's poetry: "a powerful range of emotions" that "come to grips with the conflicts of mind and flesh"; a sense of drama "that includes the psychological conflict and play of circumstances"; and "a superb sense of irony." The technical characteristics of Hardy's verse Trout discusses in his lecture are: a strict adherence to "conventional English metrics," rejection of poetic melody, "harsh diction, rough rhymes, and upside down syntax." Expanding on the last characteristic, he calls Hardy's diction "astringent" and his line and "sentence construction" as "twisted and knotted as the root of an oak tree groping for foothold in the rocks." He goes on to explain: "Hardy's condensed, aphoristic, gnomic speech occurs because the author is trying for the compressed expression of a definite thought; and his apparent clumsiness comes from conscientious struggling with subjects that poets usually do not write about, subjects that are difficult to cast into the traditional modes of English verse—and Hardy with his love of the old and the time-worn always refused to experiment with new forms."

In his summing-up of Hardy's poetry, Trout reveals his own aspirations as a poet and also what fascinated him not only about Hardy but also the appeal Villon, Donne, Dickinson, and Mew held for him. Hardy he observes, "is not pap for the young, nor delicate diet for those with queasy stomachs; but he has a value for humanity: his poetry raises subjects generally put beyond discussion; questions convention; stimulates you to make a new estimation of old standards and old dogmas and old symbols. And, as great verse must do, it stirs the emotions while it urges the reader to think again." Trout used these same criteria as a guide in creating his own verse.

Given his interest in mysticism, the occult, the Tarot, symbols, and Jungian psychology it is curious that works by Mallarmé, Rimbaud, Verlaine, Valéry, and other Symbolist poets were not among the hundreds of books Bill gave me in the 1970s. Among them I found only Arthur Symons' *The Symbolist Movement in Literature*, with the chapters on Rimbaud, Verlaine, and Mallarmé marked by Bill in the table of contents. It is possible that he either sold other books on Symbolist literature at his moving sale in 1961 or gave them away, as he did with copies of Rudyard Kipling's short stories and novels given to his student Dennis Simmons at the time. In 1963 I lent him my copy of Enid Starkie's biography of Rimbaud. Certainly Bill was aware of Rimbaud's interest in alchemy and the unconscious, his quest for spiritual experience, "beyond the veil of reality," and the way he used childhood memories as sources for his poems, particularly those in *Illuminations* (Starkie 1961, 121-122, 233-235). However, there is no mention of Symbolist writers in Trout's surviving correspondence or lecture notes, nor do any of his poems contain anything approaching the esoteric abstractions and artificial language characteristic of Symbolism. Unlike the Symbolists, Trout never entirely abandoned the physical world for the psychical. In his poems the material world does not dissolve into euphony or perplexing obscurity as it does in Valéry, Rimbaud, or Mallarmé.

Trout's assessment of William Butler Yeats (1865-1939), a key figure of early modernism, was mixed. He praised his skill as a lyric poet. And Bill's acceptance of the Jungian idea of the "collective unconscious" with its archetypes may also have disposed him toward Yeats because his poetry drew on the rich tradition of Celtic mythology and Irish folk culture. Both Yeats and Trout shared an interest in mysticism and spiritualism and their poetry strove to bring together the outer and the inner worlds. Yeats and his wife also practiced channeling and automatic writing, something Bill may have dabbled in as suggested by some of the books he read, his keeping a journal "by free association," and by his obvious interest in contacting his departed mother. He owned a copy of Evelyn Underhill's *Mysticism: A Study of the Nature and Development of Man's Spiritual Consciousness* (1957), but appears to have read only its first five chapters, the point at which his underlining and marginalia stop, suggesting his selective interest in the subject or his disappointment with Underhill. Though early on Yeats was influenced by the symbolism of Mallarmé, his symbols were not as private; nonetheless, as Vivian Del Solo Pinto observes, some of Yeats' symbols have "no precise or intelligible meaning" while others are "symbols of emotional states that defy analysis." Trout told his Contemporary Poetry class that Yeats' "search for symbols ruined him." And as with Eliot, a "conscious attempt to be obscure" he believed, compromised Yeats' poetry even though in time it became more concrete through the inclusion of material from everyday life, contemporary affairs, and the use of common speech (Pinto 1952, 94-95, 101-103). In one of his "tea-talks," Walter de la Mare recalls a gathering at Lady Ottoline Morrell's house also attended by Virginia Woolf, James Stephens, and Yeats, at which "Yeats talked and talked, but no one knew what he was trying to convey"; to which Trout wrote an emphatic "Yes" in the margin of his copy of Russell Brian's *Tea With Walter de la Mare*. Was it perhaps that the imaginative realism he looked for in the poetry of others and which informs so many of his own poems made those of Yeats seem to Trout vague and out of touch with the ordinary facts of life? Given his enthusiasm for Forrest Reid, it is safe to conclude that it was not the mysticism or spiritualism of Yeats that troubled Bill but the obscurity of his esoteric language and undecipherable symbolism.

As will be seen in the following chapter, the modernist poetry of Thomas Sterns Eliot and Ezra Pound did not strike a responsive chord in Trout, though he did not question their influence on poetry and assigned their work and those poets influenced by them, albeit sparingly, as a part the Contemporary Poetry course he taught at Millersville. On the other hand, the "New Country" poets of the 1930s (W. H. Auden, C. Day-Lewis, Stephen Spender, and Louis MacNeice), who had been influenced by Eliot but later went their own way, seem to have held some interest for Trout, though he did not share their belief in poetry as an agent of social change.

As a group these poets, all born between 1904 and 1909, and thus contemporaries of Trout, for the most part, focused on the outer world—science and the effects of modern technology, industry, urbanization, and lost faith—rather than the inner world or the consolations of nature, and drew on Marxism and Freudian psychology to write poetry of social and political commentary with a satirical edge, employing "slang, jazzy meters and imagery derived from machinery and boys' stories," and using as their means of expression "the symbolist idiom learnt from Eliot." All were anti-Fascists and flirted to varying degrees with Communism until disillusioned by the Soviet Union during the Spanish Civil War. More than the other three, Auden looked inward. Not only did he write an essay in 1935 on "Psychology and Art To-day," in which he made claims about the similarities and function of psychology and poetry Trout may not have countenanced, but also paid homage to the "father of psychoanalysis" in the poem "In Memory of Sigmund Freud." There is evidence that Trout appreciated some of Auden's poems, particularly "In Memory of W. B. Yeats." During the Second World War Auden's influence on Day-Lewis waned and his poetry developed a more traditional lyrical style more in keeping with Trout's verse. Like Bill a great admirer of Thomas Hardy, Day-Lewis arranged to be buried close to his grave in Stinsford Churchyard near Dorchester in Dorset. MacNeice, though sympathetic to Left politics, was the least overtly political of these poets, and the autobiographical nature of his verse is, as Samuel Hynes observes, touched by "his nostalgia, his melancholy sense of the present, [and] his apprehensiveness about the future," which may have sparked a sense of kinship in Trout. His "liberalism in the tradition of Shelly," perhaps explains the presence of Spender's *Selected Poems* (1947) among Bill's books. Trout was also probably aware of Auden's homosexuality and Spender's romantic affairs with men—which apparently ended with his second marriage in 1941—from the homosexual allusions made in such poems as "The Uncreating Chaos": "Whatever happens, I shall never be alone. / I shall always have a boy, a railroad fare, or a revolution", and in "Ultima Ratio Regum," in which he says of a young soldier shot and killed in battle, "He was a better target for a kiss" (Pinto 1951, 194-201; Hynes 1977, 169, 43, 66-67, 92, 167-168, 250, 333-334, 369).

There were modernist writers who held little or no appeal for Trout, among them James Joyce (1882-1941), whose novel *Ulysses* (1922) was, nonetheless, among Bill's books, and D. H. Lawrence (1885-1930), another Freud-influenced writer. Lawrence, whose raw and brutal masculinity, confused obsession with sexuality, sexist and racist views, and an authoritarian political philosophy expressed in letters to friends both during and after World War I and apparent in such novels as *Aaron's Rod* (1922), *Kangaroo* (1923), and particularly in *The Plumed Serpent* (1926), may account for Bill's reaction (6 June 1971) to the list of required readings for a graduate course I was taking on the British novel that included D. H. Lawrence's *Women in Love*. "Except for the Lawrence," he wrote, "I envy you your first meeting with those novels." Bertrand Russell claimed that Lawrence "had developed the whole philosophy of Fascism before the politicians had thought of it." W. H. Auden, though he admired Lawrence's work, called him a "dangerous figure," an "Idealogue," whose *Kangaroo* and *The Plumed Serpent* were "sinister novels." Among recent literary scholars, Terry Eagleton is not alone in pointing out the "extreme right-wing features which Lawrence shared with Eliot and Pound—a raging contempt for liberal and democratic values [and] a slavish submission to impersonal authority" (Russell 1956, 105; Nulle 1940; Hynes 1977, 95; Eagleton 1983, 42; Eagleton 2005, 258-260; Guttmann 1999; Al-Dabbagh 2011).

Former students recall that neither Joyce nor Lawrence were on the reading list for Trout's second semester novel course at Millersville, but Joseph Conrad's *Lord Jim* (1900), Arnold Bennett's *The Old Wives' Tale* (1908), and Virginia Woolf's *To the Lighthouse* (1927) were, as well as works by Thomas Hardy and Henry James. Like many professors, Bill emphasized the poetry or fiction of authors not just for their significance in literary history, but because their works corresponded to his personal and literary values. His first semester novel course included works by Henry Fielding, Sir Walter Scott, Jane Austen, Anthony Trollope, and Charles Dickens. It should come as no surprise that Trout devoted more time in his poetry course to his favorite British poets—Hardy, Housman, de la Mare, Mew and the Georgians—as well as to Gerard Manley Hopkins and Yeats, but also introduced his students to a wide range of others, including some less celebrated ones, among them John

Davidson, Francis Thompson, and Edwin Muir, whom he called a "splendid poet" from the "lower class," and lesbian writer Sylvia Townsend Warner, of whom he said a "...good poet. Slightly acid attitude, stimulating...," and whom Untermeyer characterizes as having a "low-pitched but tart tone of voice, like a feminine Thomas Hardy (Untermeyer 1958, 370). But Dianne Danz pointed out, Dylan Thomas was not among the poets Trout taught in 1962 when she took the course.

That Bill's library contained many novels by Joseph Conrad (1857-1924)—among them *The Nigger of the "Narcissus," Youth, Typhoon, Nostromo, Chance, The Shadow-Line*, and *The Arrow of Gold*—confirms the memory of his Millersville student Kenneth Gibble, who said that Trout's passion for the author "turned me into a devotee of Joseph Conrad." In his second year of teaching, Gibble wrote to Bill telling him of an after-school class he was offering to students interested in studying the novel and being "gently" warned by him that "*Heart of Darkness* might be a bit hard to handle for high school sophomores." Given his study of Jung and admiration for the works of Thomas Hardy, it is not surprising that Bill felt a special affinity for Conrad's works, particularly his *Lord Jim*.

The inner struggle created in Jim, the novel's protagonist (who thinks himself a failure), results from the conflicts between his ideals or dreams on the one hand and the contradictions, weaknesses, and imperfections inherent in human beings living in the indifferent or amoral universe. Stein, an aging German merchant and noted entomologist whose passion is collecting beetles and butterflies with whom Marlow, the novel's narrator, discusses Jim's situation, holds a philosophy with which Trout, according to Kenneth Gibble, told his Millersville students he agreed. Stein agrees with Marlow that the problem for Jim, and by implication for all of us, is "not how to be cured, but how to live"—"how to be." But there are ambiguities in the way Stein suggests achieving self-knowledge, wholeness (Jung's "individuation"). "The way," he believes, "is to the destructive element submit yourself" but to use your dreams, your ideals to stay afloat. "That is the way. To follow the dream, and again to follow the dream..." (Conrad 1923, 212-215; Schwartz 2001, 79-96; Panichas 2000). For Bill this, as we have seen, involved living to one's-self, growing a carapace, accepting the need to confront the dark side of our nature, and using Jungian techniques to explore the collective unconscious. During a period of frustration and indecision in my doctoral study, Bill proffered advice which reflects his own philosophy of life and its relationship to Conrad's *Lord Jim*. In a letter of 2 May 1971 he reminds me, "'After all, we are in the world,' the Cardinal said" and then asks: "Is it not strategy to place oneself, as soon as possible, beyond the forces of subversion? Once so ensconced, you will be as free as it is possible to be free. During this period of immersion in the destructive element, you will be able ... to make the token submission, and yet to preserve the quality of your standards."

Colleagues and students remember Trout's exploration of the byways of British and American letters. He tells Don Smith in a letter of 27 January 1941 that if he has "a yen for some fiction," he should read Mary Webb's *Precious Bane*, which he characterized as: "Poetic, unpretentious, written with uncanny insight and startling subtlety in its chronicling of the vagaries of the human heart." Responding to something Smith had written to him about German stories, Bill asks in a letter of 6 June 1945, if he knows the work of "my beloved Kay Boyle," whose "stories come alive. Do you know the magnificent stories in her White Horse of Vienna? Put her on your list as a 'must' read; the writing is exquisite." He recalls Ann Bridge's "The Burberry," as "a charming but terrifying story" published in *The Atlantic*, in a letter of 15 November 1943 to Smith. "It had," he explains "to do with a suicidal impulse that was transmuted to the wearer of a certain coat." The Powys brothers (John Cowper, Theodore F., and Llewellyn), Anne Sedgwick, and Lafcadio Hearn, all of whom he spoke of with enthusiasm, are likely not readily recognized by the reading public; nor are their books usually found on college reading lists or encountered very often in literary publications, save for those intended for literary scholars.

Novelists and short story writers including Sir Walter Scott, George Eliot, Stendhal, George Meredith (referred to in his letters), Robert Louis Stevenson, Rudyard Kipling, Virginia Woolf (mentioned in his letters), Ford Madox Ford, Aldous Huxley; and H. E. Bates and A. E. Coppard (both of whom he recommended to me), are among the authors represented in Trout's library. He revered Samuel Johnson, the British lexicographer, poet, critic, and celebrated conversationalist. During one of my afternoon visits Bill, in talking about the criteria for judging the merits of a literary work, quoted Dr. Johnson's observation that: "The only end of writing is to enable the reader better to enjoy life, or better to endure it."Since one of the courses he taught on a regular basis at Millersville was Essay, it is not surprising that his library contains collections of major essayists, among them: Montaigne, Emerson, Thomas Mann, Hilaire Belloc, G. K. Chesterton, and J. B. Priestley (a particular favorite). Other British and European poets found among his books include Robert Herrick and Andrew Marvell; Wordsworth, Shelley, and Emily Bronte; Tennyson, Clough, Gerard Manley Hopkins, and Matthew Arnold; Christina Rossetti and Swinburne; Rupert Brooke, Harold Monro, John Masefield, Robert Graves, and Richard Aldington; Heinrich Heine (the text source for many songs by Schubert and Schumann), Charles Baudelaire, the South African Roy Campbell; and Kenneth Rexroth's anthology *The New British Poets,* just one of at least half a dozen poetry anthologies. He also owned a multi-volume set of the *Greek Anthology* in Greek with the English translation on the facing page. His library contained Chinese and Japanese poetry in translation, including Shigeyoshi Obata's *The Works of Li Po: The Chinese Poet* and *Hiroshige's Tokaido in Prints and Poetry*, as well as several books on the *I Ching*, among them Helmut Wilhelm's *Change: Eight Lectures on the I Ching* (1960).

An idea of just how eclectic and voracious a reader Bill was is gained from his letters, such as one of 21 October 1940 to Don Smith in which he lists his current reading: "Euripides's *Medea, The Double Dealer* by Congreave, Shakespeare's *Richard II*, Marlowe's *Massacre at Paris*, and Ibsen's *League of Youth*." The "extra-curricular" summer reading list he made in a letter of 27 July 1953 to his Christiana School colleagues Robert and Jean Rentz includes: "Henri Murger, Vie de Boheme; A life of W. B. Yeats; A life of George Sand; Daudet, Sappho; Fielding, Jonathan Wild; Gogol, Dead Souls; Shellabarger, Lord Chesterfield and His World."

In addition to sharing what he was reading Bill was also eager to know what others were reading, as his former Millersville student Betty Curtis recalled, saying that he always asked her when she called him: "What are you reading?" Any conversation with Mr. Trout would include his suggestions for books he believed a student or friend would find interesting or valuable. And both colleagues and former students recall his ability to quote poetry and lengthy passages of prose from memory.

Chapter 8
Literary Interests — American

When it came to American literature the writers of most interest to Trout were, not surprisingly, those whose works explored social, philosophical, and psychological issues. As with the British and European authors discussed in the previous chapter, the American poets and fiction writers Bill valued most, as well as those he did not, provide clues about his ideas and values and his approach to poetry.

Trout's observations on Walt Whitman in his 1962 Contemporary Poetry class at Millersville, as his student Dianne Danz recalled, show he was no fancier of the poet. While sharing Whitman's sympathy for ordinary men and women and his anti-capitalism, there appears to have been much Bill did not like about his verse. In commenting on "Song of Myself" he acknowledges the value of using "concrete minutiae of human life," but faults him for his "jumble of themes" and failure to organize them into a "formal pattern." In short, Bill found Whitman's verse formless, its irregularities of the eye (arrangement of words on the page) and ear being little more than cadenced prose, a mere catalogue of things. In this he was in the company, albeit for him uncomfortable, of Ezra Pound and T. S. Eliot in having doubts about Whitman's poetry. In spite of its merits in capturing the images, pulse, and spirit of ordinary life in nineteenth-century America, there was more prose than poetry in Whitman's free verse. Though he probably shared Whitman's insistence that making a poem "flow" was crucial to its success, Bill appears not to have accepted his heavy reliance on creating this "flow" by using rhythms originating in the cadences of manual labor and informed by the sounds of the sea he heard while walking the shore of Long Island. Trout may well have been one of those people F. O. Matthiessen was thinking of when he wrote of "Song of Myself": "Readers with a distaste for loosely defined mysticism have plenty of grounds for objection in the way the poet's belief in divine inspiration is clothed in imagery that obscures all distinctions between body and soul by portraying the soul as merely the sexual agent" (Matthiessen 1941, 535, 565-569). Thin on thought and often lacking emotional depth, Whitman's poems were likely regarded by Trout as little more than ejaculations of pure sensation. What may also have bothered Bill was that Whitman's improvisational approach to poetry made him careless with words. By using generic or generalized terms, slang, and strange coinages, his lack of clarity undermines the communicative purpose of language. Like Trout Whitman was passionate about opera, particularly Italian opera. He attended performances frequently and while aspiring to model his poetry on music, succeeded only, according to Matthiessen, in "making his poems vaguer." In his rejection of the elements of traditional poetic form—rhyme, meter, verbal melody, assonance—Whitman precluded the possibility of making his poems musical. While Whitman "fooled himself" into thinking his verse "could rival the effects of music," Trout was not taken in by his claims that his verse was analogous to "singing," carolling," or "chanting" (Matthiessen 1941, 579-580, 558-562).

That Bill likely found little intellect and no skepticism in *Leaves of Grass* further explains his negative reaction to Whitman's verse. Moreover, the monotony and bombast characteristic of his oratory-inspired prose poetry clearly put Bill off. Then too, the insecure, private, modest, and always discreet Trout was perhaps uncomfortable with the not so subtle suggestion of eroticism in much of Whitman's poetry, specifically in his depiction of male bonding—something Bill may have recognized about himself but did not want others to know or even suspect.

The American poets Whitman lauded were Emerson, Longfellow, Bryant, and Whittier because their verse expressed what he believed American poetry should be about, capturing the national character through: "vital-tasting melody, rhym'd philosophy"; "rich color, graceful forms and incidents"; "a taste of open air ... touching the highest universal truths, enthusiasms, duties—morals"; and "the zeal, the moral energy, the splendid rectitude that founded New England." But the idealism that underpins these writers is of a piece with the optimism of Whitman's poetry, which Trout no doubt believed did not acknowledge the imperfections of human beings, the mixture of good and evil in their makeup, and the failure to recognize the dark side of the human psyche, which is the stuff of tragedy. Whitman's distaste for the writings of Edgar Allan Poe was rooted in what he saw as the "tendency of poetic culture [in the nineteenth-century] to morbidity, abnormal beauty—the sickliness of all technical thought or refinement in itself...." He called for the liberation of American poets from the bondage of foreign models, including Sir Walter Scott, Alfred Lord Tennyson, and even Shakespeare in order to fulfill "modern and scientific and democratic American purposes" (Whitman 1914, 173-174,150-151, 281-285, 320, 393-394). In spite of Whitman's criticism of American materialism and the exploitation of the poor by the rich in such unpublished notebook jottings from the 1870s as "The Tramp and Strike Question," "Who Gets the Plunder?," and the slightly qualified optimism of *Democratic Vistas* (1871), Trout probably could not stomach what David Reynolds calls Whitman's "jingoistic patriotism," his "hyperbolic reverence for America's past heroes, whom he mythologized in several stories and poems." Bill also criticizes Whitman's self-centeredness, his "blatant, unbearable egotism." Then, too, as Reynolds insists, *Leaves of Grass* "may be regarded as a sermon," saying: "The poem's prophetic tone, its stately biblical cadences, its numerous references to the soul and to God: all of these religious elements give it a sermonic flavor" (Reynolds 1988, 310-311, 26). Given Trout's objection to being preached at, as we have seen he accuses Thomas Carlyle of doing, it is not unreasonable to assume he found the same tone in Whitman's poems. Trout also may have seen Whitman's efforts to persuade readers of the virtues of America and the common man as reducing poetry to rhetoric. Next to Whitman's "Song for All Seas, All Ships" that Walter de la Mare included in a collection of poems "for the young of all ages," Trout wrote, "but what to expect from that source?"

Trout's view of Emily Dickinson's poetry was very different. Writing to Don Smith in May 1943, he admits that Dickinson had a

> tendency to be precious, but that is very explicable psychologically if one knows her life and background. She is a magnificent artist, keeping with admirable integrity, steady within her genre. Few poets have so completely translated poignant emotion—love or grief or awe—into the naked and enduring medium of language; few are so genuinely sincere. Who could [invent] anything like those innocent looking quatrains that suddenly explode in one's hands like a bomb and fill the universe with stars and colored lights.

His tattered copy of Martha Dickinson Bianchi's *The Poems of Emily Dickinson* (1932) has his favorite poems, and there are many, marked in the book's index of first lines. He also owned two other volumes of her verse and her collected letters, as well as Millicent Todd Bingham's *Ancestors'*

Brocades: The Literary Debut of Emily Dickinson (1945) and her *Emily Dickinson's Home: Letters of Edward Dickinson and His Family* (1955). He asks Don Smith in a letter of 11 June 1945 if he knows her poem "The feet of people walking home," and then says his current favorite is "I dwell in Possibility." He also wrote of Dickinson to Jean Rentz in an undated letter of the early 1950s, saying:

> You will find that she wears well. She can be so god dam[n] cute and coy and irritating at times; and on the next page will be some gigantic concept that leaves you leaning against the wall and wondering what happened to the neat little small town world you have been inhabiting. But even if you move nervously in that metaphysical world of hers, where the Hound of Heaven laps a demure bowl of milk on her door-step, and is roundly and acidly rated if He becomes insistent, you can always get slightly drunk on her poetry as such, the 'noble weather' of an exuberant and gifted expression.

He then suggests Rentz look up two poems in particular: "These are the days when birds come back" and "At last to be identified!" "But," he continues, "there are dozens that one finds one-self muttering over on dark suicidal mornings," and then by way of example goes on to quote Dickinson's "How much the present moment seems."

As noted earlier, Trout shared Dickinson's skepticism about conventional Christianity. Noting that at times she addresses God as "burglar, banker, father," he told a Millersville class: "She cannot forgive God for masking his face behind the cruelty of life and mercilessness of nature. Shame is the tint divine, she concludes, shame should be the tint divine of a deity that plays craps with his creatures and with loaded dice." Explicating for his Millersville students Dickinson's "The sky is low, the clouds are mean," Bill again reveals something about himself in what he says of her, something that shows up in much of his nature poetry: "With advancing years, her views of nature become skeptical, paradoxical, and inconclusive. The reality for her was man, and she seems to think that the possession of a conscious mind creates a gulf of sorts between man and his environment. In the end—though Emily hates to admit—nature fails us. She must turn to man, and perhaps through man to what is called the spiritual." While she knew the outer world through walks, correspondence, newspapers and magazines, as her poem "The Popular Heart is a Cannon first," with dark and sensational imagery drawn from popular culture, it was her preoccupation with the inner world that most informed Dickinson's poetry.

Like the content of Donne's poetry, so the philosophical and spiritual issues Emily Dickinson plumbed seem to have been a major reason for Trout's fondness for her. He says, perhaps with himself in mind, that her poem "A death-blow is a life-blow to some" is "the quintessence of a cruel and ugly truism—that some people cannot afford to evade pain," that only through suffering can one reach fruition, particularly in the arts. Implicit in this poem, he goes on to tell students, is the rejection of the "educator's" belief that "everybody should be adjusted." But he asks: "Will not adjustment be just mediocrity?" In this poem he sees implied the philosophical question "which everybody must solve for himself if he can: is the duality a law of the cosmos? Can there be light without darkness? Can there be no good without there is evil? Is the fruit of the Tree of Life forever inaccessible unless one has tasted the fruit of the Tree of Good and Evil?"

In a lecture on Dickinson, Bill again reveals something of himself in his discussion of her "To fight aloud is very brave." With a sense that he is speaking from personal experience, he tells students that it is "comparatively easy to be brave when the world sympathizes with our trouble and friends give us moral support." It is not such people Dickinson is writing about, he insists, but those more courageous people, the ones "who fight silently because the sight of their conflict would cause pain to others, or because their trouble is a trouble that the world would hold in contempt or would condemn the sufferer for—some flawed heredity that forces the sufferer into a desperate and anguished loneliness," a situation he alludes to in his poem "Heritage." Such people either lose their battles ("and nobody sees the defeat" but only "sees the weakling, the stumbler into ditches, the failure; or worse—the one whose unwilling ... infraction of the world's law brings him to the shame of public obloquy, the degradation of the jail"); or after "a life of spiritual campaigning" they win a Pyrrhic victory "and go to their graves, meek, self-sacrificing, self-effacing, or perhaps hard-bitten ... and no person knows the daily life of endurance without hope, the years never having another human being to confide in or to draw strength from, perhaps no spiritual comfort—no religion—to which they can turn; no human being knows of those crazy hours between two and four in the morning [hours Bill knew all too well], when the sufferer twists in his bed, biting his knuckles and staring into darkness." I would suggest that in this peroration on Dickinson's poem Bill is talking as much about himself as he is about "To fight aloud is very brave." What is the "flawed heredity," the "unwilling infraction of the world's law" that isolates him from other people and causes his loneliness and persistent self-doubt? Could it have been his sexual orientation? Whatever the cause of his mental anguish and struggle with "The Cavalry of Woe," of one thing he was certain, as the line from Morienus Romanus (a 6th-century hermit philosopher and alchemist) he quoted in an undated letter to me in the 1970s makes clear: "Exceeding narrow is the gateway to peace, and none may enter save through affliction of the soul."

"Instinctively Emily Dickinson hated the pride of the wealthy and the great," Trout insists to his students. "Her aim in life was to attain a dignity 'passing pomposity' ": an aim that could also be attributed to Bill. He noted that in some of her poems, "She assaulted a pompous God and she assaulted pompous men." A poem he often quoted from memory, always ending with a wry smile and slight chuckle, was her "I'm nobody. Who are you?" In his lecture on Dickinson he says of it: "Here again you have the swift tribute to the quietly philosophical mind that accepts life without protest—without futile ambition; the sort of mind that finds stimulus enough in what appears a prosaic existence—[paraphrasing the first two lines of William Blake's 'Auguries of Innocence'] finds the world in a grain of sand and heaven in a wild flower."

Not having the benefit of the revisionist scholarship on Dickinson, which only began to appear after he retired, Trout either ignored or overlooked her acceptance of social differences as the natural order of things. Her values, attitudes, and beliefs were, for the most part, those of the small-town New England gentry. Her contact with the working classes was limited to the services they performed for her family, friends, and neighbors. She shared the upper-middle-class concerns posed by laborers and such immigrant groups as the Irish. The myth of Miss Emily fostered by her sister Lavinia, by her niece Martha Dickinson Bianchi (who edited her poems to fit the image of the "White Moth of Amherst" and make them more acceptable to popular taste), and others, like Mabel Loomis Todd, who oversaw the publication of her poems and letters, was not seriously challenged until after Bill left the classroom (Mitchell 2000, 5, 10-13, 133-139; Hart and Smith 1998, xi-xix).

But it was not just Dickinson's themes or content that won Trout's admiration. He devoted much of his lecture on her to the technical aspects of her versification. While seemingly conventional—"the rhyme of the hymn book or the old ballad stanza"—her rhyme, he observes, is anything but conventional. "She shifts the caesura (the break in the middle of the line) and she blends (with the fixed beat of the meter) the free cadence of speech. And often the emotional force of a word is made to supply the missing beat." He praises her skill in using suspended rhyme, perhaps the most common form of approximate rhyme, assonance. What he calls Dickinson's insistent use of suspended rhyme led him to ask rhetorically: "Was she perhaps using consciously this clashing disjunction, this unharmonious harmony, to convey by the innuendo of sound her view of a world in which the pieces of the puzzle do not fit, of a world of broken sequences, of a world in which logic ravels out and becomes irrational ...?" As he points out: "Abetting the rhythmic structure is of course diction and this author's diction—vivid, apt, imperiously individual—is her unmistakable trademark." Using her poem "The soul selects her own society" by way of example, Bill insists that Dickinson "has no truck whatever with conventional poetic diction, and she often uses harsh, realistic figures with telling effect." Hers is "A world fashioned perhaps by a gleeful ironist delighting in the cruel opposition between what seems and what is." The characteristics of Dickinson's poetry he so admired perhaps gave Trout the courage to turn his back on the modernist abandonment of traditional form for ever more formless free verse and to write poetry as he did, though not in any slavishly imitative way.

The "clashing disjunction," "unharmonious harmony," "broken sequences," and logic unraveling into irrationality that Trout notes in Dickinson's unconventional diction, imagery, and rhymes may in part have had physiological origins of which he was not aware. Based on her letters and poems, research into her medical records, and the prevailing negative attitude of the day toward certain illnesses, Lyndall Gordon speculates in her 2010 biography of the poet that Emily Dickinson may have suffered from epilepsy, which may account for her reclusiveness as well as for the imagery and structure of her poetry. The frequency of earthquakes, volcanoes, explosions, and ecstatic visionary expressions of an altered consciousness in her poems may also owe something to the domestic tension occasioned by the protracted marital infidelity of her brother Austin (Gordon 2010, *passim*). But for David Reynolds the origin of such imagery does not have a physiological or familial origin but is traceable to the limitations Dickinson and other women of her day experienced in a male-dominated society, which kept them from exercising economic, social, political, and intellectual independence (Reynolds 1988, 414-415).

Edwin Arlington Robinson and Trout had many things in common, including their admiration for Charles Dickens, Thomas Hardy, and A. E. Housman

(Torrence 1940, *passim*). Their approach to versification shared a number of characteristics. Both had little interest in free verse. But whereas Robinson as he aged wrote more blank verse, Trout, for the most part, favored metered forms and rhyme. When Ellsworth Barnard points out that Robinson's "power to make feeling come alive by the magic of sound," often through his use of "assonance and alliteration," one recognizes a similar quality in Trout's poetry. Bill would have agreed with Robinson's insistence that "Poetry must be music." The economy of means—compression and concision—characteristic of both poets when combined with their penchant for suggestion, indirection, and inference are key characteristics of their poetry. What at times makes their poetry challenging for some readers is their use of historical, literary, and biblical allusions or imagery, and in Trout's case Jungian influences or references to the Tarot (Barnard 1952, 56-57, 59, 16-18).

There are also many biographical and literary parallels between the two poets, though each had different life experiences and his own poetic voice. Like Trout, Robinson spent years caring for family members and tending the family home. Living at home having to nurse his ill father, deal with alcoholic and drug-addicted brothers, and do household chores for his widowed mother, left him little time to pursue a career as a poet. Unlike Trout, Robinson had a number of close women friends, and whereas he wanted to marry and was repeatedly disappointed by women who didn't respond to his love, Trout apparently never entertained the idea of matrimony. Yet both poets were deeply committed to male friends and each shared a sense of loss and ensuing loneliness when the intimacy of these personal relationships ended as one by one the friends married and then attended to the needs of their wives and families. What Scott Donaldson says of Robinson—that he was "one of the most private persons who ever lived," was secretive and "rarely spoke of the most important events of his life," and "was notorious for keeping his friends in separate compartments"—can be said of Trout to an even greater degree. Both men were shy and uncomfortable in most social situations. As their letters testify, they had low self-respect and often were given to self-disparagement (Donaldson 2007, 5, 69-71, 124-139, 92-97, 107-109, 118, 179).

Although during childhood and adolescence Robinson enjoyed an economic security not shared by Trout, he was to experience poverty for many years after leaving Gardner, Maine, in the wake of the collapse of his family's fortunes, the result of the panic of 1893 and imprudent investments made by Herman (his businessman brother), whose jealousy over the affection his wife and daughters had for Uncle Win precipitated his leaving home. With the exception of his war-work at Lukens Steel, Trout spent his entire adult life teaching, while Robinson, who put his muse before almost everything else, worked off-and-on at a variety of odd jobs and experienced long periods of unemployment, penury, and financial dependence on friends. Although Trout never experienced near starvation, Robinson did. Trout's life was rooted—he stayed put—first in Gap and then in Lancaster. He never lived outside of Lancaster County and even there changed abodes only three times in his life, all within about a twenty-mile radius of his birthplace. Robinson on the other hand lived an itinerant life: he had no permanent home after leaving Maine, and not only did he change his address frequently during his years in New York, but over many years spent weeks if not months as a house guest of various friends (Donaldson 2007, 59, 63-65, 115, 68-71, 93, 97, 108-109, 139, 215-218, 272, 303-304).

Social criticism was a part of their poetry. For example, poems like Robinson's *Cassandra* and "The Field of Glory" and Trout's "All are headed for the river that drives on down there, in dank" and "Asylum" raise questions about America's worship of Mammon and its misplaced reliance on power and military might, what Robinson, whose Republicanism weakened over the years, called the "Trinity" of "Dollar, Dove, and Eagle." *King Jasper*, Robinson's long 1934 poem, is the story of a business tycoon who becomes royalty through rampant ambition, greed, and cutthroat competition. The antiwar sentiment expressed in two of Robinson's other long poems, *Merlin* and *Lancelot*, no doubt resonated with Trout, who held similar views on war and the military. Bill owned copies of all three works as well as *The Glory of the Nightingales* and *Matthias at the Door*, two more of Robinson's book-length, blank-verse narrative poems. Along with their opposition to war, both poets had no sympathy for American-style nationalism. Neither was a "Patriot." Like Trout, Robinson was critical of capitalism and contemptuous of businessmen and material success, though he seemed willing to accept intervention with editors from well-to-do patrons, from President Theodore Roosevelt (who also gave him a sinecure in the New York Customs House), and from successful fellow writers during the years of rejection by publishers and hostile reviews from many critics. Trout had no advocates for his poetry. Both Trout and Robinson expressed anti-capitalist attitudes in letters throughout their lives and were particularly hostile to big business (Donaldson 200, 452-454; Torrence 1940, 9, 11-12, 80, 92; Bernard 1952, 260-264). There is no doubt Trout knew of Robinson's economic views and indifference to social status and material success not only from the poems themselves but because he had owned a copy of Torrence's *Selected Letters of Edwin Arlington Robinson* since February of 1943 as well as a copy of Ellsworth Barnard's *Edwin Arlington Robinson: A Critical Study*.

The bedrock beliefs held by the citizens of Gardiner (Robinson's hometown) Donaldson says were: "a devout materialism, a strict Victorian morality, and a Puritan work ethic," as well as a commitment to rock-ribbed Republican political values. According to Donaldson, Robinson subscribed to all of these except the materialism (Donaldson 2007, 106). The same cannot be said of Trout, who lived in a small town most of whose residents likely held values similar to the citizens of Gardiner. For Bill only the work ethic, in his case coming out of an Anglo-German heritage, was the one part of small-town values to which he seems to have subscribed. However, each poet in his own way experienced the repression and spiritual impoverishment of small-town life (though early on Robinson found support for his literary interests from members of the Gardiner Poetry Society, Trout had no such support system), artistic and literary neglect, and a sense of being out of joint with his society's materialism and conventional measures of what constitutes success. And both sometimes turned to alcohol to ease their pain. There was in Robinson a vein of Puritan morality, though not censoriousness, where sex was concerned. As we know from his letters to Don Smith, Bill was accepting of other people's weaknesses of the flesh, and might be thought by some to have gently encouraged them (Donaldson 2007, 53-56, 292-293).

That so much of Robinson's poetry centered on individual human beings is no doubt another reason Trout was drawn to him. The characters in Robinson's poems that seem to have appealed most to Bill (if we take his letters and notations in Barnard's book as evidence) are those who fall into one of four categories: people like Captain Craig who are failures by the conventional standards of success (wealth, power, fame); those like Richard Cory "whose lives are outwardly illustrious but inwardly empty"; those like Aunt Imogen, the "Poor Relation"; and those in *Eros Turannos* and *Amaranth* who are either victims of self-delusion or those living in the wrong world and unable or unwilling to see the disappointing truth that may save them (Barnard 1952, 122-128, 134-137, 70, 125).

Bill tells Don Smith in a letter of 26 August 1945 that he spent "the terrible day of the 14th [of August, the day the Japanese accepted the terms of surrender] cleaning windows and porches" and glued to the radio or walking around "until 4:00 am, trying to understand, and being glad that I'm not young in this new world in which I don't belong." Bill's own sense of being a misfit and a failure may also have drawn him to Robinson's verse, which often takes as subjects small-town eccentrics, dreamers, and failures as in "Miniver Cheevy," "George Crabbe," *Captain Craig*, "Dear Friends," and, in "Calverly's," a remembrance of friends made at a West Side bar. Yet it is because of their inability to fit the conventional mold and achieve success that these people—whom Robinson views sympathetically—find themselves on the margins of "respectable" society. Not unlike the folks in Trout's "Asylum" or Lizzie in his "Lark Descending," they became victims of those who establish the norms of society, control its institutions, and judge success based on status and wealth. As their poems testify, both poets expressed sympathy and compassion for their fellow creatures (Barnard 1952, 20-23). Both poets also had an intimate understanding of and sympathy for the elderly, and often took old folks, as Robinson did in "The Poor Relation," "Isaac and Archibald," and *Captain Craig*, as the subject of some of their best poems. Although humor is often found in Robinson's poems (among them *Captain Craig* and particularly "Miniver Cheevy") it is less often encountered in Trout's—"Commencement," "Semi-Private Room," and "Lark Descending" are among the few exceptions.

Like other "Poets, rogues, and sick physicians," to use Robinson's words, "The Town Down the River," New York City, lured Robinson. He lived there for many years and even for a time was bent on writing plays for Broadway. Pointing to poems like "Calverly's," "Veteran Sirens," "The Poor Relation," and "The White Lights" whose settings or characters are urban, Louis Coxe claims he was "perhaps" America's "first and finest" city poet (Coxe 1969, 158-160), though a better case might be made for Walt Whitman. Robinson enjoyed city life and availed himself of its many attractions—including art exhibitions, plays, concerts, and operas—insofar as his skimpy income allowed. If Bill ever heard the siren call of urban life he never yielded to it.

While at a time when many poets and critics who were considered modern saw urban life and technology, whether good *or* bad, as defining modern American culture and often took them as subjects or settings for their verse, Robinson (in many of his short and medium-length poems) and Trout focused on rural and small-town life, Tilbury Town (the fictionalized Gardiner, Maine) and Gap and the countryside around it. In their verse they neither celebrated nor condemned city life or the machines spawned by industrialization, but rather focused on themselves, people they knew or observed, and on their memories of village life or the country to explore personal themes of loneliness, disappointment, torment, and courage. Whereas Robinson in such poems as "The Dead Village" and "The House on the Hill" is critical of the conventionality, censoriousness, and materialism of Tilbury Town residents—who, as Donaldson points out, confidently "misjudged others and refused to confront their own failings" (Donaldson 2007, 137)—Trout left no poems that can be said to level direct criticism on Gap. What is more, in none of his surviving letters, save one, has there surfaced to date so much as a mention of his hometown, leaving one with the impression that his attitude toward Gap may have been ambivalent. Nor, for the most part, does one find Trout committed to debunking small-town life as Edgar Lee Masters does in *Spoon River Anthology* or as Sinclair Lewis does in his novels *Main Street*, *Babbitt*, and *The Man Who Knew Coolidge*. Nonetheless, in a letter written in January 1945 to his former Gap pupil Bud Cauller, Bill reveals something of his attitude toward small-town life in saying that the "cheerful smile" of Bud's Aunt Rose, who provided him news of her GI nephew, "is one of the few pleasant aspects of Christiana," a village near Gap where Bill was teaching. And in one of his poems he sheds a bit more light on his view of small-town rural life and in so doing drops a tantalizing hint suggestive of his deepest secret:

> Handful of gravel flung against the glass
> In the small hours: should not wisdom save
> The used razor blades, since daily masses
> Nearer the ultimate war, whipped by bravado,
> And since that savant floraison will bar
> Replacement?—Thought here stumbled to a halt,
> Hearing a laughter rocket, and not far,
> Cerebral merriment in the rotten vault.
> Nervously, psychotic glanced around,
> Hunting a mask; and clutched desperately,
> And held, salvation, miraculously found:
> Here, even here, in this derisory,
> Smug town, the purple violets
> Edge the pavement, and peer at passers-by.

Who tossed the gravel against the window in the middle of the night? And to what purpose: harassment of some sort, a summons to a guilty tryst? Or was the thrown gravel merely a metaphor for something that set off a bad dream, or the subject of one? The nervous neurotic (by implication Trout himself) imagining some form of public revelation of the nocturnal event to residents of "this derisory, / Smug town" (one may assume it is Gap), seeks a way to mask himself from shame or censure in a community where even the violets that line the pavement (like townsfolk behind their curtained windows as in the poem "Removal Manqué) "peer at passers-by." Even if the thrown gravel is only a metaphor, the poem embodies Trout's paranoid fear of having people "poke and sniff" at him and helps us understand why, as he told Don Smith, he grew a carapace as a way of protecting himself from the unwanted prying of other people into his private life.

While modernist poets of the T. S. Eliot school were obsessed by the anonymity of modern society populated by modern urban types, Robinson had in poems like *Captain Craig*, "Richard Corey," and "Charles Carville's Eyes," and Trout in poems such as "Lonely wanted but companionship" and "Lark Descending" dealt with the ways in which small-town residents were socially isolated by the suspicions, indifference, petty jealousies, or personal prejudices of their fellow townsfolk. Something of the darker side of small-town and rural life is hinted at in Trout's poem "Country Sale."

> The small stone house—its adjunct acre
> Milling with males of many varied stages
> Of size and undress—racketed with the clatter
> Of the auctioneer and of women of sundry ages.
>
> Venom stewed in the three—cold, sneering hate,
> Scheming, as three heads together bowed.
> Not July's amiable coolness could abate
> Rancor from which the mind flinched, cowed.
>
> Only the old brown house retained composure,
> Its bare rooms echoing to urchin feet;
> The chimney ivy wreathed in dark leisure,
> As two stone centuries stared across the wheat.

The moral of Robinson's "Cliff Klingenhagen," the man who drank the wormwood instead of the wine, Trout told his Millersville poetry class is that, "Life is bitter, and the sooner you get accustomed to it, the better," which is as revelatory of his fatalistic view of life as is his underlining of a sentence in Ellsworth Barnard's book containing this quotation taken from Robinson's

Eros Turannos: "Take what the god has given, however harsh and desolating it may be" (Barnard 1952, 137). One doesn't need to read between the lines of Bill's letters and poems to recognize that like Hardy, he and Robinson saw the world through essentially similar lenses.

Robinson was steadfast in denying critics' contentions that his poems had a pessimistic tone. While none of Trout's poems reflects the "irremediable cheerfulness" and unsuppressed humor in the face of adversity found in Robinson's *Captain Craig*, with its repeated urgings that people "find the light" and resist giving in to despair, poems like "Henry" and those about his mother's courage, kindness, and positive outlook do act as a foil to the fatalism inherent in Trout's verse, a belief in the absurdity and meaninglessness of life perhaps no more starkly stated than in his poem:

> Remember how the old woman used to chuckle,
> Telling of neighbors on the adjacent farm?
> They had been a little unfortunate, dowered with an idiot
> child.
> He must have been eighteen or thereabouts—
> Milieu of amusing reminiscence.
> Drawn from his blankets, cleaned, combed, and fed,
> The lumbering creature, in a clement weather,
> Was placed against a sheltering southern wall.
> And then they dabbed some glue on his thumb and index
> finger—
> Each hand; and gave him a chicken feather,
> And left him safely so, to pluck and pluck
> In ordinate succession across the hours,
> Till time to feed again.—Is that not
> A sort of nice concision, birth to death?

And yet in many of his poems, particularly those about his mother, one senses his belief that (as with Robinson) fortitude is a virtue just as living without illusions is a necessity for survival (Barnard 1952, 196-197, 199, 238). A poem like " 'Forgive,' you said, over and over" may be a specific reference to the bitter split among the Trout brothers, or may more generally relate to conflicts or differences Bill had with specific institutions or with a society whose values he did not share. Perhaps this plea to put anger and resentment aside and either make peace in the family or more broadly accept in this life those things one cannot change, is one his mother made to him and is recalled later in life, after her death.

> "Forgive," you said, over and over,
> "Forgive and forbear"; although
> I brooded painfully, never
> Did my dull groping know.
> Today I hear the whispered phrase,
> No longer enigmatic; loss
> Teaches in its blunt ways—
> Salt whip and servile cross.
> "Forgive, forgive and forbear,"
> I hear, whispered prayer, plea;
> And on the ravaged, desolate way
> That I must travel yet, I share
> Truly what you said to me,
> And add, "It is but for a day."

Both poets struggled to find a creed by which to live. Robinson, though steadfastly denying his poems reflected his personal philosophy, seems, nonetheless, to have tried in a tentative way to work one out about 1897 in a series of twenty-three "Octaves," poems dealing with religion and philosophy, which served as a guide to life, a confession of faith if you will, outside of institutional religion (Donaldson 2007, 140-142, 177). Trout, as we have seen, turned to Jung for help in gaining self-knowledge as a means of finding something to replace organized Christianity and get beyond materialism and competition. And his study of Jung would no doubt have led him to agree with what W. R. Robinson claims Edwin Arlington Robinson came to recognize, namely: "When self-knowledge cannot come from communication with nature, man must turn inward or to his kind—to introspection or to what is 'between man and man' " (Robinson 1967, 49). Edwin Robinson acknowledged having little interest in the poetic possibilities of the natural world. Only after he began to summer at the McDowell Colony in the New Hampshire countryside did contact with nature begin to find its way into his verse, as in "Hillcrest," one of his best poems (Coxe 1969, 106-109). But the influence of nature on his poetry is tentative and slight in comparison to its place in Trout's oeuvre.

Robinson created such memorable figures as Captain Craig, Richard Corey, and the Clerks sometimes pretty directly from life but at other times as fictionalized characters or as composites of individuals he had known, seen, or read about (Donaldson 2007, 113, 136, 147-148, 153, 155, 179). On the other hand, Trout's portrait poems—"Henry," "Great Aunt," "Grandmother" (not included herein), "Lark Descending," "The teacher of biology—a former marine," and others—were not about fictionalized or composite characters but individuals Bill knew personally. The people Bill took for his portrait poems exhibit values, ideals, emotions, and ways of behaving he believed were undervalued in a society where status, fame, wealth, material possessions, sham appearance, and getting ahead by aggressive self-promotion were celebrated. His portrait poems are records of unassuming and unremarkable people, "salt-of-the-earth" exemplars, who are modest, dependable, honest, caring, sensitive, and self-sacrificing.

Trout's obsession with time—in many of his poems as noted earlier, including "Summer Ending" and "The small face shrivels, and the eyes grow strange"—was a theme Robinson also treated in his poems, among them "Mr. Flood's Party" and "The Clerks." The poignant and deeply moving tale of Flood's loneliness in old age caused by lost friendships in those houses in Tilbury Town whose doors were "opened long ago" to him and now are "shut," speaks to the fragility of human relationships over time. Both nature imagery and references to Mr. Flood's early life suggest the passage of time, while in "The Clerks" a former clerk finds his colleagues, who remained "a shop-worn brotherhood" though "... just as good, / And just as human as they ever were." The implication here is that the clerks have sacrificed their youthful dreams and ambitions on the altar of small-town commerce. Yet the speaker admits that he, like those with loftier visions and higher status, be they poets or kings, are still only "clerks of Time," who also struggle to improve or hold on to their social standing in "the same dull webs of discontent" (Coxe 1969, 54-55). But the implication is that most of us are also "clerks of time."

Like Robinson's clerks, Trout, as is apparent in the words and tone of his letters, never fulfilled the promise of his youth: he never achieved the literary life his classmates at Coatesville High School had predicted for him—he never became a literary critic and never published any of the poems he wrote in secrecy. We know from his letters that while he enjoyed sharing his knowledge with young people, he was apparently frustrated and unhappy with the institutional side of education—the meaningless morning devotions and later the mouthing of the Pledge of Allegiance, the dictates of a standard curriculum; the regimentation that stifles the imagination of students and aims to socialize, "adjust" them; having to teach things that made him "shudder"; the meddling of administrators; and the petty politics of institutions of learning. His practice of telling his pupils ghost stories during the lunch period and devoting a half hour after lunch to reading poetry or literary classics to them were ways he could subvert the machine of education and thus spare himself a little from what he referred to in several letters as "the mental prostitution of school teaching." In the poem "Routine," he reflects on the ways in which the habits of everyday life required to earn one's bread in the regimented world of institutional employment undermines individuality and creativity, and in so doing gives voice to what many people feel about their jobs in the factory, the office, the retail shop, and for Bill the public school or college.

> The habitual gesture gives
> Its occult solace, when grim need—
> Through held to tenuous stalemate—lives,
> And forces taut being to bleed.
>
> Coffee, at the rigorous time
> In the spruce kitchen, worn but clean;
> Departure, when the relentless chime
> Dictates the turning of the key:
>
> Such is discipline to support
> A pitiful conscript to renew
> The lost contention, to report
> At hell's arena for review.

And in the poem "Unplanned Obsolescence," likely written after he retired, he renounces the alarm clock's summons to rise and shine for work, saying:

> An abrupt click, a scornful, spinning whirr—
> Time's pestered cleric peevishly resigned,
> Profferring demission with a burr:
> Onward from Now there shall be no more time.
> —No more routine then. No more scurrying
> Of the raddled servant, tardy for review;
> No glance drooping before the stare severe
> Of the task-master: "Do you know that you. . . .?"
> Vacuously harmless is the round,
> Discoloured disk of plastic, where the slim
> Silver needle laboured long: age

Greets this friend, miraculously found;
Together, they renounce both task and wage,
And welcome penury. Let the day be dim.

The values that drew Trout to the work of Willa Cather (1876-1947) were in part similar to those that had attracted him to Robinson. He owned a copy of her collected stories, all her novels, and two biographies of her. While Cather admired those who had settled the frontier and had a deep love of the land, as her novels *O Pioneers!* and *My Antonia* make clear, she had mixed emotions about small town life in Middle America. Her reaction to the confining, stifling atmosphere of Red Cloud and Nebraska is similar to Trout's ambivalence about Gap and Lancaster County. Like Trout, Cather had an abiding interest in the personal past and history, which she indulged in short stories and in such novels as *Death Comes for the Archbishop* and *Shadows on the Rock*. In her books she expresses reverence for the land and for moral, spiritual, and aesthetic values—honesty, honor, integrity, self-reliance, hard work, self-sacrifice, craftsmanship, and beauty—that she saw as being threatened by the technology, materialism, popular mass-culture, and the relentless drive for profits and worldly success that characterized life in twentieth-century America, particularly after World War I. That she was no slave to social convention no doubt resonated with Trout. During her high school and university years she cropped her hair short, wore men's clothes, signed herself William, and developed several passionate relationships with women that went beyond close friendship. She was critical of the commercialism and shallowness of modern life; disliked the narrowness, moralizing, and hypocrisy of small-town folks; and jealously guarded her privacy. Cather, like Trout, loved classical music and opera (which was central to *Song of the Lark*, *Lucy Gayheart*, and a number of her short stories), was something of a Francophile, and valued some of the same writers, among them George Eliot, George Sand (she hung a large etching of Sand by Thomas Couture over the fireplace in her Bank Street apartment), Thomas Mann, and A. E. Housman, whose poetry inspired her to visit the reclusive poet at his flat unannounced (Brown 1953, 47-48, 220-221, 226-227, 238-239, 38-39, 301, 325, 181, 188, 106-109; Lee 1989, 10-12, 60, 57-59, 192, 333).

Both the rhythm of Cather's prose and the rhythm of Trout's poetry, which owe much to their choice of words, correspond to the rhythm of life. In a Millersville lecture he observes that Chinese poets, like the Imagists of the first quarter of the twentieth century, in presenting a concrete object could convey an emotion or thought without directly alluding to it. "Willa Cather," he goes on to point out, "says that the quality of suggested emotion is always characteristic of real literature." He supports this assertion and expands it by citing a passage from her essay "The Novel Démeublé": "Whatever is felt upon the page without being specifically named there—that, one might say, is created. It is the inexplicable presence of the thing not named, of the overtone divined by the ear but not heard by it, the verbal mood, the emotional aura of the fact or the thing or the deed, that gives high quality to the novel or the drama, as well as to poetry itself." A preference for the suggestive over the literal is also one of the salient characteristics of Trout's verse. The meaning and implications of "the thing not named" for Cather's fiction has been much discussed by literary historians and critics, and, I would argue, has relevance for Trout's poetry as well, though more broadly than the interpretation of some feminist scholars applied it in interpreting Cather's work (O'Brien 1984, 576-599).

As Hermione Lee points out: "Willa Cather's fiction is full of life stories, the recounting of autobiographies and biographies. Her characters review their own 'destinies,' or that of the person who has most influenced their own lives." She drew "very intensely and minutely on her life, on people and places she knew and stories she had been told, most especially on the material accumulated in childhood" (Lee 1989, 18-19). Certainly this fact does much to explain Trout's interest in her writing since his own poetry is so deeply informed by his life experiences and memories. The works he most admired were those which grew out of her sense of place (those most closely linked to the world in which she simmered up) or with characters whose philosophical views or psychological struggles reflect the personal conflicts and values with which he could most closely identify, among them: *Song of the Lark*, *One of Ours*, *The Professor's House*, "The Sculptor's Funeral," and "A Wagner Matinee." But he also recognized the weaknesses in her works, particularly in such late novels as *Lucy Gayheart* and *Sapphira and the Slave Girl*.

Writing to me of Cather's *Lucy Gayheart* (1935) on 30 May 1971, he characterizes it as, "a late one, showing traces of age and weariness—how one loathes himself for those remarks—but full of insights unforgettable, and instinct with understanding of music." Lucy, the novel's heroine, while studying piano in Chicago, falls in love with a middle-age singer named Sebastian, who specializes in German *Lieder*, particularly Schubert's song cycles *Winterreise* and *Die Schöne Müllerin*, which were among Trout's favorite vocal works. "*Der Doppelgänger*," a poem by Heinrich Heine that Schubert set to music is among the melancholy songs Sebastian includes in one of his concerts, and is the title Trout gave to one of his poems. Among the "insights unforgettable" that Cather provides into the emotional life of her characters, and by extension to people in real life, may include her suggestion of Sebastian's homosexuality. An example of "the thing not named," Sebastian's unhappy marriage is in part the result of having taken a "talented boy" named Marius (which calls to mind the handsome young hero of Walter Pater's novel *Marius the Epicurean*, a book Trout had read) into their home, and then had to send him away at his wife's angry insistence for reasons not made explicit but which one can intuit.

Bill didn't give a tinker's damn if the battle scenes in *One of Ours* (1922) were unconvincing according to Ernest Hemingway, whom he considered a phony with "false hair Scotch taped to his chest," as he used to say (a witty adaptation of Max Eastman's observation in a review of Hemingway's bull-fighting novel *Death in the Afternoon* in *The New Republic* of 7 June 1933). It was the corrosive effects of commercialization on American life and Claude Wheeler, the novel's hero, Cather focused on, not the war. The exploration of Claude's idealism, love of learning, loneliness, sense of being a misfit trapped in a materialist family and an intellectually and spiritually stifling small town, and his struggle to learn why he was put on earth were the things Trout believed made Cather's novel worthwhile. While serving in France, Claude realizes that after the war he could not go back to the United States. Expressing her views of postwar America (and Bill's as well), Cather says of Claude: "There was no chance for the kind of life he wanted at home, where people were always buying and selling, building and pulling down. He had begun to believe that the Americans were a people of shallow emotions" (Cather 1922, 406). But it may also be that Bill was favorably disposed because he saw himself in Cather's sensitive Midwestern farm boy, dominated by his mother's smothering love and resentful of his bullying father, filled with anxiety by his own sense of inadequacy, and emotionally attached to a fellow officer, Lieutenant David Gerhardt, a handsome, self-assured, and sophisticated New Yorker who had studied violin in Paris, given concert performances, made phonographic records, and spoke French.

In Gerhardt Cather tells us Claude had found "someone whom he could admire without reservation; someone he could envy, emulate, wish to be," and perhaps love; something he had not found with his wife or other women (Cather 1922, 411). Like Trout, both Claude and David are searching for purpose or meaning in life and find it in France through self-sacrifice and in a relationship with another man. There is an intimation of homosexuality in

Claude's feelings for Gerhardt when a German officer Claude has killed is found to have white hands and manicured nails, a silk dressing gown, a ruby pinkie-ring, and around his neck the portrait of an androgynous young man, "pale as snow, with blurred forget-me-not eyes," whom Claude naively says is "Probably a kid brother." To which the more worldly-wise David responds by touching Claude's arm and looking at him "as if something pleasant had happened in this room …" (Cather 1922, 430-432; Griffiths 1984, 266-267). Such subtle suggestiveness of "the thing not named" would not have been lost on Bill.

Many of Cather's most memorable characters are elderly—Professor Emerson Graves, Mrs. Harris, and Aunt Georgiana, to mention but three—something that is also true of Trout's poetry, which often takes the elderly as a subject. Sitting in Gap surrounded by books and listening to his classical recordings and the Met Opera broadcasts, he could identify with Emerson Graves ("The Professor's Commencement"), who had taught all his life in the local high school, never married, and lived with his widowed sister; and also with Aunt Georgiana ("A Wagner Matinee"), once a music teacher at a Boston conservatory, who had eloped with a handsome country lad and lived in isolation for thirty years as a farm wife on the Great Plains. In old age she visits a nephew in Boston—whom as a boy she had introduced to Shakespeare and mythology, tutored in Latin, given musical instruction on the old parlor organ, and told about operas she had seen in Paris—and is taken by him to a matinee symphony concert of Wagner's music. When she clutches his arm as the Pilgrim's chorus from *Tannhäuser* begins, he realizes that for her, thirty years of silence broken only by the sounds of an accordion, a parlor organ, and gospel hymns has ended. The experience brings recognition of the "overwhelming sense of the waste and wear we are powerless to combat." As the music rolls over the old lady and tears glisten on her cheeks, the nephew realizes that "the soul that can suffer so excruciatingly and so interminably; it withers to the outside eye only; like that strange moss which can lie on a dusty shelf half a century and yet, if placed in water grows green again." Bill understood the power of music and appreciated such insights, which touched him as being analogous to his own emotional response to opera. And the story no doubt reminded him of hearing his first classical music and being introduced to Shakespeare, *Gulliver*, and those books about "unfortunate kings," "houses built in trees," "ruined abbeys," and "captives sold into slavery" by his mother and grandmother, and which are recorded in poems like "So safe it was to sit beside."

Bill may have recognized something of himself in Godfrey St. Peter, a history professor and the principal character in *The Professor's House* (1925) who would not give his students "chaff and sawdust" like many instructors do, because, as Cather observes, "his misfortune was that he loved youth—he was weak to it, it kindled him" (Cather 1925, 28). And the same was oh so true of Mr. Trout. Not only is the fifty-two-year-old Professor St. Peter alienated from the values of contemporary society and unhappy about the compromise of standards in academe, his former student and friend, Tom Outland is dead, a casualty of the First World War (as Trout's pupil "Hookie" Bair was of the Second). The university where St. Peter teaches is selling out to athletics and commercialism by caving in to pressure from the state legislature and replacing liberal arts courses with vocational ones and being turned into a "trade school"—something that also concerned Trout as comments in his letters make clear. St. Peter recognizes that his best scholarly work is behind him and that his creative energy has flagged. He is an atheist stuck in a loveless marriage with a materialistic and social-climbing wife and daughters, particularly the older one who treats him to "an orgy of acquisition" in Chicago's stores. He doesn't want to leave his old house with its dripping faucets, painted tin bath tub, too-steep stairs, narrow hallways, creaky floor boards, and out-of-fashion woodwork and color schemes because it was in this house that he "had worked out his career and brought up his daughters," completed his most significant and satisfying scholarship, and developed a friendship with his brilliant and idealistic student Tom Outland that aroused the jealousy of his wife, who called their relationship a "romance of the imagination." The ugly old house was filled with memories; the new one his family insisted on having is modern, "up-to-date" but sterile and cold, without a trace of the history or humanity. Certainly part of the appeal of Godfrey St. Peter for Trout is that for both of them there are certain traditions that need to be protected as a buffer to what they see as the acquisitive, materialistic, status-seeking, intellectually shallow, cheap-and-nasty present in which integrity has been replaced by expediency and everything is measured in terms of appearance and money.

Over the years, as Doris Grumbach observes, both critics and readers have wondered what ails Professor St. Peter. A variety of explanations have been offered but for Grumbach the answer is that the novel "comes as close as Cather would allow to the question of sexual choice outside accepted social patterns" (Grumbach 1984, 338, 343). The recognition of his love for Tom Outland and suppression or sublimation of it is at the root of his unhappiness and central to understanding the novel. The young men Trout befriended in his thirties, "Hookie" Bair among them, may have done for him what Tom Outland did for St. Peter, "brought him a kind of second youth" at a time when "the morning brightness of the world was wearing off ..." (Cather 1925, 258). Like Bill's Lukens friend Jim, Outland came from poverty and was an orphan. His description of Jim to Don Smith is similar to St Peter's observations on first meeting Tom, who had a "manly, mature voice" was "fine-looking," "tall and presumably well built," with beautifully shaped muscular hands. Tom was the kind of student Bill would have been attracted to: he was imaginative; enthusiastic about learning; read Virgil in Latin while working as a manual laborer, a cowhand; loved history; and was sensitive to nature. Disillusioned by modern America's materialism and self-serving politicians, Tom had integrity, was self-assured, down-to-earth, and idealistic. Both St. Peter's love for Tom and the close bonding between Tom and his friend Roddy, which ends in a quarrel, are examples of Cather's veiled suggestions of homosexuality—"the thing not named"—and the latter is, according to Hermione Lee, the most direct one found in any of her novels (Lee 1989, 250). The novel ends after St. Peter is saved by the sewing lady from "accidental" asphyxiation and realizes that while unconscious: "He had let something go—and it was gone: something very precious, that he could not consciously have relinquished, probably." He resigns himself to going on living his diminished life (Cather 1925, 282-283). St. Peter's "letting go" reminds one (and certainly would have occurred to Bill) of the scene in *Der Rosenkavalier* when the Marschallin explains to Octavian that in love relationships those who are unable to "hold and take / hold and relinquish / will be punished by life and God."

That *The Professor's House* is a book about memory and time also goes a long way toward explaining why Bill loved it and so insistently urged me to read it. By way of enticement during one of our afternoon visits he summarized "Tom Outland's Story"—the middle section of the book—then quoted from memory the passage in which Tom first sees the adobe houses and round tower of the cliff-dwelling "through a veil of lightly falling snow." In a letter of 15 July 1961 to his former student Betty Curtis thanking her for an article on Cather she sent him, Trout says that if she has not read *The Professor's House*, "please do." And in response to her letter of 29 May 1960, in which he thanks her for a book on Cather she sent him, he mentions an unfavorable review of it by Malcolm Cowley but insists that, "No matter what anyone says, I shall go down to the everlasting bonfire squawking, 'A great writer, a beautiful writer.' "

The artist Harvey Merrick, deceased hero of "The Sculptor's Funeral," was returned from the East for burial in his Kansas hometown, a small farming and ranching community he had fled to escape an unfeeling and domineering mother who hounded her husband into submission, and from townsfolk whose intolerance and Christian hypocrisy, greed and petty dishonesty, and contempt for things spiritual and intellectual he found insufferable. Most of the townsfolk who come to the sculptor's funeral gossip and snipe at the deceased's impracticality, unconventional lifestyle, and failure to make money and be successful according to their materialistic standards. Only his father, who says, "We didn't none of us ever onderstand him," and the family's mulatto servant shed tears for Harvey. Cather leaves it to Jim Laird—the bibulous lawyer who was Harvey's friend and went to school with him back East, and who, after returning to the town to practice law, took to drink because he couldn't live with himself after all the shady and unethical things he colluded in to make local businessmen and farmers wealthy—to defend the dead man and expose the hypocrisy and corruption of those who disparage him. For someone like Trout, who had grown up in a small rural community and felt out of joint with its values, Cather's story, like Mann's *Tonio Kröger* and the subjects of a number of E. A. Robinson's poems struck a responsive chord in him and may have influenced his own choice of themes.

It is interesting to note that Trout was born in 1909, the year that master rhymester Algernon Charles Swinburne died and that Marinetti's first Futurist manifesto was published, launching Modernism's attack on rhyme, meter, and poetic diction in favor of free verse and free association of words, and the celebration of machinery, speed, change, and conflict. Though its beginnings predate World War I, Modernism to a large extent grew out of the horrors of its mechanized slaughter; to a belief that the older generation, "the old men," were responsible for the war and its consequences; to a reaction to industrialization, consumerism, and urbanization; to a repudiation of Positivism's faith in progress; to Victorian sentimentality; and to a crisis of religious faith and mistrust of established institutions and traditions, including established aesthetic values. There were also those who would have happily swept the past, including the humanist tradition going back to the Renaissance, into the dustbin of history. For others all of the old certainties seemed to be missing from modern life, which they saw as soulless and spiritually barren. The themes and mood of much modernist poetry on both sides of the Atlantic, including that of T. S. Eliot, Ezra Pound, and their offshoots, reflect such attitudes.

While William Trout shared the estrangement from modern society expressed by these and other poets of his time, he was not willing to dismiss the past completely as his adherence to traditional poetic forms and themes testifies. Yet as poems like "Then perhaps it has been so: we have embroidered," one of Trout's longest, his view of life and contemporary society was pretty bleak, as was the depth of despair with his inability to come to terms with his own lack of faith and sense of failure. Indeed, he wrote in one of his books this quotation from W. Somerset Maugham's novel *The Narrow Corner* (1939): "Life is short, Nature is hostile, Man is ridiculous." We know from letters that his disaffection with mainstream American society had begun by the time he was in his mid-thirties, if not before. But profound as his alienation was, it is qualitatively different from that of Eliot and company. Theirs is a starkly clinical, intellectualized, depersonalized malaise, as expressed by Eliot's Sweeney, in "Fragment of Agon," where he tells a woman that life/existence is a matter of birth, copulation, and death: "That's all, that's all, that's all." While Bill may have shared Eliot's judgment in the "Hollow Men" that modern man was empty and agreed that modern society as posited in *The Waste Land* was sterile, anonymous, and lacking in humanity and the spiritual, much of Eliot's verse seems to have put him off. For all of his gloom and skepticism, there is nothing in Trout's work comparable to the depravity, crime, filth, and disgusting smells one encounters in Eliot's "Rhapsody on a Windy Night."

Whereas Eliot and other modernists were preoccupied with "mass-man" or a generalized "modern man," Trout's human subjects, many of them real people he had known, are recognizable as individuals rooted in a familiar environment. If they suffer it is as individuals, sometimes at the hands of society, other times through the indifference of an unfeeling god, but often as a chance victim of Fate. As Eliot's "Rhapsody on a Windy Night" makes clear, he was horrified by the vapidity, crassness, ugliness, and brutality he believed was at the core of modern life. A view shared by Robinson Jeffers and somewhat by Trout; however, Bill tended to view the contemporary world more with contempt and disgust than horror, and, like Thomas Hardy, saw outward life as pointless. Like E. A. Robinson, Trout's focus was on cultivating the inner life, of being in the world not of it. As some former students remember, Bill expressed an appreciation of Eliot's "The Love Song of J. Alfred Prufrock"—a poem rich with imaginative imagery and a character with whom he could empathize—and might also have found his "The Dry Salvages"—with its meditations on time, life, and ageing—to his liking. Trout's use of imagery to convey both ideas and moods, as in poems like "The day's imperative history" and "Through the Shadows of the Shadowless" illustrates an ability to transform thought into feeling through the use of sensuous language in a way akin to what Eliot does in his early poems, among them "Prufrock" (Pinto 1951, 163).

> Through the Shadows of the Shadowless,
> The spirit can intrepidly,
> Steadily, serenely pass,
> By following the silver step
> Gleaming there—as here and yet
> Earth does not the touch forget.
>
> Then fall away, impotent,
> Gray shapes in chaos spawned, and creeping
> Insidious, malevolent,—
> These retreat into the deep,
> Whence the unwary soul allowed
> Invasion of the vampire crowd.
>
> The gleaming footprints do not fail,
> Pleiades, easterly, and climbing.
> Though spirit may a moment quail
> When the treacherous door of time
> Swings wide to Other, it confirms
> Soon the veritable terms—
>
> There as here—that passage wrote
> Upon earth's transitory forms;
> Here near the heart, as there remote,—
> There in peace, as here in storm,
> The traveller notes, and hastens on,
> Trusting in a western dawn.

Certainly a major difference between Trout and Eliot is that Bill was not an urban dweller, while Eliot and many if not most modernists were; hence their frames of reference were different. It is one of the parochialisms of many modernists that their interest ends at the city line, or after World War II extends only into suburbia. They ignore the hinterland. Feelings of alienation and hopelessness are part of rural and small-town life, as we have seen in the poetry of Robinson and Trout and in much of the fiction of Cather. In such places the issues are different from those in the metropolis. In a small-town environment one finds limited economic and cultural opportunities, the weight of convention circumscribing new ideas and suspicion of those who are different, restrictions imposed by family loyalties, and the constraints that come with the absence of any chance for anonymity or any hope of shedding the unwanted, troubling baggage of one's past. One is forever surrounded by the ghosts of the past. The only escape in such an environment is within, where, as Bill tells us, phantoms lurk.

The sense of utter hopelessness found in "Then perhaps it has always been so: we have embroidered," (p. 68), which questions whether anything can be done to rectify "the wreckage of this [twentieth] century" calls to mind the bleak outlook expressed by Eliot. It is a poem in which Trout questions the conventions, platitudes, and self-deceptions human beings use to abet their complacency, whose lives are not guided by things of the spirit (Saint Francis of Assisi's "dream" or Mozart's music) but by materialism ("greed"), mass culture, and organized religion ("a spired aspiration, / of stone and spirit) none of which are capable of arresting the slide into the abyss. Whereas Eliot's abstract impersonality in "The Hollow Men" sees the world ending "Not with a bang but a whimper," Trout's more personal approach in "The Road," one of his darkest poems, sees life's path ending at a "poisoned well."

> Shelling the chestnut, we have found,
> Gorged and gloating, in the meat,
> The universal worm, around
> His puckered snout coiled fat and neat.
>
> We have stopped above the wild
> Pink azalea in the gray
> Woods of spring, and then recoiled
> From the copperhead, reared at bay.
>
> Over flints that slit our feet,
> And through a heat spat from hell,
> We have plodded on—to meet
> At World's End the poisoned well.

And in "Heritage" Trout expresses, through the deft use of a simile from everyday life, the despair and failure experienced by those trapped in the past by heredity, upbringing, circumstances, and, perhaps in an allusion to his own "ugly face," physical appearance, which renders them incapable of coping with the hand life dealt and thus unable to fit into the society in which they live, himself included:

> Stuck in the past like a fly in the gummy paper.
> Releasing one appendage, only to sink another
> Into fatality, the doomed gives over;
> Despair betrays itself by the slight quiver
> As the head droops.—It is the blood, the blood—
> Doom and direction; the damned can not escape.
> And happy he, never lured to brood
> Another pattern, a less monstrous shape.

While, therefore, Trout shared T. S. Eliot's view of the spiritual emptiness of modern Western Civilization, it appears that it was the manner in which Eliot approached his subject and his narrowly religious sense of the spiritual, not the subject itself to which Trout objected. But with the exception of a few specific criticisms and some brief dismissive comments, Bill left no record of his reaction to Eliot's poetry. That he revered John Donne (as did Eliot and other modernist poets) and valued Gerard Manley Hopkins, both of whom wrote complex and intellectually challenging poetry, suggests that it was not the complexity of Eliot's poems Bill objected to but to their impersonality and what he regarded as a deliberate, calculated, self-conscious, willful intent to obfuscate meaning by over-intellectualization. He was in good company in his assessment. Louis Untermeyer in *American Poetry Since 1900* (1923), a book that went through five printings by 1927, and which Trout may well have read, faults Eliot for his "rarefied vocabulary"; his "pompous parade of erudition" using "fragments of philosophy, history, science, tea-table gossip, and fetishes of literature"—the "flotsam and jetsam of desiccated culture"—which he put together like a literary carpenter or scholarly joiner in a "picture-puzzle manner" of "severed narratives" lacking "connecting tissue." Eliot's view of modern society as soulless grew out of his narrow Anglo-Catholicism in which, as Melville observed of Hawthorne's short story "Ethan Brand," "the brain eats out the heart." What Trout seems to have recognized, was that by elevating the importance of the intellect, Eliot, Pound, Joyce, and other modernists left little if any room for compassion, brotherhood or love. It is the failure to integrate the heart and mind, intellect and emotion, by balancing culture and civilization that the great German historian Friedrich Meinecke saw as a fatal flaw in German society that underpins and helps explain the rise of Adolf Hitler (Untermeyer 1923, 352-353, 358-360; Meinecke 1950, 34-38).

Untermeyer accuses Eliot of being "scarcely a step away from Dadaism's "glorification of incoherence"; of delighting in "virtuosity for its own sake"; guilty of creating poetry "not actuated by life but by literature," that "appeals only to our acquired knowledge" and is of interest only to critics, scholars, and puzzle solvers. He does, however, credit Eliot's *The Waste Land* with "a certain authenticity" in capturing the mood of "contemporary despair" and alienation that characterizes twentieth-century Western Civilization (Untermeyer 1923, 359-362, 352-353). Edna Millay told Cass Canfield in a June 1949 letter that there was nothing "abusive," "merely murderous" about the poems she was writing—including "The cult of the occult is not adult," the poem from which the collection takes its title—satirizing Eliot's views on culture, criticism, and writing poetry (Macdougall 1951, 353). Although Bill was sparing in sprinkling some of his poems with references or allusions to Greek and Roman mythology and Tarot cards, as his student Dianne Danz remembered, he scoffed that Eliot had to write notes explaining the obscurities found in *The Waste Land.* In his "Notes" Eliot explains: "Not only the title, but the plan and a good deal of the incidental symbolism of the poem were suggested" by *From Ritual to Romance*, Jessie L. Weston's book on the Grail legend. Among his "sources" were Shakespeare, Milton, Wagner, St. Augustine, and the liberties he admitted taking with Sappho's poetry and Tarot cards. And yet Eliot's appreciation of one of the poets Bill most admired is apparent in his rhymed poem "To Walter De La Mare," written for inclusion in *A Tribute to Walter de la Mare*, a book published in honor of the poet's seventy-fifth birthday.

Louis Untermeyer placed Eliot among those twentieth-century poets he called "The Cerebralists," who turned away from naturalism, emphasized form, which they spoke of in terms of the "mathematics, the architecture of literature," in their "preoccupation with verbal craftsmanship and deliberate technic." Emotion is minimized in the "pure," "absolute" verse of these poets through its cool intellectual "detachment" (Untermeyer 1923, 348-349). In "The Anti-Poet," one of the lectures he gave at Oxford University in 1961, Robert Graves, taking the Roman poet Virgil as his subject, discussed the unfortunate influence he exerted over Western culture for two thousand years "out of all proportion to his merits either as a human being or as a poet," and whom he characterized as narrow, subservient, unimaginative and lacking "originality, courage, humour, or even animal spirits." Among Virgil's "evil bequests," he goes on to say, is "the notion that borrowing from the classics proves a poet's modesty and good sense; and that style is more important than subject," something that "fashionable, clever poets of the Establishment are still Virgilian enough to conceal recondite Classical beauties in their work, for the well-read reader to greet with self-satisfied smirks"—a passage that Trout underlined and wrote "Eliot" in the margin of his copy of Graves *Oxford Addresses on Poetry*. "Poetry must be practical," Graves insisted, and Virgil's verse was not, and for Trout who underlined the sentence, neither was Eliot's (Graves 1962, 38, 44, 53).

It may be that what underpins Trout's negative reaction to Eliot, particularly his later poetry, is what E. M. Forster in a 1949 book review says is Eliot's "purposeful interest in polemical Christianity." He goes on to observe: "We feel—and he would have us feel—that his religious faith is more important to him than anything else, and that art and literature are valid in relation to it." Furthermore, Forster asserts, for Eliot "the relation must exist" where European culture is concerned. "Where there is not Christianity there is nothing. And it has to be Christianity of an approved type ..." (Forster 1951, 260). In his 1949 *Notes towards the Definition of Culture*, the subject of Forster's review, Eliot states, "the maintenance of English culture [and by extension Western culture as a whole] is contingent upon the health of the culture of Latin Europe, and upon continuing to draw sustenance from Latin culture." He is dogmatic in believing that "Christendom should be one," for "without a common faith, all efforts toward drawing nations together in culture can produce only the illusion of unity." It is "the common tradition of Christianity," Eliot insists, "which has made Europe what it is," in its thought, its arts, its laws. "If Christianity goes," he believes, "the whole of our culture goes" (Eliot 1949, 75, 83, 126). A self-confessed "royalist in politics," Eliot once admitted being of "a Catholic cast of mind, a Calvinist heritage, and a Puritanical temperament," none of which saved him from such serious character flaws as anti-Semitism and arranging to confine his first wife to a mental hospital in 1938 and then refusing ever to visit her. Knowing what we do of Trout's life, character, and religious doubts, one can understand why Bill might have detected a whiff of hypocrisy and mendacity in Eliot's professions of faith and poetic expressions of struggle with sin and purification in poems like *The Journey of the Magi*, *Ash Wednesday*, and the *Four Quartets*, works celebrated by academics and literary critics.

Other American poets one might call "Cerebralists," though absent Eliot's theological obsession, include Ezra Pound, Wallace Stevens, and Marianne

Moore. Trout was dismissive of another pillar of the modernist *avant-garde*, when he told his Millersville students: "The vaunted learning of Ezra Pound was largely phony." And again, as his student Dennis Simmons recalled, when, in a flash of wit, he told his undergraduates that Pound's poetry was indeed "a small weight." Untermeyer's assessment of Pound was similar to Trout's. While admitting that Pound was an amazing ironist and colorist—who created delicate atmospheric effects through "subtleties of light, shadow, movement"—he regards his poetry as a descent into "tight mannerism." He characterizes his poetry as "derivative"—because of his borrowings from Robert Browning, François Villon, and the Provençal poets—and Pound as guilty of being a "connoisseur of the curious," an "archæologist," who "carefully noted, collected, tagged and set down" in his poems a plethora of gleanings from all he had read, considering nothing "too inconsequential or unworthy for preservation." He calls Pound's *Cantos* unintelligible "rag-bags of memories crammed with literary flotsam and jetsam." And as he did with Eliot, views Pound's work as a "withdrawal from life" into the "musty and deserted class-room" of formalism (Untermeyer 1923, 163, 165, 157-158, 168, 162, 167). Such an assessment seems to be in keeping with Trout's view of Pound. But there were modern American poets he valued.

In his Millersville classes Trout applauded Robinson Jeffers' antiwar sentiment (expressed in a bitterly mocking poem like "Eagle Valor, Chicken Mind"), his willingness to put forward unpopular opinions, and his hostility to the "irrational impulse of greed" that was corrupting American society. Robert Haas maintains that "Jeffers seemed to have been, politically and sentimentally an old-fashioned Jeffersonian republican ... a defender of the spartan and honest American commonwealth against the thickening of the empire" (Haas 1987, 39). As early as the 1920s in such poems as "Shine, Perishing Republic" and "Woodrow Wilson (February 1924)" Jeffers had criticized America's "vulgarity" and politicians in terms Trout no doubt agreed with. But he went much further in the 1930s and 1940s in expressing isolationist sentiments and in refusing to wave the Stars and Stripes supporting the unquestioning patriotism of the Second World War, and going so far as to make venomous attacks on President Franklin Roosevelt and intensify his condemnation of American's empire building in *The Double Axe and Other Poems* (1948), published by Random House only after ten poems had been excised and line changes made because the editors believed the work was seditious. Jeffers' reputation never recovered from the book's condemnation in literary reviews and newspapers. As we know from his letters,

Trout shared Jeffers' disappointment with the failure of the United States to live up to its lofty rhetoric of freedom for all, individualism, and democracy, as well as its self-serving foreign policy and proclivity to military intervention, but he did not share his contempt for FDR. Bill responded to Jeffers' anti-materialism and skepticism about science and technology in such poems as "Ave Caesar," "The Trap," "Shine, Republic," and "Science," which were among those he checked off as significant in his copy of *The Selected Poetry of Robinson Jeffers* (1938). He also owned a copy of Jeffers' *Hungerfield and Other Poems* (1954), where in the poem "Skunks" Jeffers tells the reader that people do not learn from the "wholesale crimes" of war or "the greed and lies of peace"; that the outrages perpetrated by political leaders throughout history in time—like the vile odor of the skunk when smelled far away is not unpleasant—are bleached of blood and the horrors they committed become mere words in books. "Distance makes clean."

Both Trout and Jeffers had a strong sense of place and love of the land, one for the meadows, fields, and woods of southeastern Pennsylvania, the other for the rugged, rocky, sometimes storm-swept, coast of central California, of which "Ocean" is representative and "Carmel Point" an example of nature's beauty "defaced" by "a crop of suburban houses." They loved animals and were angered by cruelties inflicted on them by human beings, Jeffers in "Roan Stallion," "Shooting Season," and "Hurt Hawks," and Bill in his crow poems, "One Pheasant," and "In Brief." Jeffers' view of the universe as a single organism, his "pantheism" and reverence for nature and joy in wildlife, particularly raptors, no doubt resonated with Bill, as did his disappointment with human beings. In the Preface to *The Double Axe*, Jeffers articulates his philosophic outlook, which not only attacked the egotism, self-righteousness, hypocrisy, violence, and environmental destructiveness of humankind, but also saw *homo sapiens* as only one among many species, and certainly not the best of the lot. Observing sea-lions perhaps from Hawk Tower or from Tor House—which he built himself using local stone on a cliff overlooking the Pacific Ocean, and where he lived in semi-seclusion for nearly half a century—Jeffers reflects in the poem "Animals" on the kinship of all the many "chemistries of animal life," of which human beings are only one. Despairing of the inhumanity of people, he advocated an end to the human-centered view of the universe, which places all other creatures—as well as the land, sea, and sky—at their disposal, in favor of celebrating the magnificence and beauty of all things of the earth and the cosmos. It was the poet's tone and his belief in the relationship of life forms past and present that may have reminded Trout of Jung's ideas. What also seems to have mattered to him is that Jeffers' poetry is informed by knowledge drawn from a variety of disciplines, addresses important ideas, is rooted in careful observation of nature and society, and is informed by imaginative reality. No doubt he was also struck by the undeniable grandeur and expressiveness of Jeffers' poems.

Trout shared Jeffers' bleak view of humanity and the modern world. As Frederic Carpenter points out, Jeffers "had visited the dark continents of the mind," and in explaining "the ultimates of human experience" had "seen truth itself to be ambiguous" and also found "the deepest emotions of man to be ambiguous." Trout was not, as Carpenter claims many readers are, "repelled by the apparent nihilism" of Jeffers' views. His poems explore "the elemental emotions of man" and "describe the primeval landscapes of nature," both of which are often brutal and inhuman and suggest "the abyss that lies always at the foot of modern man" (Carpenter 1962, 11, 13, 145, 151). Abyss is a word one encounters more than once in Trout's writing. Approaching his mid-sixties, Jeffers reflected on what he has witnessed in his lifetime in the poem "The World's Wonders," and sees only a continuation of the self-inflicted tragedies humanity has imposed on itself, concluding by saying: "I have learned that happiness is important, but pain gives importance." Such resignation is something Bill could understand.

The attacks Jeffers suffered for expressing his social and political views in verse may have contributed to Trout's own reticence and secrecy. But Jeffers was also savaged by the New Critics for writing poems that were too close to the realities of everyday life; too straightforward, too graphic; and lacking abstraction, complexity, and ambiguity. His answer to such criticism is found in the Foreword to his *Selected Poetry* and in the Introduction to the 1935 Modern Library edition of his *Roan Stallion, Tamar and Other Poems*, the relevant passage of which is quoted in Untemeyer's combined anthology of modern British and American poetry. In the later he claimed that the problems with modern poetry began with Mallarmé and his followers, who renounced "intelligibility" in favor of pure musicality, after which poets began to abandon "ideas," "imagery," "recognizable emotions," with the danger that in time such "austerities" would eliminate other aspects of reality and might even result in the abandonment of words, leaving nothing but "musical syllables." Three years later he said poetry was "surrendering" its "power and reality to prose" and was "becoming slight, and fantastic, abstract, unreal, eccentric." Having been struck at age nineteen by Friedrich Nietzsche's assertion that "poets lie too much," he resolved not "to tell lies in verse. Not to feign any emotion that I did not feel; not to pretend to believe in optimism or pessimism, or unreversible progress; not to say anything because it was popular, or generally accepted, or fashionable in intellectuals unless I myself believed it; and not believe it easily." His determination to remain truthful and not to follow the canons of the New Criticism led Jeffers, he explains, "to write narrative poetry, and to draw subjects from contemporary life; to present aspects of life that modern poetry generally avoided, and to attempt the expression of philosophic and scientific ideas in verse" (Untemeyer 1962, 358; Jeffers 1938, xiv-xv). For one who admired William Hazlitt and Henry David Thoreau, as Bill did, such statements could only reinforce his determination to write poetry that did not follow slavishly contemporary critical theory.

The poems in which Trout comes closest to the disillusionment, alienation, and bleak social commentary found in some other modern poets is "All are headed for the river that drives on down there, in dark obscurity," where one finds images of scientists "subsidized by the opulence of taxation" developing bombs to fill space with "flying human guts / Cooked to a turn" and of the "munitions worker" paid enough to own a Cadillac. Yet, like all of us, they are headed for the river (an allusion to the river Styx), to the grave but by a different route than "we" who follow the path of humanistic tradition and compassion for our fellow creatures and see the "dark river" streaked in gold. Here in Trout's view of the academic-industrial-military-consumer complex whose greed and lust for power have corrupted modern society, particularly in the United States, one senses the spirit of Robinson Jeffers.

> All are headed for the river that drives on down there, in dank
>   obscurity:
> The superior physicist, subsidized by the opulence of taxation,
> Devises the little formula that unlocks the sluices of creation,
> And permits to darken a nook of space with flying human guts
> Cooked to a turn;
> The generals peer, confer, caress the creases
> In careful uniforms; the munitions worker
> Touches the pay envelope in his breast pocket, drops the time card
>   in the slot,
> And singles his Cadillac in the parking lot.
> They import little really; and all are headed for the river.—
> But we—first we must bring the onion from the late September garden,
> Unsheathe the delicate tissue, brittle brown,

Slice the concentric circles—a design
Deft as the formula of the physicist—
And drop those counters in the simmering broth.
That onion smell commands meditation; far into history it retreats,
Past Acre, past the Compagna, over Delos—
Where beyond? How, from the river shadows,
All the dark faces flock, huddle, host. Is it not amusing?—
And—while the kitchen is sleepily redolent with the good perfume of
onion, cabbage, and carrot—
Look for a moment, there westward, how the last, low streaks are gold,
Over the dark river.

All of Jeffers' poems in Trout's copy of Louis Untermeyer's anthology *Modern American Poetry and Modern British Poetry* (1962) used as the text for his contemporary poetry course are annotated and many scanned, and document their being assigned to students. In a Millersville lecture he praises Jeffers' diction, his "ear for the qualitative equivalence of unstressed syllables," his "subtle variety of stress and cadence," and the musicality of his lines. His esteem for Jeffers was shared by another poet he held in high regard, Edna St. Vincent Millay, who told an interviewer in 1931 that Jeffers was the best contemporary American poet (Milford 2001, 330). And yet Jeffers was, according to Cary Nelson, one of the modern poets marginalized both because of his political views and his failure to measure up to the standards of the New Criticism (Nelson 1989, 18, 114-115, 237-238, 67), neither of which Bill would have held against him. Indeed, there was much in Jeffers' character, values, beliefs, and lifestyle, as well as in his poetry, that Trout, knowing what we do of his life and views, would have found admirable.

Among Bill's books are a biography of Hart Crane, a monograph on the poet, his collected poems edited by Waldo Frank, and a volume of letters. Although Trout said and wrote little about Crane—beyond calling him, as noted earlier, "my worthless and magnificent favorite"—the two are linked by biographical and literary ties. Both men counted Catullus and John Donne among their favorite poets, as well as the Elizabethans. As Crane's poem "To Emily Dickinson" and his reference to "Emily" in the "Quaker Hill" section of *The Bridge* testify, he shared with Bill an appreciation of her poetry and identified with the circumstances of her life that shaped it. But Trout apparently did not share Crane's admiration for Wallace Stevens' "technical ingenuity," the "meticulous precision" of William Carlos Williams, nor the "robust quality" of Whitman and Carl Sandberg. They did, however, share an interest in some of the same composers—Richard Strauss, Debussy, Wagner, and a passion for Ravel (Weber 1948, 65, 130, 142-143, 252, 300; Weber 1952, 6, 7, 108, 129, 18, 139-140).

Not only is Crane's admitted love of music apparent in his verse (his use of rhythm, musical terms, and references to sounds), but also his appeal to all the senses—the sensuousness of his poetry—was possibly another alluring element for Bill. What is more, both men rejected materialism and believed that reason and logic should be tempered by intuitive-imaginative knowledge. Trout's use of dreams in writing poetry may owe something to Crane's dream-world imagery. Crane accepted Rimbaud's belief that a poet must first study his own consciousness, an idea that Trout also seems to have taken to heart. In Crane's poetry Trout found a way to combine imagism and symbolism, and to employ cinematographic techniques to move back-and-forth between time past and time present. The use of metaphor and references or allusions to music, artists, and literary figures by both men contributed to the mystery sometimes found in their verse. But Trout did not go as far as Crane in elevating form over content (Weber 1948, 36-39, 46, 149-150, 269-270, 336-338).

In addition to certain technical aspects of Crane's poetry, what may have attracted Trout to him (though they came from different social-economic classes) was that both shared an interest in visual art and psychological fiction, felt socially isolated and alienated from commercial and middle-class values, followed a non-institutional path in their spiritual quest, were drawn to mysticism, and needed to conceal their sexual orientation (though Crane came out to some friends). For someone like Bill, who may have felt trapped by the conservative atmosphere of Gap, Crane's unconventional lifestyle and poetics were something to be admired but emulated only in his private world protected by the "carapace" he had grown. Crane's open rebellion against mainstream society and literary authority might have been approved by someone like Bill, who understood all too well what Thoreau meant by living a life of "quiet desperation" and marching to the beat of a different drummer, but whose circumstances made him unwilling or unable to be an open rebel. In spite of his guarded optimism, Crane suffered, as did Bill, from doubts and insecurities. Both had an obsession with death, though Bill didn't take Crane's suicidal plunge (Weber 1948, 6, 17, 26, 68-76, 75-77, 86, 98, 154-157, 167-169, 294-295).

Trout shared neither Crane's interest in America's urban-industrial landscape and popular culture nor his optimistic efforts to find hope and joy in a flawed world. Unlike Crane, Bill was never reconciled to the evil necessity of science and technology—"the machine." Like American painters of the 1920s and 1930s such as Gerald Murphy, Joseph Stella, Stuart Davis, Charles Sheeler, and Charles Demuth, Crane filled his poems with a rich array of urban imagery and products from factory assembly lines, hoping they might symbolize the creativity of modern man. But in the end his belief in the promise of a mechanized civilization and the democracy of popular culture was tentative at best (Weber 1948, 321; Rosenthal 1960, 169-176).

Crane came to see American popular culture as shallow, cheap, and nasty, peopled by "multitudes" of movie-goers "bent toward some flashing scene" whose promise is never fulfilled, and the plaid-clad, cigar-smoking "Czars of Golf"—"Weekenders avid for their turf-won scores"—trampling what "was the Promised Land, and still is / To the persuasive suburban land agent," as he tells us in *The Bridge*. And in "The Tunnel" section of the same poem, he describes the "hiving swarms" of subway riders "swinging from the swollen strap" "Below the toothpaste and the dandruff ads" hearing only "the monotone ... of other faces, also underground." When the car doors open, escalators lift anonymous shoes and umbrellas, "each eye attending its shoe," to the street above, where the skyscrapers Georgia O'Keeffe celebrated in her modernist, abstract paintings are called "gaunt sky-barracks" by Crane. A very different approach to the urban landscape was taken by Edna St. Vincent Millay, a more personal and intimate one, in her sonnet "If I should learn, in some quiet casual way," which sheds light on why her poems were either criticized or dismissed by the high priests of modernist poetry as being too personal and why Trout loved them while Hart Crane granted her only "genius in a limited sense" though "bound to succeed to the appreciative applause of a fairly large audience" (Weber 1952, 67).

Edna Millay, though she maintained a commitment to traditional craftsmanship, was another rebel whose unconventional life and poetry seem to have nourished Trout's verse. He owned seven volumes of her poetry, three of her plays (*The Lamp and the Bell*, *Conversation at Midnight*, and *The King's Henchman*), her *Collected Poems* (1956) edited by her sister Norma, as well as Allan Macdougall's 1952 collection of her letters, and two biographies. He collected a substantial number of newspaper clippings, magazine articles, and reviews of Millay's work. But as he told a Millersville class in the 1960s, it was in 1923 (at which time he would have been fourteen) that he first "ran across" a poem of hers—"The Curse" from her collection *The Harp-Weavers*—in a copy of the *Literary Digest* he fished from a junk-man's truck. Although admitting that it is a "slight poem," he says it has endured over the years because of its "cohering and coherent emotion, simple but always evocative vocabulary, strong but subtly varying rhythm, and imagery drawn from the experiences of the race." That Bill continued reading Millay is documented by the memory of Rhoda Hostetter Clemens, one of his Gap pupils, who recalled that among the poems he read to her eighth-grade class were many by Millay, and by his repeated references to her in his wartime letters to Don Smith. He urges him in an April 1943 letter to find a copy of her *Huntsman, What Quarry?*, and read in it the sonnet "When did I ever deny, though this was fleeting"—a poem he calls "the true vintage of Burgundy." He tells Smith in an October 1943 letter that in Gap "autumn is upon us now, a season I love," and then quotes the final quatrain of Millay's "Autumn Daybreak," a poem he recited to me from memory during one of my afternoon visits with him in the 1970s.

Trout's interest in Millay may in part stem from similarities in their childhood experiences. His father died when he was ten. Her parents separated when she was seven, and later divorced. Both of their mothers, for whom each had a deep attachment, had to work outside the home—Trout's as a teacher, Millay's as a practical nurse—to support their children. Their mothers fostered in them a love of literature and classical music. One can understand why Bill marked Millay's "The courage that my mother had" in his copy of her collected poems. This tribute to her mother's "courage like a rock," in which she had "more need of" than the "golden brooch" bequeathed her, reminds us of Bill's frequent praise for his mother's strength of character and bravery in the face of adversity, and his own sense of inadequacy and need for such courage. Both Trout and Millay grew up in poverty in small towns and had a love of nature, particularly for wildflowers and birds. Although she had been gregarious in her youth, Millay suffered from bouts of loneliness and a sense of isolation, and became increasingly reclusive in later years, as did Bill (Gould 1969, *passim*; Milford 2001, *passim*).

In a lecture on Millay he gave to a Millersville class in the mid-1960s, Trout rejects as "intolerable nonsense" the dismissal or disparagement of her work by some critics. The reasons for this hostile attitude, like earlier attacks on A. E. Housman (a poet both Millay and Trout respected), he says are not far to seek: "Today, when language is prostituted by diplomats and advertisers, the clarity, the mastery of the musical and telling phrase, the wit, the amazing modulation that both [Housman and Millay] exhibit are damning." He calls her "a great lyric, a great elegiac poet in the classical sense." He then identifies three aspects of her work that account for the pleasure he derives from her poetry: "personality, themes, and technique." As letters he wrote in 1932 testify, Housman, like Trout, held Millay in very high regard and she admired him (Macdougall 1951, 163n-194n).

Trout praises Millay's early determination to be a poet, to overcome poverty and the intellectual isolation of small-town life and not just be "some man's wife or mistress, not some child's mother, not a sacrifice to the narrow business of a picayune job." Such sentiments, which may be veiled self-criticism for his own failure to pursue his muse full-time, probably made some of his conservative and convention-bound students uncomfortable, particularly those predisposed to married life and public school teaching in rural or Levittown-communities: to others it offered an alternative to comfortable conventionality. Dedication to her art, hard work, and loyalty to friends are qualities Bill also found admirable in both Millay and George Sand.

"Always her exclusive preoccupation is with the actual world," Trout tells his students. Millay's themes, he points out, are "death; youth and the end of youth; the transience of love"; nature as Hardy saw it, not Wordsworth; "such tarnished ideas as honor, truth, integrity in a world bent on its own destruction by its own hand"; and "her own hatred of meanness, stinginess, pettiness, and expediency." As with George Sand, it was Millay's warmth, generosity, and compassion for the defeated and the downtrodden that struck a responsive chord in Bill. But his was not blind adulation. Like all poets, Millay, he acknowledges, "had written bad verse," and she "could be hysterical, appallingly arch and cute"; could "commit the grossest errors of taste"; and was (as he wrote in the margin of one of the biographies) "always the exhibitionist." Yet in the final analysis he admonishes his students, adapting a line from Sonnet XXXI of her *Fatal Interview*, "tease not her ghost with slander."

It is Millay's "capacity for feeling, for an overwhelming emotional stress," Trout tells his students, "that sharpens and makes electric her verse." She herself had told an interviewer in 1931 that her poetry was "very intense and very passionate," and like everything a poet writes, "personal" (Milford 2001, 329). Thus subjectivity, emotion, and the deeply personal nature of her verse—the same qualities that drew Bill to Beethoven's late quartets, Schubert's songs, and the music of Gustav Mahler—account for his response to Millay's poetry. He suggests that, "Perhaps the appeal of poetry, after all, is more physical than intellectual"; a belief he repeats to his Contemporary Poetry class in commenting on Millay's "God's World": "An appreciation for poetry is in the body, rather than the mind." But he also observes in commenting on her "Euclid Alone Has Looked On Beauty Bare" that, "Underneath any passionate work lies the solid geometrical design." It was her craftsmanship and interest in the details of the real world and her emotional power that set Millay's work apart from High Modernism and its progeny, which Trout observes, "has largely abandoned the effort toward intense and concentrated expression"; and which "rather scorns lyricism as such, pours out metaphors without regard to their aptness," and is "preoccupied with obscure references."

Although Millay's use of her art on behalf of progressive social and political causes (such as working in the 1920s to save the anarchist workers Sacco and Vanzetti from execution or sounding the alarm about fascism in the 1930s and later Nazi atrocities like the Lidice massacre of June 1942) was in keeping with Trout's values, his silence on her overtly political and social verse during the 1930s and 1940s is as telling as his silence on the work of other socially conscious or Left poets of the period. While clearly possessing a strong social conscience and holding progressive political, social, and economic views, Trout was neither a joiner nor an activist, which should come as no surprise from what we know of his life. Poets such as Edwin Markham (1852-1940), Genevieve Taggard (1894-1948), Langston Hughes (1902-1967), Kenneth Fearing (1902-1961), Contee Cullen (1903-1946), Edwin Rolfe (1909-1954), and Muriel Rukeyser (1913-1980), were all part of American modernism but were marginalized or repressed, particularly in the years after World War II, by anti-communist sentiment or failure to pass muster with the academic high priests of the New Criticism. Whether Bill's silence on the work of these poets stemmed from aesthetic issues, objections to subject matter, or, as a public school and college teacher from caution given the prevailing anti-communism of the Cold War era is an open question. It is interesting that while many critics and academics ignored Ezra Pound's fascist sympathies, they could not forgive Millay's poetry in support of social justice and democracy.

At a time when the sonnet was under attack by the modernists, Millay championed the form (Atkins 1964, 55-57). She was a masterful sonneteer, though one willing to take liberties with the form, sometimes switching the octet and the sestet or using unorthodox rhyme-schemes. It may have been her sonnets, as well as his love for Shakespeare's, that gave Bill the incentive to use the form at a time when it was still disparaged by many poets and critics, as was nature imagery, as he mockingly and defiantly notes in his poem:

Infringing the stricture that flowers must not be mentioned,
Let us take just this daffodil—
Cool, clear yellow, reticent, poised,
Autonomy trenchant, laconic, disturbingly demure—
And let us go back, under the gray spring sky, through this chill wind;
Let us go back, and leave these afflictions, peculiar and general,
Here in the kitchen; they will wait for us here.—
The past is a personal country: we rule that island,
Albeit precariously—a craven regency—
Province but meagrely domesticated; there is much danger there
In familiar objects—sedate, unwitting assassins—biding their time for forty years;
And shame and anguish suddenly start from a remembered door way or a time-battered chair.—
However, even death has been introduced and is familiar; little is strange,—
And out there the tuft of daffodils
Bends in the chill wind, under the naked plum-tree.

In this poem he also speaks of the past as a "personal country" over which the individual has little control and whose "memories of things past," often painful, can be sparked, a la Proust, by "a remembered door way or time-battered chair."

Another characteristic of Millay's poems that may have attracted him was the way they reflect her consciousness of time, as explored by Robert Johnson in his insightful article "A Moment's Monument." Millay and Trout were steeped in Elizabethan poetry and so were aware of the difference between Renaissance and modern concepts of time. As Johnson explains, "Renaissance time exists *outside* the human mind, as a process working toward its own ends": It is something tangible that must be "nurtured and budgeted and spent well." This notion of time informs the nature poetry of both Millay and Trout, as in her "The Death of Autumn" and his "Summer slowly takes its leave" and "Summer Ending." The modern concept of time, which developed in the course of the late nineteenth and early twentieth century and was influenced by the French philosopher Henri Bergson's idea of *duration*, regards time as a "flow of data knit into reasonable patterns," a string of momentary sensory perceptions captured in "some imaginative continuum" and used by such stream-of-consciousness writers as Virginia Woolf. The modern sense of time in the poetry of Millay and Trout is a record in one's consciousness of moments snatched from personal experience, as in her sonnets "Time does not bring relief, you all have lied" and "If I should learn, in some quiet casual way," and in Trout's "Concede the comfort of routine, alluring," "In tranced captivity the mind follows," and in the many poems about his mother that recall her character and life experiences and record their moments together over many years. The recognition that such moments slip away but can be retained in memory underpins much of the poetry of Millay and Trout and accounts for his efforts to fix them in his verse. While both notions of time inform their poetry, the use of the modern was not the cool, impersonal, distanced voice of Eliot and other modernists but rather a personal rendering of emotional experiences growing out of contact with real people and the physical realities of the world. Just as Johnson sees Millay embracing the modern concept of fluid time, so in poems like "September," "Then and Now," "Remembered," and "They," to mention only four, Trout also takes a modern view of time (Johnson 1995, 117-129).

Millay's experience of nature and gardening accounts, as does her fondness for the Elizabethan poets, for the sensitivity to smells, tastes, and sounds that fill her poems, and may in part account for Trout's attraction to her. In his poems, too, one finds the sensuous qualities of the real world: "a reek of garden loam," "smell of cucumbers," the cricket's "rackety organ," "the ebbing fumes of midnight wine," "the acrid taste of Sunday morning coffee," "the smells of fish and mint / Of cow's dung dried," and the Milkweed's "White sticky sap that oozed with lush / Indulgence … / From a leaf broken."

Like Millay's poem "Buck in the Snow" (another he marked in his copy of her collected poems), which was inspired by the sight of a deer felled by a hunter, Trout devoted several poems to such victims of human cruelty, among them "In Brief," "Crow," and "One Pheasant." But there are distinct differences between Trout's poems dealing with nature's human victims and Millay's rather sanitized "Buck in the Snow" (a noble, stately creature often romanticized, not the sort Bill chose for poems). And nowhere is the difference more apparent than in his "Entre Chien Et Loup" with its imaginative realism, sneering characterization of the indifferent hunter (a figure absent from Millay's poem), moral quandary of the witness, and overall tone. Trout's confrontation with a wounded crow raises the same dilemma Robinson Jeffers faces in his "Hurt Hawks." There are similarities and differences in the issues raised by the two poems, as well as differences in symbolism occasioned by the fact that Jeffers' bird is a hawk while in "Entre Chien Et Loup" the maimed bird is a crow. Jeffers resolves the quandary differently than Trout does.

Blinded crow, broken-winged,
Huddling there, fearfully close
To earth, the best gift life can bring
To you is death (they say, Repose,
Who would leave a house of mourning,
Silent, and its mute forlorn).
Your head jerks round, the eye pits stare,
Your beak half opens, the wing maimed
Stirs with anguish the frigid air
Of winter twilight. (Truly named,
That husky Sports-Man, ambling idly;
You witness the cosmic fratricide.)
I waver between stay and go—
To give you life-in-death, or give
Death-in-life? Yes, or no?
Either way, no reprieve
Of flinching pity can be won—
Stony, craven, done, undone.
Between the dog and the wolf is born
Quandary, blacker still,
Because the wincing self-scorning,
Grinding at its pitiful mill,
Sees in you the soul lamed,
The blinded house-mate, maimed.

The literal translation of the poem's title is "between the dog and wolf," which is a French idiomatic reference to gloaming, dusk when the dim light makes it difficult to distinguish between a dog and a wolf, and by extension refers to the familiar versus the unknown and carries an implication of uncertainty and possible danger, by which Trout says Quandary is born.

Even though he had firsthand experience of modern industry and technology working at Lukens Steel, Trout—unlike Millay, Hart Crane, Carl Sandburg, William Carlos Williams, and other twentieth-century American poets as well as visual artists—did not bring urban imagery into his verse, and made only infrequent references to trolley cars, trains, automobiles, and alarm clocks, none of which celebrate technology but rather are treated as intrusions, disturbances, or ways of regimenting or controlling people and limiting their independence and lessening imagination. Bill would have agreed with only half of Thomas Hardy's assertion that there are two good things about America: Millay's poetry and skyscrapers (Milford 2001, 290).

In spite of what he tells Don Smith in a 1943 letter, and no matter how she fell out of favor with critics and academics, Bill never abandoned his admiration for the poetry of Edna St. Vincent Millay. Nonetheless, he admits to Smith in a letter postmarked 19 January 1942 that the recording Elford Caughey sent him for Christmas of Millay reading her poetry, was "a great disappointment, with much false emphasis, an aging voice attempting to be youthful, and a distressing choice of poems. However, she does read the 'Ballad of the Harp Weaver' (a very minor dramatic poem) beautifully." What Bill probably did not know because it was not public knowledge at the time, was that Millay was suffering from back and shoulder pain from an automobile accident, addiction to morphine, and alcoholism when she made the recording. Because of her condition, Dorothy Leffler, who had done editing at Bobbs-Merrill, had been hired to assist her. Millay suggested Leffler select the poems for the recording, which she did (Milford 2001, 455-456, 458). Bill tells Betty Curtis (who had sent him a quotation from Marianne Moore's poem "What Are Years?") in a letter of 29 May 1960 that he does not understand the bird in Moore's poem, implying the modernist poet's bird imagery is obscure or does not make sense or ring true. He then quotes Millay's "Over the Hollow Land" (one of six poems she wrote honoring her poet friend Elinor Wylie, who died in 1928, in the middle of her career, at age forty-three) in which a nightingale is "shaken from the bough" in mid-song. "Now that bird I can understand," he assures Curtis. Millay championed Wylie's poetry and defended her against the narrow intolerance of those who insisted on strict adherence to social conventions.

Many critics of the day acknowledged Wylie's elegant style, startling imagery, and technical precision that combined "stunning craftsmanship with ethereal sentiments." Louis Untermeyer said her poems "sparkle without burning" and were "passion frozen at the source," while *Poetry* magazine's Harriet Monroe characterized them as "austere" and "immaculate," and Mark Van Doren applauded her "amazing liberty at rhyme." Archibald MacLeish, Malcolm Cowley, and Edmund Wilson viewed her poetry as a fusion of tradition and modernism, "the happy marriage of erudition and unexpected imagery, of intense emotion tied to a deep respect for form" (Macdougal 1951, 217,138; Olson 1979, 169, 184-187, 216-217). Such observations may have some relevance in assessing Trout's poetry, though Wiley's icy elegance and flights into fantasy did not find their way into his verse. He owned a copy of *Elinor Wylie: The Portrait of an Unknown Lady* (1935) by her sister, Nancy Hoyt, as well as the *Collected Poems of Elinor Wylie* (1932) in which he checked thirty-seven of them in the table of contents, among them "The Eagle and the Mole," "Atavism," "Wild Peaches," "Let No Charitable Hope," and "Address to My Soul," which suggests the qualities he valued most in her work.

The New Criticism's Eliot-inspired formalist aesthetic grew out of the work of a small group of poet-critics (John Crowe Ransom, Donald Davidson, Allen Tate, and Robert Penn Warren) at Vanderbilt University in the 1920s, known first as the Fugitives and later as Southern Agrarians, as well as the work of such critics as I. A. Richards and Yvor Winters. According to the practictioners of the New Criticism (the complexities of which make agreement on a precise definition of it difficult), a poem should be read and judged in terms of its "presentational meaning"—its formal qualities—not its "representational meaning" whether cognitive or affective in relation to the realities of the world, to universal ideas, to therapeutic self-illumination, or to the life or intent of the poet (Perminger 1974, 477-478, 567-568). New Critics were preoccupied with technique, praised disinterested objectivity, and disparaged as sentimentality expressions of personal, domestic emotion, and used such criteria to dismiss Millay as a popular poetic light-weight (Clark in Freedman 1995, 4-15, 18; Kaiser in Freedman 1995, 28-33, 38-40). Although Allen Tate praises Millay's sonnets in a 1924 review, in his savage 1931 review of her *Fatal Interview* he accuses her of using "shopworn materials," in creating a personal, emotional idiom, of employing "stock symbolism," of "properly speaking [having] no style," of being incapable of "profound analysis of her imagery," of "not being an intellect but a sensibility," and of being utterly dated, "the poet of ten years ago" (Brown and Cheney, 1983, 9, 120-123). Trout held the New Critics responsible for the neglect of Millay's verse, particularly in the years after the Second World War. Perhaps there is no better illustration of the aesthetic differences underpinning the poetry of Millay and Trout and that of High Modernism than to compare Ezra Pound's "The Return" with her "The Return" and Trout's "Return."

Always back, into the known,
Self slips away, glides aside—
Reversal to essential bone,
Perhaps,—all ascent denied.

But one does not deplore, excuse,
Knowing ruthless, rigorous,
The Law that men may not abuse—
Arrogance very perilous.

Life must follow primitive plan,
Pattern primally imposed;
And damned forever is the man
Who derides, or dares to doze.

With an insistence dread, minute,
The Law will clutch the wretch and thrust
On a backward way the lawless foot,
Even at the brink of dust.

Shamed, hounded by the jeers,
And pelted by the crackling laugh
From the betrayed, aborted years,
He scrawls in blood his epitaph.

Both Millay and Trout use traditional rhyme schemes in poems that explore the human condition, speaking directly to those individuals who, unable or unwilling to meet the challenges of life, give up the society of others and withdraw into themselves. Millay's poem is gentle, almost consoling in its tone while Trout's resignation to the inevitable, to Life's "primitive plan," "imposed" with a vengeance on those who dare to deride or dare to doze, reflects a bitterness found in words flung at the rebel who aspires by lifting a "lawless foot." Pound's "The Return," on the other hand, has nothing to do with the concerns of human beings but makes vague, esoteric references to the return to earth of ancient gods. The poem is primarily a showcase of Pound's compelling rhythms and vivid imagery.

Southern literary Agrarianism was not merely a response to the lampooning of Southerners and their culture by the journalist, critic, essayist, editor of the *American Mercury*, and author of the multi-volume study *The American Language*, H. L. Mencken (1880-1956), who, though he praised the culture of the antebellum Tidewater South, said of post-Civil War Dixie in "The Sahara of the Bozart" (a witty play-on-words with beaux-arts): "Down there a poet is now almost as rare as an oboe-player, a dry-point etcher or a metaphysician. It is, indeed, amazing to contemplate so vast a vacuity." And he went on: "If the whole of the late Confederacy were to be engulfed by a tidal wave tomorrow, the effect upon the civilized minority of men in the world would be but little greater than that of a flood on the Yang-tse-kiang. It would be impossible in all history to match so complete a drying-up of a civilization" (Singal 1982, 85; Mencken 1920, 136-137). Although there is no hard evidence that Trout knew Mencken's work, as one who taught a college course on the essay, it is likely he did.

What concerned the Agrarians was that with industrialization and urbanization the New South was in danger of losing its antebellum traditions, cultural values, and genteel way of life. The Southern Agrarians saw in the growing importance of secularism, science, materialism, technology, and the competitive and impersonal nature of industrial capitalism threats to the social order they had known and loved—concerns Trout shared. But as Daniel Singal makes clear, in spite of their shared desire to rekindle the Old South's "unified structure of belief ... and with it the capacity for religious faith they felt they had lost," the Agrarians differed in their individual points of view. Ransom championed the ideal of the Old South gentleman and "tranquil country life" on the English model. Davidson, the most chauvinistic of them all, whose "xenophobia, paranoia, and racism," according to Singal, "became increasingly pronounced" over the years, celebrated the heroism of the southern frontiersman in poems like his long epic *The Tall Men*. Tate's nostalgia was for the boys in gray and butternut in poems like "Ode to the Confederate Dead" and in his biographies of Thomas "Stonewall" Jackson, Robert E. Lee, and Jefferson Davis. Robert Penn Warren's short-lived and tentative association with Agrarianism was centered on its "emphasis on establishing a closer relationship between man and nature." But the fly in the ointment for all of them was their contact with the intellectual roots of Modernism (Freud, post-Darwinian science, Eliot, Symbolist poets, urban life), the very tenets of which put them in conflict with their commitment to the heritage of the Old South (Singal 1982, 200-202, 225-230, 348).

Whether Trout had read *I'll Take My Stand: The South and the Agrarian Tradition* (1930)—the proceedings of a symposium organized by Ransom and his colleagues at Vanderbilt University that reflect reactionary political and social views including acceptance of segregation—or the essays on southern topics published by Ransom, Davidson, and Tate over the years is not known, but probably not very likely. Growing up in different regions, one supportive of abolition and the other of slave holding, Trout and the Agrarians, nonetheless, shared a rural background, an interest in place, in the nature of time, in history (particularly family history and the Civil War), and in personal memory. One has only to read Trout's letters and poems to know that he was as conflicted as the Agrarians were about how to reconcile the legacy of his late-Victorian childhood and loss of faith with the demands of the rapidly changing world and the intellectual imperatives of Modernism. Yet there is little evidence, save for his markings of Ransom's poems in Untermeyer's anthology, that Bill took much interest in the Agrarians.

Among the things Bill might have found appealing in Ransom's poetry were the musicality of his lyrics, the product of deftly crafted cadences, the paring of slant rhymes, and skillful use of assonance and dissonance applied to themes rooted in his experiences and memories of the rural South, which he treats philosophically and with a touch of irony. As Daniel Singal observes, Ransom's poetry is characterized by "stoic detachment," "cool rationality and control," "wit, and dry but deadly logic" (Singal 1982, 204). His carefully crafted poems are, like "Antique Harvesters," often set in the countryside and use a rich and varied diction that includes, as in "Dead Boy," southern colloquialisms and archaic words, qualities Trout might have appreciated. Poems like his "Bells for John Whiteside's Daughter," "Blue Girls," and "Old Mansion" treat the brevity of life, the quick passing of youth and beauty, and the decay of all things material; themes also found in Trout's verse though not conveyed as Ransom does with distanced anonymity and absent emotion. Beginning about 1923, Ransom turned his attention from writing poetry to writing criticism and aesthetic theory. While recognizing the myriad choices, ambiguities, paradoxes, and tensions with which people were confronted in the modern world, Ransom came to believe that for human beings to achieve completeness and a degree of stability it was necessary to balance reason and sensibility, mind and body; hence his objection to using poetry to convey personal experiences, self-expression, emotions, or to advocate moral, social, or political causes or use it for psychic therapy (Singal 1982, 207-208). Engaged as he was in his own search for completeness, individuation, it may have been this narrowing of the interpretative function of poetry to its purely literary qualities through textual examination of image, symbol, and technical analysis that cooled Trout's interest in Ransom as well as in Tate and Warren.

Just as he cannot be seen as a poet in the mold of Wallace Stevens or Marianne Moore or John Crowe Ransom or Allen Tate, neither does Trout fit neatly into the tradition of Robert Frost, even though they share some similarities of taste, theme, and style. There are things about Frost's poetry that should have appealed to Bill, not the least of which his interest in nature and rural life, his rejection of free verse, and his quarrels with the modernists. Neither Trout nor Frost showed interest in urban-industrial America, and rather than the cosmopolitanism of Eliot and Pound, Frost cultivated a New England regionalism while Trout focused on an even narrower poetic territory.

Frost found Eliot haughty and pretentious in his affectations of Englishness and his deliberate effort to make his verse difficult and allusive, practices antithetical to his own views on the nature and purpose of poetry. Lawrence Thompson, Frost's "official" biographer, said Frost told him that Eliot, Yeats, and Pound were all fakes, a sentiment, at least where Eliot and Pound were concerned, shared by Bill. For his part, Eliot, writing in *The Dial* in May 1922, characterized Frost as "specializing in New England torpor," and in general was condescending and patronizing toward his fellow countryman. Though initially Pound had befriended and helped Frost, the two parted company in 1913 when Pound began disparaging his poetry in reviews, going so far as to call him a "backwoods, even a barnyard poet" (Meyers 1996, 197-199, 209, 106, 113, 110, 309).

Frost and Trout may have owed as much to their reading of English poets as they did to their fellow countrymen. As noted earlier, both admired Thomas Hardy and Walter de la Mare, though Trout did not seem to share Frost's fondness for Rudyard Kipling. Each had a solid grounding in Latin and was fond of the Latin poets and the Elizabethans. Frost spent the years 1912 to 1914 in England, the period that saw the emergence of the Georgian poets early in the reign of George V (ca. 1910-1922). He was associated with many of the Georgians, some of whom had formed an informal poets' colony near the village of Dymock in Gloucestershire, where for a time Frost and his family also lived (Meyers 1996, 46-47, 72-79, 92-95, 157). Like Frost, Trout's modernism has more in common with the Georgian poets than with the radical *avant-garde* represented by the Imagists, Futurists, and followers of Eliot and Pound.

In spite of the things they shared, there were important differences between Trout and Frost. They differed in the part the visual arts and music played in their lives and poetry. As Jeffrey Meyers points out, Frost's knowledge of art and music was "very limited." He showed no interest in classical music, saying he preferred band and glee club music. And he knew little about the history of art. That his favorite painters were Winslow Homer, Thomas Eakins, and Andrew Wyeth—all of whom were more linear than painterly in their work, relying more on draftsmanship than modeling with color—may in part be explained by the fact that Frost was color blind, which in turn may account for the colorless meadows, woods, seasons, weather, wildflowers, trees and leaves that figure so prominently in his poems compared to the feast of hues found in Trout's. For his part Trout, as discussed in Chapter 6, was knowledgeable about European artists, particularly those who took a more painterly approach. The difference in the musicality of their poetry may in part be attributed to what Myers calls Frost's "radical break" with those poets who followed Walter Pater's dictum that all art aspires to the nature of music, by looking instead to the "realism of the living voice," to the "tone of ordinary speech" in writing poetry (Myers 1996, 57, 38, 83). The breadth and depth of Bill's knowledge of classical music informed his poetic compositions, and may well explain the greater attention to atmosphere, mood, and tonal coloration in his poems than one finds in Frost's.

It is difficult to assess the influence of Frost's poetry on Trout since Bill mentioned him to me only once—a critical remark about Frost being a sham—and left no detailed written record of his estimate of the New England poet. However, comments written in the margins of his books provide confirmation of his dislike for Frost. Next to Frost's poem "The Runaway" included in Bill's copy of *Come Hither*, a collection of poetry put together by Walter de la Mare, he wrote: "The usual Frost pose—obtrusively false." When Russell Brian asked Walter de la Mare if he liked Frost's poems, he said he did, "and that Frost was a great friend of his. There was something Wordsworthian about him: he had an oaten voice." To which Bill responded with three large questions marks in the margin and the comment "same calculated duplicity" (Brian 1958, 80). It may be that while Frost used the vernacular to write "conversational blank verse" about nature, everyday life, and ordinary people—which should have pleased Bill—his poems may have come off as self-consciously contrived, or as clinical, objective, lacking in intimacy, emotion, and a sense of the personal that may have left Trout cold. He did tell a Millersville class in 1962 that Frost's verse lacked intensity. As Roy Harvey Pearce put it, in Frost's poetry "the ultimate equivalence of the 'I' and the 'we' has been renounced" (Untermeyer 1962, 165; Pearce 1961, 283). Of the forty Frost poems in the 1962 edition of Untermeyer's anthology of American and British poetry, Trout marked only three in his copy of this text for his Contemporary Poetry class at Millersville, and of these only "Two Look at Two" is scanned and heavily annotated. Students in his classes remember Trout assigning few Frost poems and not devoting much class time to lecturing on or discussing his work.

The literary influences, rural environment, and certain life experiences shared by Frost and Trout in part account for the similarities in their subject matter, but their personalities and values do much to explain their differences in purpose and tone and may in the last analysis account for Trout's dismissal of the New England bard. Frost was self-promoting and assertive. Trout was shy and self-effacing. Frost celebrated competition, ranked courage high on his list of virtues, and, like Ernest Hemingway, cultivated the image of the manly man, which may in part explain why Bill told a student he thought Frost was a misogynist. He mocked such posturing and had no time for sports, for two of which—tennis and baseball—Frost had a life-long passion. Frost idealized war while for the most part ignoring social and political injustice and the evils of capitalism. While his politics were conservative, his Puritanism, which included intolerance for homosexuals, did not keep Frost from having a long-term sexual affair with his secretary, Kay Morrison, the wife of a friend and fellow teacher at the Bread Loaf Writers' Conference (Myers 1996, 39, 120, 123, 158-159, 171, 210-216, 245-246, 313; Pritchard 1984, 128-131, 137, 203). As his letters to Don Smith testify, Trout was no Puritan; however, Frost's hypocrisy and character flaws no doubt put Bill off.

Apparently there was something about Frost's poetry that rang false to Bill. It may have been his deliberate effort to cultivate the myth of the "farmer-poet" who lived close to nature, tilling the soil and writing poetry when in fact he did few barnyard chores and spent precious little time in the fields, and in fact his Franconia, New Hampshire farm "consisted of some cows and a vegetable garden." With firsthand knowledge of what it was like living and working on a small farm, Trout was not taken in by Frost's "farmer-poet" myth. For one as shy and unassertive as Bill, Frost's tireless efforts to promote his own image as an amiable, folksy Yankee-farmer and cracker-barrel philosopher-poet may have poisoned Trout's opinion of him and contributed to an undeserved dismissal of his poetry as contrived, in spite of the technical excellence and characteristics of theme and tone they both valued (Meyers 1996, 52; Pritchard 1984, 122). Then, too, as Pearce observes, Frost's "people are not agonized and tormented by the thought of all the possibilities they have missed" while agony and torment are a part of Trout's view of life and find their way into his poetry (Pearce 1961, 281). Moreover, as Louis Untermeyer points out, Frost was a tidy realist who didn't want "dirt on his potatoes," and who once said: "To me, the thing that art does for life is to clean it, to strip it to form," which for Bill may have confirmed his belief that Frost was a Formalist posing as a Realist (Untermeyer 1962, 165).

For someone of Bill's temperament, life experiences, and social outlook, there is just too much self-assurance—too much ego—in Frost's public image and verse. Frost was greedy for recognition, collecting as many honorary degrees as he could, and was not above using his connections in the State Department to get both Oxford and Cambridge to confer honorary doctorates on him. That Frost was repeatedly hired by prestigious colleges and universities and required to do little if any teaching while having virtual carte blanche to conduct his poetry-reading performances around the country, may have irked a dedicated teacher like Trout, particularly since Frost was given to expounding on his approach to teaching in ways that directly or by implication disparaged the methods of public school teachers and college professors. Given his own social-political beliefs, Trout no doubt found it distasteful that the conservative Frost, during the last twenty years of his life, was a good-will ambassador for the United States government during the Cold War, the literary spokesman for the "American way," an icon of wholesome Americanism—the Grandma Moses of American poetry. Frost was the establishment's poet and had been tainted by it (Pritchard 1984, 119-120, 246-249, 253-255; Meyers 1996, 332-342).

Trout may also have suspected (based on news stories about Frost, who was interviewed frequently and written about often in the popular press, as was Hemingway) what some critics and writers reported about the New England bard's vanity and nastiness, personality traits unacceptable to Bill. Frost's treatment of E. A. Robinson, particularly his refusal to participate in a collective tribute by America's leading poets published in the *New York Times Book Review* in December 1919 on the occasion of the poet's fiftieth birthday is only one example of Frost's green-apple envy of what he regarded as his rivals (Donaldson 2007, 353, 419-420). While Lawrence Thompson's unflattering view in his three-volume biography of Frost has been softened by more recent scholarship, there seems little doubt that though he could at times be generous and supportive of other contemporary poets, he was also jealous of them, seeing them as rivals and sometimes targets for snide comments, as well as being two-faced in his relations with such fellow poets as Carl Sandburg and Edgar Lee Masters (Meyers 1996, 143-145, 173; Pritchard 1984, xi-xvii, 116-118).

What may in part have troubled Trout about Frost and Ernest Hemingway was their willingness to participate in making art an adjunct of advertising and the entertainment industry, an association that has characterized American cultural life since the Second World War. Long before Lillian Ross published her *Profile of Hemingway* in 1961, Bill thought that, like Robert Frost, he had manufactured his "image," his "public personality" to promote himself in the literary marketplace with the conscious design of making money and becoming a popular success, a "celebrity." As Scott Donaldson observes, Hemingway was "willing to cultivate and be cultivated by the rich." Like professional sports figures, movie stars, and brand name consumer goods the Hemingways and Frosts of the cultural world had the name recognition that guaranteed them a hearing and virtual carte blanche with publishers because their names sold the goods. Hemingway also had no qualms about negotiating lucrative motion-picture rights (something Willa Cather refused to do), even when the films of his novels and short stories took serious liberties with the text (Donaldson 1977, 3-4, 6-8, 13-14, 54-55, 40-42).

Trout found nothing to admire in a posturing and free-loading male chauvinist like Hemingway, who early on sponged off his upper-middle-class parents, friends, and his first two wives and their relatives; who turned on old friends who helped to advance his career (Sherwood Anderson, Ford Madox Ford, Gertrude Stein, and Scott Fitzgerald among them); who enjoyed blood-sports (bull fights, shooting birds, and slaughtering big game for adventure and to affirm his manhood); and who seemed to have had no shame or limit when it came to wooing the press and cutting deals with book publishers and popular magazines that made him rich. Both Frost and Hemingway had competitive natures, were driven by a desire to win, and were not "good losers." Though there is plenty of evidence of his childish bad temper, belligerence, and public brawls, much of Hemingway's "tough-guy" image was exaggeration or pure invention. His male chauvinism and sexual infidelities that resulted in four troubled marriages and three divorces gave further evidence to Trout of the man's untrustworthiness. He was a braggart always trumpeting his own manhood and forever bashing homosexuals. Yet in the final analysis it may have been Hemingway's hypocrisy and the aggressiveness, brutality and violence in his personality and fiction that most troubled Bill (Donaldson 1977, 60, 62-67, 81-83, 148-149, 162-169, 182-186, 49-50, 194-196, 212). While with Frost, to whose themes and poetic form Trout did not seem to object, his reaction to Hemingway apparently went beyond an aversion to his subject matter to distaste for his style with its short, choppy sentences, and the bland commonality of his diction. Writing to Don Smith on 27 January 1941, Bill asks if he has read Hemingway's *For Whom the Bell Tolls* and says: "I haven't, & don't mind ... he's a little too obtuse for me, which, of course, condemns him to festering oblivion." Nonetheless,

Trout did assign Hemingway's short story *Big Two-Hearted River* in Caroline Shrodes' and Justin Van Gundy's *Approaches to Prose* (1959), the course text for his freshman grammar and composition course.

Given his apparent preference for traditional stanza forms, meters, and rhyme, it is curious that Trout apparently found the poetry of E. E. Cummings to his liking, at least some of it. A visual artist as well as a poet, Cummings was not a modernist in the Eliot-Pound mold. He created his own poetic style, involving new grammatical usage like employing verbs, adjectives, and conjunctions as nouns; unconventional punctuation and capitalization; fragmenting words or fusing them; and abandoning the traditional arrangement of lines and stanzas, and even—drawing on his own cubist-like drawings and paintings—experimenting with spacing and visual arrangement of words to create patterned poems suggestive of musical notation in order to pace the poem's tempo. Yet throughout most of his career Cummings also wrote poems, including many sonnets, using traditional verse forms, opening him to criticism by academics and critics as being a romantic or lyric poet. Nor did he eschew subjects modernists viewed with disdain: love, depictions of everyday life, celebrations of nature, childhood and its memories, comedy, and bitterly satirical social commentary.

In a 1924 review Allen Tate praised Cummings as "a gifted painter after Pablo Picasso and a master of the line-drawing ... the most versatile practitioner of three arts in this country," and yet struck a cautionary note in saying he was "a master of a bewildering variety of forms." By the time he wrote his *Poetry* review in 1932, the caution had turned to criticism, not only for the prominent "evidence of personality" in Cummings' poems but also because: "He has a great many styles, and having these he has none at all." In a 1950 *Partisan Review* piece, Randall Jarrell, another poet-critic schooled in the New Criticism, while admitting that Cummings is "professedly modernist, experimental, *avant-garde*," strikes a condescending tone in saying that "Cummings's poems are loved because they are full of sentimentality, of sex, of more or less improper jokes, of elementary lyric insistence"; that he disguises the year-in-year-out sameness of his poems through clever technical changes; and concludes that "there is a great big moral vacuum at the heart of E. E. Cummings's poetry." In his more sympathetic 1962 *Forum* article, "E. E. Cummings and the Modernist Movement," Norman Friedman points out that Cummings' poetry contains "both modernist and romantic elements," and that it is his subjects and the way he treats them that cause modernists to label him "naïve and sentimental" (Brown and Cheney 1983, 12, 139-141;

Rotella 1984, 79-81, 160, 171). There is little doubt that Trout would have known of the critical debate about Cummings' poetry.

In his 1938 copy of *E. E. Cummings: Collected Poems*, Bill put checkmarks next to twenty-three poems, indicating those he found interesting or of merit; thus giving us a clue to the aspects of Cummings' verse he appreciated. Many of these poems take nature as their subject, among them "O sweet spontaneous" in which Cummings, linking earth and death, celebrates nature's eternal seasonal rhythms which philosophers, scientists, and theologians intellectualize in their attempts to expropriate nature for their own arid purposes and to which nature answers them "with / spring." It is not surprising that as a painter Cummings was a marvelous colorist and that Trout's own sensitivity to color drew him to such poems as "notice the convulsed orange inch of moon"; "this is the garden: colors come and go"; and "Paris; this April sunset completely utters" with its "acres of bloated rose," "cobalt miles of sky," and "the mauve / of twilight." Poems set by Cummings at twilight, at night by moonlight (as in "I go to this window"), or as with "cruelly, love" in the autumn also appealed to Bill.

But in addition to nature imagery Cummings' poems, which are intimate and deeply personal, also have themes related to love, memories, dreams, loss, or death—interests both poets shared. Poems like "somewhere I have traveled, gladly beyond" no doubt touched Bill with their combination of nature imagery and expressions of love and personal memories that may recall one of his youthful relationships or perhaps that with his mother. The remembrance of things past, which so preoccupied Bill, may account for his singling out poems by Cummings, among them "along the brittle treacherous bright streets," that treat the same subject. As with Walter de la Mare and Trout, children and childhood memories figure prominently in Cummings' poetry, as "in just," where boys play at marbles and being pirates, and girls hop-scotch and jump-rope and are tempted by the whistles of the "goat-footed / balloonMan." It is probable that Trout marked this poem not merely because of its subject matter and multiple layers of meaning but because it contains wonderful nature imagery expressed by Cummings in those delicious turns of phrase where he describes spring as a time when the earth is "mud-luscious" and "puddle-wonderful," much as a precocious child might express joy in the season and the opportunity to soil its clothes splashing and making mud pies.

Trout shared Cummings' support for individualism and his concern for social issues and spiritual values in an age when so much in American culture promoted conformity and imitation. Both were suspicious of technology and critical of materialism. They viewed American corporate values and practices with abhorrence and politics and politicians with a jaundiced eye, particularly their appeals to patriotism and popular myths to justify America's foreign policy and wars. The legendary Indian fighter and Wild West show impresario William F. Cody, who fought Indians and was responsible for the killing of thousands of bison to feed railroad construction crews, is the subject of Cummings' satiric poem "Buffalo Bill's / defunct," which seems to have appealed to Trout. The "handsome" stallion-riding, crack-shot Cody is likened to a corporation or bank gone out of business as a result of lost assets, pronounced not dead but "defunct" by Cummings. Bill would also have relished the humor, sometimes, as here, delightfully wicked, found in Cummings' poems.

A different sort of hero is celebrated by Cummings in "I sing of Olaf glad and big," which tells of the moral strength of a good-hearted conscientious objector brutalized and tortured by his fellow soldiers because he "recoiled at war" and refused to kiss their "f.ing flag." Here as always, Cummings comes down on the side of individualism against conformity and unquestioning submission to institutional thinking. Olaf, one imagines as a man of the working class, insists on being true to his principles rather than following the course of least resistance even if it means suffering and death. As Trout's letters so often make clear, his own life and his judgment of others were based on considerations of humanity, integrity, and principle, which in part explains why he noted this poem in his copy of Cummings' verse. In "next to of course god america I," another poem Bill checked, Cummings' biting satire comes through in his criticism of the appeals Americans make to their early history to justify their actions and policies—pilgrims, and the claims of the national anthem (in the words "oh / say can you see by the dawn's early / my country 'tis")—to mouthing of patriotic slogans by young men going off to war, who "acclaim your glorious name by gory / by jingo by gee by gosh by gum." He asks what could exceed the beauty of the sacrifice of "these heroic happy dead" who unthinkingly rushed to their deaths? And at the close he queries whether their deaths have kept the "voice of liberty" from becoming mute. The deaths of so many young men in World War II, including his former student "Hookie" Bair and the Manship boy, must at least in part account for Bill's checking Cummings' poem "come, gaze with me upon this dome," with its unrelenting satiric account of a young blonde college boy taking leave of his family and girlfriend to "do or die / for God and country and for Yale," to go off to war "with trumpets clap and syphilis." Trout's opposition to war and his low opinion of the military expressed to former students in letters and conversations help to explain the appeal of Cummings' irreverent antiwar poems.

Finally, the musical quality of much of Cummings' early and late poetry probably did not escape Bill's notice. Norma Pollack documents that: "At least 168 different poems, have in fact, been transformed into some 370 compositions by approximately 143 composers," among them Aaron Copland, Leonard Bernstein, Dominick Argento, Pierre Boulez, John Cage, David Diamond, Luciano Berio, and Philip Glass. Although it is unlikely Bill would have found the works of some of these composers to his liking, what is important is that he, like they, recognized the inherent musicality of Cummings' verse. As Pollack points out, "the poems that have generated the most musical settings suggest that composers are drawn to fantasy, whimsicality, mystery, ambiguity, naiveté, romance, fervent expressions of love, and distinctive sensory expressions." And she goes on to observe that composers gravitated toward those poems that dealt with "the traditional subject matter of lyric poetry, such as love, subjectivity, and the cycle of life and death," and toward those poems that communicate through multisensory means—"kinetic, visual, aural"—the very subject matter and means the proponents of High Modernism and the New Criticism disparaged. Among the poems most frequently used for musical compositions were "in Just," "All in green went my love riding," "this is the garden:colours come and go," and "O sweet spontaneous," all of which Bill had checked in his copy of Cummings' collected poems (Pollack 1995, 121-122, 124, 129). A similar appeal, and one of another sort, seems to have attracted Trout to the poetry of Conrad Aiken.

There are a number of factors that may account for Trout's interest in Aiken's work, though his friendship with Ezra Pound and Eliot's influence on his poetry certainly were not among them. However, his edition of selected poems by Emily Dickinson published in 1924, which contributed to a revival of interest in her work may have been. The trauma of the murder-suicide of his parents when he was eleven years old gave rise to life-long bouts of depression and led Aiken to take a serious interest in psychology, particularly in Freud and later in Jung. His childhood experience and extensive reading in analytical and depth psychology influenced both his novels and poetry, which focus on self-understanding, and led to Freud's praising his novel *Great Circle* as a masterpiece of analytical introspection. Roy Harvey Pearce contends: "Aiken's essential theme is modern man's search for his identity, which develops into a search for a means of discovering that identity, which in turn develops into a conviction that the seeking and what is sought are one. In the end that identity is proved to be a kind of non-identity, and man to be just another product of cosmic process." Both Pearce's views and Louis Untermeyer's assessment that Aiken's "subtly subjective poetry" brought "tortured self-analysis to a pitch of pure poetry," were certainly interpretations that would have attracted someone like Trout, so much of whose poetry is informed by an interest in analytical psychology. With much of his own poetry devoted to the inner person and aimed at his own efforts to achieve self-knowledge, Aiken's poetry was sure to appeal to Bill. Aiken's use of interior monologue, like Charlotte Mew's, may also have drawn Trout to him since many of his own poems use the same technique (Pearce 1961, 349; Untermeyer 1962, 420).

Untermeyer sees Aiken's early work as that of a "natural musician" who leavened his playing with "new rhythms" and "haunting cadences" with "injections of T. S. Eliot's conversational idiom." He says of Aiken, "he is one of the finest verbal musicians in this country; his work is rich in color and incident, thoughtful without losing itself in the jungles of the mind, distinguished without being flagrantly bizarre." He likens Aiken's poetry to "a subaqueous music, strangely like the magic of Debussy," and claims he makes poems "as much like symphonies as possible." But the anthologist later faults him for his "over insistence on sound" and his too close "*liaison* between poetry and music," which places "so much importance on the rise and fall of syllables" on "the sensuous side," while losing "the vitality of speech which is the very blood of poetry." Pearce also criticizes Aiken for trying to make "words work like music," for his "grandiose attempts to make poems reach the state of music—the poem being the equivalent of the score, the performance being the real thing, and for moving too deeply into the unconscious" (Untermeyer 1923, 170, 176, 180-181; Untermeyer 1962, 419-420; Pearce 1961, 353, 355).

Allen Tate, faulting Aiken in a 1926 review in *The Nation* for "diffuseness" created by "a great deal of rhetorical padding," in a *New Republic* review of 1931 accuses him of "aimlessness" resulting from his penchant for "psychological theory and musical form" (Brown and Cheney, 1983, 40, 133-134). Yet Untermeyer applauds Aiken for recording "the interplay between man's dreams and his casual acts, the mingling of memory and the living moment, the hundred daily clashes between realism and fantasy," and credits him with being a "sensitive recorder of the half-illusory, half-elusive states of mind" (Untermeyer 1923, 175-176). As we have seen, these were the very qualities Trout looked for in poetry and may further explain his attraction to Aiken's verse. His copy of Untermeyer's single-volume anthology of modern American and British poetry has Aiken's poetry heavily underscored and annotated. And his student Dianne Danz, whose course notes include direct quotations from Trout, remembered his enthusiasm for Aiken. He told his class that Aiken was a poet who kept "a receptive mind to the incongruity of ideas, emotions, and verse form," and that he recognized "Poetry is constructed out of conflict."

The literary context in which Trout began to think about poetry and to write it was summarized by Untermeyer, who saw American poetry in the years between the two world wars—during which time Bill attended high school and college, began his teaching career, and was reading everything he could lay his hands on (including that Millay poem retrieved from the garbage truck and his first copies of Charlotte Mew and May Sinclair)—as a period when "many tendencies were in the air at one time." It was, he says, a time when the "classicism" of Eliot coexisted alongside "cool scholasticism," aesthetic intellectualism, "restrained sentiment," social realism, and the "emotional directness" of Millay. The lyric was changing from a "fixed form to an almost dissolving line" in the poems of Conrad Aiken, the Benét brothers, John Hall Wheelock, and George Dillon, while a revived interest in the late Elizabethans influenced the verse of Louise Bogan, Léonie Adams, and Elinor Wylie. In the years after the American economy collapsed in 1929, "such highly idiomatic poets" as William Carlos Williams, Horace Gregory, and Delmore Schwartz continued growing in importance in the face of a split in poetry into two distinct camps. The one, using the vernacular and focusing on social and economic problems, the plight of the common man, and popular culture, grew strident and "polemical." The other, which in large measure grew out of the Fugitives and their disciples, appealed to the "exceptional man" through wit, "adroitly elaborate ... yet remote" intellectualism, in language "allusive in a pedantic way." For their part, the Surrealists ignored both the Great Depression and World War II, concerned only with "self-expression" and championing "the almost forgotten 'Art for Art's sake' " (Untermeyer 1962, 24-29). Although Untermeyer's anthology of modern American verse reflects the richer diversity of poetry being written and published in the years 1920 to 1945 (including such left-leaning social critics as Genevieve Taggard, Langston Hughes, Kenneth Fearing, and Muriel Rukeyser) than does the Cleanth Brooks and Robert Penn Warren *Understanding Poetry* (which did so much to restrict the poetic canon), it did not include such working-class poets and Marxists as Mike Gold and Edwin Rolfe. The "many tendencies" of the inter-war years gave way after 1945 to other trends in poetry, which reflect both the prosperity and the tensions of life in Cold War America and will be explored in the following chapter.

As with the British poets Trout chose to teach in his Millersville poetry course, so the American poets on the syllabus showed a desire to give students a representative introduction to American verse from Whitman and Dickinson to the mid-twentieth century. As one might expect, there was lots of Dickinson, Robinson, Wylie, Millay, Jeffers, and Aiken; with Whitman, Eliot, Pound, and Frost getting shorter shrift. Some of the leading lights of modernist verse were either ignored or given only a nod, among them William Carlos Williams, Wallace Stevens, Marianne Moore, John Berryman, and Robert Lowell. Ransom, Jarrell, Stephen Vincent Benét, MacLeish, Peter Vierick, and others were chosen by students either to read aloud and explicate in class or to write about in short analytical papers. With the work of seventy-seven American poets in the textbook and eighty British poets (from Hardy to Charles Tomilson), it would have been impossible to provide more than a cursory survey of modern Anglo-American poetry in a sixteen-week semester. Yet from his markings in Untermeyer's anthology and from the class notes and recollections of former students, it is clear that Trout devoted time to poets outside the canon, including such lesser-known ones as Edwin Markham and Lizette Woodworth Reese.

In addition to those American writers discussed earlier who seem to have had an influence on Trout, there were others whose works were a part of his library and reflect the breadth of his reading. Among his books on American poetry were collections of poems by John Greenleaf Whittier, Joyce Kilmer, Edgar Lee Masters, Sara Teasdale, Dorothy Parker, Steven Vincent Benét, and Ogden Nash, as well as a number of anthologies.

Like Emily Dickinson, Bill enjoyed reading biography and autobiography. Both also kept abreast of current events by reading newspapers and magazines, which left its mark on the themes and imagery of their poetry (Reynolds 1988, 428-437). Trout's letters from the 1940s contain references to biographies he was reading when still a junior high school teacher, long before he would have had need of such information to prepare college-level lectures. He read about the lives of noteworthy people, including a fair number of literary biographies, not merely out of personal interest in human beings and fascination with history, but as a way of understanding the possible sources of literary and artistic creativity, and no doubt in part to better understand himself and his own desire to give expression to his ideas and feelings through verse. He was obviously interested in what made artists of any discipline different from the common run of humanity. His library contained a significant number of biographies and autobiographies. In addition to the literary biographies mentioned elsewhere in this study, he owned books on the lives of such writers as Lord Byron, the Brontes, Shelley, Madame Edmond Adam (Juliette Lamber, a contemporary of Sand, Berlioz, and Wagner), Herman Melville, and Edith Sitwell, among others.

Among his books were the collected letters of Lord Byron and Lafcadio Hearn, in addition to those already mentioned. He was interested in people and in understanding the human experience, particularly what it was that made poets, composers, artists, and fictional characters like Tonio Kröger more aesthetically sensitive and better able to give voice to their emotions than the Hans Hansens and Ingeborg Holms of this world, but also what it was that artists suffered or had to give up for their art—why they were often on the margins of society and how they coped with being there. He believed that to understand their creativity it was necessary to know about them as human beings and be familiar with their life experiences and the times in which they lived, which in turn might help him better understand himself.

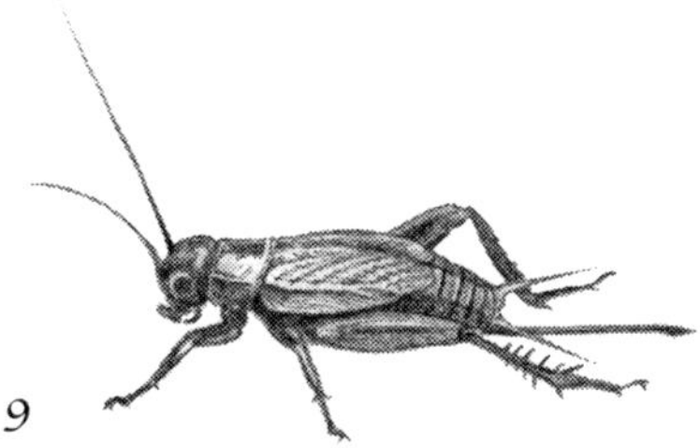

Chapter 9
The Poet and His Contemporaries

"Poetry begins in reading books," Robert Frost observed, and the poet "writes out of the eddy in his mind of all the books he has ever read..." (Meyers 1996, 69). The writers William Trout admired and his wide range of reading in various disciplines discussed throughout this volume give important clues to the qualities he valued in life and in literature and sought to express through his own poetry. It would have been impossible for such an omnivorous and eclectic reader as Trout not to absorb subconsciously the ideas and spirit of others. However, in his poetry their influences are not merely assimilated but transformed and given the imprint of his personality and voice. But he was part of no particular literary movement. In addition to any "influence" other writers may have had on his poetry, it should be recognized that in the final analysis his verse was the product of genius and "the accidents of personal experience," as Frank Swinnerton rightly observes is true of all first-rate writers (Swinnerton 1956, 78). This chapter summarized the characteristics of Trout's verse, his relationship with his literary contemporaries, and explores the possible reasons why he chose not to publish his poems.

Like most good writers of verse or fiction, Trout wrote about what he knew best—his environment, personal experiences, family and friends, and himself—but did so in such a way that others can find themselves in his words. He saw in lived reality the beauty and the ugliness of life, and the deeper significance of the emotions ordinary people experience, particularly what many at times suffer: a frustrating search for meaning in life, dashed hopes and compromised ideals, missed opportunities, self-doubt, lost faith, emotions that cannot be shared, fear of the unknown, sorrow, isolation, and loss. The insights he gained through his own personal losses and hardships inform his poetry and explain his ability to render intense suffering in poems like "Her endless, silent monologues of age," "The small face shrivels, and the eyes grow strange," "And still she sings, the Marschallin," and "There at the wood's edge, in the pitted snow" expressed with a depth of tenderness absent from the work of most of his contemporaries. While his poems record external events and experiences, they contain deeply personal reflections of his inner thoughts, and like his letters are about loneliness and companionship. But he also wrote of those things that gave him comfort or pleasure. Two different qualities merge in Trout's personality—intellect and sensibility—the capacity to reason and to feel deeply, qualities that manifest themselves in his poetry and his personal relations. Robert Frost observed in a 1915 letter to W. S. Braithwaite that in writing poetry the "effects of actuality and intimacy are the greatest aim an artist can have. The sense of intimacy gives the thrill of sincerity" (Pritchard 1984, 93). And it is the intimacy of Trout's realism and imagination that accounts for the authenticity and sincerity of his verse. Yet his poems reflect not only his doubting and inquiring mind, but his preference for exploring internal conflict to recording external events and acts.

Although nature is central to much of Trout's poetry, his sensitivity to social and economic injustice also figures as a subject or subtext of his poems. Just as he did not play at recess with his schoolmates, so later in life it was not in keeping with his personality to be an activist; hence his unwillingness to join causes or advocate collective action, as did the poets of the literary Left. His social and political poems have an elegiac tone; they are not exhortations or calls to action; their influence is indirect and reflective; they raise issues and consciousness and encourage contemplation rather than seeking to effect change directly. Here he seems to be at one with W. H. Auden in believing that "Poetry makes nothing happen," as Auden says in his poem "In Memory of W. B. Yeats." While poetry might raise consciousness, it is not instrumental in the sense of changing political, social, or economic institutions and practices or in altering the course of history. Trout's poems often carry moral messages without either moralizing or seeking social change through moral instruction, as Auden's do. His are instructive without being didactic. They offer lessons to those who are sensitive and at an angle to conventional society in which they are forced to live misunderstood and unappreciated. But the root of Trout's genius is his receptivity, his remarkable powers of sympathetic observation, imaginative assimilation, adaptation, and transmutation.

While he saw the society of his day as driven by materialism, consumerism, advertising, mechanization, and the perversion of democratic ideals by finance and its political lackeys, he wrote few poems of cultural criticism, focusing instead on the personal, including his own inner world. The private content of his poems is characteristic of lyric poetry. Because he was plagued by doubts and uncertainties and used poetry in his search for self-knowledge, it is not surprising that indirection and even obscurities are found in his poems. Unlike Emily Dickinson, who organized fair manuscript copies of two thirds of her total poetic output into forty-nine packets of poems tied together with string (suggesting she at least thought about posthumous publication of her work), Trout seems to have given little time to arranging his poems into any particular order and little thought to publication (Johnson 1960, viii). Since at times he was writing for himself, not a wider public, the deeply personal nature of his poems can make grasping their meaning or intent difficult. Knowing something of his life and times makes it possible to have a richer appreciation of his verse.

Many of Bill's poems take the form of reminiscence, interrogation, or interior monologue, and in some he poses questions to the reader or to himself, creating a dialogue about an idea, issue, or emotion. For him memory becomes a mirror for introspection, a reflection on his life and the world he lives in that carries implication for others. Often the past and present are found in the same poem; sometimes flashbacks and flash-forwards seem almost simultaneous. Both irony (something he appreciated in other writers) and, to a lesser degree, satire, are found in Trout's verse.

As Bill's letters and poems reveal, his life embodied the earthy, the intellectual, and the spiritual. And paradoxical though it may seem for one who isolated himself from the wider world, his life confirms his belief that, as he tells Don Smith in a letter of 18 July 1943, "any artist is richer for a variety of experiences, whether he be musician or writer." The realism of his poems, which unites the tactile and the visual, is not merely descriptive but appeals to the reader's imagination and is leavened with idealism and mysticism. There is not only reality but also immediacy in poems like "Sic Transit," "On the Back Porch," "One Pheasant," and "Crow." That Trout saw poetry as a part of everyday life, his immediate reality, not as something academic or esoteric is apparent in many of his poems, among them "Now Anonymous," "Country Sale," and "Forecast." While he did not reject science out of hand, he recognized its limitations where the acquisition of knowledge—particularly inner- or self-knowledge—is concerned.

He never dismissed the importance of the intellect but believed that intuition and the imagination were at least of equal if not greater importance, and too often ignored by people. Interest in the metaphysical, in trying to find meaning in what lies beyond the senses and consciousness, informs much of his poetry. Central to his verse is the attempt to understand those intangibles that underpin physical reality, to grasp the ultimate mysteries of life. He also insisted that the irrational—the dark side of the psyche—had to be acknowledged and explored with care if personal wholeness is to be realized, however imperfectly, and some understanding of the world achieved, however incomplete. And his poetry is informed by the interplay of reality and fantasy; it merges sensation and reflection.

It was passion, craftsmanship, and the exploration of the experience and meaning of life for the individual, the self that Trout looked for in the poetry of others and was central to his own work. And yet for all the evidence in his letters and the memories of those who knew of his expressions of emotion, there is in his poems a sense of detachment in his observations of nature, people, situations, and himself, a quality illustrated by such poems as "Remembered," "A Dry Leaf," and here in "Winter Afternoon":

> Completed picture. The warm silent room;
> Beyond, the soft push of snow against the pane,
> Folding, hushing all, muting the trucks upon the highway,
> And burying the bush of barberry on the lawn;
> The silver dial of the clock upon the wall
> Spins ceaselessly, minutely hums.
> Alone,
> Detached, emotion drained away. Completed picture,
> Suspended in memory, subtracted from the sum of time,
> Perfumed by the sheaf of freesias on the table,
> Set to the metronomic beat of blood
> Slowed from the heart.

Unlike Eliot, Pound, and other modernists, Trout did not set out to break with the past, to be innovative, "cutting edge," but rather sought to stamp tradition with his own voice and personal concerns and interests. His verse techniques are rooted mainly in the work of the English poets and a few Americans: Emily Dickinson, E. A. Robinson, Edna Millay, Robinson Jeffers. Like many of the modern poets he most admired—Mew, Robinson, de la Mare, Millay—he remained true to traditional forms, usually structuring his poems into quatrains, sestets, or sonnets, and creating a richly melodic style by using combinations of end rhyme, internal rhyme, assonance, consonance, and judicious alliteration. Nonetheless, he did occasionally abandon meter and rhyme, to write narrative poems like "Then and Now," "The

Book," and "Then perhaps it has always been: we embroidered." But he did not completely eschew sophisticated diction, what some might call "literary language," for that of everyday speech. Rather, he combined it with simple words and common phrases like those found in the poems of his contemporary Winfield Townley Scott while avoiding the colloquialisms of Robert Frost and the slang used by E. E. Cummings and Theodore Roethke. Nor did he experiment with formulating new language and new grammar, as did Gertrude Stein, Cummings, and other modernists. In E. A. Robinson, Trout found a poet whose aversion to Symbolist poetry he appears to have shared, up to a point. While he avoided the most esoteric devices of Symbolist abstraction, Bill's interest in Jungian psychology, mythology, and the occult led him to employ symbols and literary-historical references or allusions, few of which, however, are as abstruse as the symbolism of Yeats, Eliot, and Pound or as introverted as that of Theodore Roethke.

To say that Trout rejected the modernists out of hand is too simplistic a conclusion to be drawn either from his poetry or from statements he made in letters or to his students. While he did not share their obsession with Freudian sexual explanations for conduct or subconscious experiences, their repudiation of moral standards and all conventions, and their relegation of the lessons of history to the scrap heap, he did share their alienation from contemporary society, and their interest in the unconscious, the issue of relativity, and questions about the nature of time. It is also well to remember that he valued the poetry of Hart Crane, Robinson Jeffers, Conrad Aiken, and E. E. Cummings. My conclusions about Bill's attitude toward Modernism are somewhat conjectural given the paucity and brevity of direct statements he made about it. However, at the risk of being accused of equivocation, it seems reasonable to say that in his poetry he was neither a practitioner of the genteel tradition nor a card carrying member of the *avant-garde* but a modern traditionalist whose *personal values*, like those of his mother and some of the writers he most admired, were rooted in the years immediately before and after the Great War—between 1900 and 1920—and were colored by his own experiences of its social and economic aftermath.

Trout was essentially a lyric poet with a marked tendency toward the elegiac in his reflections on the tragic aspects of life. He took the principal themes of lyric poetry—nature, love, and death—as subjects for many of his poems. Conspicuous by its absence in any of Bill's lyrics (though not as we have seen in his letters) is evidence of romantic love or the eroticism of physical attraction most of us experience in our lives. Rather than focusing on romantic love, as is the lyric norm, he created memorable poems devoted to maternal love and age, an innovation that deserves recognition. Nor does the mood or tone of his nature poetry bring to mind Herrick, Keats, or Wordsworth, but rather Hardy, Frost, and Jeffers. Although he experimented with a variety of forms, much of his poetry uses meter and rhyme and exhibits the attributes of the lyric: brevity, subjectivity, sensuality, passion, rich imagery, and most particularly the tonal variation that confirms its melodic origins and sets its mood. As Alex Preminger and his fellow editors point out: "The irreducible denominator of all l[yric] poetry must, therefore, be those elements which it shares with the musical forms that produced it … it is representational of music in its sound patterns, basing its meter and rhyme on the regular linear measure of the song"; or on "cadence and consonance" to create "poetic lyricism" (Preminger 1974, 461-462). Most of Trout's extant poems are short or medium-length and some, like "The three-legged ant," "Aubade," and "Abendrot," are almost epigrammatic. He may well have been following the lead of Emily Dickinson in the brevity of his own work, as suggested by an observation he made on her poems to his Contemporary Poetry class: "A poem must be brief because the essence is so volatile." Of his favorite poets—Emily Dickinson, Thomas Hardy, E. A. Robinson, A. E. Housman, Walter de la Mare, and Edna Millay—Dickinson, Housman, and de la Mare limited their work to short and medium-length poems. While some of his poems are narrative, none are ballads or epics. Trout used a variety of line lengths and though apparently preferring to write in either quatrains or sestets, did compose poems in quintets, septets, and octaves.

At a time when the sonnet was under attack by the New Critics and modernist poets, Bill would probably have agreed with Wordsworth, who began one of his, "Scorn not the sonnet," and closed another saying that "Within the Sonnet's scanty plot of ground," he had found "brief solace there." Trout's many sonnets are one of the chief glories of his poetry. Among his best "Trust in neither God nor man," "Her endless, silent monologues of age," "Before the Sale," and "Now a light along the room" are English, Shakespearean in form, consisting of three quatrains and a final couplet, rhyming ababcdcdefefgg.

The subtlety and nuance of Trout's nature poems refine one's perceptions by drawing attention to those things often overlooked; they not only help one to see, hear, and smell the natural world but to *feel* it in poems like "Summer Ending" and "Light Snow." In his multi-layered sonnet "Fourth Act" he combines the most telling characteristics of his poetic imagination with undisputable technical skill. He engages all our senses, some directly and others through indirection or intimation. Through his keen attention to specific visual details he paints a vivid but not a dramatic picture of a late autumn day containing such things as "lichened stone," "shell-bark hickory trees," "sleepy woods," a flapping crow, and particularly through his sensitivity to color shows us how the umber and rust hues appear to make the "ragged slope" "smoulder." His choice of words suggests the subtlety of both sound and movement in the scene: smoldering colors of autumn on a nearly still day with the sound of a shivering cricket clacking his "mill," punctuated at times by the noise of boys playing baseball under the trees and the strident caws of a passing crow. Trout's obsession with time, specifically with the transience of life, is patent in the references to the changing seasons—August gone, September fled, October waning, and the threat of impending winter at hand. And in the final couplet—expressed in typical Troutian terms of soft sorrow, regret, and resignation—one finds Bill's preoccupation with death. The cricket might be taken as a metaphor in that like Man he has not granted, not accepted that his time is running out—that like the seasons of the year the cycle of life is inevitable. The presence of boys playing ball further underscores the implicit message of "Fourth Act" and injects a modern element:

> Umber and rust on the ragged slope
> Smoulder; almost the day is still,
> Save for the cricket under the cope
> Of lichened stone—he clacks his mill,
> Shivering there, not granting yet
> That August is gone, September fled,
> October waning, and the threat
> Of winter leveled at his head;
> And boys with clubs now shout and throw
> Under the shell-bark hickory trees;
> And over the sleepy woods the crow
> Flaps and caws his stridencies.
> But, cricket, be quiet, for all is over—
> Be decently quiet, and under cover.

In other sonnets, Trout takes a variety of liberties with the rhyme scheme but does not go as far as his contemporary Merrill Moore (1903-1957), whose "And to the Young Men" is an apt example of what Louis Untermeyer says about his sonnets: "His rhyme-schemes seem as haphazard as they are numerous—the rhymes themselves are suspiciously unorthodox" and his lines "divide themselves anywhere with what seems sheer perversity." Moore was a medical doctor and psychiatrist, a graduate of Vanderbilt University, was one of the Fugitives, and is reputed to have written more than 50,000 sonnets. His hybrid "American sonnets," praised for their vitality and improvisation, were well received by New Criticism critics (Untermeyer 1962, 572-573).

Trout was aware of Moore's work if for no other reason than that his sonnets were represented in the textbook he used for his Contemporary Poetry course, but also because he was one of the writers who participated in Millersville's Contemporary Writers' Lectures. While Bill knew the rules of versification he, like Emily Dickinson, Charlotte Mew, and Edna St. Vincent Millay, was not averse to bending them, though not as much as Merrill Moore did. Indeed, Bill's iconoclasm comes through in his occasional polemics against unalterable Laws, be they the conventions of social behavior, institutions of the dominant culture, religious straight-jacketing, or literary rules. He was no more a slave to metrical purity than were Dickinson or Millay, but the beauty of his wording and the strength of his ideas justify the liberties he sometimes took with metrics. The melodic quality of his verse is influenced by his use of the dash both as terminal line punctuation and within the line as a visual means of pacing or rhythmical flow. While at times complex and unconventional, his punctuation brings out what Amy Lowell called the "organic rhythm" of the speaking voice. Also contributing to this musicality is his skillful use of caesura, a pause within a line or at its end and the hastening or slackening of the rhythm by varying the lengths of syllables. Setting off qualifying information or explanations in parentheses as though the writer were making an aside to the reader or to himself is another distinguishing feature of Trout's poetry that influences its rhythm. Enjambment, which is also characteristic of Trout's writing and contributes to the rhythmic quality of his verse, is the run-over of one line to the next, a commonplace with the Elizabethans and Milton, which went out of fashion in the eighteenth century but was revived by English Romantics (Preminger 1974, 241).

There is good reason to believe that Bill so internalized the classical music he listened to that his thought processes were akin to those of a musician or composer and contribute to the musicality of his verse. His ability in mathematics (as his pupils and others testified), his annotations of musical scores, and, as noted earlier, his observations on the "symphonic" quality of Thomas Mann's works and the relationship between the Chinese poetry text and Mahler's score for *Das Lied von der Erde* all suggest that Bill thought like a musician. He may in fact have seen poems as word-songs. Further evidence of the close linkage between music and literature in Trout's mind is found in letters he sent to Don Smith on 26 April and 10 May 1943, in which he mentions the possibility of turning Herman Melville's *Moby-Dick* into "an opera on the Wagner-Strauss-Verdi plan." He tells Smith he is "sketching a libretto on the fly-leaves of the book as I read. It has everything—physical action, emotional drive, splendid characterization, a ripping chance for scene-painting, stupendous vocal possibilities, and a terrific, surging climax, with all the inherent catharsis of great tragedy, both physical and spiritual—the impotent but indomitable human spirit in doomed conflict with the impersonal forces of the universe." Bill recognized the complex philosophical issues in Melville's novel, what David Reynolds refers to as the archetypical "resonances" represented not only in the symbolism of the sea and the whale but also by its characters, particularly in the bonding of the "savage" Queequeg and the "civilized" Ishmael with its intimation of homoeroticism, and most strikingly in the "mythic stature" of Captain Ahab, who combines "the evil Ahab described in I Kings … the doomed overreacher of Renaissance dramas [and] … Faust, Lear, Prometheus" (Reynolds 1988, 546, 551). It was not until April 2010 that Jake Heggie, who composed *Dead Man Walking* in 2000, premiered his *Moby-Dick*, which was commissioned by the Dallas Opera jointly with four other opera houses, accomplishing what Bill had envisioned sixty-seven years earlier. Finally, Trout's poetic vocabulary reveals just how important the *sound* of words, their music, was to him. His choice of words, influenced by sensitivity to color both in the visual and musical sense, shows him to be a poet with a good ear and a rich visual imagination. Generally speaking—though not necessarily where his "horror" or social criticism poems are concerned—the dynamic quality of the sound conveyed by Trout's word combinations and the overall tone color of his poems might best be characterized by the musical terms *piano* and *diminuendo*—an overall softness. Yet though music underpins his poetry it never submerges the energy of the spoken word.

Trout's mastery of diction, apt word choices, owes much to his unusually rich vocabulary, no doubt the legacy of his eclectic interests and passion for books and reading, and is one of the hallmarks of his poetry. His poems document a belief that one's daily surroundings are the basis of poetry and must link the senses to the intellect through words that appeal to the emotions and imagination of the reader. Bill loved words, as his former pupils recalled. They remembered the emphasis he placed on expanding their vocabulary, as his Millersville student Robert Smiles mentioned in an email to me, explaining: "When he [Trout] came upon one of my unfortunate word choices [in an essay], he would not only point it out, but he would also suggest 10 other words that would have been better." Trout's choice of words shows how much he savored the sound of language. Archaic or little used words appealed to him. He was a master at using imaginative or invented word forms like "beggarly" to characterize a roadside ditch in which wild chicory grew, to describe the gray chill air of a graveyard as "a little gritted, a little grimed," or to call the arthritic hands and knees of an old black man "knobbly." He selected words (often preferring the English to the American spelling, or taking the second rather than the first spelling offered by the dictionary) for their communicative power, not merely for their direct meaning, but for their secondary meaning, for the overtones or nuances they convey as well as for the way they sound. His apparent interest in the morphology of language, particularly the origins and changes in words—influenced by his knowledge of Latin, French, and German—manifests itself in his poems. It is interesting to note how many of the words Trout uses are French or have French roots: ambuscade, manqué, benison, derogation, and revenants, to mention but five. And he often employs a single powerful word to invoke a mood. His objection to modernist writers of poetry and fiction, and perhaps also to those who used verse as an instrument to support a cause or bring about social change, may in part be to their deliberate choice of the simplest of words (much as advertising, journalism, and war propaganda does), to their efforts to "desophisticate" language, which he saw as robbing language if its richness, variety, and beauty.

It is clear that Bill mourned the ever-shrinking and more commonplace vocabulary used by a majority of Americans, which resulted not only from the influence of popular culture and advertising, but was abetted by the language of the street employed by writers of fiction and poetry in their attempt to be "relevant" and to reach a wider market for their work. He would probably have agreed with William Faulkner, who quipped that Hemingway "has never been known to use a word that might send a reader to the dictionary." His interest in the visual arts is apparent in the color choices of his language and the composition of his placement of words. The aptness of his word choices amplifies Trout's unusually acute powers of observation and the variety and density of his imagery as in such poems as "The groping mind turns back to May, where bides," "From memory's scattered fragments, scraps," and "You know how the spirit clings."

Bill's interest in visual art comes through in the sensitivity to color reflected in the rich and varied palette he uses to render landscapes, flora and fauna, and the weather. In "Abendrot" (Sunset), he gives us an insight into how one of his poems came into being, the inspiration for which came as he caught glimpses of the sky as he graded students' papers or wrote lecture notes. He captures the stages of a sunset in short, condensed, staccato-like lines reminiscent of Emily Dickinson's poem "A slash of Blue" or of E. E. Cummings in poems like "here's a little mouse) and," "cruelly, love," and "O sweet spontaneous":

> Looked up once;
> The sky was pink—
> Suffusion, brimming
> Steady rose.
>
> Bent again to pen and ink—
> Bread and butter's
> Evening woes;
>
> Later looked,
> By accident,
> Between the willow
> And the pine:
>
> The west was gold
> And umber, blent—
> A sudden and
> A heady wine.

Both specificity and nuance are apparent in Trout's color choices, which go beyond the usual primary and secondary colors to include more varied and subtle hues such as crimson, cream, charcoal, bronze, blue-gray, turquoise, scarlet, rust, lemon, gray-white, amber, and umber. Much of his verse, particularly his nature poetry, is filled with appeals to the senses—to odors, colors, textures, tastes, sounds—as, for example, in "Sur Le Noël":

> Under the white oak, in the snow,
> We scratched with stiffened fingers, found,
> Sturdy in the black ground—
> In soft leaf-mold—green below

The white crust, fruit and leaf,—
Partridge berries. Scarlet bright
The berries, like a steady light
Burning in that gray, brief,
December afternoon; the green
Oval leaf, precise and neat:
To find these, our numbed feet
Had stumbled uphill, on between
Rail fence and hawthorn bush.
We scraped snow and leaves away,
And crouching under dwindling day,
Tasted, in the wintry hush.
Icy fire in nose and lung
The air was, on the hill,
Above the valley, blue and still.
But Sinbad spice twitched at the tongue.

And in this untitled poem, which casts up a memory of sparkling jewels, peeling paint, smoky haze, shadows, and the scent of spicewood.

From memory's scattered fragments, scraps
Of emerald, amethyst, and pearl,
Of weathered paint, flaking perhaps
Even as I thought, I unfurled
Painfully the April promise
Of freakish spring, after the grim,
Dragging winter. From the hush
Of smoky haze, I drew the glimmer
Of spicewood bushes, among the thin,
Slanting shadows of the woods
Yet attenuate. Central then
I put your smile—the hardihood
Of steady courage. I closed my eyes.—And over all,
Winter-sudden, swept the ultimate snowfall.

But one of the most striking features of Trout's diction is his frequent use of adverbs and adverbial phrases and clauses and his skillful use of past participles. The imaginative use of action verbs is also characteristic of his work. Things are in motion as lines from four of his poems make clear: "To cascade in the iron trough / Then whirl and gurgle and be off"; "Pell-mell fear sped our bare feet / And legs abbreviate"; "They glide and slide, they slink and peer"; "shiver of sudden gooseflesh raced the spine." But not all of his verbs relate to speedy movement. He is also gentle in such lento phrases as: "An umbered drift"; "the leaf's down-drifting grace"; "Soft airs of April freak / The shattered wing, nudge the parted beak"; "The saunter into autumn has begun"; and "But western fire sinks to umber, / And the ship of summer begins to list." His word choices also show a preference for subtlety and understatement rather than for the dramatic or sensational. Here again one might think of Trout's choice of words and word combinations in relation to music, specifically tempo signatures ranging from *lento* and *adagio*, through *andante* and *moderato*, to *allegretto* and *presto*.

Much of Trout's poetry, whether the subject is nature, the aging process, or psychological states, is informed by mysteriousness and transcendence—a view which owes as much to the music he most loved as it does to his lived reality and reading of literature, philosophy, and Jungian psychology. The works of Mahler discussed earlier and Richard Strauss' *Death and Transfiguration*, *Metamorphosen*, and the *Four Last Songs* are meditations on life and the transformational experience of departing earthly existence. Strauss' description of the "program" of his tone-poem *Death and Transfiguration* (1889) as a musical rendering of the final hours of an artist whose thoughts wander through his past life with its unfulfilled desires and aesthetic strivings, ends as the soul departs the body into infinite space with the implicit recognition that the ideal to which artists aspire is not something achievable on earth. That such philosophical issues are so gloriously rendered through Strauss' music no doubt left its mark on Trout.

Ambiguity is characteristic of much modern art, as well as some of its precursors, particularly in the visual arts and poetry. Preferring inference to direct statement, Bill once justified such indirection to Don Smith in a letter of 22 May 1943 regarding poems by Don's girlfriend, Tuck, enclosed in a letter to him: "too much is stated, too little inferred; she underestimates her readers, always a fatal thing to do." He also cautioned about "over-writing" since it "clutters up the picture and clouds the firm outlines of a fine poem." But he praised Tuck's "gift for a telling phrase," "depth of feeling," and "good sense of rhythm and cadence." Bill was given to indirection, suggestion, nuance, and the interplay of light and shadow to create mood or atmosphere in his poetry much as a painter uses chiaroscuro or as Strauss and Mahler create rich and varied tone color in their symphonic works through their instrumentation.

However, the intimacy and brevity of his poems, it seems to me, probably owe more to German *Lieder* and chamber music than to grand symphonic works. Given the advice he offered Don Smith's girlfriend, it is no surprise that many of Trout's own poems are quite dense. There is, nonetheless, a certain complexity and degree of ambiguity in his poetry, and it is these qualities that help make it so intellectually appealing. His use of parentheticals notwithstanding, compactness, concision is characteristic of many of his poems. And such lines as "Mooed her delicate malaise"; "March brooms the empty countryside"; "Throbbed through at noon"; "In three-jowled fascination"; "The flocks of phantoms, rising fast"; "The gleaned grain of mythic sheaves"; "Her endless, silent monologues of age"; and "The fiddles sighed exquisite pain" document his mastery of the telling phrase.

We can learn about Trout's own poetry by looking into his approach to teaching the poetry of others, as was done in part in Chapters 7 and 8. In teaching about poetry it was the poem itself and the biography and cultural-historical context of its creator that received Trout's attention, not the views of critics. His personal library contained only a few volumes of literary criticism, among them: Henri Bergson, *The Philosophy of Poetry: The Genius of Lucretius*; A. E. Housman's *The Name and Nature of Poetry*; collections of E. M. Forster's essays; Edmund Wilson's *The Shores of Light: A Literary Chronicle of the Twenties and Thirties*; both volumes of Virginia Woolf's *Common Reader* and her *The Moment and Other Essays*; and Robert Graves *Oxford Address on Poetry*. He may well have owned others, which he disposed of at the public auction in 1961 when he left Gap for Lancaster, or, more likely, gave to friends and students. He had easy access to two college and one public library and, given his low opinion of criticism in general, may have borrowed such books rather than buying them.

As his students remember, he stressed the centrality of the text in the study of literature, but not in the same way as the "close reading" of the New Criticism. Such a method he regarded as too clinical, too scientific, and limiting in its narrow focus on formal elements such as diction, rhyme, and meter to the exclusion of biographical information, cultural-historical context, poetic intent, attention to content, and the emotional effect on the reader. Unlike the New Critics, he did not accept the absolute autonomy of the poem stripped of the contexts in which it was created and free of external evidence to aid its interpretation. Neither would he have been likely to accept all of the criteria the New Critics favored in poetry, which according to Stephen Burt and Jennifer Lewin, include: "difficulty, seriousness, violence, frequent allusions, complex syntax and Christian symbolism." Nor would he have been entirely sympathetic to the practices of poets guided by the New Criticism, who: "describe or enact psychological dilemmas, [insist on] closure, incorporate contrasting tones or complex symbols, suggest tragic or irresolvable dilemmas, and evoke moral sentiments only through symbols," though certain of these elements are also found in some of his poems (Burt and Lewin in Roberts 2001, 154-155, 163).

But what Trout seems to have objected to most was the New Criticism's insistence on impersonality, which originated with Eliot's pronouncement that "the poet has, not a 'personality' to express, but a particular medium, which is only a medium and not a personality … Poetry is not a turning loose of emotion, but an escape from emotion; it is not the expression of personality, but an escape from personality" (Eliot 1975, 42-43). What Eliot advocated was the use of metaphor, simile, and a multiplicity of associations and extended comparisons to create intellectual *not* reflective poetry. He believed that the multiplicity and complexity of twentieth-century Western Civilization required that "The poet must become more and more comprehensive, more allusive, more indirect, in order to force, to dislocate if necessary, language into his meaning" (Eliot 1932, 242, 247-248). It is important to note that while Trout made a concerted effort to live to himself, he was in his own way a people-centered person. For all his obvious interest in ideas and emotions, it is the embodying of ideas and feelings in individuals, *real people* (and animals) rather than disembodied abstractions that mattered to Bill as documented by his reading of biographies; by the work of specific writers, composers, and visual artists; by his correspondence with former students and soldier friends; and by the subjects of many of his poems (his mother, the teacher of biology, Lizzie, Henry, a mentally retarded young man, an old maid, and animals like a maimed crow and a trapped muskrat). It may, therefore, have been the *person* of J. Alfred Prufrock and his ability to identify with him rather than what Eliot's invention represents that garnered Bill's approval.

As discussed in Chapters 7 and 8, Bill objected to the impersonality, the lack of expressions of personal emotion that characterized much modernist poetry and was drawn to those modern poets—Mew, Millay, Aiken, Cummings, Jeffers—who examine their own experiences and explore their own inner lives, as Trout does in such poems as "Search" and "Not knowing what to do, I wait," "Here I clung, threading maze," a meditation on his life experience and the importance of his mother in his life, written when Trout was in his late fifties and caring for his mother in their Lancaster apartment, which he calls "partly junk-yard, partly tomb."

Here I clung, threading maze
Unconsciously, in other days
Darkened, harried, by repeated
Groping, destined to defeat.
At the end, now, she and I
Watch the mocking cycles ply;
Hand in hand we drowse and wait,
Seeing to wither desolate
The paltry years, priced too high
By the Shylock of the sky.
But I win, in some way,
Because the spat-on yesterday—
Loathed, hated, cursed, lived through—
Joins the evil shadow-crew
Grimacing in the rented room,
Partly junk-yard, partly tomb.
Poised between the dusk and dark,—
Here the grave, there the stark
Machine of doom against the east—
I guard my grudged and meagre feast.
Now, finally, have I come,
Past the occult crossways, home.
Like a clearing in a wood,
Here rests immutable certitude,
In this timid, frail bird-claw
That in my clutch alleges law—
For me—assures me to have come,
Past the gallows-crossroad, home.

Bill also seems to have been wary of the approaches to criticism that came into vogue late in his career: Phenomenology, Hermeneutics, and Structuralism. Writing to Betty Curtis on 15 July 1962, (between terms) he told her: "Ever since school stopped, I have been trying to get the … novel course in order, and the effort has necessitated scanning (with a basin handy) a good deal of criticism; that effort has completed the cure—I shall never take a critic seriously. Even the deer of the Arctic—really noble-looking creatures—are attacked by innumerable parasites. Criticism should confine itself to pointing out beauties that we blunt-witted people miss. That, and no more."

We of course know from his lectures and from former students that Trout did much more than merely point out the beauty found in prose and poetry.

Writing to me on 11 June 1971 about "critiques" of literature by "supposed experts," he asked: "Do you sometimes think of Gulliver at the Academy of Lagado?" At this institution of learning in the fictional country of Balnibarbi, Gulliver met a number of scholars: one had spent eight years "extracting Sun-Beams from Cucumbers" and storing them in vials until released "to warm the Air in raw inclement Summers." Another "contrived a new Method for building Houses, by beginning at the Roof, and working downwards to the Foundations." A third was devising a way "to reduce human Excrement to its original Food." And the professors in the School of Languages were at work shortening "Discourse by cutting Polysyllables into one, and leaving out Verbs and Participles; because in Reality all things imaginable are but Nouns." In the same letter Bill goes on to tell me, apropos of the Academy of Lagado: "I recall (involuntarily and retchingly) how my gorge rose when the PhD's at MSC [Millersville State College] spoke of 'analysis in depth' and of 'depth psychology' applied to—well, to Miss [Jane] Austen's Emma. But after the impulse to vomit had been mastered, 'Mr. Weston's good wine' [a bitterly witty reference to T. F. Powys' 1927 novel *Mr. Weston's Good Wine*] came to the rescue." Trout's attitude toward psychological analysis of literature perhaps grew out of Jung's criticism of Freud's "reductive" approach to the interpretation of art (Jung 1966, 68-69).

But there were critics Bill respected, among them Donald A. Stauffer, whose *Nature of Poetry* and Robert Hillyer's *First Principles of Verse*, he recommended his students read. And as Dianne Danz (a student in his 1962 Contemporary Poetry course at Millersville) noted in her textbook, he drew on Stauffer to lay out for students the standards to be looked for in good poetry. Drawn from Danz's class notes are Stauffer's characteristics of what poetry should be (herein cited in italics) interlaced with brief quotes from Trout's gloss. A poem should be *exact, intense* ("demanded by the brevity of life"), and *significant* in that its key idea is "applicable to a phase of life." It should be *concrete*, free of "verbal abstractions" so that its "emotional content can't be missed." Though "necessarily *complex*," a good poem should not be "obscure" but make an honest attempt to render "an intangible reality as accessible as possible." And it should be *rhythmical* and *formal*, though adhering to the poet's "own creed" (Stauffer 1946, *passim*).

What may in part have drawn Bill to Stauffer's book was the emphasis the author places on certain key qualities of poetry, including diction as a means of creating "a state of consciousness" through "pure sound," using the poet's own vocabulary not that of "great artists of the past, or … contemporary convention." Suggestiveness achieved by sound-conscious word choices rather than directly stating emotions and sensory images, and compressing language and rhythm—which (as Wordsworth argued) provides intellectual, aesthetic, and physiological pleasures essential to good poetry—are qualities found in Trout's verse (Stauffer 1946, 50, 66-67, 76, 138, 150, 193, 195, 199). Bill no doubt agreed with Stauffer's observation that "far too many modern critics and readers assume that sentiment and even sentimentality are not fit parts of human experience." And as Stauffer goes on to say, in addition to expressing feeling, the use of "restraint and understatement," "profound thought," and "the convolutions of a controlled argument" can "produce equally powerful emotional effects" (Stauffer 1946, 18). Bearing in mind, as noted earlier, that Trout regarded his own poetry-making as therapeutic rather than as work intended for the public, one might still use the standards noted above as a guide to his intent and a measure of his success in achieving a satisfying result.

Robert Hillyer's cultivation of traditional forms, his "classicism," and what Louis Untermeyer calls his "deceptively quiet voice," and his association with Elford Caughey, may in part account for Bill's recommendation of his book *First Principles of Verse* to students (Untermeyer 1962, 481). Hillyer's views on versification and the qualities to look for in well-crafted poems can also be found in Trout's poetry.

Hillyer stresses the importance of diction, particularly words which imparted not merely literal meaning but secondary meanings—the "deft manipulation of overtones or suggestions." While he believes poetic diction should be "simple, definite, and fresh," it is "exactitude of thought" that matters most in making word choices. For him "adjectives should be chosen with scrupulous care and reduced in number" and "verbs should move actively, as is their function." Just as important as the "overtones of meaning" conveyed by words are their "overtones of sound." In matters of diction the poet should be sensitive to all sorts of sound, from the melodious to the discordant. The good lyric, Hillyer insists, should not only have something to say but should sing; it should be musical and sensuous without resorting to embellishments. The reader should be "moved by the sound of words." He praises the simplicity, terseness of Emily Dickinson and the Chinese poets. "Abstractions are to be shunned," he insists, and warns against overuse of alliteration, assonance, random internal rhymes, and inversion of syntax. He admonishes poets and readers to be wary of the importance all too many critics give to so-called originality and "freedom from tradition," though he acknowledges that "scarcely any great poet—if, indeed, any at all—has been rule-perfect" (Hillyer 1950, 3, 6, 9, 17, 21, 23, 90-91, 94, 105, 118).

Poetic temperament is described by Hillyer as "that faculty which perceives the most ordinary events of life as something wonderful and interesting, the most ordinary objects of life as something beautiful or significant." And he maintains that it is the poet's responsibility "to set forth an idea or emotion shared by the majority of the race" with intensity and in "concentrated and heightened form." Then two pages later, at the end of the chapter on "Temperament," he warns of the grave situation facing poetry at the time (1949-50), saying: "Obsequiously devoted to the pedantry of T. S. Eliot and the incoherencies of Ezra Pound, a loose confederacy, with a nucleus of unscholarly reviewers and analysts calling themselves the 'New' critics, have seized as much power as has ever fallen into the hands of any band of literary adventurers." He then observes that young college professors have been seduced by the New Critics and are spreading "a wholly false set of artistic values" to their students (Hillyer 1950, 85). Though Trout's negative opinion of High Modernism and the criticism based on it may have predated the publication of *First Principles of Verse*, it is likely that Hillyer's views confirmed his dislike of its aesthetic philosophy and critical practice.

Trout's progressive social and political views would also have put him at odds with some of the most committed modernists and New Critics. His attitude toward modernist writers appears to have gone deeper than distaste for their experiments with language, their esoteric references and shadowy allusions, their hostility to traditional literary forms, and the impersonality of their formalism. He may have sensed or detected in their lives and work what recent scholarship has confirmed about the connection between modernism and reactionary or right-wing politics (see Jameson 1979, Redman 1991, Sherry 1993, Hewitt 1993, Morrison 1996, Carlson 1998, Suretta 1999, Ferrall 2001, Antliff 2007).

As Barbara Will's research makes clear, while Gertrude Stein's experimental approach to writing was revolutionary and carried the hallmarks of modernist aesthetics in its use of language and its rejection of traditional methods of composing fiction, drama, and poetry, her political and economic views were reactionary. She took up residence in France after World War I and remained there throughout World War II, protected by Pétain sympathizers and Bernard Fay (Stein's "dearest friend during her life" according to Alice Toklas), who was an official in the Vichy government, a confidant of its president, Henri Philippe Pétain (1856-1951), and a Nazi collaborator. In her actions and letters to friends she comes across as an unapologetic champion of the authoritarian regime of General Pétain whose speeches she began to translate into English with the intention of publishing them to win support in the United States for his government, and to "educate" her fellow countrymen about his political philosophy. Even after the war ended, she tried to interest Bennett Cerf at Random House in publishing the general's speeches. In a series of articles on "Money" published in *The Saturday Evening Post* in 1936, Stein used harsh language to attack Franklin Roosevelt's New Deal efforts to lift the United States out of the Great Depression, charging that FDR's policies were dangerous, contrary to American values, and a threat to freedom. In "The Winner Loses, A Portrait of Occupied France," another of her Vichy propaganda pieces, published in *The Atlantic Monthly* in 1940, Stein's muddled and often contradictory political thinking is apparent in her claim that in their defeat by the Germans in 1940 the French people under Pétain had won a victory, a chance to begin anew by abandoning the corrupt and decadent parliamentarian democracy of the toppled Third Republic in favor of Pétain's vision of a peaceful agrarian nation in which tradition, Catholicism, daily life, hard work, and habit were valued and the social strife and lack of discipline born of the Revolution of 1789 would no longer exist (Will 2011, 134-140, 188-189, 9-11, 94-95, 103-105, 6-7). Since we know that Trout read periodicals, some of which, *The Atlantic* for example, published his cousin Elford's poems, it is not unreasonable to think that he knew about or had read Stein's articles as well as newspaper stories about her. Thus Bill had both literary and political reasons for apparently never mentioning Stein.

But Gertrude Stein was not the only right-wing modernist. Ezra Pound, a notorious anti-Semite, lived in Italy during World War II and actively supported Mussolini, for which he was arrested for treason after the war and confined in a psychiatric hospital in Washington D. C. from 1946 to 1958. T. S. Eliot's conversion to Anglo-Catholicism contributed to a deepening conservatism on his part. Those poets and New Critics with Southern affiliations known first as the Fugitives and later as the Agrarians—John Crowe Ransom, Donald Davidson, Allen Tate, and Robert Penn Warren—were tainted, as noted earlier, by reactionary regionalism and allowed their "anti-liberal predispositions" (including with some of them racism and homophobia) to influence their cultural and political writing (Burt and Lewin in Roberts 2001, 155-156; Nelson 1989, 169-171; Kalaidjian 1996, 300-302, 304-306, 308-

311). Whether Bill knew of the social and political views of the Fugitives/Agrarians is uncertain since he left no record of his assessment of their work.

Characterizing the American poetry scene in the 1940s and 1950s as an "exquisite chaos," M. L. Rosenthal goes on to say: "Everywhere in [Randall] Jarrell the world seems to be locked in a grisly dream of the endless victimization of man. This mood is one shared by a great many other poets of his generation ..." among them, I would argue, William Trout (Rosenthal 1960, 246). Certainly the horrors of World War II, from the mechanized slaughter on the battlefield to Axis atrocities and war crimes, to the mass civilian deaths caused not only by the Axis but also by Allied saturation bombing and incendiary raids on such cities as Hamburg and Dresden, and use of the Atomic Bomb against Japanese civilians, were the roots of the "grisly dream" that haunted those poets who experienced the war first hand. Many poets of this generation served in the military, though not all of them in combat units or even overseas. Randall Jarrell operated a celestial navigation tower in the Army Air Corps and learned about combat from the newspapers and the stories told him by pilots. Richard Eberhart was a gunnery instructor in the Navy. Neither was deployed overseas, and so their poems about the war reflect neither impressions nor emotions based on personal experience; however, Eliot's dictum that personality and sentiment be kept out of poetry gave them license to write about things of which they had no direct knowledge, which explains why, as William Pritchard maintains, Jarrell's poems "are about the army in its dailiness" not about the war, and accounts for their "anonymity of viewpoint" and "flatness of tone." They also reflect Jarrell's beliefs about the dangers posed to individuality by the state and mass society. In a letter to Allen Tate in 1945, he said that the atmosphere in which soldiers lived "was entirely one of lying, meaningless brutality and officiousness, stupidity not beyond belief but conception—the one word for everything in the army is *petty*, what Paul Fussell describes as "chickenshit" (Pritchard 1990, 100, 104, 111, 127; Fussell 1989, 80-84). Trout came to the same conclusion without benefit of military service as is apparent from his letters to Don Smith and conversations with those in uniform. Both John Ciardi (1916-1986) and Louis Simpson (1923-2012) served in combat units, one in the Pacific and the other in Europe, which helps to account for the difference in Jarrell's "The Death of the Ball Turret Gunner," "A Pilot from the Carrier,"

"The Wingman," "A Camp in the Prussian Woods" and Eberhart's "The Fury of Aerial Bombardment" on the one hand and Ciardi's "Two Songs for a Gunner," "Elegy," "Sea Burial," "The Health of Captains" and Louis Simpson's "Carentan, O Carentan."

None of these poets wrote flag-waving, God-and-country hymns celebrating patriotism and heroism: they penned anguished cries about the killing, suffering, and utter senselessness of war and the physical and psychological scars left with those who participated in, witnessed, or saw photographs of atrocities, slaughter, and horrific destruction. But far and away the most unsettling of American war poems, it seems to me, was by another non-combatant, the quiet, gentle Winfield Townley Scott whose "The U. S. Sailor with the Japanese Skull" is a chilling piece of imaginative writing based on the tale of a "trophy" a young sailor brought home from Guadalcanal, which reveals not only the dehumanizing and barbaric effects of war on those involved in combat but recognizes what Joseph Conrad tells us in *Heart of Darkness*: that deep in the unconscious we all harbor dark drives and desires kept in check by the moral and ethical conventions and institutions of society; something Trout also understood from having read Jung. What is particularly disturbing about Scott's poem is the implicit racism of the act (that Allied forces treated the Japanese with greater brutality than they did German or Italian soldiers and civilians is well-documented); the matter-of-factness with which "our Sailor boy" told listeners (the poet among them) of severing the head, skinning, curing, and polishing it; and the absence of moral comment about the actions of this unidentified twenty-year-old, who, like other American servicemen strolled among enemy corpses after battles hunting for souvenirs: swords, pistols, gold teeth, insignia, identity tags, family photographs. Scott's poem reminds us that war not only physically maims and kills young men but also injures them psychologically and damages their moral compass. Win Scott was a life-long pacifist who spoke against all wars, including the one in Vietnam, and it may have been his objections to war that prompted him to write "The U.S. Sailor with the Japanese Skull." What all of these poems share—save perhaps for Ciardi's which, though formalist, are a little less impersonal—is the anonymity of the subjects who are not identified as individual human beings but as a ball turret gunner, a carrier pilot, a wingman, a master-sergeant, captains and lieutenants, "our Bluejacket," or, as in Eberhart's poem, last names on a military roster "whose faces I do not recall." Like their white bell bottoms or khaki uniforms, the metal dog tags with their serial numbers, their mess kits, and trench spades, these young men—mere boys, really—are just more Government Issue, GI Joes, who as Jarrell tells us in his poem "The Lines" stand in an endless succession of queues waiting for inoculations, chow, mail, liberty passes (Donaldson 1972, 41; Goldstein 2002, 59-64; Fussell 1989, 63, 66-67, 70, 75, 117, 134).

While the impersonality of the war poems of Jarrell, Eberhart, and others mirror the institutional realities of military life, it is also well to remember that they reflect the cardinal characteristics of the prevailing modernist aesthetic set down by T. S. Eliot: the artist's "extinction of the personality" and avoidance of personal emotion. Trout's soldier boys were not anonymous, faceless, undifferentiated, or interchangeable parts. They had names (like Hardy's "Drummer Hodge"), personal histories, and identifiable characteristics—"Hookie" Bair's love of motorcycles, Don Smith's musical talent, Jim's Gaelic good looks and interest in art, the Manship boy's incredible beauty, and the nineteen-year-old veteran of Guadalcanal who taught Bill "Waltzing Matilda." Though he never saw military life first hand, Bill read it in the letters and faces and actions of the young service men he knew. If he wrote poems about the experiences of any of the service men he knew, or "portrait poems" of them none have survived. Yet a war poem that may have touched Bill personally, given his own correspondence with service men, was Jarrell's "Burning the Letters," about the memories and reflections running through the mind of the widow of a pilot killed in the Pacific who destroys his letters to her several years after his death—a poem one of Bill's Millersville students chose either to write a paper or discuss in class.

Although Trout was rejected for military service on medical grounds, he did war work at Lukens Steel (where fellow workers told him of their sons' experiences) and had a brother and friends who served, including at least one who died on active duty. There is evidence that Trout's students confided in him, but how willing and candid his young soldier friends were in talking about their military experience, particularly those who had seen combat, is uncertain. As Paul Fussell observes, the letters soldiers and sailors sent home, in addition to being censored, were "composed largely to sustain the morale of the folks at home," and keep loved one from worrying and thus gave little information about realities at the front or the actual emotions of the writers. Those who wrote to service men and women no doubt wanted to keep their spirits up and so would refrain from asking about conditions at the front. What is more, combat veterans were reluctant to talk even among themselves about what they had undergone in battle. As the poet Louis Simpson, who had fought in the Battle of the Bulge and was a member of what he called "the generation of silence" said: "We didn't want to discuss what we had seen...." It took Kurt Vonnegut, who served as an infantry private and was captured in the Battle of the Bulge, twenty-four years to break his silence about the emotional impact of witnessing the Allied fire-bombing of Dresden, where he had been imprisoned, by writing his 1969 novel *Slaughterhouse-Five* (Fussell 1989, 145, 151, 134). We know from Bill's letters how much he agonized over the war and worried about the safety of friends and loved ones. Yet he wrote neither war poems, which is not surprising since he always wrote about what he knew and had no first-hand experience of military life, nor home-front poems, which is more difficult to explain given the feelings and views expressed in his war-time correspondence.

But, as we have seen, Bill did write poems about the victimization of animals, particularly small animals, in "There at the wood's edge, in the pitted snow," "One Pheasant," "In Brief," and "Entre Chien Et Loup." There are some interesting implications for Trout's poetry in the link M. L. Rosenthal sees between the experiences of Bill's poet contemporaries and their poems about the death of animals: Jarrell's "Loss," Richard Wilbur's "The Death of a Toad," Eberhart's "For a Lamb," and particularly his "The Groundhog," to mention only four. By focusing on the death of a single creature, Rosenthal argues, these poets were in part reacting to the impersonality of modern mass-society, which tends to treat as statistics "the victims of every sort of catastrophe from industrial and automobile accidents to war" (Rosenthal 1960, 247-248). The close-up, detailed, and sometimes gruesome descriptions of the dead animal, as in Eberhart's "For a Lamb" where the "putrid lamb" lying on a "slant hill" "propped with daisies" had its "guts" out "for the crows to eat" contrasts with the clinical manner in which the media deals with the lives and deaths of individuals, contributing to the de-sensitizing of the public to suffering of all kinds.

Trout's many nature poems, in which he gives close and detailed examination of small creatures like birds, spiders, and crickets and lavishes attention on "weeds" and weather, may in part be his reaction to the way most mid-twentieth-century Americans, so preoccupied after World War II with making and getting and so wedded to technology and mass culture, ignore the natural world and the valuable lessons of life it can teach. Not until the mid-1960s was there sufficient public interest in the environment to pressure politicians into passing legislation creating the Environmental Protection Agency (1970). Trout recognized that many Americans in the second half of the twentieth century had lost touch with nature and that the anonymity of urban life and the vapidity of suburban living had isolated them not only from wildlife and the rhythms of the natural world but also from their fellow human beings. His poems are in part a reaction to this situation, though not a back-to-nature call.

Among poets who were Trout's near contemporaries two are of particular interest: Richard Eberhart (1904-2005) and Winfield Townley Scott (1910-1968). Like Trout they rejected the detached, ambiguous, and esoteric approach to poetry of Eliot and Pound, and maintained as well their independence of contemporary stylistic fashion. While their poetry is identifiably twentieth-century, their individualism kept them from being labeled members of any "school" or "coterie." In their poetry they place stress on the human, on reality and actual people and individual life experiences.

Win Scott's life was burdened by insecurities born of childhood experiences, fears and self-doubts, and personal struggles with the values of contemporary American society. The familiarity of Scott's themes and plain-speaking did not fit the modernist mold or that of his successful contemporaries—Robert Lowell, Theodore Roethke, Randall Jarrell, and John Berryman—who early in their careers followed the lead of Eliot and Auden. The later work of Lowell, Jarrell, Roethke, and Berryman also held little if any appeal for Scott, save for a shared fascination with dreams. Rather, he sympathized with and supported those poets—among them E. E. Cummings and Edwin Arlington Robinson, both of whom he admired—who were pushed aside or neglected by the general public and by critics and those poets who had won recognition and honors. And unlike the luminaries of contemporary verse, Scott was not adept at playing "the game of literary politics" (Donaldson 1972, 36-37, 41-42, 48-49, 20, 245-247). Much the same can be said of Trout's experiences as a person and a poet.

There are similarities of theme and tone in the poetry of Win Scott and William Trout, which set them apart from their fellow postwar poets. They shared a fascination with the historical and personal past and had a strong sense of place. Old people, particularly women, influenced them in part by fostering an interest in history through the recollections they shared, thereby helping to explain the importance childhood and memory play in their poetry, for example Scott's "Shoetown" and "Blue Fish in a Blue Sky" and Trout's "Great Aunt" and "Boy with a Kite." Like Trout Scott was deeply attached to his mother and grandmother and wrote poems about them: "Memento" and "My Grandmother Townley's Funeral." Dreams are recurrent themes in Scott's poetry, as they are in Trout's. For Scott Traman (a persona he created which is derived from *Traum*, the German word for dream) mirrors the fantasies, insecurities, and sense of failure of the poet himself, as in the poem "Traman Walks to Work." While both poets took death and ghosts as subjects they did not necessarily convey the same tone or mood as in Scott's "All Memory" and Trout's "With supplicating eyes, the dead return." A nostalgic, sentimental longing for the past informs many of Scott's poems, as with "Memorabilia," "Fourth of July, Old Style" and "Broken Shell," whereas Trout's tentative and muted nostalgia is apparent in such poems as "Before The Sale" and as here in "Then And Now":

> In those days nothing ever was crueller than
> The despair of the mother's infrequent illness.
> Negligibly, a schoolmate's mockery, or toothache, perhaps,
> Was sovereign irritant, worth a passing rebellion;
> On the other hand,
> Deprivation, the shabby clothes,
> All poverty's make-shifts—these were accepted,
> Defended angrily if they were aspersed....
> (But sometimes excitement and shallow-breathed suspense
> Were wholly valid,—for instance, at Christmas. In mid-afternoon
> The woods grew twilit; the cedar tree on the spring-wagon
> Dreamed almost black, pungent to the nostrils, prickly
> To the hand; and the snow clung frozen
> To baskets of crowsfoot, wintergreen, and lionspaw.
> In the resonant, brittle air, the horse's breath fumed like smoke,
> And, half-hidden by the smooth snow-drifts,
> The black creek whispered its intermitted mysteries.
> The jolting ride home,
> The stumbling one's way through darkness, the brave kitchen light
> At last shining, and then the stable smell—
> All these were valid. Later, the tree, as yet untinseled,
> Stood slenderly dark and mysterious in the shabby sitting room.)
> Almost always in those days
> Cruelty had frontiers, was manageable.
> Now is another matter.

Scott used nature settings for a number of his narrative, story poems in addition to writing some fine nature poetry. But with few exceptions—"Seven

Lines," "Sixteen Lines," "Summer Afternoon," and "Late Summer" among them—his nature poems lack the sensuous detail, intimacy, and sensitive nuance one finds in Trout's poems, particularly "Summer Ending" and "Summer slowly takes its leave." The "portrait poems"—Scott's "Mrs. Severin" and "Gert Swasey" and Trout's "Henry" and "Lark Descending"—no doubt have roots in their mutual admiration for Edwin Arlington Robinson. Scott's interest in American history and what Scott Donaldson describes as a "lifelong dedication to the nation's political leaders" and "worship of American heroes," fed a patriotism not found in Trout's more critical reading of the nation's history and its leaders, past and present. They both held the work of Emily Dickinson, Thomas Hardy, Willa Cather, and Robinson Jeffers in high regard. While Scott never achieved the level of critical and popular recognition he craved, his poems did appear in respectable journals and were anthologized, nine books of his verse were published, and he was the recipient of a number of book awards; nonetheless, there is no record that Trout ever read any of Win Scott's poetry, which is strange given what they had in common as poets (Donaldson 1972, 332, 3-4, 12-14, 19-21, 29, 40, 228, 331, 249, 352, 283-284; Scott, 1962, 30, 157, 153, 283, 22, 164, 271, 154, 156, 4, 291, 132).

Richard Eberhart, who admitted philosophizing about everything, found philosophical issues and moral lessons in nature and the lives of ordinary people. He took real people and experiences as his subject matter rather than following the example of Eliot's detached, impersonal approach. Harkening back to nineteenth-century poets, among them Emily Dickinson, he never abandoned completely the rhyme and meter of traditional American verse, which is another characteristic, in addition to subject matter and tone, he shared with Trout. As Joel Roache observes, Eberhart, using detailed descriptions of earthly reality, takes death or "life-in-death" as a theme in such poems as "I walked over the grave of William James," "Cover Me Over," "For a Lamb," and "The Groundhog." Coming upon a dead woodchuck in a field, its body simmering with maggots in the June heat, and then returning in the autumn and again the following summer to look for the remains, Eberhart's fascination with the loathsome sight turns to thoughts of the transitoriness of life and material things as he thinks about the passing of great civilizations and great people: Alexander the Great, Montaigne, and Saint Theresa. Similarly, in the earthy realism Trout uses in "Crow" and "There at the woods' edge in the pitted snow" are moral questions and philosophical musings about life and death. Roache maintains that Eberhart's "most important work of the 'thirties, among them 'The Groundhog' and 'If I Could Only Live at the Pitch That Is Near Madness,' however much they are based in concrete reality, are fundamentally examinations of his own mind: his isolation had forced him to look inward." The same can be said about much of Trout's poetry. But whereas in the 1940s, as Roache points out, Eberhart's "eye clearly turns to the outer world and its problems" (as in "The Horse Chestnut Tree," "Cousin Florence," and "Clam Diggers and Diggers of Sea Worms"), Trout's eye over the years turns ever more deeply inward, to the "self," the "I" linking him to the dominant theme in the later poetry of what Bruce Bawer and others call the Middle Generation of American twentieth-century poets (Roache 1971, xv-xvii, xxv-xxvi, xxii-xxv, 34, 89, 114, 194, 236, 239, 241-242, 252; Bawer 1986).

Trout had things in common with the Middle Generation, the poets about his own age working from the 1930s through the 1960s, specifically Theodore Roethke (1908-1963), Delmore Schwartz (1913-1966), Randall Jarrell (1914-1965), John Berryman (1914-1972), and Robert Lowell (1916-1977). Bill and these poets shared personal experiences and attitudes that influenced their verse. All had difficult childhoods. Death or divorce robbed Roethke, Schwartz, Jarrell, and Berryman of their fathers, while Lowell was estranged early on from his, and left them with overly protective, dependent, or domineering mothers. All were disaffected from contemporary American society, particularly from its popular culture, which they saw as shallow and banal. Schwartz, Berryman, and Lowell were both fascinated and fearful of homosexuality and did their best to sublimate their same-sex urges, as Trout seems to have done as well. There is ample evidence that Trout stayed up late at night and into the wee hours of the morning, suggesting that like Schwartz, Jarrell, and Berryman he suffered from insomnia. All the Middle Generation poets were interested in philosophy and psychology, as was Trout. Schwartz majored in philosophy as an undergraduate, a subject Berryman also studied in college and whose theological questions led him to Kierkegaard, Hegel, and Wittenstein, while Jarrell immersed himself in Bertrand Russell, Alfred North Whitehead, and Sigmund Freud. Lowell's dissatisfaction with New England Calvinism drew him to St. Thomas Acquinas and such neo-Thomists as Jacques Maritain and Etienne Gilson. But *unlike* Trout these other Middle Generation poets were, for the most part, devout Freudians, particularly Jarrell. While Bill's shyness, desire for privacy, and sense of inadequacy kept him on the margins of society, his Middle Generation contemporaries believed themselves to be outcasts and craved recognition, even fame. They were deeply troubled, damaged human beings. As Edward Hirsch puts it: "There was something broken in each of these poets, I suppose, something that could not be mended—was there ever a generation of poets more prone to alcoholism, more stormed and afflicted by mental illness, more devastated by suicide?" (Bawer 1986, 5-15, 20-21, 31-33, 37-38, 41-47, 25-28; Burt 2002, Chapter 3; Hirsch 2000, 12).

Randall Jarrell was five years younger than Trout. From an early age both were avid and eclectic readers, with Trout reading at home and during school recess and Jarrell spending hours in Nashville's Carnegie Library, which he recorded in such poems as "The Carnegie Library, Juvenile Division" and "Children Selecting Books in a Library." Early on Jarrell fell under the influence of the Fugitives; however, his Marxist leanings made their reactionary agrarian political and social views unacceptable to him, as did their formalist New Criticism approach to writing and reviewing poetry. While Jarrell wrote his master's thesis on an aspect of A. E. Housman's poetry, it was T. S. Eliot and particularly W. H. Auden who had the greatest influenced on his early work. Later he looked to Walt Whitman, William Carlos Williams, and Robert Frost. Among contemporary poets, his closest friends were Robert Lowell and Elizabeth Bishop. Though neither Trout nor Jarrell played an instrument, they were passionate about classical music and opera, including Mozart, Robert Schumann, and Tchaikovsky, and shared a particularly fondness for Beethoven, Mahler, and Richard Strauss, whose opera *Der Rosenkavalier* Jarrell alludes to via an epigraph—"Die alte Frau, die alte Marschallin" (nicknames, you will recall Trout used for his mother)—he placed at the beginning of "The Face," a poem that deals with time and the aging process. Their favorite *Lieder* and opera singer was Lotte Lehmann, though both also adored the great contralto Ernestine Schumann-Heink, whom Jarrell mentions in his poem "A Man Meets a Woman in the Street." Jarrell, like Trout, wrote several poems on works of art, among them "The Old Masters and the New Masters," "The Bronze David of Donatello," and Dürer's "The Knight, Death, and the Devil." But Bill did not share Jarrell's fascination with clothes, fast cars, and sports, specifically tennis, football, and auto racing. While Trout was rooted in Lancaster County, living there all his life and rarely venturing beyond the county line, Jarrell resided for extended periods of time in nine states and the District of Columbia and took holidays in other states and five foreign countries (Pritchard 1990, 15-16, 138-141, 227-228, 144-146, 159-160, 271-272, 289-290; Burt 2002, 4-5, 7, 226-230, 260n, 5, 26, 178-179, xii-xv, 61-65).

Educated at Vanderbilt University, Jarrell switched his undergraduate major from English to psychology and then again to English. While Trout, as we have seen, was steeped in Jungian psychology, "Gestalt terms and Freudian theories together," Stephen Burt claims, "gave Jarrell a critical vocabulary in which he could discuss at once perception and desire, form and feeling...." Moreover, according to Burt, the Freudian doctrines of "oedipal desire and hostility, repression, the idea that the libido explains most if not all of our hidden motives," and that the most "interesting differences between men and women are biological," manifest themselves in his poems, particularly those involved with dreams such as "The Black Swan," "A Hunt in the Black Forest," and "Field and Forest." While Jarrell probably read Jung, he apparently found Freud's approach to psychoanalysis with its emphasis on drives and biological urges more congenial. Trout's poems—"Encounter," "Recurrent dream: I stand knee-deep in reeds," and "Some flagged corridor of exit – more"—on the other hand, reveal traces of Jung's key concepts: the "collective unconscious," the meaning of archetypes, the importance of intuition, the quest for "individuation" among them (Burt 2002, 85-117, 248n).

Both poets had an abiding interest in children and childhood (Jarrell wrote stories and books for children, some of them illustrated by Maurice Sendak), which manifests itself in poems that grew out of childhood memories such as Jarrell's "The Elementary Scene," "Moving," and "Sick Girl," and Trout's "Boy with a Kite," "Garden Toad," and "So safe it was to sit beside." Basing poems on their own childhood experiences (and in Jarrell's case observations of adolescences), were in part attributable to their interest in fairy tales, particularly those of the brothers Grimm, and, for Jarrell, Rainer Maria Rilke; while, as we have seen, for Trout it was the work of Walter de la Mare. Although Jarrell appreciated de la Mare, as his 1946 review of his *The Burning Bush* testifies, his poetry did not reflect as directly as did Trout's de la Mare's influence. As Jarrell observes, "de la Mare was not primarily interested in ordinary rational or practical life" or "mechanical and rationalized routine," but rather in nature, children, the supernatural. Dreams, intuition, emotions, and perceptions are what mattered most to him. But among nonfiction writers it is arguably Marcel Proust who had the most profound and lasting influence on the work of Jarrell and Trout, both of whom were obsessed by time and memory (Pritchard 1990, 279-283; Jarrell 1946, 134-135; Burt 202, 146, 148-149, 142-143, 150-156, 160).

According to Stephen Burt, Jarrell said Proust was "the greatest of the writers of this century," and, as noted earlier, Trout told Don Smith he was "a way of life ... a religion." They reread *Remembrance of Things Past* several times over the years and repeatedly refer to Proust in their letters, as

Jarrell does also in the poem "A Man Meets a Woman in the Street." In "The Christmas Rose," "The Face," and "A Ghost, A Real Ghost." Jarrell wrote about aging; and these poems, like those on childhood, are informed by his reading of Proust, as are Trout's poems, among them "Now Anonymous," "Her endless, silent monologues of age," "The small face shrivels, and the eyes grow strange." Photographs—which by marking specific points in time document its passing and record how things and people have changed or disappeared—figure prominently in the verse of both poets, as in Jarrell's "The Player Piano" and Trout's "Remembered" and "See on the right, there just in the corner." What Stephen Burt says of Jarrell's poems—that they acknowledge "we come to identify our real selves so thoroughly with now unavailable persons, roles, behaviors as to feel stranded, unknowable, unreal"—is something that Trout also recognized in his search for self-knowledge. Whereas Proust, according to Burt, "wants to rescue interiority from Time, the people Jarrell depicts [in his poems] want not to live outside of time but to live with others in it," as one sees in such poems as "Gleaning" and "Thinking of the Lost World." Like Strauss' Marschallin, who stops all the clocks in her home but knows the impossibility of arresting time, so Bill acknowledges Time's relentlessness in his poems "Burn now the calendars, and halt the clocks" and "Let us now stop Time forever at ten o'clock" (Burt 2002, 121-139, 252n, 2).

Both Jarrell and Trout recognized the failures and the dangers inherent in the mass culture of modern industrial society, which Jarrell in part learned by reading the works of his close friend, the political theorist and historian Hannah Arendt, and that Bill got from reading Henry Adams and Erich Kahler. The postwar intellectual climate of opinion in the United States, given voice in books like David Riesman's *The Lonely Crowd: A Study of the Changing American Character* (1950) and William H. Whyte's *The Organization Man* (1957), no doubt left its mark on Jarrell and Trout. Both were what Riesman would characterize as "inner-directed" personalities. They were confirmed individualists whose poetry focused on inner experience. They were critical of mass culture and mass media, of the impersonality and institutionalization of modern life, and the theory and practice of the New Criticism, a position Jarrell came to over time. They shared concerns about the changes taking place in postwar American society. Both recognized the threat posed to childhood, individuality, private life, art, and intelligent discourse by advertising and consumer capitalism, popular culture, and the growing institutionalization of all aspects of life. But whereas Bill expressed criticism primarily in letters and conversations with friends but in only a few poems, among them

"All are headed for the river that drives on down there, in dank obscurity" and "Asylum," Jarrell proclaimed his in such essays as "A Sad Heart at the Supermarket" (1960), in public addresses, and poems like "Next Day" and "Windows" (Burt 2002, 14-15, 48, 11, 50-55, 58-59, 81-83, 162-166; Pritchard 1990, 100, 188, 267). Trout had things in common with another of his poet contemporaries, Theodore Roethke.

Roethke grew up in Saginaw, Michigan, where his father and uncle Charles owned greenhouses and a flower business. Sensitive, awkward, lonely, and introverted, he seems not to have had any close friends as a child and adolescent and had a difficult relationship with his stern and hard-to-please German-born father. Ted had not yet turned fifteen when in a matter of a few months the greenhouses were sold after the brothers had a falling out, his uncle committed suicide, and his father died an excruciating death from cancer. Like Trout, Roethke grew up in an area of the country lacking opportunities for intellectual stimulation and indifferent or unsympathetic toward those with aesthetic interests. Roethke's entry in his notebooks recording the "absolute ... cultural loneliness of the American provincial creative intellectual" no doubt also expressed Bill's sentiments about growing up in rural Pennsylvania. Roethke received his A.B. and M.A. from the University of Michigan and studied at Harvard, where he received encouragement from Robert Hillyer. By the mid-1930s, he was publishing poems in periodicals, and in 1941 brought out his first volume of verse. After teaching at several colleges, he took a position at the University of Washington in 1947, remaining there until his death. Over the years he won a number of awards and honors, including the Pulitzer Prize in 1954. Yet, according to Rosemary Sullivan, the death of his father "induced in Roethke a pathological fear of his [own] inadequacy" with which he struggled all his life and which may in part account for his manic-depression and periodic psychological breakdowns (Seager 1968, 39, 42-43; Malkoff 1966, 1-2, 5-9, 11; Sullivan 1975, 5-8, 16).

Roethke's poems record an abiding interest in nature (birds and plants, but particularly lower forms of animal life like snails and slugs, frogs and snakes), childhood experiences and memories, the nature of time, philosophical/theological and psychological questions, and the search for identity through exploration of the unconscious. That much of his poetry appears to be informed by Jung's theories—particularly those relating to the collective unconscious, archetypes, regression and progression, individuation, and the spirit or soul—might have drawn Bill to him. Both poets wrote verse in part as therapy, as a means of purging their demons and coming to an understanding of themselves by applying Jung's ideas to poetry as a way of achieving self-knowledge, individuation. Each recognized the limitations of reason and looked to intuition to explore other forms of consciousness and to delve into the unconscious, though in time Roethke became "profoundly antirationalistic," adhering to a "primitivism" that took "being" and "knowing" as antagonistic opposites; a view to which Trout did not subscribe. The poetry of John Donne and Emily Dickinson influenced both poets (Malkoff 1966, 59-66, 73, 120, 199, 18-20, 29; Sullivan 1975, 32, 42, 64, 4, 12-13, 26, 166). Yet in spite of all these similarities of outlook, intellectual interest, and personal experience, there is no evidence that Trout spoke of, wrote about, or taught Roethke's poems, though some students in his Contemporary Poetry course apparently chose to discuss them in class or write papers on them, as suggested by the names he placed next to Roethke's poems in the course textbook.

Although Roethke claimed that he had read little psychology, both his wife and his close poet friend Stanley Kunitz said he had read Jung, and in his notebooks Roethke mentions two of Jung's works: *Psychology and Religion* and *Two Essays on Analytical Psychology*. Rosemary Sullivan maintains that while he "may have read little Freud or Jung, he was familiar with certain of their disciples." However, Jenijoy La Belle makes a convincing case that Roethke's knowledge of the Swiss psychoanalyst's work was secondhand, coming to him mainly through reading Maud Bodkin's *Archetypal Patterns in Poetry: Psychological Studies of Imagination* (1934). Bodkin was one of Jung's literary disciples and her book, as Sullivan explains, would have given Roethke an understanding of how some of Jung's key ideas could be presented in poetry. The frequency with which his poetry includes imagery of sexuality of both the conjugal and generative biological type, as well as questions of repression, allusions to psychological complexes and Freudian symbols suggests that Freud was as much or more of an influence on Roethke than was Jung (Kunitz 1965, 25; Malkoff 1966, 52-53, 59, 70-74, 78, 81, 97; Sullivan 1975, 32-33, 71n, 73n; La Belle 1976, 179).

Moreover, La Belle believes that much of the influence attributed to Jung in fact comes from literary sources, particularly William Blake, Samuel Taylor Coleridge, and T. S. Eliot, but also, according to Sullivan and Malkoff, from Rimbaud and William Butler Yeats as well. La Belle observes that Roethke's metaphors are "based upon archetypal patterns rooted in the natural world and experienced through the poetry of his tradition, rather than upon the mystical transcendence of the natural world," concluding that it seems more "likely that the center from which his poetry flows is other poetry rather than abstract psychological theories" (Kunitz 1965, 25; Malkoff, 1966, 150-151, 157-58; Sullivan 1975, 10-13, 91-99; La Belle 1976, 180-193). As documented in Chapter 5, Trout's knowledge of Jung came not from secondhand interpretations or applications of his ideas but from years of intense reading and rereading of many of his seminal works; and he may therefore have regarded Roethke's Jungianism as superficial and adulterated by Freudian ideas.

John Ciardi, who during the 1950s wrote a number of articles in which Roethke was either among the poets discussed or was the subject, and who participated in several Contemporary Writers Conferences at Millersville during the same period in which Trout also lectured, would likely have included Roethke in his lectures on contemporary poetry, assuring that Bill would have been aware of his work. One might expect poems like "In a Dark Time" and "Meditation at Oyster Bay" (both of which were included in the Untermeyer anthology) to have appealed to Bill. Some of Roethke's poetry was written in traditional form using meter and rhyme (particularly slant/near rhyme much used by Emily Dickinson), and containing well-crafted rhythms and cadences, which should also have appealed to Bill. But Roethke's adoption of Walt Whitman's "catalogue" technique of stringing words together in long lines of free verse, Sullivan maintains, move him "in the direction of formlessness," something Bill would not have found appealing (Sullivan 1975, 152-154).

In spite of Roethke's concerted effort to use only simple words, his imagery is often abstract, his associations, coming from what Allan Seager calls "deliberate flights of free association," are patently subjective, and the meaning of his metaphors are at times so obscure that, as Sullivan says, readers have "no possible way" of understanding their meaning. Even Sullivan, who is favorably disposed to his poetry, admits that Roethke's "symbolism is in danger of reductivity" and at times "stretches even intuitive comprehension" (Seager 1968, 189; Sullivan 1975, 79, 82-89). Bill would have had no sympathy with such contrived obfuscation. It is also possible that he found Roethke's mixing of Jungian archetypes with his own personal symbols and a too generous use of murky metaphors as going off the deep end of visionary poetry into hazy mysticism, the very sort of obscurity he objected to in the poems of Eliot and Yeats. Then, too, Bill may have been put off or simply wearied by Roethke's obsessive exploration of his own sexual neurosis using Freudian psychoanalysis in the poems of both *The Lost Son* sequence and the *Praise to the End* sequence.

Trout may also have agreed with such critics as M. L. Rosenthal and Stephen Spender, among others, who saw Roethke's poetry as both egocentric and myopic. He was so narrowly focused on exploring his own psyche, confronting his own demons, and searching for his own identity that his poems do not take into account the rest of the human world. There is little in his poems beyond his personal struggles with self-doubt, fear, failure, inadequacy, self-hate, and search for spiritual peace. For the most part they fail to universalize or generalize his personal experiences, to open paths to readers who are also struggling with similar problems. It is as though he lived in total isolation from the rest of humanity (Sullivan 1975, 192-196), which Trout in spite of his reclusiveness did not, for the most part, do in his poetry. Readers are more likely to find their own or similar experiences in Trout's poems than in those of Roethke.

Although some of Trout's poems are also self-centered, he is innocent of egocentrism in part by the fact that he probably never intended to publish these "therapeutic" pieces, and by the fact that many of his poems acknowledge the outside world: the realities faced by other people ("Autumn/ Watching," "Asylum," "Remember how the old lady used to chuckle"), the experiences of daily life ("Concede the comfort of routine," "Semi-Private Room," "Unplanned Obsolescence"), family life and personal relationships ("Great Aunt," "Lark Descending," "Henry," "Country Sale"), the natural world of plants and animals ("Crow," "Frost tonight you said, and took," "Wild Chicory"), and the social and historical context in which people live ("Encounter" and "They must reverse the arrogant pilgrimage"). His poems of personal memories, "The small face shrivels, and the eyes grow strange," "And Still she sings, the Marschallin," and "The Book" among them, can be recognized easily by people who shared such experiences. Even in his most introspective poems, such as "Not knowing what to do, I wait," "Unprofessional Psychiatry," and "Onset," Trout's imagery and symbolism are not so personal or so abstruse as to keep most readers from recognizing similarities between the emotions raised by his internal struggles and those they may also have had. Although the "fiends," "ghosts," "phantoms," and unintelligible symbols that invade our sleep and sometimes haunt our waking hours may have different origins and meanings, we can all identify with the psychic disturbance Trout describes.

From the late 1930s to the early 1950s the poetry of the Middle Generation poets, as Bawer explains, reflected the ideas and sensibility of T. S. Eliot, W. B. Yeats, and W. H. Auden (Bawer 1986, 57-62, 65-67, 80-88, 91, 97, 101). Their poems were intentionally complex, cerebral, esoteric, impersonal, dispassionate, and unrelated to lived reality, which Trout's poetry, on the whole, was not. In the course of the 1950s Middle Generation poets moved away from Eliot in order to accommodate their growing desire to explore their own personal lives, emotions, doubts, obsessions. They looked to such American poets as Edgar Allan Poe, Walt Whitman, Stephen Crane, Emily Dickinson, and the Beats, as well as to the Symbolist poets in exploring life and the unconscious. They explored dreams and questions of aging, mortality, and the nature of time (either trapped in it or unable to arrest its passage), themes that occupied Trout was well (Bawer 186, 119-120, 124, 137-138, 142-143, 149-150). In the morning hours of a new day Delmore Schwartz says in his poem "In the naked bed, in Plato's cave," one becomes aware of "the mystery of beginning / Again and again, / While Time is unforgiven." And he ends "For Rhoda" with "Time is the school in which we learn, / Time is the fire in which we burn." While in Schwartz's "Seurat's Sunday Afternoon Along the Seine," Jarrell's "In Those Days" and "Nestus Gurley," and John Berryman's "Winter Landscape" as in many of Trout's poems, among them "Let us stop Time forever at ten o'clock," the poet wants to halt the passing of time, to freeze the moment not only for his mother or grandmother in "the kitchen rocking-chair," but for all death's victims be they soldiers, the hospitalized, or prisoners on death row. But Trout acknowledges the impossibility of stopping "Time's hands."

Let us stop Time forever at ten o'clock
On this sunny Sunday morning of October: the neighbors now
Are all at church, and filled with holy thoughts;
The dying snake of the sky has only a feeble sting,
And earth goes deathward in coronation robes;
And death's next victim, whom we cherish so,
Reads a book in the kitchen rocking-chair;
And the nourishing oven, faintly redolent,
Performs grandmotherly functions by a dial.
Just here to stop Time's hands....
But no, and no. No.
The soldier northward in the frozen mud,
The marked quarry on the sterile bed,
The duped checkmated with the shaven head—
These, and others, lack even such oasis,
Ringed with chrysanthemums and the migrant warblers.

Just as Trout takes dreams or nightmares as subject matter for his poems and examines them from a Jungian perspective, so the extent to which other Middle Generation poets relied on Freud is apparent in Schwartz's "The Dream of Knowledge" and *In Dreams Begin Responsibilities*; Jarrell's "Dreams," "The Dream," and "The Dream of Walking"; Berryman's *The Dream Songs*; and Lowell's "Dream of Fair Ladies," "Harriet's Dream," and many more dream poems, which over time abandoned the cold intellectual and reasoned objectivity of Eliot's symbolism for the emotional subjectivity of individual human experience given expression in the poet's own personal voice. Trout's dream poems are unlike those of the other Middle Generation poets who accepted Freud's view that neurosis is rooted in sexuality and that dreams are the fulfillment of wishes and in which they could find, as Bawer and others claim, an explanation of and temporary release from the tortures experienced in their everyday lives. Indeed, Lowell wrote: "My dreams are more rewarding than my actuality" (Bawer 1986, 45-50).

There is little evidence of just how much "new" poetry Bill read from the early 1960s on. Among the hundreds of books he gave me in the 1970s, only a few were by contemporary poets, among them: John Ciardi's *As If: Poems New and Selected* (1955), the 1955 edition of Elizabeth Bishop's *Poems: North & South – A Cold Spring*, and Dorothy Roberts' *Twice to Flame* (1961). Although he no doubt used books from the Millersville and Franklin & Marshall College libraries in his course preparation, it is unlikely that he purchased much "new" poetry. After his mother's health began to deteriorate about 1959, and particularly after her death in 1967 and his retirement the following year, he may have abandoned any effort to "keep up" with current poetry. Nowhere in his letters, conversation, or the memories of former students and colleagues is there any acknowledgement by Trout of Projective/Open Verse, the Beats, or the American Confessional Poets.

As M. L. Rosenthal points out, "self-analytical monologues" from Eliot's "Prufrock" to Muriel Rukeyser's *Elegies*, have been, along with social criticism, hallmarks of twentieth-century poetry (Rosenthal 1960, 237). How well acquainted Trout was with the work of America's Confessional Poets is a matter of conjecture. It is *Heart's Needle* (a collection of deeply personal autobiographical poems), W. D. Snodgrass' first book and winner of the 1960 Pulitzer Prize, which literary scholars often take as the inaugural work of modern American "confessionalism." John Berryman, Robert Lowell, W. D. Snodgrass, and Anne Sexton were represented in the 1962 edition of Untermeyer's anthology of American and British poetry Trout used as a course text. But his acquaintance with the later work of America's Confessional Poets is undocumented.

There is autobiographical content in many of Trout's poems. But whether the nature of these reminiscences puts him in the company of his "confessional" contemporaries, and those like Randall Jarrell, Delmore Schwartz, Stanley Kunitz, and Theodore Roethke, whose poetry also contains confessional elements, merits examination. Although as noted earlier, Bill saw both keeping a journal and writing poetry as "therapeutic," his self-revelations are neither as matter-of-factly nor as boldly stated, immodest, indiscreet, and even sensational as those of Lowell, Berryman, Anne Sexton, or Sylvia Plath. Whereas the Confessional Poets use the technique of "dramatic monologue" to bare their demons for all to see in unequivocal, everyday language and with a specificity, even rawness, no one could misunderstand, Trout often masks his by indirection; by using symbolism and literary allusions; or through obscure and indeterminate language, which may owe as much to Jung as to Bill's desire to conceal.

Unlike Lowell, Trout did not seem to be obsessed with sin; burdened as M. L. Rosenthal claims Lowell was with "moral guilt," which as a New Englander, he felt for the legacy of Puritan hypocrisy, repression, and commercialism. In his *Life Studies*—a work Rosenthal calls "impure art," "unpleasantly egocentric," and "a series of personal confidences, rather shameful, that one is honor-bound not to reveal"—Lowell discredits his "father's manliness and character, as well as … the family and social milieu of his childhood" (Rosenthal 1960, 231-239). On the other hand, Trout's poems picture his childhood as a time of economic struggle within the fold of a supportive and caring extended family headed by his widowed mother in poems like "So Safe it was to sit beside," "Great Aunt," and as here in "The Book."

> There was one Christmas: I remember scraps of it,
> As we see a range of hills through drifting clouds.
> It was a very cold day,
> But the sitting-room was warm; the stove glowed, and sometimes
>   a coal dropped through the grate, shockingly loud.
> The smell of cedar hovered in the room;
> And on the Christmas Tree the poor, few ornaments shone softly
> In the gray morning, redolent of snow.
> I remember the cardboard angel with pale gold hair, and the
>   mysterious tinsel spider, that we were always half-afraid of.

And there were three plates under the tree, with little heaps
of cheap candy,
And stockings and handkerchiefs in white tissue paper with
diminutive bright seals.
To the north, far beyond the naked front porch—
Over the lonely fields, and above the road, with its line of bare
trees—
The hills bulked, crisped with snowy rectangles among the black
areas of woods.
But most of all, there was the Book—
The Surprise, that you had, so secretly, managed with tea tickets—
saved for half a year—
And forty cents—saved from selling eggs.
In the corner of the threadbare sofa, I read all that gray day,
Till early darkness dimmed the adored page,
And night crept in across the snowy fields.
Now, after so many years, I search what grim regret
Flits through the gray corridors of the mind.

In poems like "Not knowing what to do, I wait" and "Street Scene," Trout alludes, as in "Through the ebbing fumes of midnight wine," to his use of alcohol to relieve his frustrations, sorrows, doubts, loneliness, and sense of inadequacy. And yet in looking at the "dark pink geranium" he senses something beyond the material world, something the conscious mind and intellect cannot grasp. He senses an out-of-the-ordinary, supernatural light—perhaps akin to the one that blinded Paul on the road to Damascus, the occasion of his conversion to Christianity—or a summons or calling forth that boldly imprints itself on the self-doubt or absence of religious faith that he feels holds him securely in its grip. The sight of the geranium creates a ray of hope that shines "beneath the mind, and far from the dark heart."

Through the ebbing fumes of midnight wine,
Through the acrid taste of Sunday morning coffee,
Through the clear, blowing air and the late September sunshine,
This dark pink geranium, in its modest miracle of round leaves,
Glows.
Immobilized, preternaturally lucent,
It is apparition suspended remote, striking at the sense of sight,

But striking too at something beneath the mind, and far from the
 dark heart:
Miniature Damascus, minute evocation,
Bold assertion printed vehemently
Upon the tangible fastnesses of doubt.

In other poems, among them "Lonely wanted but companionship," he admits both his loneliness and some seemingly innocent act on his part that earned him unexpected and humiliating social censure. And as in "Heritage," he despairs about his "monstrous shape" and the limitations handed him by heredity—"the blood, the blood"—and circumstances. These poems like many of the "horror" poems discussed in Chapter 5—among them "Onset," "Threat," Compulsion," and "Unprofessional Psychiatry"—are "confessional" in nature. And there is one short poem which suggests that some neurotic who suffers from violent mood swings, perhaps Bill himself, might do everyone a favor by committing suicide:

Let us leave him here in the hallway, go in, and shut the door
Upon his repellent posturing, his feeble twittering, his congenital
 insincerity,
His neurotic shifts of mood from gloom to laughter:
We have been patient with that fatuity heretofore,
But sterner fates condemn and disallow such charity.
Toss him a rope, and indicate the chair, the convenient rafter.

Neither these nor any of Trout's other "confessional" poems come close to the sensational revelations of Lowell, Sexton, and Plath. What is more, while he genuinely thought that by applying Jungian psychology to the process of making poetry he might be able to effect a type of spiritual healing, the Confessional Poets, though honest and even courageous in their self-revelations, seemed content to record their alcoholism, phobias, neurotic behavior, struggles with personal relationships, and experiences in asylums without applying insights gained from psychoanalysis to their poetry-making in an effort to heal themselves. For them it seemed enough to "just get it out." Sexton, for example, addresses one of her poems, "You, Doctor Martin," to her psychiatrist, in which she chronicles a day of her life in the mental hospital. There is no evidence that Bill sought help from a therapist, as did a fair number of his contemporaries, and not just the Confessional Poets. He turned his dreams, his fears, his doubts into poems and tried using them to gain self-knowledge and make sense of his life, whereas, as Sexton told an interviewer (among other things) writing poetry didn't cure her mental illness: "It isn't as simple as my poetry makes it, because I simplified everything to make it more dramatic." Indeed as both the daughter and the wife of a salesman, and with the ambition to make it big in the literary world, Sexton gave increasing attention to "making contacts"—cultivating other writers and critics (who did not always give her favorable reviews)—and to tailoring her poems to the marketplace. She was a showman who knew how to work the crowd at her reading performances and according to Diane Middlebrook was "assiduous in the business end of poetry" and "an active self-promoter." Along with Sylvia Plath, she is a heroine to many feminists, willing to give voice to women's issues in such poems as "Menstruation at Forty," "In Celebration of My Uterus," and "The Abortion" (Marx 1965, 560-570; Middlebrook 1991, 83, 382, xix-xx, 95-96, 151). Trout did not simplify or dress up his "confessions" to make them more accessible and certainly not with an eye to popularity. It would never have occurred to him to turn his personal problems into a marketable commodity, describe sexual acts and bodily functions, or make a spectacle of himself in front of an audience.

Lowell, Berryman, Sexton, and Plath—all of whom suffered from clinical depression—were tortured human beings who expressed their sufferings in their published poetry. Trout kept his quiet desperation mostly to himself though in his "confessional" poems the "phantoms," as he calls them, come to light but were not tailored for public display. There is something muted, tentative, guarded about his "confessions"—something not characteristic of Sexton or Plath. For him personal struggles were private matters not to be broadcast to the world. He was searching for answers for himself, not as a means of getting into print. Everyone knew of Lowell's alcoholism and very public troubled marriages; of Berryman's emotional instability and excessive drinking; of Plath's struggles with her unfaithful husband (the British poet Ted Hughes) and with being a woman in a male-dominated world; and of Sexton's marital problems, infidelities, alcoholism, drug addiction, and mental illness. But apparently few people, judging from my interviews with those who knew him, suspected Trout's psychological struggles.

In her book *Touched with Fire: Manic-Depressive Illness and the Artistic Temperament*, Kay Redfield Jamison, a professor of psychiatry at The Johns Hopkins University School of Medicine, makes a good case that research shows "strong scientific and biographical evidence linking manic-depressive illness and its related temperaments to artistic imagination and expression," and that artists (poets, writers, painters, and composers) suffer from mood disorders at "a vastly disproportionate" rate compared to the general population. Family history (evidence of depression, mania, psychosis, alcoholism, drug abuse, institutionalization in a psychiatric hospital, suicide, or attempted suicide, particularly among first-degree relatives: parents, siblings, or children) strongly suggests a genetic cause for depression and manic-depression (Jamison 1993, 5, 240, 58-59). Among the artists whose lives show clear symptoms of major mood disorders are such painters as Vincent van Gogh, Edvard Munch, Arshile Gorky, and Mark Rothko; composers like Robert Schumann, Hector Berlioz, Gustav Mahler, and Hugo Wolf; writers, among them Herman Melville, Hermann Hesse, Ernest Hemingway, Eugene O'Neill, and Virginia Woolf; and poets, including Lord Byron, Edgar Allan Poe, Edward Thomas, Edna St. Vincent Millay, Hart Crane, Delmore Schwartz, Randall Jarrell, and Theodore Roethke, in addition to Robert Lowell, John Berryman, and Anne Sexton (Jamison 1993, *passim*).

It is apparent from his letters written over many years and his poems that Trout had a melancholic temperament, but determining the type of mood disorder he may have suffered from is difficult given the available evidence—and certainly beyond my competence—but may have been Cyclothymia, a mild chronic mood disorder without the more dramatic and violent emotional ups and downs characteristic of manic-depressive illness. Both his letters and verse suggest that Bill's mood swings were episodic or rhythmic and may have been related to the seasons, thereby in part explaining his ability to convey so deftly transience and transition in his nature poems. Mood change related to time of year as well as the use of one's art as a therapeutic means of escaping or relieving pain is not uncommon among artists with mood disorders according to Dr. Jamison (Jamison 1993, 118-130).

That Trout experienced bouts of deep depression, as noted earlier, as well as his compassion for those who did not fit into conventional society, may have made him sympathetic to the troubled lives of Berryman, Sexton, and the others. However, the raw sexual content of their poetry—and particularly Sexton's exploration of issues like menstruation, abortion, masturbation, and adultery—he would probably have deemed beyond what a poet ought to express in print. Although Bill was no prude, as his letters to Don Smith testify, his personality, upbringing, and the social-cultural milieu in which he simmered up would not have allowed him to so directly and unabashedly expose the sorts of private details of his life as did writers numbered among the American Confessional Poets of the 1960s and '70s. He suffered his mental anguish alone and in silence, conditioned by the values instilled in him by his courageous and compassionate mother, values that taught self-reliance and solving one's own problems as best one could. In sympathetic letters to me about my personal problems and discontents, which were trivial in comparison with his mental suffering, he proffered advice he no doubt took himself—what "Aeneas told his handful of Trojans, huddling together, as Troy burns: Durate (Hang on)." In exploring his unconscious, he was seeking wholeness through self-examination as Jung advised. While his efforts and the poems that came out of them may not have produced a "cure," they may have saved him from the fate of Berryman, Plath, and Sexton, who took their own lives, as Randall Jarrell and Winfield Townley Scott may also have done. Finally, though it may be uncharitable or cynical to say, Lowell and the others appear, though struggling with real and painful mental illness, to have written their "confessions" with the conscious intent of publishing them and obviously with an eye on the critics, book contracts, and a hoped-for positive response from a public in the 1960s and '70s in rebellion against all sorts of conventions and authority and inclined to "let it all hang out." But it should also be acknowledged that their candid confessions may have given assurance to readers who themselves were suffering in similar ways that they were not alone. For his part Trout probably never dreamt of submitting his most personal poetic creations to the "poking and sniffing" of strangers. He was trying to reconcile both his own individuality and the values and traditions of the pre-World War I agrarian society (not all of which he appears to have approved of) experienced in his formative years with the dramatic changes wrought by Modernism in all aspects of American life. Through his pursuit of self-knowledge Bill was trying to be at home with himself even if he was unable to be at home in a world in which he felt so out of place. In this he was at one with many American artists and intellectuals in the middle years of the twentieth century.

Without knowing of Bill's private doubts an understanding and appreciation of his achievements as a poet, teacher, and human being would not be possible. Knowing about his personal conflicts and struggles does not diminish him but rather increases our admiration for him. For in the face of such problems he not only met responsibilities to his mother and students and created a credible body of poetry, but did it all with equanimity, gentleness, kindness, and concern for others that earned him widespread and long-lasting respect and love from those who knew him. And in the final analysis, what M. L. Rosenthal wrote of Robert Lowell and writers like him is, I believe, also true of William Trout: that through their "self-analytical monologues," their explorations of "the lost Self," they affirm that "their individual lives have profound meaning and worth, and their therapeutic confessions will lead to the realization of these values" (Rosenthal 1960, 237).

The years 1965 to 1968 must have been particularly difficult for Bill given his mother's worsening physical and mental deterioration and the tensions occasioned by fractious political turmoil within the college community. In September 1965 Robert Christie, a historian and vice president at New York's Hofstra University began his thirty-four-month tenure as Millersville's tenth chief executive and ended when the trustees requested his resignation in December of 1967, which he submitted effective August of 1968. An "outsider" brought in to guide the institution's transformation from teacher-training institution to liberal arts college, Christie soon ran afoul of the newly formed faculty senate over matters of governance, and of faculty "old timers" who objected to his interference in departmental decisions on faculty teaching assignments, promotion, and retention. That Trout felt threatened by Christie's efforts to "upgrade" the faculty by culling members without advanced degrees in liberal arts disciplines to make room for recruits with doctorates in these fields is suggested by a conversation Byron Detwiler (one of Bill's former students and a member of the Foreign Language Department) told me he had in Trout's office, in which Bill related, in whispered words lest colleagues in neighboring offices heard, the pressures being placed on him to resign, jerking his head toward the president's campus residence to indicate the source of the pressure.

Difficulties between Christie and Dr. Lynwood Lingenfelter, who for many years ran the English Department pretty much as he pleased, came to a head in the spring of 1966 over objections raised by some faculty members to the classes he had assigned them to teach in the fall semester, particularly the number of sections of freshman composition they were given. A few instructors wrote to President Christie explaining their objections to the class assignments, and one in her letter cites a litany of "persecutions" she suffered at the chair's hands over the years. Christie stepped into the fray and removed Lingenfelter as chair of the department. The defrocked chair continued teaching until his retirement in the spring of 1968. The English faculty was deeply divided over the affair and the petty gossip, back-biting, and sniping which is an unhappy part of academic office politics was made even worse by articles and letters to the editor that appeared in local newspapers. All through the Lingenfelter affair the health of Trout's mother continued to deteriorate, ending with her death in November 1967. Bill wanted to resign immediately but was persuaded by his colleague Joseph Rhen, who argued that he had responsibilities to his students, to postpone his leaving until the end of the academic year. In a one-sentence letter of resignation sent to President Christie on 6 February 1968, Bill at the age of fifty-nine ended his thirty-seven year career as a teacher (Downey 2004, 157-163; Robert Christie Papers, MU Archives). There can be little doubt that the personal and professional stresses of 1966-1967 exacerbated Bill's melancholic disposition.

Although in theme and tone Trout's poetry shares some characteristics with other American poets of the mid-twentieth century, what seems to distinguish him from them is that his poems do not shed British influences for Whitmanesque Americanism; are rooted in continuity, the context of traditions and community and history; express the primacy of personal emotions and values (kindness, compassion, dedication, and self-sacrifice); focus on the relationship between inner life and the outside world; and call for contemplation and introspection by raising timeless issues concerning nature, the meaning of life, matters of faith, reason versus imagination, the aging process, and death.

Trout's attention to craftsmanship and the fact that he titled many of his poems suggests that the possibility of publication was at least in the back of his mind. Responding to my enthusiasm for his poems, he wrote to me in November 1971, saying:

> Your self-effacing generosity amid the harassments of your existence fills me with a sort of baffled chagrin, since—God knows—the paltry matters that relate to me do not merit your benevolence. What you say of the doggerel leaves me wavering between the incredulity of self-contempt and a dim relief to think that perhaps I may not yet be a candidate for Charenton [a French mental asylum founded in 1645 and known for its humane treatment of patients]. But beyond that relief, obstinately attacked by the incredulity, I do not care. For a year or so, I supported the idea (and was supported by it) of perhaps, perhaps publishing one in some respectable magazine. I would not care to be accepted by The Farm Journal, Baer's Almanac, or the modern equivalent of True Story; but then beggars are always quixotic. Later, a little common-sense returned; I still scrawl, as Flaubert says the bourgeois turns napkin rings

> on the lathe in his attic—or as another collects buttons or makes bird houses—which the birds haughtily refuse to inhabit. Shock had dulled momentarily the result of long self-observation; a psyche questionably endowed to begin with, and corroded by almost forty years of mental prostitution and warped by the crazy stresses of a penurious existence. You are welcome to any of the jingles that you care to have, but I am unable—wholly unable to judge any of the stuff.

Assuming that Trout began writing poetry on a regular basis in the 1940s, or perhaps somewhat earlier, one would have to place him within the poetic context of those writing at the same time, from the 1940s to the 1970s. Based on three popular anthologies of modern verse—*A New Anthology of Modern Poetry* (1946) edited by Selden Rodman, the revised edition of Oscar Williams' *A Little Treasury of Modern Poetry* (1952), and the 1962 edition of Louis Untermeyer's combined *Modern American Poetry* and *Modern British Poetry* (all of which Trout owned)—there are twenty-four American poets who were contemporaries of Bill's (if one accepts as his contemporaries those born five years either side of him, 1904-1914), who were among those submitting poetry to book publishers and journal editors from about 1935 to 1975, and therefore would have been judged by publishers along with Trout, had he in fact been submitting work for publication. The list of his anthologized contemporaries, in addition to those already discussed in some detail, include Robert Penn Warren and Elizabeth Bishop, whose fame has endured, and others like Eunice Clark, Reuel Denny, and Robert Fitzgerald, whose notoriety has faded with time. There were also many poets like Elford Caughey who published in respectable magazines and journals but are now forgotten. We are left with trying to understand the circumstances or reasons why Trout did not seek to get his poems into print.

Most of Trout's anthologized poet contemporaries were born or resided in urban centers; were educated in selective liberal arts colleges or major universities; had lived abroad or traveled widely; were part of a literary milieu that included regular attendance at poetry readings and academic or literary conferences; gave public readings of their work; in general were part of a literary network; had published mentors (Robert Hillyer for Theodore Roethke and Elford Caughey and John Crowe Ransom for Randall Jarrell, to cite but three); knew each other from their student days at such places as Harvard, Dartmouth, Brown, Vanderbilt, Vassar, Barnard, or Kenyon College; held academic appointments at selective colleges or universities; and were both poets and critics. In other words, all these poets had "literary connections." Trout, on the other hand, had none. He lived and worked in isolation and obscurity.

Attending Millersville State Teachers College had most likely not been the liberating experience for Bill that college was for the published poets who were his contemporaries. Millersville was a teacher-training institution most of whose student body were residents of Lancaster and surrounding counties. The financial difficulties faced by the approximately 450-500 students enrolled during the Great Depression meant that the majority were, like Trout, commuters, "day" students who were hard pressed to come up with the $105 tuition plus fees per semester and could not afford to live on campus. College administrators had to make cuts to non-essential programs like clubs and other extracurricular activities, further reducing opportunities for organized student interaction outside of classes (Downey 2004, 102-105). Millersville students came from middle- or lower-middle-class homes with conservative religious and political beliefs. Bill's brilliance and consuming interest in things of the mind probably were not matched by most of his fellow students and left him without a soul mate his own age. Among his classmates Bill would have found doubters and questioners like him as rare as hens' teeth. It is also unlikely he would have met among his classmates the more cosmopolitan, sophisticated, or just financially better-off students found at liberal arts colleges or universities. Then, too, when classes ended, Trout, a commuter student, would have taken the trolley or bus back to Gap. He probably had few opportunities to associate with college faculty outside the classroom and no chance, even if he managed to overcome his innate shyness, to find the kinds of campus organizations and companions Willa Cather found at the University of Nebraska in the 1890s, or opportunities to engage in the sort of discussions and late night bull sessions with fellow students living on campus which do so much to connect one to a wider world, challenge one's beliefs and values, and foster youthful rebelliousness. There is no evidence that Bill made any close or lasting college friendships.

Trout was not alone among poets in having to work a day job and write poetry in his spare time; however, his income was probably less than that of many of his contemporaries. William Carlos Williams was a pediatrician, Wallace Stevens a lawyer and businessman, Merrill Moore a psychiatrist, and Winfield Townley Scott worked for newspapers and a radio station. And unlike poet-professors such as Tate, Jarrell, Berryman, and others who had reduced course loads and usually taught seminars and advanced courses with small enrollments, at Millersville Trout taught a four- or five-course load, including specialized courses and surveys like freshman grammar and composition and World Literature. He had no teaching assistant to grade papers but read the quizzes, tests, and weekly compositions of his freshmen himself, always returning the papers promptly, filled with his corrections, suggestions, and critical comments penned in red or green ink. For a quarter of a century before going to Millersville he taught in the public schools (and during part of this time worked in a steel mill), where he taught seventh and eighth graders Latin, social studies, health, and other subjects in addition to English. At Octorara High School he taught a five- or six-period day and was the adviser to the school newspaper, which his journalism class initiated.

In addition to his teaching schedule with its multiple course preparations and paperwork, he cared for his aging mother and was kept busy doing chores around the house and property. Yet he managed to keep writing poetry, often in the wee hours of the night, or in time stolen from postponed yard work, which he mentions in letters to Don Smith. In a letter of 21 April 1945 to Smith he chronicles his chores, saying he "mowed the lawn and dug the garden all day ... But the hedge needs trimming ... I must plant the endive and take down the storm door and review for final examinations." Writing to Smith on 22 July 1945 he tells him,

> yesterday I trimmed the hedge ... and mowed the lawn, finishing at nine o'clock, with my shadow going on before me in the moonlight. After scrubbing, I was no longer sleepy, so I played all through Rosenkavalier, Tapiola, a Mozart piano concerto, some Debussy songs, and ended with the old [Schubert] lullaby – Schlafe mein susses Kind (?) – just to hear Lehmann give the ineffable caress to the Leibling, gute nach at the end. Then I read Millay's Collected Lyrics (!) – my only birthday gift – until three o'clock. Then in came a seventeen-year-old, who had borrowed the antiquated Plymouth to take his girl to a carnival and he stretched out on the sofa and told me the delights of a moonlight summer night. So life runs on, and I shall lose my mill job [at Lukens Steel] after next week: cancellation of orders - hopeful sign – is bringing about endless lay-offs. Don't know what I shall do till September [when he would begin teaching at Christiana School].

Bill's reluctance to seek publication of his verse goes beyond demands on his time to his insecurity about its quality, "relevance," or fear that it might be rejected. Certainly he had contact, albeit very limited when compared with the published poets of his day, with people in the literary world—Alida Monro, Professor Boll, and his cousin Elford Caughey—who might have been willing to give him advice and use their contacts in publishing to help get his poems into print. During the 1950s and '60s Dr. L. S. Lingenfelter, the English Department Chair, invited noted writers to give lectures at Millersville and also organized a Contemporary Writers Conference during the summer. Among those who lectured or taught in the summer Writers Conference were such poets, fiction authors, and critics as Carl Sandburg, Margaret Widdimer, John Ciardi, Conrad Richter, Richard Wilbur, Merrill Moore, Peter Viereck, E. E. Cummings, Malcolm Cowley, and Louis Untermeyer. English Department faculty (fig. 14) including Trout shared instruction in summer workshops with the literary luminaries. During one of these Writers Conferences, for example, he lectured on the British poet Walter Savage Landor (English Dept. Files and MSTC *Journal*, 1959 in Millersville University Archives). Trout would thus have come into direct contact with some of the most successful contemporary writers in America. But given his shyness and self-deprecation, it is unlikely he spoke with any of them about his own poetry.

Bill was certainly aware of the reluctance of Emily Dickinson to publish her poems, preferring to send handwritten copies to a few select friends and relatives, an example Trout apparently did not follow. He may even have read her poem that begins "Publication – is the Auction / Of the Mind of Man" and decided he didn't want to submit his poems to the tender mercies of some literary huckster. As Domhnall Mitchell and others have explained, Dickinson, who seems to have seen writing poetry as a private act, had reason to be suspicious of editors and publishers, since the few poems of hers that were printed in her lifetime were altered without her permission. She knew that to publish was to risk losing control of one's creation, not just through changed words, punctuation, line breaks, and so forth but by being misinterpreted by readers and critics (Johnson 1955, chaps. 4 and 5; Mitchell 2000, 10-11). Given Trout's suspicion of established institutions, part of his unwillingness to submit poems for publication may have been a similar mistrust of commercial and academic publishing—a fear that he might lose control of his poems to editors and printers as he must have known happened to other poets, including Charlotte Mew and A. E. Housman. He was also aware of the years of rejection and disappointment suffered by E. A. Robinson, whose poems were returned by one publisher after another. But the most likely reason for his reluctance even to show his poems to others, let alone seek publication, was that to do so would have constituted an invasion of his privacy, since they were deeply personal expressions of his own experiences and reflections on life. Publication would expose his thoughts and feelings, as well as some of his most intimate secrets, to the world, which he had spent most of his life trying to keep out by "growing a carapace" to foil those who would "poke and sniff" at him. Publication would shine a light on him (and on his mother); draw attention to him; suck him into associations and contacts he had done his best to avoid and which would wreck his solitude. Why he chose to show his poems to me, to this day I do not know.

During the 1930s and early 1940s, about the time Bill was probably beginning to write verse, the New Criticism was codifying the conventions of modernist poetry; and poets he admired, Millay among them, began to be marginalized, even savaged by critics like Allen Tate, and fall out of favor. From the late 1930s through the 1950s, poets of the Eliot-New Criticism persuasion held editorships of important journals. Cleanth Brooks and Robert Penn Warren authored *Understanding Poetry* (1938), which went through three editions between 1938 and 1960 and was arguably the most widely used undergraduate text in college poetry courses; thus inculcating several generations of American college graduates with the gospel of the New Criticism and thereby influencing their reading habits, their literary tastes, and the poetry books they purchased (Burt and Lewin in Roberts 2001, 153-155, 162-166). Even three of the four modern poets Trout valued—Hart Crane, Conrad Aiken, Robinson Jeffers, and E. E. Cummings—were not particularly well received by the New Critics. In the 1960 edition of *Understanding Poetry* neither Millay nor Aiken is included; Hart Crane and Cummings were given only three poems apiece, and Jeffers allotted only one.

Other influential literary scholars and critics, among them Roy Harvey Pearce, also dismissed some of the modern poets Trout valued. Pearce maintains: "No one kind of poem, no one style, is Aiken's. Above all, he is an 'influenced' poet, and absorptive poet. He has no form or manner which is really his own," and "seems never to have been quite clear as to his subject." "Reading through the bulk of Cummings," Pearce claims, "one begins to feel that what he is reading is so often mere technique; and the feeling is an unhappy one ..." since, he suggests, the reader feels manipulated by the technique. Furthermore, he views the poet's penchant for comedy and satire as "perhaps the other side of the coin of sentimentality ..." (Pearce 1961, 349, 358-359, 364-365). The manifestations of romanticism and sentimentality found in Cummings' poetry also troubled M. L. Rosenthal, though he thought his "more colloquial tones" helped him keep those more personal emotions in check. (Rosenthal 1960, 150). While Millay is named but not discussed by Pearce, Jeffers is not even mentioned by him in his seminal book *The Continuity of American Poetry*. Jeffers and Aiken were among those modern poets Rosenthal believes "maintained a certain traditionalism in [their] art and thought—at a crucial cost, however" (Rosenthal 1960, 159). If even these certifiably modern poets could not pass muster with the critics of the 1940s and '50s Bill must have resigned himself to not being published.

In the decades from World War II on, writing poetry became professionalized and institutionalized in the halls of academe, where writers' workshops and MFA degrees in creative writing proliferated, and whose faculties and graduates set the tone for literary life in the postwar years. The harshness with which a number of the poet-critics—John Crowe Ransom, Allen Tate, Randall Jarrell, and John Ciardi among them—treated poets in their reviews may also have contributed to Trout's reluctance to expose himself to such treatment, particularly since his poetry would likely have been dismissed, I believe unfairly, like Robinson's and Millay's was by the New Criticism as "dated," an example of the amorphous absurdities of "literary speak." Trout's poetry is rooted in values that do not change according to the fashions and vagaries of the market place whether commercial or literary. The sonnet was a favorite form for Trout, as it was for Cummings and Millay, whose sonnets had fallen into disfavor by the 1940s. The modernist poet William Carlos Williams insisted in 1938 that "the sonnet is an outmoded form" save for those by Merrill Moore (1903-1957), whose work "has broken through the binding, stupid formality of the sonnet" and convinced Williams that the "sonnet ... is not a form at all but a state of mind" (Witemeyer 1989, 25-26). The extreme liberties Moore took in writing his "American" sonnets made a mockery of its traditional forms. For someone of Trout's temperament, such a hostile climate for traditional poetic forms would have been a significant deterrent to any thought of publication. And then in the 1950s Projective Verse, also known as Open Verse or Composition By Field, appeared.

In 1950 Charles Olson (1910-1970)—a member of the faculty at Black Mountain College in North Carolina along with other leaders of the *avant-garde* such as Joseph Albers, Willem de Kooning, Franz Kline, Buckminster Fuller, Walter Gropius in the visual arts; John Cage and Roger Sessions in music; and Merce Cunningham in dance—published in pamphlet form his influential essay *Projective Verse*. This approach to poetic composition rests on the notion that a poem transfers "energy" from the poet to the reader by having one perception lead directly and immediately to the next perception. Focusing on the syllable and the line, according to Olson, creates the spontaneity of the poem, which is determined by breaths the poet takes in the process of composition. Projective Verse abandons the conventions of meter, rhyme, and cadence and replaces content and description with dramatic formlessness. Poetry thus became a matter of strung-together single breaths (lines) uttered by the poet and exemplified by Olson's "The Kingfishers" and Paul Blackburn's "The Assistance." The progenitors of Projective Verse were Walt Whitman, Ezra Pound, and William Carlos Williams, poets Trout seems not to have appreciated (Rosenthal 1960, 268-272). The strong connection between Projective Verse and the Beats is apparent to anyone who has read Allen Ginsberg's "Howl." Thus the cultural climate of post-World War II America fostered art forms that ran counter to all Trout loved in the arts. And as his brother Frank observes in a letter to Don Smith on 25 May 1980, after Bill's death: "The current state of literature, music, and art saddened him. Those were the things he cared most about."

Certainly the urbanization of nature by postwar poets as typified by John Ciardi's "March Morning"—a poem written by a city dweller for other city dwellers—is one of the things that would have saddened Trout and made him realize that for many Americans early spring was not as he had imaged it in his poem "March," but was for them a matter of streets fouled by "Black snow," "black slush," and "Oil slick puddles" splashed onto sidewalks by traffic, as recorded by Ciardi in his impersonal, detached formalist manner. In "Thoughts on Looking into a Thicket," Ciardi uses nature as an opportunity to voice his philosophical view of the world and life through the clever use of words, similes, and metaphors; esoteric references to religion and to two American entomologists; and allusions to Darwin's theories. Not a religious person, Ciardi uses information on insects gleaned primarily from books rather than habitual observations of the natural world to support his belief in "the neutral mindlessness of nature" (Ciffelli 1997, 196). Robert Lowell's "Mr. Edwards and the Spider" has little if anything to do with an arachnid save as a symbol or metaphor for the poet's theological/philosophical musings. Compared to Trout's spider poems, which combine philosophical reflection with careful observation of the tiny creatures, those of Ciardi and Lowell are impersonal and use spiders merely for abstract intellectual and aesthetic ends. Again in "Two Egrets," Ciardi uses nature as a means to literary abstraction in which the birds are aesthetic devices and symbolic formal elements devoid of emotion and unconnected to lived reality. And by likening "globular clusters" of frog eggs to "the pomegranate of Mother Church" in which the "saints are such seeds," in his poem "Tommy's Pond," Ciardi again uses nature for purely literary ends. No wonder Trout despaired of getting his poems published. And yet the fact that he owned a copy of Ciardi's *As If: Poems New and Select* (1955) suggests that he had respect for the poet's commitment to traditional forms of poetry and for his study of etymology—the history of words, their origins, and how their meaning changed over time.

The growth of suburbia in the postwar years and the beginning of the interstate highway system during the Eisenhower administration changed American society dramatically and made the America Bill wrote about less and less familiar to the "Togetherness"-conscious baby-boom moms and dads who reared their children in the "little boxes made of ticky-tacky" (to quote Pete Seeger) in one Levittown community after another, and who took their families to see the USA in their Chevrolets. The novels and short stories acclaimed by critics and purchased by those who read good fiction—books by such authors as Sloan Wilson, John Updike, John Cheever, and Jack Kerouak—focused on the lives of Americans living in cities or subdivisions or the emerging counter-culture types who took to the road, not the rooted residents of places like Gap and its agricultural hinterland. Life in suburbia—housewife blues, the pressures of unfulfilling office jobs and the vapidity of efforts to escape them (including by watching TV), consumerism and social climbing, country clubs and cocktail parties, playing golf and bridge, marital infidelities and alcoholism—or going "on the road" to escape it—all must have made Bill realize that he was swimming against the tide of critical and popular opinion, which would have thought his poems "irrelevant" to their "other-directed" way of life. The "other-directed" majority of postwar Americans described by sociologist David Riesman in *The Lonely Crowd* were more conformist, more susceptible to public and peer opinion, more willing to work in modern bureaucracies and participate in an economy of pleasure and consumption than were "inner-directed" people like William Trout.

Finally, even given the streak of Puritanism Americans are thought to carry in their DNA, stoicism is not something they willingly embrace, particularly not the consuming "Ozzie and Harriet"-types of postwar America, who groomed their children to be homemakers or to join the ranks of the gray flannel suits making the daily commute from suburbia to office buildings in the metropolis only to see them rebel, stuff Salinger's *Catcher in the Rye* in their hip pockets and, lured by rock 'n' roll into hedonism, be carried into Hippiedom on the "beat" of Ginsberg's and Ferlinghetti's poetry. Trout's view of life and his poetry were certainly steeped in stoicism and would have been regarded as "square" by many of his postwar contemporaries, literary and otherwise. If back in 1907 Henry Adams had thought Americans "always take tragedy lightly," the tragic sense of life that colored so much of Trout's poetry would not have been understood nor appreciated by most of his fellow citizens who had seen the end of the Great Depression, the winning of World War II, the rise of the United States as the most powerful and materialistic nation in the world, and the economic prosperity of the Eisenhower years. In the "can-do" optimism of Americans in the postwar years—the threat of Communism and nuclear annihilation notwithstanding—Bill no doubt thought his poems would fall on deaf ears.

This was, as Herbert Gold called it, "The Age of Happy Problems," (an essay Trout assigned to Grammar and Composition classes in 1961), a generation "particularly distinguished by its worry about making wives happy, about doing right by its kids, about acquiring enough leisure and symbols of leisure, which it hopes to cash in for moral comfort" (Gold 1957, 59). Trout's poems are not about "happy problems" or living the postwar myth of the "American dream." In the Introductory Note to his posthumously published collection of poetry, *Winter Words: In Various Moods and Meters* (a copy of which Bill owned), Thomas Hardy complains that his previous volume of verse "was pronounced wholly gloomy and pessimistic by reviewers"; and even though he believed that "the licensed tasters had not willfully misrepresented the book," he questions whether they had in fact read it. Aware of the tone of much of his poetry, and not wishing to be rejected as Millay's *Second April* was years earlier by a publisher because of its purported pessimism, or dismissed by "the licensed tasters" as "gloomy," it is no wonder Bill felt out of place and was reluctant to submit poems for publication that ran counter to the optimistic mood of the dominant culture which believed in America's exceptionalism. Given the poets and fiction writers who got into print in postwar America, Bill no doubt realized that sales-conscious publishers would reject his poems. Being new, innovative, and cutting-edge were what mattered most to America's "bottom-line" literary entrepreneurs. Valuing the intrinsic rewards of writing poetry rather than the extrinsic ones, Trout was apparently unwilling to tailor his verse to popular taste, the marketing concerns of publishers, or the dictates of contemporary criticism.

But it may be unnecessary to go beyond Bill's philosophy of living to one's self for an explanation of why he chose not to publish. John Cowper Powys in his *Autobiography* gives the crux of this "philosophy of solitude":

"Independence! Independence! That is the secret of all philosophy. To be independent of the opinions of your neighbours, of your relations, of your friends; to be independent of this ridiculous itch for 'being heard of'; to take the neck of your desire to compete and wring it ..." (Powys 1934, 569).

On that December afternoon in 1970 when Bill first showed me his poems, we sat on drab and worn upholstery chairs opposite each other in the dim winter light of the sparsely furnished living room of his Lancaster apartment. He took one poem at a time from a manila file-folder resting on his knees and passed it to me. Watching me with an intensity that was unnerving, he would snatch the poem back saying "No good" if he detected what he thought was any sign in my facial expression (pursed lips, slight turn of the head, raised eyebrow, quizzical expression) of confusion, uncertainty, doubt, or disapproval. About two months later (February 1971) he wrote: "As to the doggerel, I learned intuitively from you, in spite of your gentle magnanimity, that which I needed to know—that which I knew, I think, in spite of my mental confusion: that the trash would not even yield one scrap that might be published." And in a letter of 4 August 1972, he urged: "You must not pay any more heed to that insane doggerel"; and then likened himself to "Robinson's [poet] Elaine Amelia Watchman (in Amaranth)," who "writes and writes and writes."

There is evidence that in the final months of his life Bill was reading *Come Hither*, a collection of British and American rhymes and poems "for the young of all ages" compiled by Walter de la Mare. The marginal notes Bill made in it suggest that he was reviewing events in his own life relating to his family, particularly his mother. Next to Padraic Colum's "An Old Woman of the Roads" he wrote: "Long ago, my dear, in a little anthology that you bought for school." And next to "I Remember" by Thomas Hood he noted, "Often read to you—1959-1967" (the years his mother was an invalid). His sister Susanna's dates (9. 30. 1904 - 4. 14. 1911) were inscribed next to Robert Herrick's "Upon a Child that Died"; and his father's death was recorded with: "About 2:00 P.M., Friday, February 14, 1919" next to a line by Sir Henry Wooton: "And Birds Had Drawn Their Valentines." In the last letter Bill wrote me, which is postmarked 7 March 1980, he tells me:

> The twelve-year exile from the bitter farce of 'teaching' has cast an unendurable light on my natural incapacity, on my lack of education, on my protracted lodging on the lower levels of the 'schools,' on my entire unsuitability for the job at M[illersville]U[niversity]. (But that job let me hang on a little longer, pay the bills, do what had to be done.

> At the expense of the 'college students'? No doubt. But I did not seek the job). And the twelve-year exile has thrown into farcical relief my own pathetic inability to write, my blindness, even, to the contemptible results of that inability (But no longer blind.).

In the same letter he mentions being ill, saying he is "still burdened by the misery. 'Got the, miz'ry' as my negro pupils, first school [Mt. Airy], used to say." Knowing that he would volunteer no details and would resent inquiry, I let the matter drop, though because he was a heavy smoker all his adult life—and for much of it unfiltered Camels, though in his last years he switched to menthol filtered Salems, which he smoked with a cigarette holder—I could surmise his "misery." His letters to me from the late 1970s record the effects of the aging process including apologies for difficulties in typing or controlling "the arthritic vulture claw in order to induce legible script," claims of lapsing "into hopeless desuetude," and of being "incapable of coherence, and my powers of 'composition'—always feeble, God knows—have fled the sinking ship" (4-19-77, 1-24-79, 10-27-79). In a letter of 27 October 1979, he mentions having "some sort of pleurisy" but "like an old cat, I just crept under the back porch and waited for the fit to pass." But what Bill was experiencing was not pleurisy, and he probably knew it. That he had a premonition of his impending death seems almost certain from two marginal notations he made in his copy of *Come Hither*, which Frank gave to me after Bill's death. He underscored these lines of Henry King's "The Exequy": "My last good-night! Thou wilt not wake / Till I thy fate shall overtake," put an "x" next to "I am already on my way," and placed two upright lines bracketing the poem's final lines: "Each minute is a short degree / And every hour a step towards thee...." In the margin next to the poem he wrote two dates, 1967 (the year his mother died) and 1980. At the bottom of the final page of text de la Mare placed the words, "*And so, Farewell*," which Bill marked with a wavy line and wrote the date—1. 26. 80.

According to his brother Frank, Bill became ill in February but refused medical treatment until he at last had to be taken to hospital. He died in Lancaster General Hospital on May Day 1980 of cardio-respiratory arrest caused by bronchogenic carcinoma and was buried next to his sister, Susanna, in the Bellevue Presbyterian Church Cemetery in Gap. At Bill's insistence no obituary appeared in the papers, a final effort to guard his privacy and perhaps a belief that no one would or should care about his passing. Like so much else in his life, the prospect of his own death moved him to verse. In the poem "Incurable" (written one imagines after his diagnosis) his stoicism; his penchant for imaging personal memories and emotion and giving them universal appeal through the language of common speech; his compact, concentrated means of expression; and his self-mocking, cynical humor come through even so near the end. Like single-frames in a film, he flashes through memories of his life—students and young friends; the Lukens plant; traffic passing his childhood home and the house he later shared with his mother, both on U.S. 30 (the Lincoln Highway); and the trains that went through Gap and sometimes got him out of it.

> So there is nothing now except death—
> The impassive fact before whose granite face
> The hand of custom, the pathetic human hand,
> Falls limp and sweating.
> The brutal energy of the young; the smoke
> From the steel mills; the trucks upon
> The summer highways; in winter the lighted train
> Streaking through darkness: what mockery in these,
> For the sunk-eyed watcher in the sterile room,
> Counting the daily cost from now to then,
> Wondering whether he has money to afford
> The so luxurious necessity of death.

CODA

William Trout placed self-fulfillment above self-advancement and valued thought and feeling more than action. He was, for the most part, a soft-spoken iconoclast where the assumptions and values of mainstream American society were concerned. Having to confront the ambiguities of life can make any of us bundles of contradictions, but particularly those who are deeply sensitive and intellectually gifted. The public Trout, the one most of those who crossed his path knew, was a kind, generous, and gentle man whose ethics were based not on narrow religious morality, but on a humanistic commitment to do the right thing. The private Trout, the one of his letters and poems, comes across as an insecure, lonely, unhappy, and perhaps guilt-ridden neurotic always searching for the purpose and meaning of life in a society and time from which he felt alienated. He honestly and frankly confronts the fact that all people, and some more than others, experience loss, sorrow, and pain and must grapple with unhappiness. For Trout, who was spiritually awakened rather than religious, life was a tragedy, which helps explain his profound consciousness of suffering. The manner in which he lived his life suggests an acquaintance with Schopenhauer's view that "everything that happens... happens of necessity," and "a man steeped in the knowledge of this truth" will "do what he can" and "endure what he must." Whether Bill was a philosophical fatalist, determinist, necessitarian, or just a disillusioned realist with a touch of idealism is too fine a point to argue here.

Yet for all of the darkness in many of his poems, he never escaped into mysticism and spirituality (though these inform his poetry), never evaded the responsibilities of everyday life, never abandoned hope, but kept on if not singing at least humming in the lifeboat of his intellectual and aesthetic interests. While his nature poetry focuses on autumn and winter rather than the sunny months of spring and summer, it is more contemplative than nostalgic—never morose—and testifies to his love of the earth and pleasure he took from it as revealed in the sensitivity and sensuousness with which he depicts the actuality of its creatures and captures the subtle beauty of its weather and seasons. No matter how gloomy some people may find his poetry, the fact remains that he never stopped exploring and questioning. And he kept on writing. As his marginalia proves, his critical faculties remained sharp and his skepticism robust as he "debated" the authors whose books he read and challenged or lampooned politicians and public policies he read about in magazines and newspapers. He did not give up, become a dysfunctional alcoholic, take the gas pipe, or quit inquiring, learning, and writing poetry in his search for answers to the riddle of life. Because of his wide-ranging curiosity and the breadth of his intellectual interests, his pastimes merged with and enriched his vocational responsibilities, and help explain why people, particularly students, enjoyed talking with him.

Certainly loneliness and a desire for companionship are themes that run through his correspondence and poetry; however, his pastimes since childhood were, after all, solitary ones—reading, observing nature, and listening to classical music—activities most people do by themselves. Like William Hazlitt, Henry David Thoreau, Emily Dickinson, and John Cowper Powys he made a conscious decision to "live to himself," to follow a road "less traveled by," as Robert Frost put it. Would having taken a more conventional, mainstream route given him as rich an intellectual, imaginative, and spiritual life as the one he experienced? He did cultivate friendships by sharing his interests and ideas with the students who visited him or those invited to listen to recordings and Metropolitan Opera broadcasts, through conversations with his friends, and in letters to colleagues, friends, and former students. As his correspondence with those serving in the military confirms, he tried hard to maintain friendships. Nonetheless, his only long-time companion was his mother, and when she passed away there was no one to fill the void. Not only the years he gave to his mother's care but also the people among whom Bill sought companionship—younger men and married couples—as well as the unresolved question of his sexual/affectional orientation, go a long way toward explaining why he had no other committed companion. If there had been another "someone," of which faint hints of infatuations can be found in his letters to Don Smith—and suggested by the initials of male students he wrote in books—society's hostility toward such liaisons and Bill's inability to leave his mother would have made such a relationship impossible.

The sorrow of losing his mother only in part accounts for Trout's reclusive behavior during the last twelve years or so of his life. It is also traceable to his life-long proclivity for "living to one's-self" and to his reading of Jung. In the "On Psychic Energy," "Stages of Life," and "The Soul and Death" sections of *The Structure and Dynamics of the Psyche* (which Bill read in 1966 and then again in 1973, 1976, and 1979), Jung explains that the "truths and ideals" that guide the external and expansive goals and behaviors of youth (centered on employment, social achievement, family) are not appropriate, are indeed harmful, if people try to carry them into the evening of life, where the focus should not be expansion but contraction—"simplification, limitation, and intensification" of *personal* cultural goals. "The second half of life," Jung says, "does not signify ascent, unfolding, increase, exuberance, but death, since the end is its goal." And those who fail "to go along with life ... get wooden in old age; they look back and cling to the past" unable to accept that: "Waxing and waning make [a single] curve" (Jung 1960, 60, 398-402, 406-407). Confirming his acceptance of Jung's observations on aging, Bill wrote on the beginning page of Section IV: "the descent toward life's afternoon demands simplification, limitation, & intensification—individual culture."

Bill chose to "age in place," as the current gerontology jargon describes senior citizens living on their own in their own homes. Certainly he suffered protracted unhappiness because of his mother's death and his alienation from a society whose values he did not share, yet he maintained an active intellectual life spending his days reading, listening to music, writing poetry; contacting secondhand dealers to buy books he had not read or borrowing those he had from the library; polishing his knowledge of the French language and keeping up his Latin; corresponding with the likes of Professor Boll and Alita Monro; answering occasional letters from friends and former students; and trying to make sense of himself, life's mysteries, and what lay beyond this world, all of which are examples of the content of "individual culture" Jung said that people should pursue' in the evening of life. This way of life merits sympathetic understanding not pity. It is well to remember that rather than being confined in an assisted living facility playing basket bingo, joining in sing-alongs, and making pinch pots, or being left exposed on a bed pan by an over-worked nursing assistant—as Frank Trout was when I last visited him at a Lancaster nursing home in December of 1990 (he died in 1991)—Bill lived in his own apartment on his own terms until he was taken to hospital a few days before he died. During his last years he shared the apartment with his brother Frank, with whom he could talk about family and past experiences; discuss their mutual interests (history among them) and what they read in *The New York Times* and news magazines to which Frank, a retired social studies teacher, was addicted; and kvetsh about the sorry state of American politics and society. Bill never lost his sense of humor, of that I can testify, though it may have become more bitingly satirical or sometimes cynical over time.

Bill's tireless dedication to his profession, his selfless devotion to his mother, and perhaps most of all his low self-esteem and the need to hide his deepest beliefs and desires took a toll on him, as did his mother's passing. But his poems—the fruit not only of his knowledge and sensitivity but also of solitude, sublimation, and loss—will make all who read them richer for the experience. His poems show us nature from a perspective different from that of many of his contemporaries; they examine concerns about aging, death, personal doubt, and the dark side of human nature many of us share but are reluctant or refuse to admit and confront; and they alert us to the dangers of either forgetting the past or dwelling in it. He was a poet steeped in literature from the ancients to his own day and knowledgeable of its historical context, whose poetry, informed by this rich literary tradition, grew out of his own time and personal experience and speaks to us of timeless human values and concerns. His poetry makes a plea on behalf of traditional poetic forms and the importance of craftsmanship in a time when free verse, contemporary prose poetry, and related types of verse have all but obliterated the distinction between poetry and prose. There is a singularity about Trout's voice, which is characterized by the richness and distinctiveness of his diction, by the beauty of his rhymes and rhythms, by his memorable lines and marvelously turned phrases, and by his technical skill. For all of these reasons, and for the profundity and thoughtfulness of the ideas and the insights he offers us, William Trout merits recognition and a place in twentieth-century American poetry.

Although in his lifetime he neither sought nor received recognition for his poetry, and therefore would not be counted a success by the standards of our society, William Trout's triumph lies in the integrity with which he lived life, his admirable dedication to the duties that lay nearest him, to the memories of his kindness and humanity held by those who knew him, and to his commitment to his muse that in the face of difficult circumstances resulted in the creation of over 750 poems whose quality compares favorably with those of his published contemporaries.

Appendix
Selected Poems

These small and sad allies that man
Has made his comforters, to go
Upon the dark and hopeless span
With him, to perjury are slow.
A shy cup, a humble chair,
A tolerant mirror on the wall.
Some treacheries of time repair—
Entities theological.
When love has flung himself outdoors
In anger, never to return,—
When death upon the lintel scores
The hieroglyph man shrinks to learn,
The humble cup, the loyal chair
Their mute alleviations wear.

Come back, come back, across this wind:
So often have I called, it seems
Bewildered retrogression spins,
Ambushed by negation's whim,
And drops into the languid jaws
Of the unutterable Law.

I seem to see, diminutive,
The scarlet robe, the radiance
That tames the wolfish-raging wind,
The smile that calls to age afraid,
Terror-struck, to see the only
Good swept under, lost alone.

Can you not—when now the dial
Coldly points the matin Two—
Bring the diamond-reply
Affirmative: Say that you,
As always, denizen of day,
At the Wood's entrance show the way?

❧ ❧ ❧ ❧ ❧

Concede the comfort of routine, alluring
The candid craven (the condemned man shaves and eats his
breakfast).
Little tasks divide and meekly subdivide the gray
extensions of the day,
To limit the desert (only as far, now, as to the shoulder
of that dune).
Thus, the period ended, we go slowly home
Through the vague evening, haunted teasingly by ghostly
daffodil.
We go dully back
To the garrulous newspaper, wearily superfluous,
To a page of Shelley, across the coffee cup;
To fatigue creeping numbly in the marrow.
And day's periphery, sulky still with threat,
Recedes grudgingly.

❧ ❧ ❧ ❧ ❧

Not we the white wind-flower
That stands in April's wood
Ever again shall gather—
Or would we if we could.

If any lesson sharply
To the blunt mind is taught,
It is, to let rest darkly
The Past, in Time's net caught.

And yet, that tree and chimney,
That roof-line on the sky

Set something stirring dimly
That in its dust should lie:

Scent of childhood stairway,
Step upon the stair—
And we are recklessly daring
What wise men do not dare.

Individuation

Yonder is something lost; I think it is a child—
Here, in this falling snow, with evening coming on
Too fast. I know it is something wild;
It hurries from bush to rock, gray and fleet,
Gliding like a shadow, on swift, silent feet.
(It must be a changeling, then, a gnome's child,—not human.)
It does not heed even the most tranquil call,
More frightened, seemingly, by a voice than by this ominous
snowfall.
Slipping from ditch to tree, from root to bush,
It flies before us, fading into the hush
Of night and snow. (It may be a child.)
Perhaps it would stop if you would call?

You know how the spirit clings—
That obstinate Gray Impotence—
To rags, to withering, broken things,
Allusive, far beyond the sense.
You know. Therefore beneath the curse
That leads astray, confuses signs,
Transposes landmarks, and reverses
Law, whereby one might divine
Direction: then old head-in-hands—
Despair-in-heart, that wanderer—
Gently dispels the quarrelling,
Ungovernable servitors,

And turns again, intuitively
To attend the senile sage
Muttering in drowse.—You
Understand the need to wage
Once more the fight, blindly at bay.—
So begins the lightless day.

We gathered cress, fished it from the icy
Water of the choked, neglected spring.
"Snake," you said, pointing the lank device
Of a masterless demoniac, singing
His stave gone stale a little. Culling the crisp
Sprays from webs of pallid, inter-tressed
Grass, we heard a hawthorn sparrow lisping
Gospel to a Shadow gliding west.

Ritually washed with water from
The pump, our cress redeemed its chipped plate.
We set out salt and butter, cut the bread,—
And then agreed that Snake, posing Its head
On the zenith of a Cross, and Shadow-baited,
Might gladly share our crust of Kingdom Come.

Near All Hallows

Stealthily, the autumn wind
Roams the porch and tries the door,
Doubly latched, iron-pinned,
Bolted—not as heretofore.

Now with dry ash leaves confers
That picklock, in a sibilant
Parley, couched in brittle whispers,—
Conspiracy too evident.

Bough-shadows on the pallid blind
Signal fiercely, and subside

To stillness, ominously bland,—
Espials coded, conned, and cried.

The night grows colder, and the year
Shallows, deepens, ages, stills;
The fête of All the Hallows near,
The strange wind walks the hills.

Intuition

From within, some truth grows out,
Imposes logic and design
On chaos. Not decree devout,
Not script inspired, not grail of wine
Sanctifies. Let suffice
The arbitrary artifice.

One burnishes the little room,
Rafterless, a globe of foam,
Fragility, that assumes
Hearth and threshold, and is home,—
Shelter, that a truth accretes,
Growing out. Sly Paraclete.

A Dry Leaf

You pressed your cool, withered cheek
Against my fingers, as I knotted
The blue-gray scarf.—How the bleak
Mind becomes a Camelot—
A moment only, it may be,
But with incisive verity.

Bowed beneath such accolade,
But strengthened from the secret source,
Grief does not find illusion odd,—
Welcomes it without remorse;

And, with effrontery serene,
Eludes the guards of doom's demesne.

The fingers scrawling now the line—
I stare at them in disbelief;
Fleet—but yet here broods a fine
Autumn; from this brittle leaf's
Crumbling verge, the blue-white jay
Shouts across the gold day.

❧ ❧ ❧ ❧ ❧

Hawk in February

Gold outline naked to the undazzled staring eye,
The waning disk of sun hung in the gray western sky
That was still spitting snow.
Then, there, in the southeast—marvellous to relate—
We saw, above the woods, against a sky of slate,
The inverted symbol—the gray blunt-headed hawk,
Beak downward, the wings spread, and the tail.
We saw the emblem as upon a shield,
Upon the hard breast of a coat of mail:
And suddenly against the darkness was the swerving flight concealed.
It was a grave appearance, there in the welling twilight, the
    silence, and the spitting snow,
To the startled watchers, half-frightened now, but slow to
    turn and go.

❧ ❧ ❧ ❧ ❧

Past All Hallows, past All Saints,
Beyond All Souls—the autumn keeps
A dignity of age, though tints
Are muted now, and raked in heaps.

But even so, the sun refuses—
Solstice-somnolent—to turn
From our appeal; it pours on you
The alms that it must soon adjourn.

A blue jay screams; a yellow painted

Leaf spirals slowly. On so fine
Conceived finale, past All Saints,
We cross the unnoteworthy Line.

❧ ❧ ❧ ❧ ❧

Out of the Dark

The porch lamp's watery blur
Illuminates the dash
Of April's cold downpour,
The slanting, pelting splash;

Catches the yellow face
Of the bowing daffodil,
And prints conclusive grace
Upon a wavering will,

That with a sigh resigns
The metaphysical
To slanting crystal lines
And grace reciprocal.

❧ ❧ ❧ ❧ ❧

"Neat," he said. "A place for everything,
And everything in place." Yet he moved
Unhurriedly amid the sprawling sheaves
Of objects wildly mis-allied and shoved
Randomly: meerschaums never smoked,
Bobbing poles lodged aloft to season,
Seed bags labeled reconditely, broken
Cider spigots, damaged single-trees.
In the midst of haymaking, he made no bones
To quit placidly the clover lying
Prime for raking, and he to search the sunfish
In the June meadow-creek,—Let make fun
The hustlers, what conclusively atoned
That slackness was his knowing how to die.

❧ ❧ ❧ ❧ ❧

Time now to thumb the page's edge
To see one does not turn two leaves
Instead of one; time to allege
Hope's crazed desertions—and reprieves:
But there negation, since I would
Assert timidly that I have
Time, and time lets obtrude
The strange eternity of the grave.
Fluid, fluent, pliable,
Bending to thought's unskillful touch,
Teaching thought to cede without
Offense to the inscrutable
Unfettered power: time is as much
Strength in storm as nagging doubt.

Cliché

That the banal should reveal itself as valid,—
Sententious aphorism should be unveiled
As verity: who would have credited
Such traffic yonder, in a past assailed
By cynicism, bitterly by the wind
Of insolent indigence, which winnowed lean
The flesh, and then poised, chiseled and thinned,
A desperate mind, necessitously keen?
Now we are old, that jeering wind slacks,
And veers obliquely off; indigence sinks
To patched poverty. And near these graves,
Some sunken and some new, the mind, grown lax
Through grief, now astonishingly thinks—
Too late—that only love matters, and saves.

Burn now the calendars, and halt the clocks,
Do you not think? Becoming skeletal,
Transience doffs its rags in faded flocks

Of ravellings, conveniently annulled
By time-tide flowing out. (Anemones
Of March forlornly trail their delicate
Rose-pointed petals on the ragged hem
Of wintry drift whirled off upon the swell.)
Thus matter, turning immaterial,
Webs in change the withering creature, drawn
Dully from dust. But some horizon-lightening
Undimensionally flashes, shearing
Pedantic number's transitory law,
And frees time's slave for migratory flight.

In tranced captivity the mind follows
The gentle revolution of the flow
That you evoke in time, and so recalls
Your worn fingers, moving surely slow
At winter weaving, in the brief sun
Of the south window. Down that diamond noon,
The juncos fed, the greedy gray squirrel ran,
Scanning the web of rose, white, and blue.

So now, self-effaced, with unassuming
Mandate, on time's essence you impose
A double fugue; and grief, staring dimly
Tranced, sees to gather, glimmering,
Child, bride, Saint Joan in the room,
As age weaves slowly, white, blue, and rose.

Wavering wedge of wild geese crying hoarsely
In the March morning, under a gray roof,
And over the soppy meadows where the coarse
Skunk-cabbage rankly thrust: such sight was proof
That a loose practice, which might yet be law,
Was regnant slovenly, lightly banning
Upstart presumption, though the rule seem flawed

By some indulgence with regard to man.
Now the unwavering liner trails its scream,
Driving obsession into fantasy
To dread the whistling missile—March and spring
Re-ordered to the trousered simian's dream
And no retreat. Insanity the van,
Rear dare not lag, to mourn the migrant wings.

Omitted

"Now," the clock said, and the sun, suspended
At winter zenith, cried from the pale dazzle,
"Now"; but forces disparate contended—
Congealed in terror, and in doubt frozen.

And thus, between the curve of the cup and the trembling
Fingers, dwindled by age and pain, appeared
The diamond instant, blazing before the fumbling
Mind, which must apprehend, must clutch—yet feared.

"Too late," the clock said, pronouncement past appeal,
Icy finality; and the scornful sun
Swooped to nadir, leaving night to seal
The interdiction that faltering had spun.

il en faut peu....

Well, and at the moment, this was lovely:
A paper napkin—better than Giotto's Saint Francis,
Than Breughel's Winter, that the Bridge at Arles—
Suddenly assumed supremacy, lying reticently there upon the tray,
Lying obliquely beside the coffee cup steaming, beside the silver
spoon.
It underwent translation, shimmered, throbbed with an underswirl
of taunt intent,
Curved in deamond-foam that fused sunlight and starlight
In equivalent potencies, dissolving material density,

To leave only the Other, an incarnation that stormed through
consciousness in a gale of light.
And yet—a square of pale gray paper, folded,
On which a single narcissus, Easter-white,
And carelessly drawn, stooped in a chilly wind.

Aubade

Dull impulse, to make clean
The shabby corner, where
Life persists—the scene
Of ruin past repair:

Habitual needs no thought,
Because the hand's reflex
Replies, almost unsought,—
Simplicity complex.

The milkman at the door,
The junco on the bough,—
All as heretofore,
Must such be answered now,

But mutely, lest they note
A broomstick, magicked by
Some wizard, moves remote,
With coins and seeds, whereby

Surely to send away
The tradesman and the beak,
Satisfied—a fray
Where is no need to speak.

Averted from the mount
Abrupt, with stone stark,
The mind stumbles, hunting,—
Across the dark.

I.

Autumn

So many chestnuts in that last October—
Tom sold bushels; the grove was in its prime
Just then. And despite life grown sombre,
Since Jane was dying, the farm allowed scant time
To encounter grief; the steers had to be driven
From the station stockyard, and on the northern slope
The orchard raced to ripen. No fugitive
From life might deny the lavish hope.
And she did not deny; she signed amen
To the heedless cycles: knowing that Alice might,
At any hour of the day or night,
Need the doctor, she twistedly maintained
The thought in her delirium, for she smiled,
And cradled in thin arms the unborn child.

II.

Watching

Below the portrait in the west parlor—
The mother in her wedding gown, painted
By her brother, dead almost four-score
Years before this night, a suicide (tainted
Thus the family line)—beneath that girl's
Sad face, Jane lay calm at last,
Her dark hair brushed back smoothly, no curls,
As in the picture, and her hands severely clasped.
Beside the lamp, its yellow flame lowered
Respectably, Maria darned a sock,
But Kate and Sue sat mutely idle; gathered
In the next room, the brothers talked of livestock,—
And in the sycamores, the October wind
Roamed and murmured, among boughs leaf-thinned.

They

Can we not halt time here, in this blue October,
When you were thirty-two, and stood by the tall husband
With your hands on the little girl's shoulders? Would it not be better
To stop so? Ahead lies such desolate country, such gaunt desert-land,
That it seems better, wiser, to pause so, to linger always here, and
  to remember.
There is a small sting latent in this drowsy light—gold, crisp,
On the clear horizon to the north, where all the changing leaf-stains
  fuse
To purple, to grape-colour, colour that smells of wine. Chrysanthemums,
Small and bronze, poise by the gray pickets; and in the orchard
  beyond, the Baldwins bruise
Against the bough as they fall, to nestle in the streaming grasses
  that bend and whisper over them.—
Let us stay here, for ahead is darkness, and winter, and
Earth opened in graves, to hold what love's arms have spanned.

Remembered

Somewhere there is a photograph:
A faded, yellow picture glued on cardboard,
Of the two of them, he bald, with his sleeves rolled up,
She pinch-waisted, angular-elbowed, with a nervous mouth.
They stand in the backyard, looking at a young tree,
A mere sapling—an exotic, an apricot.
A Plymouth Rock hen is blandly pecking in the background,
And the dish-rag flaps on the little clothes-line.
  Today we remember that, when she lay dead
In the darkened parlour, the air heavy with the scent of funeral
  tube-roses and carnations,
Lil came and put three red roses in the folded, gnarled hands:
But later he came in, and took away the roses,
And going out into the yard, he cut, with his old, bone-handled
  jack-knife,
A pink-white spray from the blossoming apricot—

Then, in early May, an irregular house of bloom, murmuring with the
drowsily incessant,
Intent humming of the honey-bees—
And shuffling back, he placed in the stiff hand
The little laughing bough.

In March

One task awaits the baffled will;
But yesterday, kneeling there,
I foresaw the ineffable
Less ambiguous to face
Alone, despite the lack of grace…

Then lightly, down the Easter air,
Brittle in its rigorous chill,
Three amber bees rowed carefully
Near, to spy, with musing hum,
Heather and chrysanthemum.

I stared dully as I knelt,
Querying resurrection brave
Enough to quest what honey dwelt
Meagre by a three-years' grave;
And heart felt—though mind despised—
A rune, cruelly disguised.

Sources

Note on Manuscript and Archival Sources

The manuscript and archival sources on which this book is based are of two types: those records available in public institutions, and documents in the possession of the author and not yet available to the public. Archival records are drawn from historical societies and federal, state, and local government agencies in Washington D. C., Pennsylvania, and Massachusetts, and include military service and pension records, newspaper obituaries, family wills, probate documents, court records, county directories, state department of education records, census data, public school and college publications and transcripts. The institutions that extended research privileges and/or provided documents are: The National Archives and Records Administration, Lancaster County Court House, Lancaster County Historical Society, Senator John Heinz Pittsburgh Regional History Center, Coatesville High School, Octorara High School, Pequea Valley School District, Millersville University Archives, Graystone Society/National Iron & Steel Heritage Museum (Lukens Steel Company materials), Boston Public Library, Harvard University Library, New England Conservatory of Music, and the Boston Symphony Orchestra Archives. Documents in the author's possession include, in addition to the poems themselves, manuscripts of lectures Trout gave in his Millersville classes, original letters or copies of letters Trout sent to friends and acquaintances; these include those sent to me and those sent to Donald Smith, Robert and Jean Rentz, Betty Curtis, Bud Cauller, Alida Monro, Mrs. Ralph Hodgson, and T. E. M. Boll. Oral sources include my own memories of Trout and telephone and tape-recorded interviews I conducted with Trout's niece, Alice Trout Smith (the only surviving relative who knew him), and with former colleagues, public school pupils and college students, and friends, some of whom were in their eighties or nineties when interviewed between 2005 and 2013. In addition, email remembrances and completed questionnaires were received from former public school pupils and college students. The names of individuals who provided letters or oral or written reminiscences are referenced in the narrative text but not in the General Index. Trout's scrapbooks of pictures, postcards, magazine and newspaper cuttings, together with the contents of his library, numbering hundreds of books, *most of them heavily annotated*, which he gave to me in the 1970s constitute another category of archival sources. However, the books given me do not represent all of those he owned over the years. When he and his mother sold their house in Gap and moved to Lancaster in 1961, they had a public auction at which Bill sold some of his books and gave others to friends and former students as Dennis Simmons who attended the sale testified. The books people read, and particularly those they reread, provide important insights into their intellectual development and personality, which is why I have treated the books Trout owned and filled with marginalia and markings as primary sources. My belief in the usefulness and importance of marginalia as a primary source was validated by Hermione Lee's article "From the Margins," *Guardian* (April 3, 2010), in which she discusses the notes British novelist and biographer Penelope Fitzgerald made in books she owned. Documentation of archival sources is provided within the narrative text.

Note on Print Sources

The print sources used for this book consist of the articles and books listed below. I have cited copies of books or articles that were part of Trout's library; those mentioned by him in correspondence, conversation, and lectures; or that would have been available to him in order to provide some idea of what he read in the course of his creative years. Books from his library, as noted above are taken as archival sources, and are marked with an asterisk * in the bibliography to differentiate them from the others consulted for this study. More recent scholarly books have been used to provide context in discussing various aspects of Trout's life, thought, and poetry. *The Chicago Manual of Style*, 14th Edition (1993) was used when citing printed sources.

Books and Articles

Adams, Henry. 1918. *The Education of Henry Adams*. Boston: Houghton Mifflin.

*Adler, Gerhard, ed. 1973. *C. G. Jung Letters, 1906-1950*. Princeton, NJ: Princeton University Press.

*_____, ed. 1975. *C. G. Jung Letters, 1951-1961*. Princeton, NJ: Princeton University Press.

Antliff, Mark. 2007. *Avant-garde Fascism: The Mobilization of Myth, Art, and Culture in France, 1909-1933*. Durham, NC: Duke University Press.

*Atkins, Elizabeth. 1964. *Edna St Vincent Millay and Her Times*. New York: Russell & Russell, Inc.

*Baker, Herschel. 1962. *William Hazlitt*. Cambridge: Harvard University Press.

*Barnard, Ellsworth. 1952. *Edwin Arlington Robinson: A Critical Study*. New York: The Macmillan Company.

Barnett, Andrew. 2007. *Sibelius*. New Haven, CT: Yale University Press.

Bawer, Bruce. 1986. *The Middle Generation: The Lives and Poetry of Delmore Schwartz, Randall Jarrell, John Berryman, and Robert Lowell*. Hamden, CT: Anchor Books.

Blum, Jerome. 1994. *In the Beginning: The Advent of the Modern Age, Europe in the 1840s*. New York: Charles Scribner's Sons.

Boll, Theophilus E. M. 1973. *Miss May Sinclair: Novelist*. Rutherford, NJ: Fairleigh Dickinson University Press.

*____. 1970. The Mystery of Charlotte Mew and May Sinclair: An Inquiry. *New York Public Library Bulletin* 74: 445-450.

Boritt, Gabor S. and Adam Boritt. 1983. Lincoln and the Marfan Syndrome: The Medical Diagnosis of a Historical Figure. *Civil War History*. 29: 213-229.

*Brain, Russell. 1958. *Tea with Walter De La Mare*. London: Faber and Faber.

Brooks, Cleanth and Robert Penn Warren. 1960. *Understanding Poetry*. 3rd ed. New York: Holt, Rinehart and Winston.

Brower, Daniel R. 1975. *Training the Nihilists: Education and Radicalism in Tsarist Russia*. Ithaca, NY: Cornell University Press.

Brown, Ashley and Cheney, Frances Neel, eds. 1983. *The Poetry Reviews of Allen Tate*, 1924-1944. Baton Rouge, LA: Louisiana State University Press.

*Brown, E. K. 1953. *Willa Cather: A Critical Biography*. Completed by Leon Edel. New York: Alfred A. Knopf.

Burns, Charlene P. E. 2009. Wolfgang Pauli, Carl Jung, and the Acausal Connecting Principle: A Case Study in Transdisciplinarity. In *The Global Spiral* 11: 6.

Burt, Stephen, and Jennifer Lewin. 2001. Poetry and New Criticism. In *A Companion to Twentieth-Century Poetry*. Edited by Neil Roberts. Malden, MA: Blackwell Publishers.

Burt, Stephen. 2002. *Randall Jarrell and His Age*. New York: Columbia University Press.

*Campbell, Joseph. ed. 1957. *Man and Time: Papers from the Eranos Yearbooks*. Vol. 3. Translated by Ralph Manheim and R. F. C. Hull. New York: Pantheon Books.

*Carlyle, Thomas. 1881. *Reminiscences*. Ed. James Anthony Froude. New York: Harper & Brothers.

Carlson, Erin G. 1998. *Thinking Fascism: Sapphic Modernism and Fascist Modernity*. Stanford, CA: Stanford University Press.

*Carpenter, Frederic I. 1962. *Robinson Jeffers*. New York: Twayne Publishers, Inc.

*Carrel, Alexis. 1935. *Man, The Unknown*. New York: Harper & Brothers.

*Cather, Willa. 1922. *One of Ours*. New York: Alfred A. Knopf.

*____. 1925. *The Professor's House*. New York: Alfred A Knopf.

*____. 1965. *Willa Cather's Collected Short Fiction*. Introduced by Mildred R. Bennett. Lincoln, NB: University of Nebraska Press.

Ciffelli, Edward M. 1998. *John Ciardi: A Biography*. Fayetteville, AR: University of Arkansas Press.

*Cirlot, J. E. 1962. *A Dictionary of Symbols*. Translated by J. Sage. New York: Philosophical Library.

Clark, Kenneth. 1969. *Civilization, A Personal View*. New York: Harper & Row Publishers.

Clark, Suzanne. 1995. Uncanny Millay. In *Millay at 100: A Critical Reappraisal*. Edited by Diane P. Freedman. Carbondale: Southern Illinois Press.

Commanger, Henry Steele. 1950. *The American Mind*. New Haven: Yale University Press.

Conrad, Joseph. 1923. *Lord Jim*. Garden City, NY: Doubleday, Page & Company.

Cook, Matt. 2003. *London and the Culture of Homosexuality, 1885-1914*. Cambridge, UK: Cambridge University Press.

Coxe, Louis. 1969. *Edwin Arlington Robinson: The Life of Poetry*. New York: Pegasus.

Craven, Wayne. 1968. *Sculpture in America*. New York. Thomas Y. Crowell Company.

*De Marliave, Joseph. 1961. *Beethoven's Quartets*. Translated by Hilda Andrews. New York: Dover Publications.

Donaldson, Scott. 1977. *By Force of Will: The Life and Art of Ernest Hemingway*. New York: The Viking Press.

_____. 2007. *Edwin Arlington Robinson: A Poet's Life*. New York: Columbia University Press.

_____. 1972. *Poet in America: Winfield Townley Scott*. Austin, TX: University of Texas Press.

*Doumic, Rene. 1910. *George Sand: Some Aspects of Her Work*. Translated by Alys Hallard. New York: G. P. Putnam's Sons.

Downey, Dennis B. 2004. *We Sing To Thee: A History of Millersville University*. Millersville, PA: Millersville University of Pennsylvania.

Eagleton, Terry. 1983. *Literary Theory: An Introduction*. Minneapolis: University of Minnesota Press.

____. 2005. *The English Novel: An Introduction*. Chichester, UK: Wiley-Blackwell.

Ebersole, Mark C. 2006. German Religious Groups and Slavery in Lancaster County Prior to the Civil War. *The Journal of the Lancaster County Historical Society*. 107: 158-187.

Eliot, T. S. 1949. *Notes towards the Definition of Culture*. New York: Harcourt, Brace and Company.

_____. 1932. *The Metaphysical Poets. Selected Essays, 1917-1932*. New York: Harcourt, Brace and Company.

_____. 1975. Tradition and the Individual Talent. *Selected Prose of T. S. Eliot*. Edited by Frank Kermonde. New York: Harcourt Brace Jovanovich.

Ellis, Franklin and Samuel Evans. 1883. *History of Lancaster County, Pennsylvania*. Philadelphia: Everts & Peck.

English, David. 2008. Understanding Aging: A Medical Humanities Approach to "Death in Venice." In *Berkeley Undergraduate Journal* 20, 1: 1-35.

Ferguson, George. 1961. *Signs & Symbols in Christian Art*. London: Oxford University Press.

Ferrall, Charles. 2001. *Modernist Writing and Reactionary Politics*. Cambridge: Cambridge University Press.

Fitzgerald, Penelope. 1984. *Charlotte Mew and Her Friends*. London: Collins.

*Forbes, Elliot, ed. 1970. *Thayer's Life of Beethoven*. Princeton, NJ: Princeton University Press.

Forster, E. M. 1951. *Two Cheers for Democracy*. New York: Harcourt, Brace and Company.

Frank, Mortimer H. 2002. *Arturo Toscanini: The NBC Years*. Portland, OR: Amadeus Press.

*Frank, Waldo, ed. 1946. *The Collected Poems of Hart Crane*. New York: Liverright Publishing Company.

Franklin, Peter. 1991. *Mahler: Symphony No. 3*. Cambridge, UK: Cambridge University Press.

Franklin, Ralph W, ed. 1998. *The Poems of Emily Dickinson*. Cambridge, MA: The Belknap Press of Harvard University Press.

Fussell, Paul. 1975. *The Great War and Modern Memory*. New York: Oxford University Press.

_____. 1989. *Wartime: Understanding and Behavior in the Second World War*. New York: Oxford University Press.

*Gibb, Jocelyn, ed. 1965. *Light on C. S. Lewis*. New York: Harcourt, Brace & World.

Gibson, Walter S. 1977. *Bruegel*. London: Thames & Hudson Ltd.

_____. 1973. *Hieronymus Bosch*. London: Thames & Hudson Ltd.

Gold, Herbert. 1957. The Age of Happy Problems. *The Atlantic Monthly* 199: 58-61.

Goldstein, Laurence. 2002. "The Imagination Problem": Winfield Townley Scott and the American Wars. *War, Literature, and the Arts* 14: 59-77.

Gordon, Lyndall. 2010. *Lives Like Loaded Bombs: Emily Dickinson and Her Family's Feuds*. New York: Viking Press.

*Gould, Jean. 1969. *The Poet and Her Book: A Biography of Edna St. Vincent Millay*. New York: Dodd, Mead & Company.

Grant, Joy. 1967. *Harold Monro & the Poetry Bookshop*. Berkeley, CA: University of California Press.

*Graves, Robert. 1962. *Oxford Addresses on Poetry*. Garden City, NY: Doubleday & Company, Inc.

Griffin, Roger. 2007. *Modernism and Fascism: The Sense of a Beginning Under Mussolini and Hitler*. Basingstoke, UK: Palgrave Macmillan.

Griffiths, Frederick T. 1984. The Woman Warrior: Willa Cather and *One of Ours*. *Women's Studies* 11: 261-285.

Green, Harvey. 1992. *The Uncertainty of Everyday Life, 1915-1945*. New York: Harper Collins Publishers.

Grumbach, Doris. 1984. A Study of the Small Room in *The Professor's House*. *Women's Studies* 11: 327-345.

Guttmann, Allen. 1999. Sacred, Inspired Authority: D. H. Lawrence, Literature and the Fascist Body. *The International Journal of the History of Sport*. 16: 2, 169-179.

Haas, Robert. 1987. Robinson Jeffers: The Poems and the Life. *American Poetry Review* 16: 6, 33-41.

Harrison, T. R. 1998. *Harrison's Principles of Internal Medicine*. 14th ed. Edited by Anthony S. Fauci, et al. New York: McGraw-Hill.

Hart, Ellen Louise and Martha Nell Smith. 1998. *Open Me Carefully: Emily Dickinson's Intimate Letters to Susan Huntington Dickinson*. Ashfield, MA: Paris Press.

Hawkins, Maude M. 1958. *A. E. Housman: Man Behind the Mask*. Chicago: Henry Regnery Company.

Heilbut, Anthony. 1996. *Thomas Mann: Eros and Literature*. New York: Alfred A. Knopf.

Hewitt, Andrew. 1993. *Fascist Modernism: Aesthetics, Politics, and the Avant-garde*. Stanford, CA: Stanford University Press.

Hillyer, Robert. 1950. *First Principles of Verse*. Boston: The Writer, Inc.

Hirsch, Edward. 2000. One Life, One Writing: The Middle Generation. *The American Poetry Review*. September/October: 11-16.

Hollis, Matthew. 2011. *Now All Roads Lead to France: The Last Years of Edward Thomas*. London: Faber and Faber Ltd.

Horowitz, Joseph. 1987. *Understanding Toscanini*. London: Faber and Faber.

*Housman, A. E. 1956. *The Collected Poems of A.E. Housman*. New York: Henry Holt and Company.

*_____. 1933. *The Name and Nature of Poetry*. New York: The Macmillan Company.

*Hudson, W. H. 1939. *Afoot In England*. London: J. M. Dent & Sons Ltd.

Hughes, H. Stuart. 1958. *Consciousness and Society: The Reorientation of European Social Thought, 1890-1930*. New York: Alfred A. Knopf.

Hynes, Samuel. 1977. *The Auden Generation: Literature and Politics in England in the 1930s*. New York: The Viking Press.

Jameson, Frederic. 1979. *Fables of Aggression: Wyndham Lewis, the Modernist as Fascist*. Berkeley, CA: University of California Press.

Jamison, Kay Redfield. 1993. *Touched with Fire: Manic-Depressive Illness and the Artistic Temperament*. New York: Free Press.

*Jankelevitch, Vladimir. 1959. *Ravel*. London: John Calder Ltd.

*Jeffers, Robinson. 1938. *The Selected Poetry of Robinson Jeffers*. New York: Random House.

Johnson, Robert. 1995. A Moment's Monument: Millay's Sonnets and Modern Times. In *Millay at 100: A Critical Appraisal*. Edited by Diane P. Freedman. Carbondale: Southern Illinois University Press.

Johnson, Thomas H. 1955. *Emily Dickinson: An Interpretative Biography*. Cambridge, MA: Harvard University Press.

_____, ed. 1960. *The Complete Poems of Emily Dickinson*. Boston: Little, Brown and Company.

*Jung, C. G. 1959. *Aion: Researches into the Phenomenology of the Self*. Translated by R. F. C. Hull. New York: Pantheon Books.

*_____. 1958. *Answer to Job*. Translated by R. F. C. Hull. New York: Princeton University Press.

*_____. 1962. Commentary. In *The Secret of the Golden Flower: A Chinese Book of Life*. Translated by Richard Wilhelm. New York: Harcourt, Brace & World, Inc.

*_____. 1973. *Memories, Dreams, Reflections* (rev. ed.). Recorded and Edited by Aniela Jaffé. Translated by Richard and Clara Winston. New York: Pantheon Books.

*_____. 1963. *Mysterium Coniunctionis: An Inquiry into the Synthesis of Psychic Opposites in Alchemy*. Translated by R. F. C. Hull. New York: Pantheon Books.

*_____. 1961. *Psychological Reflections*. Selected and Edited by Jolande Jacobi. New York: Harper & Row.

*_____. 1968. *Psychology and Alchemy*, 2nd ed. Princeton, NJ: Translated by R. F. C. Hull. Princeton University Press.

*_____. 1971. *Psychological Types*. Translated by H. G. Baynes and R. F. C. Hull. Princeton, NJ: Princeton University Press.

*_____. 1956. *Symbols of Transformation: An Analysis of the Prelude to a Case of Schizophrenia*. Translated by R. F. C. Hull. New York: Pantheon Books.

_____. 1966. *The Spirit in Man, Art and Literature*. Translated by R. F. C. Hull. Princeton, NJ: Princeton University Press.

*_____. 1960. *The Structure and Dynamics of the Psyche*. Translated by R. F. C. Hull. New York: Pantheon Books.

*_____. 1953. *Two Essays on Analytical Psychology*. Translated by R. F. C. Hull. New York: Pantheon Books.

*Kahler, Erich. 1957. *The Tower and the Abyss: An Inquiry into the Transformation of the Individual*. New York: George Braziller, Inc.

Kaiser, Jo Ellen Green. 1995. Displaced Modernism: Millay and the Triumph of Sentimentality. In *Millay at 100: A Critical Reappraisal*. Edited by Diane P. Freedman. Carbondale: Southern Illinois University Press.

Kalaidjian, Walter. 1996. Marketing Modern Poetry and the Southern Public Sphere. In *Marketing Modernisms: Self-Promotion, Canonization, Rereading*. Edited by Kevin J. H. Dettmar and Stephen Watt. Ann Arbor, MI: The University of Michigan Press.

Keneagy, Carolyn Neuhauser. 1966. *A Gap in My Memory*. Privately Published.

Kennedy, Michael. 2000. *Mahler*, 2nd ed. Oxford: Oxford University Press.

_____. 1999. *Richard Strauss: Man, Musician, Enigma*. Cambridge: Cambridge University Press.

Klein, H. M. J., ed. 1924. *Lancaster County Pennsylvania: A History*, New York: Lewis Historical Publishing Company.

Kroen, Collin. 2007. Abraham Lincoln and the 'Lincoln Sign.' *Cleveland Clinic Journal of Medicine*. 74: 108-110.

Kunitz, Stanley. 1965. Roethke: Poet of Transformations. *New Republic*. 152: 23-29.

La Belle, Jenijoy. 1976. Theodore Roethke's "The Lost Son": From Archetypes to Literary History. *Modern Language Quarterly*. 37: 179-195.

Lane, Gary. 1976. *I AM: A Study of E. E. Cummings' Poems*. Lawrence, KS: University Press of Kansas.

Langbaum, Robert. 1959. The New Nature Poetry. *The American Scholar* 28: 323-340.

Lawrence, D. H. 2002. *The Letters of D. H. Lawrence*. Edited by George J. Zytaruk and James T. Boulton. Vol. 2, June 1913-October 1916. Cambridge: Cambridge University Press.

_____. 2002. *The Letters of D. H. Lawrence*. Edited by Warren Roberts, James T. Boulton and Elizabeth Mansfield. Vol. 4, June 1921-March 1924. Cambridge: Cambridge University Press.

Lee, Hermione. 1989. *Willa Cather: Double Lives*. New York: Pantheon Books.

Leopold, Richard William. 1940. *Robert Dale Owen: A Biography*. Cambridge, MA: Harvard University Press.

Levey, Michael. 1975. *High Renaissance*. Harmondsworth, UK: Penguin Books, Ltd.

*Lodge, Sir Oliver. 1929. *Why I Believe in Personal Immortality*. Garden City, NY: Doubleday, Doran & Company, Inc.

Lorenz, Joan M. 2002. *A History of Salisbury Township, Lancaster County, Pennsylvania*. Morgantown, PA: Masthof Press.

*Lucas, Veronica. 1930. *Letters of George Sand*. London: George Routledge & Sons, LTD.

*Macdougall, Allan Ross, ed. 1951. *Letters of Edna St. Vincent Millay*. New York: Harper & Brothers Publishers.

Malkoff, Karl. 1966. *Theodore Roethke*. New York: Columbia University Press.

*Mann, Thomas. 1936. *Stories of Three Decades*. Translated by H. T. Lowe-Porter. New York: Alfred A. Knopf.

*____. 1939. *The Magic Mountain*. Translated by H. T. Lowe-Porter. New York: Alfred A. Knopf.

*March, Harold. 1948. *The Two Worlds of Marcel Proust*. Philadelphia: University of Pennsylvania Press.

Marx, Patricia. 1965. Interview with Anne Sexton. *Hudson Review* 18: 560-570.

Matthiessen, F. O. 1941. *American Renaissance: Art and Expression in the Age of Emerson and Whitman*. New York: Oxford University Press.

*_____, ed. 1950. *The Oxford Book of American Verse*. New York: Oxford University Press.

*McCrosson, Doris Ross. 1966. *Walter de la Mare*. New York: Twayne Publishers, Inc.

McKusick, Victor A. 1991. Abraham Lincoln and Marfan syndrome. *Nature* 352: 80.

McLaughlin, William G. 1955. *Billy Sunday Was His Real Name*. Chicago: University of Chicago Press.

Meinecke, Friedrich. 1950. *The German Catastrophe*. Boston: Beacon Press.

Mencken, H. L. 1920. *Prejudices: Second Series*. New York: Alfred A. Knopf, Inc.

Meyers, Jeffrey. 1996. *Robert Frost: A Biography*. New York: Houghton Mifflin Company.

Middlebrook, Diane Wood. 1991. *Anne Sexton: A Biography*. Boston: Houghton Mifflin Company

Milford, Nancy. 2001. *Savage Beauty: The Life of Edna St. Vincent Millay*. New York: Random House.

Mitchell, Domhnall. 2000. *Emily Dickinson: Monarch of Perception*. Amherst, MA: The University of Massachusetts Press.

Moore, R. Laurence. 1977. *In Search of White Crows: Spiritualism, Parapsychology, and American Culture*. New York: Oxford University Press.

Mudge, Jean McClure. 1975. *Emily Dickinson & the Image of Home*. Amherst, MA: The University of Massachusetts Press.

Nelson, Cary. 1989. *Repression and Recovery: Modern American Poetry and the Politics of Culture Memory, 1910-1945*. Madison, WI: The University of Wisconsin Press.

Nulle, Stebelton H. 1940. Lawrence and the Fascist Movement. *New Mexico Quarterly* 10: 3-15.

O'Brien, Sharon. 1984. "The Thing Not Named": Willa Cather as a Lesbian Writer. *Signs: Journal of Women in Culture and Society* 9: 576-599.

Olson, Stanley. 1979. *Elinor Wylie: A Life Apart*. New York: The Dial Press.

Panichas, George A. 2000. The Moral Sense in Joseph Conrad's *Lord Jim*. *Humanitas* XIII: 1, 10-30.

Parekh, Pushpa N. 1994. Nature in the Poetry of E. E. Cummings. *Spring* 3: 63-71.

*Pater, Walter. 1907. *The Renaissance: Studies in Art and Poetry*. New York: The Macmillan Company.

Pearce, Roy Harvey. 1961. *The Continuity of American Poetry*. Princeton, NJ: Princeton University Press.

*Philip, Lotte Brand. 1956. *Hieronymus Bosch*. New York: Harry N. Abrams.

Pickvance, Ronald. 1984. *Van Gogh in Arles*. New York: The Metropolitan Museum of Art.

Pierrot, Jean. 1981. *The Decadent Imagination*. Translated by Derek Coltman. Chicago: University of Chicago Press.

Pollack, Norma. 1995. Poems of Cummings Set to Music. *Spring* 4: 121-129.

Powys, John Cowper. 1934. *Autobiography*. New York: Simon and Schuster.

Praz, Mario. 1933. *The Romantic Agony*. Translated by Angus Davidson. London: Oxford University Press.

Preminger, Alex, ed. 1974. *Princeton Encyclopedia of Poetry and Poetics*. Princeton, NJ: Princeton University Press.

Pritchard, William H. 1984. *Frost: A Literary Life Reconsidered*. New York: Oxford University Press.

_____. 1990. *Randall Jarrell: A Literary Life*. New York: Farrar, Straus and Giroux.

*Rakoczi, Basil Ivan. 1954. *The Painted Caravan: A Penetration into the Secrets of the Tarot Cards*. The Hague: L. J. C. Boucher.

*Regardie, Israel. 1945. *The Middle Pillar*. Chicago: The Aries Press.

Rettew, L. D. 2006, *Treason At Christiana, September 11, 1851*. 2nd ed. Morgantown, PA: Masthof Press.

Rewald, John. 1978. *Post-Impressionism: From van Gogh to Gauguin*, 3rd ed., rev. New York: The Museum of Modern Art.

Reynolds, David S. 1988. *Beneath the American Renaissance: The Subversive Imagination in the Age of Emerson and Melville*. New York: Alfred A. Knopf.

Roache, Joel. 1971. *Richard Eberhart: The Progress of an American Poet*. New York: Oxford University Press.

Robertson, Priscilla. 1952. *Revolutions of 1848: A Social History*. Princeton, NJ: Princeton University Press.

Robinson, Edwin Arlington. 1922. *Collected Poems*. New York: The Macmillan Company.

Robinson, W. R. 1967. *Edwin Arlington Robinson: A Poetry of the Act*. Cleveland, OH: The Press of Western Reserve University.

*Rodman, Seldon, ed. 1938. *A New Anthology of Modern Poetry*. New York: The Modern Library.

Rosenthal, M. L. 1960. *The Modern Poets: A Critical Introduction*. New York: Oxford University Press.

Ross, Alex. 2007. *The Rest is Noise: Listening to the Twentieth Century*. New York: Farrar, Strauss and Giroux.

Ross, Robert H. 1965. *The Georgian Revolt, 1910-1922: Rise and Fall of a Poetic Ideal*. Carbondale, IL: Southern Illinois University Press.

Rotella, Guy. 1984. *Critical Essays on E. E. Cummings*. Boston: G. K. Hall & Co.

Russell, Bertrand. 1956. *Portraits from Memory*. London: George Allen and Unwin.

Rydell, Robert W. 1993. *World of Fairs*. Chicago: The University of Chicago Press.

Schwartz, Daniel R. 2001. *Rereading Conrad*. Columbia, MO: University of Missouri Press.

Schwartz, Harold. 1964. Abraham Lincoln and the Marfan syndrome. *Journal of the American Medical Association* 187: 473-479.

Scott, Winfield Townley. 1962. *Collected Poems: 1937-1962*. New York: The Macmillan Company.

Seager, Allan. 1968. *The Glass House: The Life of Theodore Roethke*. New York: McGraw-Hill Book Company.

*Sergeant, Elizabeth Shepley. 1953. *Willa Cather: A Memoir.* Philadelphia: J.B. Lippincott Company.

Sheridan, Alan. 1999. *Andre Gide: A Life in the Present*. Cambridge, MA: Harvard University Press.

Sherry, Vincent. 1993. *Ezra Pound, Wyndham Lewis, and Radical Modernism*. New York: Oxford University Press.

Singal, Daniel Joseph. 1982. *The War Within: From Victorian to Modernist Thought in the South, 1919-1945*. Chapel Hill, NC: The University of North Carolina Press.

Starkie, Enid. 1961. *Arthur Rimbaud*. Norfolk, CT: New Directions Books.

Stauffer, Donald A. 1946. *The Nature of Poetry*. New York: W. W. Norton & Company.

*Stechow, Wolfgang. 1968. *Pieter Bruegle the Elder*. New York: Harry N. Abrams, Inc.

St. Armand, Barton Levi. 1984. *Emily Dickinson and Her Culture: The Soul's Society*. New York: Cambridge University Press.

_____. 1977/78. Emily Dickinson and the Occult: The Rosicrucian Connection. *Prairie Schooner* 51: 345-357.

*Sullivan, J. W. N. 1960. *Beethoven: His Spiritual Development*. New York: Vintage Books.

Sullivan, Rosemary. 1975. *Theodore Roethke: The Garden Master*. Seattle: University of Washington Press.

Surette, Leon. 1999. *Pound in Purgatory: From Economic Radicalism to Anti-Semitism*. Urbana, IL: University of Illinois Press.

Sutton, Matthew Avery. 2007. *Aimee Semple McPherson and the Resurrection of Christian America*. Cambridge, MA: Harvard University Press.

Swinnerton, Frank. 1956. *Background with Chorus: A Footnote to Changes in English Literary Fashion Between 1901 and 1917*. New York: Farrar, Strauss & Cudahy.

Tate, Allen. 1932. Personal Convention. *Poetry* 39: 332-337.

Taylor, Brian. 1980. *The Green Avenue: The Life and Writings of Forrest Reid, 1875-1947*. Cambridge: Cambridge University Press.

Thompson, Lawrence. 1966. *Robert Frost: The Early Years, 1874-1915*. New York: Holt, Rinehart and Winston.

_____. 1970. *Robert Frost: The Years of Triumph, 1915-1938*. New York: Holt, Rinehart and Winston.

_____ and R. H. Winnick. 1976. *Robert Frost: The Later Years, 1938-1963*. New York: Holt, Rinehart and Winston.

*Thoreau, Henry D. 1910. *Walden*. New York: Grosset & Dunlap.

Thurston, Michael. 2001. *Making Something: American Political Poetry Between the Wars*. Chapel Hill, NC: The University of North Carolina Press.

*Torrence, Ridgely. 1940. *Selected Letters of Edwin Arlington Robinson.* New York: Macmillan Company.

Trachtenberg, Alan. 1982. *The Incorporation of America: Culture & Society in the Gilded Age.* New York: Hill and Wang.

Untermeyer, Louis. 1923. *American Poetry Since 1900.* New York: Henry Hold and Company.

*____, ed. 1962. *Modern American Poetry & Modern British Poetry.* New York: Harcourt, Brace & World.

Wainwright, David and Catherine Dinn. 1989. *Henry Scott Tuke 1858-1929 Under Canvas.* Carshalton, England: Sarema Press.

*Waite, Arthur Edward. 1959. *The Pictorial Key to the Tarot.* New Hyde Park, NY: University Books.

Walter, Bruno. 1966. *Gustav Mahler.* New York: Alfred Knopf.

Watson, George L. 1957. *A. E. Housman: A Divided Life.* London: Rupert Hart-Davis.

*Weber, Brom. 1948. *Hart Crane: A Biographical and Critical Study.* New York: The Bodley Press.

*_____, ed. 1952. *The Letters of Hart Crane, 1916-1932.* New York: Hermitage House.

Weber, Daniel B. 1983. The New Friends of Music: Democracy, Chamber Music and the Mass Audience. *Journal of American Culture* 6: 4, 44-48.

Webster, Michael. 2000. The New Nature Poetry and the Old. *Spring* 9: 109-124.

*White, Stewart Edward. 1943. *Anchors to Windward.* New York: E. P. Dutton and Co.

*_____, 1948. *The Job of Living.* New York: E. P. Dutton and Co.

Whitman, Walt. 1914. *Complete Prose Works.* New York: Mitchell Kennerley.

Witemeyer, Hugh, ed. 1989. *William Carlos Williams and James Laughlin: Selected Letters.* New York: W. W. Norton.

Wolff, Cynthia Griffin. 1986. *Emily Dickinson.* New York: Alfred A Knopf.

Wyatt, David M. 1977. Completing the Picture: Williams, Berryman, and 'Spatial Form.' *Colby Quarterly* 13: 4, 246-262.

Zeller, J. Terry, ed. 2008. *Time & Memory: Poems By William S. Trout.* Baltimore: American Literary Press.

_____. 2006. William S. Trout: Teacher, Poet, Friend. *Millersville Review* 119: 12-15.

Index of First Lines and Titles

Page numbers refer only to the page on which the poem itself is found.

General Index

CPSIA information can be obtained at www.ICGtesting.com
Printed in the USA
BVOW03s1841280514

354597BV00007B/43/P